Environmental Justice and Environmentalism

Urban and Industrial Environments
Series editor: Robert Gottlieb, Henry R. Luce Professor of Urban and Environmental Policy, Occidental College

For a complete list of books published in this series, please see the back of the book.

Environmental Justice and Environmentalism

The Social Justice Challenge to the Environmental Movement

edited by
Ronald Sandler and Phaedra C. Pezzullo

The MIT Press
Cambridge, Massachusetts
London, England

MIT Press books may be purchased at special quantity discounts for business or sales promotional use. For information, please email special_sales@mitpress.mit.edu or write to Special Sales Department, The MIT Press, 55 Hayward Street, Cambridge, MA 02142.

This book was set in sabon by SPi and was printed and bound in the United States of America.

Printed on recycled paper.

Library of Congress Cataloging-in-Publication Data

Environmental justice and environmentalism : the social justice challenge to the environmental movement / edited by Ronald Sandler and Phaedra C. Pezzullo.
    p.   cm.—(Urban and industrial environments)
Includes bibliographical references and index
ISBN-13: 978-0-262-19552-2 (alk. paper)
ISBN-10: 0-262-19552-6 (alk. paper)
ISBN-13: 978-0-262-69340-0 (pbk. : alk. paper)
ISBN-10: 0-262-69340-2 (pbk. : alk. paper)
    1. Environmental justice. 2. Environmentalism. I. Sandler, Ronald D. II. Pezzullo, Phaedra C.
GE220.E578   2007
363.7—dc22
                                                          2006046648

10 9 8 7 6 5 4 3 2

This book is dedicated to all those who are struggling, whatever their self-identification, to realize a more environmentally sustainable and socially just world.

Contents

Acknowledgments

We would not have met each other if Robbie Cox and Kirstin Replogle had not actively persuaded us to try to find a way to work within the environmental movement to help achieve environmental justice. This volume was born out of our volunteer experiences, both inspiring and frustrating, by their sides. We hope this volume helps illuminate the limitations and possibilities of such attempts.

In addition to the contributors, we would like to thank Clay Morgan at The MIT Press and series editor Robert Gottlieb for their support of this project. We also thank the anonymous MIT Press reviewers for their many helpful comments and suggestions.

We thank John Basl, William Currie, and Benjamin Miller for their research assistance and help in preparing the manuscript. Ron is fortunate to work with such enthusiastic and capable undergraduates.

Above all we thank our families, including our partners Ted Striphas and Emily Mann, for their support.

Contributors

Kim Allen is a doctoral candidate in the Department of Anthropology at the University of North Carolina–Chapel Hill. Her research focuses on racial formations in the United States, environmental activism, and regimes of nature.

J. Robert Cox is a professor of rhetoric and social theory in the Department of Communication Studies at the University of North Carolina–Chapel Hill. He has served twice as the president of the national Sierra Club (1994–1996, 2000–2001) and currently serves on its board of directors. His published work includes critical studies of the rhetoric of civil rights, antiwar protest, labor, and the environmental movement. His recent work has included studies of the challenges to transparency and the participation of civil society in neoliberal free-trade agreements, as well as a textbook on public environmental discourse in the United States, *Environmental Communication and the Public Sphere* (Sage, 2006).

Vinci Daro is a doctoral candidate in the Department of Anthropology at the University of North Carolina–Chapel Hill. Her research is on globalization and transnational activist networks, discourses of democracy, and edge effects within and around social movements.

Kevin DeLuca is an associate professor in the Department of Speech Communication and the Institute of Ecology at the University of Georgia. He is the author of *Image Politics: The New Rhetoric of Environmental Activism* (Guilford Press, 1999) and numerous essays on visual rhetoric, critical theory, environmental activism, and the virtues of violence. His research concentrations include rhetorical theory and criticism, media theory and criticism, environmental discourse, visual studies, and critical cultural studies.

Giovanna Di Chiro teaches in the Environmental Studies and Gender Studies programs at Mount Holyoke College. She is a coeditor of the anthology *Appropriating Technology: Vernacular Science and Social Power* (Minnesota, 2004) and the author of numerous articles on the science and politics of environmental justice.

Daniel Faber is an associate professor of sociology and director of the Green Justice Research Collaborative at Northeastern University. His research is focused in the areas of political economy, environmental justice and policy, Central America and underdevelopment, social theory, economic crisis theory, social movements, and philanthropy. He is the author of *Environment Under Fire: Imperialism and the Ecological Crisis in Central America* (Monthly Review Press, 1993) and editor of *The Struggle for Ecological Democracy: Environmental Justice Movements in the United States* (Guilford Press, 1998) and Foundations for Social Change: Critical Perspectives on Philanthropy and Popular Movements (Rowman and Littlefield, 2005). He is currently writing a book entitled *Green of a Different Color: Environmental Justice Politics in the New Millennium*. He is also on the board of the Alliance for a Healthy Tomorrow in Massachusetts.

Dorothy Holland is the Cary C. Boshamer Professor of Anthropology at the University of North Carolina–Chapel Hill. A former chair of the department and former president of the national Society for Psychological Anthropology, her latest published book, *History in Person: Enduring Struggles, Contentious Practice, Intimate Identities* (School of American Research Press, 2001), is one of five that she has coedited or coauthored. Holland's current research interests concern identity, local democracy, activism, and the environmental movement.

Dale Jamieson is a professor of environmental studies and philosophy at New York University. He is the author of *Morality's Progress: Essays on Humans, Other Animals, and the Rest of Nature* (Oxford, 2002) and editor of *A Companion to Environmental Philosophy* (Blackwell, 2001). He is currently completing a book on global environmental change and coauthoring an environmental science textbook.

M. Nils Peterson is an assistant professor in the Department of Forestry and Environmental Resources at North Carolina State University. His research addresses how human culture and household dynamics influence conservation. He has published the results of his research in *Communication and Critical/ Cultural Studies, Conservation Biology, Ecological Modelling, Journal of Wildlife Management, and the Wildlife Society Bulletin*.

Markus J. Peterson is an associate professor in the Department of Wildlife and Fisheries Sciences at Texas A&M University. He previously served as the Upland wildlife program leader for Texas Parks and Wildlife. He has published the results of his research in *Birds of North American, Communication and Critical/Cultural Studies, Conservation Biology, Ecography, Ecological Modelling, Environmental Values, Journal of the American Veterinary Medical Association, Journal of Wildlife Diseases, Journal of Wildlife Management, Proceedings of the National Quail Symposium, and the Wildlife Society Bulletin*.

Tarla Rai Peterson holds the Boone and Crockett Chair in Wildlife Conservation and Policy at Texas A&M University, where she is a professor in the Department of Wildlife and Fisheries Sciences. She is also an adjunct professor in the Communication Department at the University of Utah. Her research focuses on how the intersections between communication, environmental policy, and democracy constrain sustainable development. She has published the results of her research in *Sharing the Earth: The Rhetoric of Sustainable Development* (South Carolina, 1997) and her edited volume *Green Talk in the White House: The Rhetorical Presidency Encounters Ecology* (Texas A&M, 2004), as well as in scholarly journals such as *Agriculture and Human Values, Communication and*

Critical/Cultural Studies, Conservation Biology, Ecological Modelling, Environmental Practice, Environmental Values, Quarterly Journal of Speech, Journal of Applied Communication Research, and Journal of Wildlife Management.

Phaedra C. Pezzullo is an assistant professor of rhetoric and public culture in the Department of Communication and Culture, as well as an adjunct professor of cultural studies and American studies, at Indiana University, Bloomington. She served on the Sierra Club's National Environmental Justice Committee from 1999–2005 and continues to serve as an advisor to the committee. She also participates in local environmental and environmental justice activism. Her research focuses on antitoxic environmental justice struggles, environmental communication, social movements, identity, democracy, and tourist studies. She is completing a book on the rhetorics of travel, pollution, and environmental justice on toxic tours (University of Alabama Press, 2007) and editing a special issue of the journal *Cultural Studies* on the environment.

J. Timmons Roberts is a professor of sociology and director of the Environmental Science and Policy program at the College of William and Mary. After completing his doctorate in the sociology of comparative international development at Johns Hopkins University, he taught for ten years at Tulane University in Louisiana. In addition to more than thirty published articles and book chapters, he is author of *From Modernization to Globalization: Perspectives on Development and Social Change* (with Amy Hite, Blackwell, 2000), *Chronicles from the Environmental Justice Frontline* (with Melissa Toffolon-Weiss, Cambridge, 2001), and *Trouble in Paradise: Globalization and Environmental Crises in Latin America* (with Nikki Demetria Thanos, Routledge, 2003).

Ronald Sandler is an assistant professor of philosophy in the Department of Philosophy and Religion at Northeastern University. His research is in the areas of environmental ethics, ethical theory, ethics and technology, and the history of ethics. He is author of *Character and Environment* (Columbia University Press, 2007) and a coeditor of *Environmental Virtue Ethics* (Rowman and Littlefield, 2005). He served on the Sierra Club's National Environmental Justice Committee from 2002–2004.

Steve Schwarze is an associate professor of communication studies at the University of Montana at Missoula. His principle area of research is the rhetoric of environmental controversies. He has published in the journals *Argumentation and Advocacy, Management Communication Quarterly, Quarterly Journal of Speech Philosophy and Rhetoric,* and *Rhetoric and Public Affairs.*

Peter Wenz is an emeritus professor of philosophy and legal studies at the University of Illinois at Springfield. His published books are *Environmental Justice* (SUNY, 1988), *Abortion Rights as Religious Freedom* (Temple, 1992), *Nature's Keeper* (Temple, 1996), *Environmental Ethics Today* (Oxford, 2001), and *Political Philosophies in Moral Conflict* (McGraw-Hill, 2007).

Introduction
Revisiting the Environmental Justice Challenge to Environmentalism

Phaedra C. Pezzullo and Ronald Sandler

The two environmental movements could not be more different as black and white is truer than it sounds.
—M. Dowie[1]

People don't get all the connections. They say the environment is over here, the civil rights group is over there, the women's group is over there, and the other groups are here. Actually all of them are one group, and the issues we fight become null and void if we have no clean water to drink, no clean air to breathe and nothing to eat.
—C. Tucker[2]

The environmental and environmental justice movements would seem to be natural allies. Indeed, one might expect that a social movement dedicated to environmental integrity and preservation and a social movement dedicated to justice in the distribution of environmental goods and decision making would not be two distinct social movements, but rather two aspects of one encompassing movement. After all, both have chosen the core term of "environment" to name their passions, mobilize their constituents, and send their message to those they aim to persuade. Moreover, there are ample opportunities for joint efforts in the cause for environmental health, sustainability, and integrity. All of our environments—from urban to wilderness areas— are being stressed, polluted, and commodified, while corporations and governmental agencies increasingly are challenging the general public and local communities for control over them. So it would seem reasonable that the movements would be, at minimum, coalition partners in a broad array of social and political struggles. Therefore, it is somewhat unexpected that the relationship between the environmental movement and the environmental justice movement in the United States often has been characterized as one of division and even hostility, rather than one of cooperation.

Since at least the early 1990s, activists from the environmental justice movement consistently have criticized what they consider the "mainstream" environmental movement's racism, classism, and limited activist agenda, charges against which environmental organizations have responded in ways ranging from defiance to varying degrees of acceptance.[3] For its part, the academic community's reaction to these critiques, both initially and in subsequent years, primarily has been to investigate the validity of the various charges, as well as to try to better understand the sources—the social, cultural, racial, economic, conceptual, institutional, historical, and rhetorical factors—that generate the tensions between the two movements. This scholarship was and remains important work, and it provides the basis for the next step: exploring how the two movements might be able to overcome, move beyond, or dissolve what divides them, to foster productive cooperation toward accomplishing their goals. The aim of this volume is to provide a stimulus for moving academic dialog in that direction. It consists of ten original essays, each of which considers some aspect of the environmental justice challenge to environmentalism and the relationship between the two movements in terms of what divisions remain, how interactions between the movements have fared in the past, and what the limits and possibilities are for the future. Without neglecting significant conceptual and practical points of tension, and while recognizing that there are times when collaboration is not appropriate or desirable, the collection as a whole emphasizes productive responses to the challenges environmental justice poses to environmentalism and the ways both movements have the potential to accomplish a great deal when they work together.

That the goals of both the environmental justice movement and the environmental movement are urgent and worth advancing is something all the contributors to this volume embrace. What is ultimately at issue is *not* whether one movement has more worthwhile goals or moral authority over the other, but, rather, *how the goals of both movements might be achieved together effectively*. As such, the contributors to this collection do not approach their topics from the "side" of either the environmental or environmental justice movement. Nor do they all approach the theme of this volume from one particular academic discipline. Among the fields represented are anthropology, environmental studies, natural resource sciences, philosophy, public policy, rhetoric, and sociology. The contributing authors thus provide a range of scholarly perspectives, methods, and frames. This diversity is appropriate to the multifaceted relationship between the two movements and the complexity of the social, political, conceptual, evaluative, historical, and rhetorical terrain in which they operate. A comprehensive assessment of the prospects for these two movements to work together requires that each of these perspectives be considered, without encumbrances from disciplinary boundaries.

The remainder of this introduction is intended to serve, first, as a primer for those who are not already familiar with two key events in the early 1990s—the letters to the "Group of Ten" and the First National People of Color Environmental Leadership Summit—that have since then largely framed the relationship between the two movements and significantly oriented the scholarship regarding the challenges that environmental justice poses to environmentalism. It then provides a brief discussion of what both activists and scholars have identified as major sources of division between the two movements. Finally, it provides a brief overview of the chapters, locating them within the questions, issues, and themes that drive this volume.

The Letters

On January 16, 1990, the Gulf Coast Tenant Leadership Development Project sent a letter to the "Group of Ten"[4] national environmental organizations, declaring, "Racism and the 'whiteness' of the environmental movement is our Achilles heel."[5] Two months later, on March 16, 1990, the Southwest Organizing Project sent a second letter to the Group of Ten. This letter, which included 103 signatories, invited "frank and open dialogue" regarding the following charges:

Although environmental organizations calling themselves the "Group of Ten" often claim to represent our interests, in observing your activities it has become clear to us that your organizations play an equal role in the disruption of our communities. There is a clear lack of accountability by the Group of Ten environmental organizations towards Third World communities in the Southwest, in the United States as a whole, and internationally.

The letters accused the Group of Ten of ignorance, ambivalence, and complicity with the environmental exploitation of communities of color within the United States and abroad. Although they often emphasized that environmental tenets are universal, the Group of Ten's pursuit of their conception of environmentalism had failed, according to the letters, to take into account the ramifications of their agenda for "working people in general and people of color in particular." The letters also claimed that the voices and representatives of communities of color too often were marginalized from environmental decision making by the very organizations that claimed to be representing their interests on a variety of issues ranging from grazing of sheep on public lands to "debt-for-nature swaps," in which Third World countries are invited to trade some rights over parts of their land for reduction of their national debt. Overall, the letters called for the environmental movement to review comprehensively and address its own culpability in patterns of environmental racism and undemocratic processes, including its hiring practices, lobbying agenda, political platforms, financial backers, organizing practices, and representations of Third World communities within the United States and abroad.

This was not the first time such concerns were expressed, but in this case environmental justice activists succeeded in raising the social, political, ethical, and institutional challenges to environmentalism in a way that gained the attention of the national mainstream press.[6] In light of the bluntness of these public allegations, it seemed impossible for the environmental movement to plead ignorance any longer about accusations of its own responsibility in patterns of racism and elitism. Meanwhile, the environmental justice movement only seemed to be gaining momentum.

The First Summit

One year later, on October 24–27, 1991, the First National People of Color Environmental Leadership Summit (Summit I) was held in Washington, DC. The gathering brought together more than a thousand activists from across the United States, as well as Canada, Central America, and the Marshall Islands. In the words of then Executive Director of the United Church of Christ Commission for Racial Justice, Reverend Benjamin F. Chavis, Jr., Summit I was "not an independent 'event' but a significant and pivotal step in a crucial process whereby people of color are organizing themselves and their communities for self-determination and self-empowerment around the central issues of environmental justice" (1991, p. i).[7]

On the final day of the Summit, the delegates adopted the seventeen "Principles of Environmental Justice," which has since served as the defining document for the environmental justice movement. (The Principles of Environmental Justice can be found in Appendix A of this collection.) The Principles embody an expansive conception of environmental issues, and locate them within an encompassing social, political, and ethical outlook. They call for a robust activist agenda and a wide range of spiritual, ecological, sustainable, educational, and social justice commitments. They articulate a desire for universal protection and self-determination domestically and internationally. Overall, the Principles emphasize that the environmental justice movement is not only an effort for racial justice; it is a movement for justice for "all peoples."

At Summit I, a prominent corollary to articulating a vision for the environmental justice movement was addressing the relationship between environmental justice communities and environmental organizations. For example, Pat Bryant, executive director of the Gulf Coast Tenants Organization, outlined conditions for dialogue with environmental organizations.

I think there is fertile ground for coalition and cooperation. But it cannot happen unless we adhere to some very basic principles.... We cannot join hands with anybody who will not join with us and say that we have the right to live. And having the right to live means that we also have the right to housing, health care, jobs and education.... We need our friends who are environmentalists to look at a total program for human uplift. (1991, p. 85)

During Summit I, a session was dedicated to the relationship between the environmental justice movement and the environmental movement. Moderated by Chavis, it was entitled "Our Vision of the Future: A Redefinition of Environmentalism." The speakers for that session included African American, Latino/a, Asian American, and tribal representatives of the environmental justice movement from across the United States, as well as two environmental movement leaders, John H. Adams, executive director of the Natural Resources Defense Council (NRDC), and Michael Fischer, executive director of the Sierra Club.

Both environmental leaders noted that their organizations had done previous work on pollution and public health campaigns. "The Sierra Club works a lot on rocks and trees and mountains and scenic beauty," Fischer acknowledged, but added, "[it] is not all we do. It is most important to know that, particularly in the last 10 to 15 years, much more of our energy has gone into a very broad mission" including toxics and urban sprawl (1991, p. 99). He also pointed out that the Sierra Club had recently given its highest award to Wangari Maathai, a Kenyan grass-roots activist who established a women-led organization to reforest their lands. On a similar note, Adams reminded those attending the Summit that NRDC was an organizer of Summit I itself. A dedication to environmental justice, he argued, was not unusual for his organization: "For 20 years, NRDC has relentlessly confronted the massive problems associated with air, water, food and toxics. These issues form the core of NRDC's agenda, a public-health agenda" (1991, p. 101).

Nevertheless, both speakers could go only so far in situating their agenda within the emerging discourse of Summit I. Although both Fischer and Adams described the work of their organizations on what might be called "environmental justice issues" (for example, air quality and toxics), they stopped short of claiming that their groups' interests were equivalent to those voiced at the Summit. Instead, they claimed a desire to forge alliances. As NRDC's Adams put it, "I did not come here just to talk or just to listen, but I came here to engage in a new partnership" (1991, p. 101). Each insisted that this required efforts from not only environmentalists, but also from those delegates who attended Summit I. Adams observed, "What we need now is a common effort" (1991, p. 102). Fischer concurred:

We know we have been conspicuously missing from the battles for environmental justice all too often, and we regret that fact sincerely.... I believe that this historic conference is a turning point, however, and while we can still say the *mea culpas* from time to time, this is a charge to all of us to work and look into the future, rather than to beat our breasts about the past.... We national environmental organizations are not the enemy. The divide-and-conquer approach is one that the Reagan and Bush administrations have used all too successfully for all too long. (1991, p. 99)

Thus, representatives of both movements hoped that the Summit might mark a starting point toward better communication, understanding, responsiveness, and alliances.

Cautious about any "quick fixes," however, Dana Alston, senior program officer of the Panos Institute of Washington, DC, responded with hesitation to the prospects of collaboration. First, she emphasized the importance of an expanded appreciation of "environmentalism," which involved a broader agenda than traditional conservation or preservation discourses included:

For us, the issues of the environment do not stand alone by themselves. They are not narrowly defined. Our vision of the environment is woven into an overall framework of social, racial and economic justice. The environment, for us, is where we live, where we work, and where we play. (1991, p. 103)

Second, she described what a basis for a "just partnership" between the two movements would require:

What we seek is a relationship based on equity, mutual respect, mutual interest, and justice. We refuse narrow definitions. It is not just ancient forests; it is not just saving the whales or saving other endangered species. These are all very important. We understand the life cycle and the inter-connectedness of life. But our communities and our people are endangered species, too. We refuse a paternalistic relationship. We are not interested in a parent-child relationship. Your organizations may be or may not be older than ours. Your organizations definitely have more money than ours. But if you are to form a partnership with us, it will be as equals and nothing else but equals. (1991, pp. 105–106)

Understanding the Challenge

In the aftermath of the letters and Summit I, scholars began investigating further why these charges arose and analyzing the challenges they posed to the environmental movement. Several prominent themes emerged, including racism, classism, and sexism, as well as conceptual, rhetorical, historical, evaluative, and cultural differences.

As the letters and Summit I indicated, the primary impetus for the environmental justice movement's criticisms was the failure of the environmental movement to make racism a priority, internally or externally. Leading environmental justice scholars and activists Beverly A. Wright, Pat Bryant, and Robert D. Bullard echoed the letters by reiterating that a major barrier between the two movements is the whiteness of the environmental movement: "That seems to be the strategy of leaders of major environmental organizations. These groups cannot reach out to African Americans and people of color as long as they are nearly all white" (1994, p. 121).[8] In 1980, when the Group of Ten was established, the leaders of each organization were white.[9] One implication of this racial divide was the way it shaped agenda setting, particularly insofar as certain places became the focus of protection and other places—usually more populated and with more people of color inhabiting them—drew less attention from the environmental movement (Figueroa 2001; Lawson 2001). Moreover, by marginalizing the people, places, and issues important to those in the environmental justice movement, the environmental movement was limiting possibilities of alliance building, even when people of color approached them. "We knew we needed allies," Bryant explained, "but when we reached out to the Sierra Club, we found that only one Sierra Club member could understand us. ... Somehow, racism has made itself palatable to the intellectuals and to the environmentalists" (1991, p. 84).[10]

Although race has been established as a separate, and often more significant, predicting factor of environmental discrimination and exclusion than economic status, elitism and economic disparity are also significant factors in the unequal siting of environmentally undesirable land uses, routine marginalization from environmental decision-making processes, and denial of just compensation and informed consent in environmental matters.[11] As environmental justice activist Lois Gibbs and others have noted, poor, white working-class communities also felt ignored by the Group of Ten. Despite occasional efforts to use the resources and clout of the more established movement—particularly in lobbying Capitol Hill—they found such attempts at collaboration often forced them to lose their own voices in setting the agenda (Schwab 1994, pp. 389, 391). As a result, the issues working-class communities wanted to focus on were often marginalized. And, although labor activists and environmentalists had worked together on some occupational health and safety legislation in the past, the often false choice of "jobs versus the environment" remained a dominant frame and influenced many local struggles (Obach 2004; Levenstein and Wooding 1998). In addition, "debt-for-nature" swaps were perceived as signals that, when the environmental movement engaged global issues of deforestation and global warming, it failed to take into account the needs of indigenous peoples and the Third World poor in those negotiations.[12]

Exacerbating the environmental justice movement's racial and economic critiques of the environmental movement was a sex and gender divide between the two movements. Although they have played various roles throughout the history of the U.S. environmental movement, women's contributions largely have been undervalued. Moreover, their roles have been more at the grassroots level, rather than in national or international leadership positions (Merchant 1996). Conversely, housewives and mothers, often mobilized by environmental health crises in their homes and communities, quickly emerged as leaders in the environmental justice movement and challenged traditional notions of gender roles. The attitudes and practices of the predominantly male leadership of the environmental movement further exacerbated tensions between the two movements when empowered, often self-taught grassroots leaders of the predominantly female-led or, at minimum, co-led environmental justice movement found themselves less respected and less represented by the environmental movement.[13]

In addition to challenges of race, class, and sex, there were also conceptual, cultural, and rhetorical differences. Both before and after the letters to the Group of Ten, environmental justice activists openly complained of the difficulties of articulating their views and concerns within the prevalent terms and conceptual frames of environmental organizations.[14] Although there was widespread awareness and concern about toxic pollution and public health within the environmental movement since at least the publication of Rachel Carson's (1962) best-seller *Silent Spring*, the Group of Ten remained most commonly identified by those both inside and outside the movement with the preservation of scenic wilderness areas and the protection of endangered species (Bullard and Wright 1992, p. 42). In her account of efforts to stop the location of a 1,600-ton-per-day solid waste incinerator in a South Central Los Angeles neighborhood in the mid-1980s, Giovanna Di Chiro reports, "These issues were not deemed adequately 'environmental' by local environmental groups such as the Sierra Club or the Environmental Defense Fund" (1996, p. 299ff.). Thus, when residents of the predominantly African American, low-income community approached these groups, "they were informed that the poisoning of an urban community by an incineration facility was a 'community health issue,' not an environmental one" (1996, p. 299).[15] On the other coast, in meetings in New York City, critics observed that it was clear "that the mainstream environmental community is reluctant to address issues of equity and social justice, within the context of the environment" (Alston 1990, p. 23). Episodes of this sort not only indicated to many in the environmental justice movement that the environmental movement was indifferent to their issues, they also suggested that the environmental movement was not interested in significantly challenging the established social and political power structure. Environmentalism failed, on this view, to provide a much-needed radical cultural critique (Bullard 1993; Hofrichter 1993).

Exasperated with the perceived narrowness of the environmental movement's social agenda and the marginalization of their issues and experiences, environmental justice activists began to emphasize self-definition (Di Chiro 1998). As is apparent from Alston's statement at Summit I, environmental justice activists were reinventing the concept of "environment" to reflect their diverse range of voices and cultures.[16] In *We Speak for Ourselves*, Alston (1990) insists that environmental justice "calls for a total redefinition of terms and language to describe the conditions that people are facing" (quoted in Di Chiro 1998, p. 105). And according to the National Environmental Justice Advisory Council, the movement "represents a new vision borne out of a community-driven process whose essential core is a *transformative public discourse* over what are truly healthy, sustainable and vital communities" (1996, p. 17). Indeed, one of the primary goals of the movement was, in the words of environmental justice activist Deehon Ferris, literally "shifting the terms of the debate" (1993). For example, the language of environmental justice activists drew on the legacy of the civil rights movement, but terms like "racism," "economic blackmail," "justice," and "rights" were not the predominant environmental discourse at the time. As Dorceta Taylor (2000) has argued, from the beginning the environmental justice movement effectively reframed environmental discourse by communicating its grievances and goals in a frame that inextricably linked social justice with the environment. This broadened dialogue about the "environment" worried some environmentalists, who wondered whether the already marginalized concerns for animals and wilderness would be placed even further on the back burner by this seemingly more anthropocentric set of values and terms.

In addition to redefining terms, the environmental justice movement also sought to redefine knowledge, by emphasizing how grassroots communities express their experiences and the knowledge they have to share. The environmental justice movement, for example, recognizes the importance of storytelling as an epistemology, in addition to more traditional scientific and economic discourses (Krauss 1994, p. 259). This way of knowing and critically interpreting the world contrasts with environmental reports that rely heavily on scientific and economic data and challenges particular conceptions of what an educated presentation entails.

As even this concise and selective discussion shows, in the 1990s the environmental justice movement was challenging the environmental movement in many ways and promised to do nothing short of transform the political and cultural landscape of environmental practice, theory, and discourse. Initial attempts by the environmental movement to respond to these charges were perceived with suspicion. For instance, when several large environmental organizations began environmental justice efforts, some environmental justice activists immediately expressed concern that such gestures were merely attempts to raise more money from foundations—money that environmental justice groups then would be unable to receive (Di Chiro, 1998, p. 112). Some environmental justice activists also questioned whether there was even a role for environmentalists in the environmental justice movement (Ferris and Hahn-Baker 1995). But all the criticisms, disappointments, and suspicions of the environmental movement not withstanding, this was a time of substantial optimism within the environmental justice movement. As Fred Setterberg and Lonny Shavelson have put it, "The 1990s, they hoped, would be their decade" (1993, p. xiii). Indeed, most scholars and activists seemed to agree. According to Jim Schwab, "The new movement had won a place at the table. The Deep South, the nation, would never discuss environmental issues in the same way again" (1994, p. 393).

Time to Reassess

It now is well over a decade since the environmental justice critique of environmentalism was laid out in the 1990 letters to the Group of Ten and Summit I was convened. Much has changed within, transpired between, and happened around the two movements over that time. For example, in 1994 President Clinton signed Executive Order 12898, Federal Actions to Address Environmental Justice in Minority Populations and Low-Income Populations. Among the executive order's outcomes was the formation of the National Environmental Justice Advisory Council (NEJAC) to the EPA.[17] In this way, among others, the environmental justice movement has become increasingly institutionalized over the last ten years. Also, on October 23–27, 2002, a second National People of Color Environmental Leadership Summit (Summit II) was convened in Washington, DC, to mark a decade of accomplishments and to discuss directions for the future of the movement.

Moreover, there have been significant shifts in receptivity to environmental justice and environmental concerns within the national political landscape, particularly at the federal executive level. Whereas President Clinton was an outspoken advocate for environmental justice efforts targeted toward minority and low-income communities, President George W. Bush has reduced environmental justice efforts at the EPA and has proposed redefining environmental justice in a way that does not reference the historical environmental inequities and disproportionate environmental burdens of those communities.[18] Although neither President Clinton nor Vice President Gore became the leaders for which the environmental movement had hoped (there was widespread disappointment, for example, with their failure to support the Kyoto Protocol to curb global warming and with the signing of the North American Free Trade Agreement), both political leaders were preferable over the subsequent Bush administration, which has attempted to defund, roll back, revise or otherwise undermine many significant existing federal environmental policies and regulations and has stymied almost all new initiatives to expand environmental protections.[19] As a result of the current political climate, there are ongoing conversations within both movements regarding the viability and direction of their futures.

Other relevant changes to the environmental justice and environmentalism landscape since the early 1990s include: the emerging prominence of new issues, such as globalization, global warming, and human genetic research; the development by several environmental organizations, including the Sierra Club and Greenpeace, of active environmental justice campaigns and programs; the hiring of some people of color into prominent positions in environmental organizations[20]; and an increased circulation of the environmental justice framework globally, where it has begun to have an impact on transnational conversations, summits, and meetings.

Thus, it is time to reconsider the environmental justice challenge to environmentalism, as well as the relationship between the environmental and environmental justice movements more broadly to reassess the prospects for working together in the future. How and to what extent has the environmental movement responded to the challenges posed to it by the environmental movement? What are the points of division between the movements now, given the changes in the movements and the shifting social contexts in which they operate? Have new challenges, points of tension, or opportunities for cooperation emerged as a result of issues that have become increasingly urgent in recent years? Has the dialogue invited in the letters to the Group of Ten and in the speeches by Fischer and Adams at Summit I been realized to any significant degree, in at least some locales and on at least some issues? If so, what do these efforts teach us? How should the environmental movement respond to the challenges that remain? Are overcoming the divide, finding common ground, and promoting alliances or unity between the two movements appropriate aims? Do the two movements tend to work more productively when independent of one another, or have collaborations been effective in advancing both environmental and environmental justice goals? Do the events of the past decade signal future directions for the two movements? Do they adumbrate a collective or unified movement in which there is widespread appreciation of the importance of social justice to environmentalism and of environmentalism to social justice?

The essays in this collection address these and related questions. As noted, they do so from diverse academic perspectives and employ diverse research methodologies, including ethnographic participant observation, interviews, critical analysis of case studies, quantitative economic and ecological research, and philosophical analysis. Again, we believe this variety in perspectives and methods is appropriate to the multifarious dimensions of the dynamics between the movements. Only by expanding the dialogue within and beyond any one academic approach and bringing together various scholarly frames, techniques, and conceptual paradigms can an appropriately multifaceted understanding of the environmental justice challenge to environmentalism and the relationship between the two movements be achieved.

This is not to suggest that the selections in this collection represent all relevant perspectives. Rather than exhausting and closing down discussion, it is hoped that this polyvocal, but selective, gathering of academic voices will provide stimulus for a progressive and ongoing discussion of where the relationship between the two movements stands right now and how it might be developed to the benefit of both movements in the future.

The Chapters

This collection consists of ten original works—written specifically for this volume—which are divided into three parts: "Conceptual Issues," "U.S. Environments," and "International Environments." The rationale behind this division is that, although some aspects of the environmental justice challenge to the environmental movement and the possibilities for the relationship between the two movements can be discussed in abstraction from specific domestic or international circumstances, other aspects vary substantially between contexts. Both movements originated in the United States, and, as the chapters illustrate, the issues associated with the domestic relationship between them often differ substantially from the issues that arise in international contexts to which they have been exported.

In part I, "Conceptual Issues," the authors consider the environmental justice challenge and the relationship between the two movements in terms of their conceptual or value orientations, as well as the implications of that relationship for the coordination (or lack thereof) of their practical agendas. In "A Wilderness Environmentalism Manifesto:

Contesting the Infinite Self-Absorption of Humans," Kevin DeLuca argues that there are compelling reasons to maintain a biocentric environmental movement oriented around valuing wilderness. Moreover, he argues that there are both philosophical and practical problems with environmental organizations adopting environmental justice as a goal. However, rather than claiming that either environmentalism or environmental justice is more important than the other, he asserts that each promotes worthy ends and should be commended and supported for those struggles.

Peter Wenz disagrees. In "Does Environmentalism Promote Injustice for the Poor?" he argues that, despite the different conceptual underpinnings and prioritized values of the two movements, "there are no inherent conflicts between the goals of environmentalism and environmental justice." Wenz points out that there are cases where worthy goals are at odds even within the construct of a single ethical outlook or social movement, and, therefore, we cannot expect perfect congruence in all cases between these two movements. Nevertheless, he claims that, in general and under present circumstances, the goals of environmentalism favor social justice, and vice versa.

In the final contribution of the first section, "Justice: The Heart of Environmentalism," Dale Jamieson maps out a third position. He argues that concerns about justice are very much at the heart of traditional environmentalism both conceptually and historically. Moreover, he claims that recognition of this dimension of environmentalism can help reconcile the sometimes hostile divisions within the movement and counter its "tendency toward misanthropy and pessimism." Yet, Jamieson concludes, although justice is at the heart of environmentalism, it does not exhaust our ethical relationships with the environment.

In part II, "U.S. Environments," the authors consider the relationship between the environmental and environmental justice movements by examining the challenges and possibilities in specific contexts of the United States. In "Becoming an Environmental Justice Activist," Kim Allen, Vinci Daro, and Dorothy Holland present an analysis from their extensive ethnographic interviews with environmental justice activists in North Carolina. Their findings suggest that, whatever practical convergence the two movements might have "in theory," there are considerable differences between how environmental justice and environmental activists problematize environmental issues and conceptualize their practices "on the ground." Allen, Daro, and Holland, also emphasize the importance of telling the story of the relationship between the two movements in the development of what they call "the figured world of environmental justice."

In "A More 'Productive' Environmental Justice Politics: Movement Alliances in Massachusetts for Clean Production and Regional Equity," Daniel Faber reports on several initiatives in the Commonwealth of Massachusetts that are being promoted by coalitions of environmental, environmental justice, housing justice, labor, and other activist groups. In light of the obstacles that environmental justice and environmental efforts currently face at the national level, he notes that state- and local-level initiatives are critical to generating momentum, growing the movements, and moving toward accomplishing social justice and environmental sustainability. In Massachusetts, there are ongoing alliances working on environmental justice legislation and toxic reduction and substitution initiatives, as well as on regional equity initiatives. This integrated and comprehensive agenda, Faber argues, is being aggressively promoted by diverse social advocacy groups and appears to be largely motivated by recognition on the part of coalition members that in the long run environmental justice, environmental sustainability, and regional justice will either be accomplished together or not at all.

In "The Silences and Possibilities of Asbestos Activism: Stories from Libby and Beyond," Steve Schwarze tracks the hazards of Zonolite asbestos insulation from the point of extraction at a vermiculite mine and processing facility outside Libby, Montana, to, among other places, its release into the Manhattan environment as a result of the World Trade Center collapse. Schwarze argues that, despite the ubiquity of the asbestos problem, it does not fit the standard environmental justice or the standard environmental frames well. Schwarze takes this as exemplifying a more general point: there remain environmental public health struggles that neither movement appears particularly well oriented to address as of yet. So, although the current frames of both movements address urgent environmental issues, we ought not think that even taken together they adequately address all problems that fall under the rubric of the "environment."

In the final chapter of part II, "Moving Toward Sustainability: Integrating Social Practice and Material Process," M. Nils Peterson, Markus J. Peterson, and Tarla Rai Peterson study the environmental and environmental justice attitudes and activities of border residents of Cameron and Hidalgo counties, Texas (USA). Their approach combines a personally administered survey, informant-directed interviews, participant observation of the social situation, and field notes. From this research, they argue that the concept of sustainable development offers potential for environmental movements and environmental justice movements to work together. They believe that realizing this possibility "requires 'movement fusion,' or thoughtful integration of physical processes typically stressed by environmental movements with social practices stressed by environmental justice movements."

In part III, "International Environments," the authors consider the challenges for and possibilities of the environmental justice and environmental movements working together in international contexts. In "Golden Tropes and Democratic Betrayals: Prospects for the Environment and Environmental Justice in Neoliberal 'Free Trade' Agreements," J. Robert Cox examines the relationship of environmental justice and environmentalism within the context of neoliberal trade agreements such as the North American Free Trade Agreement (NAFTA), the Free Trade Agreement of the Americas (FTAA), and the General Agreement on Trade in Services (GATS). Advocates of such agreements commonly claim that the economic gains they provide will inevitably lead to improvement in environmental quality. Cox argues both that the evidence in favor of this claim is less than decisive and that the conditions and constraints neoliberal trade agreements place on national governments undermine their capacity to implement environmental protections. Because it is the poor and politically marginalized who most often and most severely suffer from environmental degradation, Cox emphasizes how neoliberal trade agreements are more likely to compromise the environment and promote environmental injustice than promote environmental quality and environmental justice.

In "Indigenous Peoples and Biocolonialism: Defining the 'Science of Environmental Justice' in the Century of the Gene," Giovanna Di Chiro considers the promise that genetics, through such initiatives as the Human Genome Diversity Project and the Environmental Genome Project, can find cures and treatments for many of the environmental illnesses disproportionately affecting people of color and low-income communities across the globe. Di Chiro reports that many environmental justice activists are skeptical of such claims, in view of the social backdrop and historical precedence against which they are made. Further, Di Chiro finds the critique offered by many Indigenous activists around the world in response to the "geneticization" of environmental and health problems to be particularly telling. The push to commodify "life itself" is neither novel nor radical; it is a continuation of the centuries-old pattern of colonization (in this case, biocolonialism) through commodification. Di Chiro concludes that Indigenous voices provide a robust critique of the genetics movement that is not yet fully integrated as part of the standard discourse of either the environmental or environmental justice movements.

In the final chapter of the section, "Globalizing Environmental Justice" J. Timmons Roberts reflects on the growing transnationalization and globalization of the environmental justice frame. He claims that the result has been the forging of a number of diverse, unexpected, and broad-based international coalitions focusing on both environmental and environmental justice issues. Although Roberts has some reservations about the robustness of many of these alliances, he is nevertheless optimistic about their potential, because there have already been some successes, such as the establishment of the Brazilian environmental justice network. Moreover, he believes that the environmental justice movement has "lost some traction" within the national context and, therefore, international environmental justice struggles hold some of the greatest promise for the future of the environmental justice movement.

In the concluding chapter of this collection, "Working Together and Working Apart," we assess what these contributions taken together tell us about the ways that the environmental movement can effectively respond to the challenges of environmental justice, as well as the possibilities for creating a productive relationship between the two movements. We argue that, although they provide a strong case against the environmental movement radically redefining its core mission and commitments or attempting to somehow merge with the environmental justice movement, they demonstrate that effective, mutually beneficial alliances that advance both movements' missions are possible over a wide range of issues and contexts. Moreover, they indicate several conditions, including mutual respect and well-defined goals, that make those alliances and collaborations successful.

The perspectives and voices represented in this collection are in some ways diverse—the authors are from a variety of scholarly fields, reflect a range of activist orientations, and do not all agree, but in other respects they are quite narrow. For example, the authors are all academics, but the concerns posed in this volume are not merely academic issues. With this in mind, our intent is that this set of essays will be *a part* of a rethinking of the relationship between the environmental justice and environmental movements. To be sure, whether, when, and how the two movements can work effectively together will ultimately be settled by events on the ground, not in the pages of any book. Still, our hope is that readers will come away from these essays with some new insights and renewed motivation to discuss the continuing environmental justice challenge to environmentalism, as well as what these movements can and cannot offer each other in the context of our current and emerging environmental struggles.

Notes

1. Dowie (1995, p. 127).

2. Environmental Justice Activist Cora Tucker, in Kaplan (1997, p. 69).

3. To differentiate between the environmental movement and the environmental justice movement, many scholars call the former the "mainstream environmental movement." We choose not to use the word "mainstream" because it suggests that the tenets of this movement have been widely accepted in dominant society. At this time, with the U.S. federal government ignoring or actively rolling back most initiatives of the environmental movement, environmentalism hardly appears "mainstream." For a discussion of additional limitations of this label, see Gottlieb (2005, p. 162).

4. "The Group of Ten" was the nickname for the major environmental organizations that met regularly to coordinate efforts to respond to the backlash against the environmental movement during the Reagan Administration. It included the Audubon Society, Environmental Defense Fund, Friends of the Earth, Izaak Walton League, National Parks and Conservation Association, National Wildlife Federation, Natural Resource Defense Council, Sierra Club, Sierra Club Legal Defense Fund, and The Wilderness Society.

5. "About the same time, the Network for Environmental and Economic Justice wrote to Greenpeace, the National Toxics Campaign, and the Citizens' Clearing

House for Hazardous Wastes, expressing deep appreciation for their support of grassroots struggles in communities of color. The letter pointed out, however, that their organizations were still led and controlled by whites and were thus more likely to advocate *for* rather that [*sic*] *with* communities of color" (Dowie 1995, p. 147).

6. See, for example, Shabecoff (1990).

7. This and all subsequent quotes from the Summit are excerpted from a transcript of the Summit Proceedings compiled by the United Church of Christ Commission for Racial Justice.

8. It is interesting that this critique and many like it have been published by Sierra Club Books.

9. Gottlieb (2005, p. 165).

10. This "one Sierra Club member" is most likely Darryl Malek-Wiley, a European American who, at the time, was an employee of the Gulf Coast Tenants Association and one of the original signatures in the first letter to the Group of Ten. He also helped support the BASF lockout and the Great Louisiana Toxics March. In 2004, the Sierra Club hired him as an Environmental Justice Grassroots Organizing Program organizer for southern Louisiana.

11. The Council on Environmental Quality (CEQ) released a report in 1971 acknowledging a correlation between income and environmental quality. In 1982, protests in Warren County, North Carolina, prompted a U.S. General Accounting Office (GAO) study and a study commissioned by the United Church of Christ Commission, both of which established race to be a primary factor influencing waste siting. See, also Bullard (1990), Bullard and Wright (1987), United Church of Christ Commission for Racial Justice (1987), Lavelle and Coyle (1992), Moses (1993), and Faber and Kreig (2001).

12. Buttel (1995), Weissman (1993), and Bello (1993).

13. For more on the role of women as mothers and housewives in the environmental justice movement, see Freudenberg and Steinsapir (1992), Krauss (1993), Bullard (1994), and Kaplan (1997). For more about sex and gender divisions in the two movements, see Dunlap and Mertig (1992), Di Chiro (1992), and Gottlieb (1993, 2005).

14. For evidence of such complaints, see Austin and Schill (1994, pp. 58, 60), Bullard (1993), Dowie (1995, pp. 172–173), Pulido (1996, pp. 24–29), and Schwab (1994, p. 386).

15. Di Chiro notes, "Eventually, environmental and social justice organizations such as Greenpeace, the National Health Law Program, the Center for Law in the Public Interest, and Citizens for a Better Environment would join Concerned Citizens' campaign to stop [the proposed facility] LANCER" (1996, p. 527n).

16. Di Chiro, (1992, 1996, 1998); Dowie (1995, p. 124).

17. Executive Order 12898 requires "inter-agency coordination for eliminating discriminatory siting of polluting facilities." For more on NEJAC, see the

government's official webpage: http://www.epa.gov/compliance/environmental justice/nejac/overview.html

18. A 2003 report issued by the U.S. Commission on Civil Rights called *Not In My Backyard: Executive Order 12898 and Title VI as Tools for Achieving Environmental Justice* notes that, despite the limited success of these legislative landmarks, their implementation has not yet been adequately realized (online at http://www.usccr.gov/pubs/envjust/ej0104.pdf). The commission reiterated this assessment of the progress of implementation in *Redefining Rights in America: The Civil Rights Record of the George W. Bush Administration, 2001–2004* (online at http://www.usccr.gov/pubs/bush/bush04.pdf, pp. 72–79). According to the report, the Bush administration has yet put in place a comprehensive strategic plan for realizing the order, has yet to establish performance measures for assessing implementation, has yet to make Executive Order 12898 part of the EPA's core mission (and has instead deemphasized the disproportionate exposure of minority and low-income communities in its approach to addressing environmental hazards), and has failed to increase participation of affected minority and low-income communities in meaningful decision making processes. This evaluation echoes many of the concerns raised by the EPA Office of Inspector General's March 1, 2004, evaluation report: *EPA Needs to Consistently Implement the Intent of the Executive Order on Environmental Justice, Report No. 2004-P-00007* (online at http://www.epa.gov/oigearth/reports/2004/20040301-2004-P-00007.pdf). And on June 22, 2005, Bush's EPA introduced an "Environmental Justice Strategic Plan Outline" and "Framework for Integrating Environmental Justice," which do not include mention of the history of unequal protection in its definition of environmental justice.

19. For an accessible summary of the antienvironmental policies of the Bush administration's first term, see Kennedy (2004).

20. Most notably, in 2005, Jerome Ringo became the first African American chair of a major environmental organization, the National Wildlife Federation.

References

Alston, D. *We Speak for Ourselves: Social Justice, Race, and Environment.* London: Panos Institute, 1990.

Austin, R., and M. Schill. "Black, Brown, Red and Poisoned," in R. D. Bullard, ed., *Unequal Protection: Environmental Justice and Communities of Color.* (San Francisco Sierra Club Books, 1994), 53–76.

Bello, W. "Global Economic Counterrevolution: The Dynamics of Impoverishment and Marginalization," in R. Hofrichter, ed., *Toxic Struggles: The Theory and Practice of Environmental Justice.* New Society Publishers, 1993, 197–208.

Bryant, B. *Environmental Justice: Issues, Policies, and Solutions.* Washington, D.C.: Island Press, 1995.

Bullard, R. D. *Unequal Protection: Environmental Justice and Communities of Color.* San Francisco: Sierra Club Books, 1994.

Bullard, R. D. *Confronting Environmental Racism: Voices from the Grassroots.* Boston: South End Press, 1993.

Bullard, R. D. *Dumping in Dixie: Race, Class, and Environmental Quality.* Boulder, Colo.: Westview Press, 1990.

Bullard, R. D., and B. H. Wright. "The Quest for Environmental Equity: Mobilizing the African-American Community for Social Change," in R. E. Dunlap and A. G. Mertig, eds., *American Environmentalism: The U.S. Environmental Movement, 1970–1990.* New York: Taylor and Francis, 1992, 39–49.

Bullard, R. D., and B. H. Wright. "Environmentalism and the Politics of Equity: Emergent Trends in the Black Community," *Mid-American Review of Sociology,* 12 (1987): 21–37.

Buttel, F. H. "Rethinking International Environmental Policy in the Late Twentieth Century," in B. Bryant, ed., *Environmental Justice: Issues, Polities, and Solutions.* Washington, D.C.: Island Press, 1995, 187–207.

Carson, R. *Silent Spring.* New York: Houghton Mifflin, 1962.

Di Chiro, G. "Environmental Justice from the Grassroots: Reflections on History, Gender, and Expertise," in D. Faber, ed., *The Struggle for Ecological Democracy: Environmental Justice Movements in the United States.* New York: Guilford Press, 1998, 104–136.

Di Chiro, G. "Nature as Community: The Convergence of Environment and Social Justice," in William Cronon, ed., *Uncommon Ground: Rethinking the Human Place in Nature.* New York: W.W. Norton, 1996, 298–320, 527–531.

Di Chiro, G. "Defining Environmental Justice: Women's Voices and Grassroots Politics," *Socialist Review,* 22, no. 4 (1992): 92–130.

Dowie, M. *Losing Ground: American Environmentalism at the Close of the Twentieth Century.* Cambridge, Mass.: MIT Press, 1995.

Dunlap, R. E., and A. G. Mertig. *American Environmentalism: The U.S. Environmental Movement, 1970–1990.* New York: Taylor and Francis, 1992.

Faber, D., and E. Kreig. *Unequal Exposure to Ecological Hazards: Environmental Injustices in the Commonwealth of Massachusetts.* Boston: Philanthropy and Environmental Justice Research Project, Northeastern University, 2001.

Ferris, D. "Environmental Justice: Continuing the Dialogue." Audio tape of presentations by D. Ferris, R. M. Augustine, et al., at a meeting of the Society of Environmental Journalists, Third National Conference, Duke University, Durham, N.C., October 21–24, 1993.

Ferris, D., and D. Hahn-Baker. "Environmentalists and Environmental Justice Policy," in B. Bryant, ed., *Environmental Justice: Issues, Policies, and Solutions.* Washington, D.C.: Island Press, 1995.

Figueroa, R. M. "Other Faces: Latinos and Environmental Justice," in L. Westra and B. E. Lawson, eds., *Faces of Environmental Racism: Confronting Issues of Global Justice*, 2nd ed. Lanham, Md.: Rowman & Littlefield, 2001, 167–184.

Freudenberg, N., and C. Steinsapir. "Not in Our Backyards: The Grassroots Environmental Movement," in R. E. Dunlap and A. G. Mertig, eds., *American Environmentalism: The U.S. Environmental Movement, 1970–1990*. New York: Taylor and Francis, 1992, 27–38.

Gottlieb, R. *Forcing the Spring: The Transformation of the American Environmental Movement*. Washington, D.C.: Island Press, 1993.

Gottlieb, R. *Forcing the Spring: The Transformation of the American Environmental Movement*, revi. and updated ed. Washington D.C.: Island Press, 2005.

Hofrichter, R. "Introduction," in R. Hofrichter, ed., *Toxic Struggles: The Theory and Practice of Environmental Justice*. New Society Publishers, 1993, 1–11.

Kaplan, T. *Crazy for Democracy: Women in Grassroots Movements*. New York: Routledge, 1997.

Kennedy, R. F., Jr. *Crimes Against Nature: How George W. Bush and His Corporate Pals Are Plundering the Country and Hijacking our Democracy*. New York: Harper Collins, 2004.

Krauss, C. "Women of Color on the Front Line," in R. D. Bullard, ed., *Unequal Protection: Environmental Justice and Communities of Color*. San Francisco, Sierra Club Books, 1994, 256–271.

Krauss, C. "Blue-Collar Women and Toxic-Waste Protests: The Process of Politicization," in R. Hofrichter, ed., *Toxic Struggles: The Theory and Practice of Environmental Justice*. Philadelphia: New Society Publishers, 1993, 107–117.

Lavelle, M., and M. Coyle. "Critical Mass Builds on Environmental Equity." *National Law Journal*, Washington Briefs, sec. 5 (September 21, 1992).

Lawson, B. "Living for the City: Urban United States and Environmental Justice," in L. Westra and B. E. Lawson, eds., *Faces of Environmental Racism: Confronting Issues of Global Justice*, 2nd ed. Lanham, Md.: Rowman and Littlefield, 2001, 41–56.

Lester, J. P., D. W. Allen, and K. M. Hill. *Environmental Injustice in the United States: Myths and Realities*. Boulder, Colo.: Westview, 2001.

Levenstein, C., and J. Wooding. "Dying for a Living: Workers, Production, and the Environment," in D. Faber, ed., *The Struggle for Ecological Democracy: Environmental Justice Movements in the United States*. New York: Guilford Press, 1998, 60–80.

Merchant, C. *Earthcare: Women and the Environment*. New York: Routledge, 1996.

Moses, M. "Farmworkers and Pesticides," in R. D. Bullard, ed., *Confronting Environmental Racism: Voices from the Grassroots*. Boston: South End Press, 1993, 161–178.

National Environmental Justice Advisory Council Subcommittee on Waste and Facility Siting, *Environmental Justice, ban Revitalization, and Brownfields: The Search for Authentic Signs of Hope* (Wasington, D.C.: U.S. Environmental Protection Agency, 1996).

Obach, B. K. *Labor and the Environmental Movement: The Quest for Common Ground.* Cambridge, Mass.: MIT Press, 2004.

Pulido, L. *Environmentalism and Economic Justice: Two Chicano Struggles in the Southwest.* Tempe: University of Arizona Press, 1997.

Schwab, J. *Deeper Shades of Green: The Rise of Blue-Collar and Minority Environmentalism in America.* San Francisco: Sierra Club Books, 1994.

Setterberg, F., and L. Shavelson. *Toxic Nation: The Fight to Save Our Communities from Chemical Contamination.* New York: John Wiley and Sons, 1993.

Shabecoff, P. "Environmental Groups Told They Are Racists in Hiring," *New York Times* (February 1, 1990): 20A.

Taylor, D. "The Rise of the Environmental Justice Paradigm," *American Behavioural Scientist,* 43 no. 4 (2000): 508–580.

United Church of Christ Commission for Racial Justice. *Toxic Wastes and Race in the United States,* B. A. Goldman and L. Fitton, eds. Cleveland, Ohio: United Church of Christ, 1987.

U.S. General Accounting Office [GAO]. *Siting of Hazardous Waste Landfills and Their Correlation with Racial and Economic Status of Surrounding Communities.* Washington, D.C.: Government Printing Office, 1983.

Weissman, R. "Corporate Plundering of Third-World Resources," in R. Hofrichter, ed., *Toxic Struggles: The Theory and Practice of Environmental Justice.* Philadelphia: New Society Publishers, 1993, 186–196.

Wright, B. H., P. Bryant, and R. D. Bullard. "Coping with Poisons in Cancer Alley," in R. D. Bullard, ed., *Unequal Protection: Environmental Justice and Communities of Color.* San Francisco: Sierra Club Books, 1994, 110–129.

I
Conceptual Issues

1

A Wilderness Environmentalism Manifesto: Contesting the Infinite Self-Absorption of Humans

Kevin DeLuca

The world is nature, and in the long run inevitably wild.... Wilderness is a *place* where the wild potential is fully expressed.
—G. Snyder, *The Practice of the Wild*

For the past two decades, the core of the environmental movement, wilderness preservation, has suffered from a two-pronged assault, one political and the other theoretical. On the front of political practice, the attack has come from the so-called environmental justice movement.[1] This movement is better conceived as the human justice movement. My renaming is not a slight. Human justice is a fine goal, but it is not environmental justice. As even a cursory reading of the environmental justice literature suggests, the main concern of the environmental justice movement is humans. The nonhuman is only of interest insofar as it affects humans. Therefore, although the environmental justice movement is often concerned to clean up the environment, at other times it is content to support practices that harm the environment and the nonhuman in support of some human concern, frequently jobs. Never is the environmental justice movement primarily concerned with wilderness. Fundamentally, the environmental justice movement does not support environmental issues that impinge on human interests or rights. Indeed, the environmental justice movement attacks environmental groups that support wilderness or endangered species as racist and classist.

The environmental movement also has been attacked as being in favor of something that does not exist—namely, wilderness. From a position heavily indebted to postmodernism, wilderness has been savaged as a racist and classist human construct invented by elite whites and corporations.

The chief proponent of this position is William Cronon, though roots go
to the work of Raymond Williams and many have participated, including myself.[2] This theoretical deconstruction often spawns cruder arguments that (1) wilderness does not exist, (2) the construct of wilderness
is discriminatory, and, therefore, (3) it makes no sense to attempt to preserve wilderness.

The response of some in the environmental movement has been, in a
word, appeasement. Mainstream environmental organizations, such as
the Sierra Club and Greenpeace, have been quick to turn to environmental justice issues. In this chapter, I want to suggest that the environmental
movement's surrender of wilderness is premature. There are good reasons
to defend wilderness ferociously. In what follows I will review and critique the positions of the environmental justice movement and the postmodern critics of wilderness. I then will defend wilderness as both a
crucial rhetorical trope in environmental political battles and an a priori
reality that makes possible the human. Finally, I will review two cases that
show the benefits and possibilities of wilderness environmentalism.

Environmental Justice: All Humans, All The Time

The environmental justice movement in the United States has achieved
extraordinary success. Whether one ties its origin to Lois Gibbs, Love
Canal, and the antitoxins movement or to Robert Bullard, Warren
County, and the environmental racism movement, the environmental
justice movement has raised to a national level public awareness of the
disproportionate impact of environmental degradation on minorities and
lower classes, changed corporate practices, and transformed government
policies. Some of the more obvious successes include the stopping of
numerous hazardous waste sites, the establishment of the Superfund law,
and the signing of Executive Order 12898. That order mandated that
"each Federal agency shall make achieving environmental justice part of
its mission by identifying and addressing, as appropriate, disproportionately high and adverse human health or environmental effects of its programs, policies, and activities on minority populations and low-income
populations."[3] The federal government established the National
Environmental Justice Advisory Council (NEJAC) and the Interagency

Working Group on Environmental Justice (IWG) to help implement environmental justice goals, defined as follows:

Environmental Justice is the fair treatment and meaningful involvement of all people regardless of race, color, national origin, or income with respect to the development, implementation, and enforcement of environmental laws, regulations, and policies. In sum, environmental justice is the goal to be achieved for all communities and persons across this Nation. Environmental justice is achieved when everyone, regardless of race, culture, or income, enjoys the same degree of protection from environmental and health hazards and equal access to the decision-making process to have a healthy environment in which to live, learn, and work.[4]

This national mandate has trickled down to regional levels. For example, the city of Los Angeles includes environmental justice in its general plan:

Assure the fair treatment of people of all races, cultures, incomes and education levels with respect to the development, implementation and enforcement of environmental laws, regulations, and policies, including affirmative efforts to inform and involve environmental groups, especially environmental justice groups, in early planning stages through notification and two-way communication.[5]

It is clear that the environmental justice movement has benefited thousands of people. It has changed government policies and laws and has helped specific communities protect their homeplaces from the depredations of corporate polluters. For its many successes, for its dedication, and for its effective redress of race and class discrimination, the environmental justice movement is to be celebrated.

As it has gained national stature, the environmental justice movement has also challenged and transformed the environmental movement, especially with respect to its focus on wilderness and nonhuman nature. This challenge has been both implicit and explicit. Environmental justice activists have redefined "environment" to focus on humans. Gibbs articulates this new definition:

Over the past ten years the Movement for Environmental Justice has redefined the word environment. No longer does the media, the general public or our opponents see the environmental movement as one that is focused on open spaces, trees, and endangered species alone. They have finally got it! The Environmental Justice Movement is about people and the places they live, work and play.[6]

Bullard echoes Gibbs: "The environmental justice movement has basically redefined what environmentalism is all about. It basically says that the environment is everything; where we live, work, play, go to school, as well as the physical and natural world."[7]

Words have consequences. They direct thoughts and actions. Gibbs and Bullard are right. Environmental justice activists have successfully shifted the meaning of environmentalism from a wilderness focus to a human and human habitat focus. For example, at the landmark first National People of Color Environmental Leadership Summit (Summit I), out of the seventeen Principles of Environmental Justice (Appendix A), only one has a focus on nature not connected to humans. Even the last principle, which focuses on preserving "Mother Earth's resources," connects that preservation to human self-interest: "to insure the health of the natural world for present and future generations." There is no need to explicitly state humans. It is understood.

This shift in environmentalism is manifested in environmental justice actions.[8] Gibbs's Center for Health and Environmental Justice (CHEJ), "the only national environmental organization founded and led by grassroots leaders," is concerned with multiple issues affecting human health but has no room for wilderness issues. Bullard's Environmental Justice Resource Center (EJRC) focuses on "environmental and economic justice, environmental racism, land use and industrial facility permitting, brownfields redevelopment, community health, transportation equity, suburban sprawl, and smart growth."[9] Wilderness is noticeably invisible. The insignificance of wilderness for environmental justice activists makes sense, in light of their experiences and focus. As Gibbs's CHEJ defines it, environmental justice is "the principle that people have the right to a clean and healthy environment regardless of their race or economic standing."

So, environmental justice activists shift the focus of environmentalism from wilderness and nature to people. On its own, this is neither surprising nor noteworthy. The problem for wilderness advocates is that environmental justice groups, not content to have their own "environmental movement" focused on people, directly challenge and berate the environmental movement for not focusing on people and their problems, in other words, for being environmental groups. In the now famous 1990 letters to the Group of Ten, the Southwest Network for Economic and Environmental Justice indicted wilderness advocacy as racist and colonialist:

Your organizations continue to support and promote policies which emphasize the clean-up and preservation of the environment on the backs of working people in general and people of color in particular. In the name of eliminating environmental hazards at any cost, across the country industrial and other economic activities which employ us are being shut down, curtailed, or prevented while our survival needs and cultures are ignored.[10]

These charges of racism and classism raise the shibboleth of jobs versus the environment, the ghost that haunts the environmental movement. Far from being a call for environmental justice, this letter demonstrates a most pernicious form of anthropocentrism, wherein only human interests count. From such a position, no wilderness area or national park should be preserved because it would necessarily cost human jobs when the trees cannot be cut, the minerals mined, the grasses grazed. No poisons, such as DDT, could be banned because someone would lose a job when the production line was shut down. Environmental devastation is big business, and stopping it will cost jobs (at least in the short run).

The culture issue is also used to smear the protection of ecosystems and species. For example, if one's culture tends to favor fishing an endangered species, that is their human right, and too bad for the fish: "although these Latino communities support conservation efforts, they are concerned that state restrictions on activities such as fishing 'will deprive them of an opportunity for contact with nature by restricting their ability to use the catch as an occasion for generosity to family, friends, and neighbors.'"[11] The environmental crisis is the result of a multitude of human practices. If we are going to make any progress in stopping environmental destruction, we are going to have to give up many cultural practices, no matter how much we like them. For example, in the South, from where I am writing, cars and the right to drive them whenever and wherever one wants are considered part of one's cultural heritage—note the devotion to NASCAR. When it comes to saving ecosystems and the planet's health, culture is often the problem and should not be a trump card used to stop protecting species and ecosystems.

Indeed, environmental justice responses to protecting endangered species represent another damaging aspect of human self-absorption. Giovanna Di Chiro writes, "So the trademark slogans of mainstream environmentalism, such as 'Save the whales' or 'Extinction is forever,' are seen to reflect concerns of white people who are blind to the problems of

people of color."[12] To put it bluntly, from an environmental justice perspective, to be worried about the extinction of nonhuman species is a
form of racism. African American journalist Paul Ruffins articulated
(with regret) the position of African American environmentalists: "We
have attacked white environmentalists for their concern with saving
birds and forests and whales while urban children were suffering from
lead paint poisoning."[13] The absurdity of this position is obvious. Is the
environmental movement not allowed to care for wilderness or other
species until every human being is safe and happy? Because humans are
so expert at hurting each other, such a position amounts to disbanding
all conventional environmental organizations.

Environmental justice groups attempt to claim the moral high ground
on this issue by claiming endangered species status for themselves: "We
feel that many of these communities are just as much endangered species
as any animal species."[14] Although Di Chiro lauds this position—"The
question of what (and who) counts as an endangered species is therefore
another crucial aspect of the environmental justice movement's recon-
ceptualization of the relationships between nonhuman and human
nature and the emergence of new ideas of nature and new forms of environmentalism"[15]—in truth the position represents either a woeful ignorance of science or a stunning example of human self-centeredness. No,
humans are not an endangered species and a subset of humans cannot
constitute an endangered species. Yes, many species are endangered as a
result of human cultural practices.

Silencing Wilderness: The Gag of Humanism

Despite the logical inanity of the environmental justice positions and the
blatant use of the race and class cards, many environmental movement
groups have acquiesced to environmental justice demands.[16] The Sierra
Club, America's preeminent environmental organization both historically and politically, is the paramount example.[17] At a Sierra Club centennial celebration, then executive director Michael Fischer called for "a
friendly takeover of the Sierra Club by people of color... [or else it will]
remain a middle-class group of backpackers, overwhelmingly white in
membership, program, and agenda.... The struggle for environmental

justice in this country and around the globe must be the primary goal of the Sierra Club during its second century."[18] This marked turn toward social justice was institutionalized in 1993: "The Board of Directors of the Sierra Club recognizes that to achieve our mission of environmental protection and a sustainable future for the planet, we must attain social justice and human rights at home and around the globe." This utopian humanitarian mission was elaborated upon with a 2001 declaration of their own "Environmental Justice Principles."[19]

So, what is wrong with the Sierra Club and other environmental organizations adopting "environmental justice" as a goal? The problems are both philosophical and practical. The startling innovation that wilderness preservation introduced into modern industrial civilization with Yosemite in 1864 is the idea that other living beings have a right to existence outside of their service to humans. In thinking about Yosemite, David Brower suggested that Frederick Law Olmsted was one of the first to attempt to speak for the trees: "Mountains have a voice, and Olmsted was one of the first to try to speak for them. He proposed the rights for nature implicit in the national park idea."[20] The attempt of the Sierra Club to accommodate environmental justice activists represents a retreat from speaking for the trees to once again speaking for people, just like everyone else. It is, according to Aldo Leopold, to shun the light of Darwin's wisdom:

that men are only fellow-voyagers with other creatures in the odyssey of evolution. This new knowledge should have given us, by this time, a sense of kinship with fellow-creatures; a wish to live and let live; a sense of wonder over the magnitude and duration of the biotic enterprise. Above all we should, in the century since Darwin, have come to know that man, while now captain of the adventuring ship, is hardly the sole object of its quest, and that his prior assumptions to this effect arose from the simple necessity of whistling in the dark.[21]

There are many organizations that speak for people and their myriad concerns. I do not insist that they become environmental organizations and speak for the trees. It is important for environmental organizations to retain their unique perspective, speaking primarily for sentient beings that have no human voice. The Sierra Club's board of directors is wrong to claim that, "to achieve our mission of environmental protection and a sustainable future for the planet, we must attain social justice and human rights at home and around the globe."[22] Indeed, in the case of population control, the nondemocratic Chinese government provides a clear counter-example. It is highly doubtful that a democratic China could have curbed its population as effectively as China has through its strict one-child policy. Democratic India has been an abject failure at controlling its population. Population control is not a popular idea. Democracy is not an a priori condition for environmental integrity.[23] Social justice and human rights around the globe are not a priori conditions for environmental protection. Indeed, the protection of endangered species around the globe often requires the violation of human rights and social justice. Environmental protection often increases human suffering. When people are prevented from hunting rhinos for money to feed their families or poaching turtle eggs for profit and food, human suffering is increased. Some environmental protection requires the shutting down of destructive industries and the loss of jobs. If the environmental movement adopts the human-centered perspective of the environmental justice movement, they will be unable to make the hard decisions that increase human suffering, that require putting other beings and ecosystems, not humans, first. Putting humans always first is a crucial cause of the environmental crisis we now face.

In practical terms, abandoning wilderness and environmental protection as a first principle leads environmental groups to abandon environmental criteria as a means of judging practices and policies. Environmental justice activists quite explicitly put human, cultural, and economic concerns over environmental concerns. Gibbs's and Bullard's definitions of "environment" make that clear. The berating of wilderness activists moved to save whales and trees while there are still children suffering from lead paint poisoning or starvation makes that clear. When environmental groups put human rights, social justice, economic concerns, and respect for cultural diversity ahead of wilderness preservation and ecosystem health, it becomes impossible to condemn human practices on environmental grounds and judge among competing cultural practices. For example, backpacking, off-road four-wheeling, recreational vehicle "camping," and fishing are all cultural practices, but they have different environmental consequences and should be judged in light of those consequences, not their importance to the groups that practice them.

When the right of minorities to have jobs is the paramount concern, it becomes difficult to condemn jobs and work practices harmful to the environment.

The controversy in California and Canada over leaf blowers is another example. When local groups tried to convince towns to do something as simple as ban leaf blowers, a recent extraneous and ecodamaging invention, they were charged with being elitist and racist, because many landscape workers in California are Latino. Despite the environmental and human health costs, especially for workers, groups such as the Association of Latin American Gardeners of Los Angeles and the Bay Area Gardeners Association insisted on a right to leaf blowers. As one proponent of the ban noted, "To convince urban gardeners that it is their God given right to work with leaf blowers is akin to the United Farm Workers demanding the retention of the short handled hoe and DDT in their day."[24] Sheldon Ridout, a veteran of what he terms "combat gardening," started a landscaping company called the Silent Gardener. He was motivated by "coming home smelling like fuel every day, always being in a cloud of dust and being surrounded by noise."[25]

The point cannot be emphasized enough. The world is facing a catastrophe of historic and unique proportions, and it is not a crisis of social justice and human rights. Arguably the state of social justice and human rights is better now than at any other time in human history. Regardless, social injustices and human rights violations are not new. As documented annually by the World Watch Institute and others, however, humans are threatening the vital signs of planetary health in a manner and scale unprecedented in human history. Air and water pollution, chemical contamination, topsoil loss, collapse of multiple fisheries, forest loss, desertification, and loss of biological diversity are the threats that must be confronted if we are to achieve the environmental movement's mission of environmental protection and a sustainable future for the planet.[26]

Another important consequence of the ethos of environmental justice groups is the deferment to the local. Following the lead of environmental justice groups, environmental groups like the Sierra Club and Greenpeace not only agree to take on environmental justice issues, but also agree to defer absolutely to the experiences and decisions of local environmental justice groups. This is a problem. Although local groups can have insights peculiar to their experiences and place, they are by no means the sole repository of wisdom and can often act for short-sighted self-interests against the interests of the greater community and the larger good. An obvious and painful example comes from recent U.S. history. If left up to the "wisdom" of the local majority in the South in the 1960s, Jim Crow segregation would have remained the law of the region. With respect to environmental issues, the intervention of national or international bodies is often necessary to overcome the resistance of the local. In the controversy over the slaughter of ancient forests in the Pacific Northwest, local communities often vociferously have opposed any protections of trees or animals that impinge on what they perceive to be their self-interests. Locals have physically assaulted environmentalists and proudly displayed their feelings toward the endangered spotted owl on bumper stickers: "Kill an owl. Save a logger."[27] On the global level, nations repeatedly have asserted their local self-interests over global interests. Paramount examples in this respect would be the U.S. refusal to ratify the Kyoto Protocol on global warming and Brazil's refusal to heed international suggestions for protecting the Amazon rainforest. To idealize the local is a dangerous act for environmental groups. Leopold's famous story about shooting a wolf is instructive. "I thought that because fewer wolves meant more deer, that no wolves would mean hunters' paradise. But after seeing the green fire die, I sensed that neither the wolf nor the mountain agreed with such a view."[28] It is difficult for people facing pressing local needs (hunger and employment) to "think like a mountain."

Even romanticizing "native peoples" is problematic. Americans' romanticization of Native Americans is both racist and historically inaccurate.[29] In Thailand, grassroots activists idealize the hill tribes, arguing that they live in harmony with the forests while ignoring the damage hill tribes are doing to headwaters forests. As Buddhist monk Achan Pongsak Techadhammo, a leader of Green Buddhism, notes, "Man coexisting with the forest: that's a romantic idea, little more than wishful thinking. People still talk about it because that's the way they'd like things to be. The hill tribe population is growing rapidly. They just don't farm to live; they farm to sell and with the support of vested interest groups. They have TVs, motorcycles, and cars."[30]

A final concern with the turn to environmental justice issues at the expense of wilderness is brutally political. Although Fischer argues that the Sierra Club needs to turn away from backpacker issues to environmental justice issues to avoid "losing influence in an increasingly multicultural country,"[31] such a stance is either politically naïve or utopian. The United States is not a democracy with power equally divided among each person and his or her vote. Quite clearly, political power rests in the hands of corporations and the upper and middle classes (largely white) and will continue to do so for many more decades. To these groups, wilderness issues and preservation appeals are more likely to be persuasive then discussions of toxic waste sites. The environmental movement makes this political reality an implicit calculation in their widespread rhetorical appeals through calendars, photography, books, and wilderness vacations. In a recent year, the Sierra Club's five calendar entries were *Wilderness*, *Wildlife*, *Birds*, *Butterflies*, and *Adventure Travel*. I have yet to see the toxic-waste-site calendar.

Wilderness is a Fiction: Your Point?

The environmental justice denigration or neglect of wilderness is echoed and reinforced by the postmodern deconstruction of wilderness. From this perspective, wilderness is a fiction, a social construction of a particular time, place, and people. More to the point, wilderness is the invention of rich, white European and American males in the 1800s, which involved practices that excluded woman, other classes, and nonwhite races and visited genocidal destruction upon Native Americans. The upshot is that, if wilderness is not natural, what is the point of preserving it, especially if such preservation entails racist, classist, and sexist practices? The source of much of this critique of wilderness is William Cronon's essay, "The Trouble with Wilderness; or, Getting Back to the Wrong Nature." Cronon's polemical title encourages dismissing wilderness, which is a misreading of his essay and a misunderstanding of the postmodern theories undergirding his own writing.

In deconstructing wilderness, Cronon is advancing the deconstruction of nature more broadly, suggested by Clarence Glacken, R. G. Collingwood, Raymond Williams, Donna Haraway, and Neil Evernden, among others, to the idea of wilderness. His essay continues in a more pointed fashion from work such as Roderick Nash's groundbreaking *Wilderness and the American Mind* and Max Oelschlaeger's comprehensive *The Idea of Wilderness*. In a nutshell, Cronon argues, "Far from being the one place on earth that stands apart from humanity, it is quite profoundly a human creation—indeed the creation of very particular human cultures at very particular moments in human history. . . . [T]here is nothing natural about the concept of wilderness."[32]

In much of my own work I have detailed how a "white wilderness" was created in the United States. Through Carleton Watkins' Yosemite photographs, William Henry Jackson's Yellowstone photographs, Thomas Moran's paintings, and John Muir's writings, among others, the values of elite "white" culture were inscribed in a vision of pristine, sublime wilderness that subsequently became a foundational value of the preservation movement.[33] To move from the deconstruction of wilderness to the dismissal of wilderness in favor of privileging humans and their concerns, however, is to misunderstand postmodernism. If postmodernism can be reduced to a central impulse, arguably, it would be the questioning of modernism's foundational concepts and Truths.[34] Far from privileging the human, postmodernism represents an even more sustained questioning of the human than of wilderness. Foucault puts this questioning most succinctly at the end of *The Order of Things*: "Taking a relatively short chronological sample from within a restricted geographical area—European culture since the sixteenth century—one can be certain that man is a recent invention within it. . . . As the archaeology of our thought easily shows, man is an invention of recent date. And one perhaps nearing its end." Foucault concludes that, if the cultural discourses that made possible "man" were to change, "then one can certainly wager that man would be erased, like a face drawn in sand at the edge of the sea."[35]

If one accepts the postmodern deconstruction of wilderness, the same logic dictates the deconstruction of the human. Our contact with the world, with the Real, is always already mediated through multiple discourses. This is the meaning of Jacques Derrida's infamous line, "*il n'y a pas de hors-texte* [There is nothing outside of the text]."[36] The response, then, is not to dismiss wilderness as a fiction and turn to the human, but, rather, to ask what are the benefits and costs of the fiction of wilderness. To Cronon's credit, despite his polemical title, this is what he does. The very first sentence of his essay, which stands alone as its own paragraph, reads, "The time has come to rethink wilderness."[37]

Cronon calls for this rethinking because of the importance of wilderness: "Although wilderness may today seem to be just one environmental concern among many, it in fact serves as the foundation for a long list of other such concerns that on their face seem quite remote from it. That is why its influence is so pervasive and, potentially, so insidious."[38] Cronon points to several insidious effects. The idea of pristine, sublime wilderness posits an ontological separation between humans and wilderness, because the very presence of humans destroys wilderness. A focus on pristine wilderness condemns civilization to being a narrative of environmental devastation, the despoiling of the Garden of Eden. Valorizing pristine wilderness devalues other habitats. A focus on wilderness leads environmental groups to ignore other issues, such as pollution and social justice.

It is important to recognize, therefore, that Cronon is critiquing the *idea* or *concept* of wilderness: "By now I hope it is clear that my criticism in this essay is not directed at wild nature per se, or even at efforts to set aside large tracts of wild land, but rather at the specific habits of thinking that flow from this complex cultural construction called wilderness. It is not the things we label as wilderness that are the problem—for nonhuman nature and large tracts of the natural world *do* deserve protection." For Cronon, the deconstruction of wilderness provides an opportunity to figure out and nuance our appreciation of the ecological, social, and political value of wilderness, not to analyze away its worth. Perhaps the greatest value of wilderness is that it prods us humans out of our infinite self-absorption. "The striking power of the wild is that wonder in the face of it requires no act of will, but forces itself upon us as proof that ours is not the only presence in the universe. Wilderness gets us into trouble only if we imagine that this experience of wonder and otherness is limited to the remote corners of the planet, or that it somehow depends on pristine landscapes we ourselves do not inhabit."[39]

Cronon and I agree on both the deconstruction and vital nature of wilderness, though we disagree on the ecological and political valuation of wilderness. In a later lecture tellingly titled "Humanist Environmentalism: A Manifesto," Cronon reaffirms the value of wilderness but reduces it to one among many humanist values: "A humanist environmentalism strives to protect nature but also other, equally important values: responsible (wise?) use, social justice, democracy, fairness, tolerance, community, generosity (forgiveness of the other), love, humane living, beauty, good humor, joy. Wilderness is a crucial measure of our success in building a more just and humane environmentalism."[40] Instead of a humanist environmentalism, I want to propose a wilderness environmentalism, wherein wilderness is the measure of all things.[41]

Salvaging Wilderness

I propose a wilderness environmentalism because I think it is crucial that the environmental movement be grounded in wilderness, not humanism. That said, in proposing a wilderness environmentalism, I acknowledge the deconstruction of wilderness and suggest wilderness not as the pristine and sublime ideal, but as the a priori condition of our being that surrounds and grounds us. The resources for such a move come from a surprising list of both famous environmentalists and social theorists. After briefly noting these thinkers, I will look at wilderness environmentalism on the ground and in the trees, with the examples of Julia Butterfly Hill and WildAid.

In his essay "Walking" Thoreau elaborates on his sentiment, "In Wildness is the preservation of the World": "I wish to speak a word for Nature, for absolute freedom and wildness, as contrasted with a freedom and culture merely civil—to regard man as an inhabitant, or a part and parcel of Nature, rather than a member of society."[42] Karl Marx, even while noting that nature is "not a thing given directly from all eternity, remaining ever the same, but the product of industry and the state of society" also admonishes, "Man *lives* from nature, i.e., nature is his *body*, and he must maintain a continuing dialogue with it if he is not to die."[43] It is important to keep in mind that both Thoreau and Marx note not only humanity's essential connection to nature, but also that humans are not apart from but a part of nature/wilderness. Even Muir, often credited as a chief architect of sublime wilderness as a realm apart from humans, writes, "Mountains are fountains not only of rivers and fertile soils, but of men. Therefore, we are all, in some sense, mountaineers, and going to the mountains is going home.... [W]ildness is a necessity."[44] Here Muir is advocating wilderness as home, not as vacation destination.

Writing in exile from Germany during World War II, Frankfurt School theorists Max Horkheimer and Theodor Adorno proposed that the domination of nature results in such horrors as the Holocaust, so that "the fully enlightened earth radiates disaster triumphant." For Horkheimer and Adorno, "world domination over nature turns against the thinking subject himself.... As soon as man discards his awareness that he himself is nature, all the aims for which he keeps himself alive—social progress, the intensification of all his spiritual and material powers, even consciousness itself—are nullified."[45] It is important to emphasize here that Horkheimer and Adorno, urban Jewish intellectuals who in no way supported the Nazi romanticization of the earth, insist that the very possibility of social progress depends on how humans relate to nature. Their position exactly reverses the claim of environmental justice groups and the Sierra Club that "to achieve our mission of environmental protection and a sustainable future for the planet, we must attain social justice and human rights at home and around the globe."

Aldo Leopold echoes the primacy of wilderness: "Wilderness is the raw material out of which man has hammered the artifact called civilization.... Wilderness gives definition and meaning to the human enterprise." In advocating for the primacy of wilderness, Leopold also prescribes humanity's place in the wild with his famous land ethic, which "changes the role of *Homo sapiens* from conqueror of the land-community to plain member and citizen of it."[46] Lacking Leopold's poetic sensibility, ecoactivist Dave Foreman puts it bluntly, "It [wilderness] is the natural world, the arena for evolution, the caldron from which humans emerged, the home of the others with whom we share this planet.... The preservation of wildness and native diversity is *the* most important issue. Issues directly affecting only humans pale in comparison."[47]

These theorists do not suggest neglecting the human, but, rather, recognizing that wilderness/nature grounds and circumscribes the human. What does such a perspective look like in practice? The practices of Julia Butterfly Hill and WildAid suggest another response to the specter of jobs and the incessant cry of humanity that seem to so easily defeat environmentalism—one that does not abandon wilderness. It is a response that does not ignore human issues, but also does not turn the environment into another subset of the human domain. It is a response that respects the nonhuman and humbles humanity in relation to the rest of creation. It is a response that honors Thoreau's dictum, "In Wildness is the preservation of the World," in its most fundamental senses.

Speaking for Trees and People

Julia Butterfly Hill lived for two years in Luna, a 1,000-year-old redwood targeted for cutting, descending only when Pacific Lumber agreed to spare the tree. Tree-sitting is a tactic made popular by the radical environmental group Earth First! as a way of saving ancient forests. The particular tree-sit that Butterfly joined had started in October 1997 and was significant for its location. It was not in pristine wilderness but on a hillside above the town of Stafford, California. The members of Earth First! chose this location after a mudslide caused by clearcutting destroyed seven homes in Stafford. Significantly, Stafford is a lumber town. The site of this Earth First! tree-sit links wilderness and social concerns. This linkage is echoed in Butterfly's rhetoric, which explicitly articulates the inextricable twining of wilderness and social issues.[48]

In numerous interviews, Butterfly deftly weaves wilderness issues with human concerns and a critique of corporate practices that manages to displace the jobs-versus-environment debate. Instead of letting jobs or social justice be the test of all wilderness issues, Butterfly places wilderness as the grounds for environmental and social concerns. Further, she does this all the while consistently claiming that she and her actions are merely symbols for larger struggles against environmental devastation and corporate avarice.

Speaking to *Time Magazine Online*, Butterfly said, "After being up here a few days, I realized that what was happening here was not only destroying the environment, but people's lives as well. I gave my word to this tree, the forest, and to all the people whose lives are being destroyed by the lumber companies, that my feet would not touch the ground and until I had done everything in my power to make the world aware of this problem and to stop the destruction." In an interview with

Monica Mehta on *MOJO Wire*, Butterfly elaborated on many of these points:

I feel pretty good. It's been really, really hard, but as hard as it's been on me physically, all I have to do is think about the seven families in the town of Stafford who no longer have a home. And all I have to do is think about the animals whose homes are these forests that are being destroyed. I felt raising public worldwide awareness is very important. And right now this sit has gained a much-needed spotlight that we can shine on the forests and on the issues and love and respect. I look at *Earth First!* more as a movement than as an organization, in that when we put ourselves first we suffer, but when we put the Earth first then everyone is helped.[49]

Butterfly presents an engaging and sophisticated analysis of justice that encompasses environmental and social dimensions through a grounding in wilderness. Instead of people first, it is wilderness first but with a recognition that caring for wilderness *is* caring for people. For Butterfly, adding people is not merely a polite gesture, but a recognition of the essential connection between wilderness and people. Consistently, Butterfly links the tree *and* forest *and* people. She is a tree-hugger and a people-hugger. In this position Butterfly is reaffirming the fundamental insight of the Frankfurt School's analysis of the domination of nature: that in the domination of nature people are inevitably dominated. Clearcutting the redwoods destroys people's homes. Butterfly is also proffering a complicated notion of wilderness. It is not out there, far away. It is in many places and it is intimately connected to human lives. Indeed, wilderness is the ground of our being. We do not so much live in an environment as dwell in wilderness.

The position Butterfly advocates fundamentally transforms Cronon's "humanist environmentalism" by moving the emphasis from "humanist" to "wilderness" so that wilderness is not merely an important value and a crucial measure of our success but the ground that makes possible our existence. Wilderness environmentalism holds out hope for shifting away from the multiple anthropocentric worldviews that have done enough harm. In the end, Butterfly is offering and enacting a wilderness environmentalism that grounds caring for people in caring for wilderness. This is a different vision than the myth of pristine wilderness and offers the possibility of reimagining human-wilderness relations.[50]

Founded in 1999, the radical, direct-action group WildAid uses armed confrontations with poachers, undercover espionage, and high-profile media campaigns in an attempt "to decimate the illegal wildlife trade within our lifetimes." Using such tactics, WildAid cofounders Steve Galster, Suwanna Gauntlett, Steve Trent, and Pete Knights have helped save tens of thousands of wild animals, reduced consumption of shark-fin soup in Thailand by 30 percent, and solicited millions of dollars to put armed patrols in parks and wildernesses. WildAid is a good case study for two reasons. First, it is confronting one of the main threats to global ecosystem health: loss of biodiversity. As E. O. Wilson explains, "The sixth great extinction spasm of geological time is upon us, grace of mankind. Earth has at last acquired a force that can break the crucible of biodiversity."[51]

Second, WildAid is working in regions (largely in Southeast Asia) where endangered animals are at risk from desperate people and embedded cultural traditions. The $5 billion annual illegal trade in "protected" wildlife is largely supplied by poor villagers. In Myanmar (Burma), where annual per capita income is $300, one clouded leopard skin fetches $114, aloe wood can wholesale for $1,000 per kilo, and Malayan sun bear skins and gall bladders sell for $1,000 each.[52] The largest source of consumer demand is from China, where there is a cultural belief in *ye wei*, or wild taste: "the belief that exotic fare endows them with added social status and the traits of the animal consumed, such as bravery, long life or sexual prowess."[53] China's increasing economic wealth has led to a sort of economic democracy that is devastating to wildlife and ecosystems. Wild fare that was once the province of only the wealthy is now accessible to the many. Roughly 20 million seahorses are used each year to "treat" asthma, heart disease, and impotence. In just eight months in 2003, 10,000 pangolins (scaly anteaters) were seized on their way to China from Indonesia. In Southeast Asia, up to 10,000 tons of freshwater turtles are used annually.[54] As Galster describes it, the fauna and flora of the region face "the Chinese vacuum cleaner, sucking up Southeast Asia's wildlife left and right."[55]

In this human war on wildlife and wild places, WildAid is clearly on the side of the wild. Cofounder Gauntlett explains, "There are 30,000 parks in the world, most of which are not protected at all. That's why we dedicate ourselves to direct protection of wildlife preserves in developing countries."[56] A *New York Times* reporter states it a bit more harshly in describing WildAid's work in Cambodia: "In a country where there is little help for the people, a new generation of environmentalists is trying to protect the ebbing populations of wildlife in Southeast Asian bush. And they are doing it the way so much gets done these days: with troops and guns."[57] WildAid's work in Asia puts in stark relief the consequences of giving up on wilderness in favor of an environmental justice approach to people, their work, and their cultural practices. If we put people first, we will stand by and watch as the last rhino horn, the last tiger penis, and the last seahorse are ground up and consumed in desperate attempts to increase the world's human overpopulation. If we put people first, we will stand by and watch as a poor villager eradicates the last clouded leopard in a futile attempt to eradicate poverty.

Putting wilderness first, as WildAid does, involves brutal choices. While raiding a Cambodian wildlife restaurant at gunpoint and rescuing long-tail macaques, turtles, and cobras, WildAid does not concern itself with the young teenage girls working as waitresses and prostitutes. As the accompanying reporter notes, "I can't resist the rude observation that while we have saved some turtles, we have left the girls behind . . . punishing a lady for having a turtle while abandoning child prostitutes."[58] This example, however, suggests the futility of the Sierra Club position that to achieve environmental protection "we must attain social justice and human rights at home and around the globe." If environmental protection depends on eradicating prostitution, we may as well all go buy SUVs and retire to the beach.

Putting humans first dilutes the focus and efforts of environmental groups. Further, because many human issues involve abstractions, such as social justice and human rights, they are Sisyphean tasks with no clear way to even define victory. Putting wilderness first, however, does not mean abandoning humans, as the case of Butterfly suggests. Though not as eloquent as Butterfly, WildAid definitely attends to human issues by attending to wilderness issues. WildAid lists five goals: to decimate the illegal wildlife trade in our lifetimes; to bring wildlife conservation to the top of the international agenda; to protect wilderness areas effectively and affordably; to ensure that endangered species populations rebound; and to enable people and wildlife to survive together. WildAid elaborates: "We want a world where our invaluable natural resources are not ravaged, one in which local communities can improve their lives without destroying their environment, and where humanity can survive together with wildlife for generations to come."⁵⁹ More then just words on a website, WildAid has put humans and wilderness in dialogue through several practices under the rubric "Surviving Together." First, many of the park rangers that WildAid hires and trains are former poachers. Second, WildAid hires local people to act as staff and informants. Galster hopes, by 2030, to be "turning its overseas offices into locally run NGOs [nongovernmental organizations] with all-local staffs, as he has already done with the Phoenix Fund in Russia."⁶⁰ Third, WildAid helps former poachers turn to more sustainable practices, such as mushroom and flower farming. As former poacher Sampong Prachopchan explains, "When I was a poacher, a middleman sent me into the forest to get aloe wood. We all knew that if we shot an elephant or tiger, he would buy that, too. But after I was arrested, I decided to leave poaching. If we keep on destroying the forest, there will be none left for the next generation."⁶¹

The Upshot

Understanding is always a dicey proposition. I want to be as clear as I can here. The environmental justice movement is a good thing. The work that environmental justice groups perform is needed and makes a significant difference for human health and well-being. I am in no way suggesting that environmental justice groups should change their focus on human health, toxic wastes, and race and class bias. For people living in the midst of severely degraded environments, such a focus makes perfect sense. That said, accusations of racism against groups that support wilderness issues and encouraging the environmental movement to move away from wilderness are both wrong and a mistake.

The Sierra Club is an amazing organization that has done invaluable work for decades. Their move to adopt the principles of environmental justice at the expense of a focus on wilderness, however, is a grievous error. The Sierra Club is not unique in this error. In a promotional video celebrating thirty years of "Making a World of Difference," the World Wildlife Fund spends roughly half of the program discussing the problems of people and tells contributors, "[Y]ou've enabled local people to improve their lives today and preserve the earth's irreplaceable natural resources for future generations." Even Earth First!, originally a no-compromise radical wilderness group, so turned to human issues like jobs for loggers in the 1990s that cofounder Foreman left to start an organization with a focus on wilderness (The Wildlands Project).

To make alliances with diverse groups is important. The stances of environmental justice advocate Bullard and wilderness advocate Foreman are instructive. In an interview with Earth First!, Bullard says, "I don't think you can get any more radical than fighting racism."[62] Foreman argues, "The idea of wilderness, after all, is the most radical in human thought—more radical than Paine, than Marx, than Mao. Wilderness says: Human beings are not paramount, Earth is not for *Homo sapiens* alone."[63] While retaining their radically different positions, both Bullard and Foreman advocate alliances with others. In speaking with Earth First!, Bullard says, "I'm not saying that you are gonna get a lot of people of color inundating your organization with membership but we can work together without being members and that's where the I think the collaboration, coalitions and signing onto supporting specific campaigns has really made a difference."[64] Although insisting that, "[i]n everything human society does, the primary consideration should be for the long-term health and biological Diversity of Earth," Foreman suggests, "[c]onservationists should try to find common ground with loggers and other workers whenever possible."[65] Such common ground among environmental, human justice, labor, native peoples, civil rights, women's rights, and peace activists is even more crucial now in the face of the onslaught of corporate global trade and the acronyms of that apocalypse (WTO, GATT, NAFTA, IMF/WB).

Still, I think Bullard and Foreman are right. It is important that environmental justice and wilderness environmental groups with different ideas retain their distinct identities and orientations even when forming alliances when it makes strategic sense. For the environmental movement, that identity revolves around wilderness. This is true even if one finds compelling, as I do, the deconstruction of wilderness. The lesson of postmodernism is not that wilderness is a deconstruction and, therefore, we should all be humanists. Rather, the lesson is that the mediated world we think in is necessarily a product of multiple social discourses, so the question is not one of truth but of rhetorical force, not one of ontology but of politics. The human and human rights are just as much social constructions as wilderness. China makes this very point when contesting the United Nations' Universal Declaration of Human Rights as a political ploy by Western nations in the thrall of the ideology of individualism and neglectful of community. The question, with respect to wilderness, then, is what sort of political, ecological, and social work does it enable environmentalists to do?

First, wilderness historically has been a politically effective trope that enables the environmental movement to improve the environment for both wildlife and people. The constant use of wilderness images via photography, calendars, screen savers, books, and ecotourism by the environmental movement testifies to the political and rhetorical force of wilderness. For example, using an image-based strategy proponents of the Arctic National Wildlife Refuge have staved off determined attempts to open the area to drilling. Although the refuge remains under threat, it is important to remember that it has taken the Republicans decades of rancorous struggle, repeated attempts, millions of dollars, appeals to national security in the wake of the September 11 attacks, and an election that increased the Republican majorities to even approach this goal. In addition, as part of this campaign, pro-drilling advocates realized they would have to portray the area in a way that challenged its worth as wilderness. As Ann Klee, Secretary of the Interior Gale Norton's top advisor, asked department biologists while preparing a slide show, "Don't you have any ugly pictures of ANWR"?[66]

The idea of wilderness also continues to spread around the globe and enables nations and activist groups to save significant areas. Thailand, for example, has preserved roughly 12 percent of its land. The recent awarding of the Nobel Peace Prize to Kenyan environmental activist Wangari Maathai suggests an international recognition of the primacy of nonhuman nature. As Nobel committee chair Ole Danbolt Mjoes explained, "It is clear that with this award, we have expanded the term 'peace' to encompass environmental questions relating to our beloved Earth. . . . Peace on earth depends on our ability to secure our living environment."[67]

Second, as Dave Foreman and Howie Wolke argue in *The Big Outside*, wilderness, especially when designated over large areas, is crucial to preserving ecosystems and maintaining biodiversity. With mass extinction one of the major threats facing the planet, wilderness is a crucial strategic response: "big wildernesses, particularly if adjacent to or connected via corridors with other wild areas, are best able to support the full array of indigenous species in a given region."[68]

Finally, wilderness provides a context and restraint for humans. With a humanist orientation, humans lose all sense of perspective and place and succumb to the fatal illness of species solipsism, believing "man is the measure of all things." Wilderness as the a priori ground of humanity provides a powerful antidote. Cronon succinctly expresses this important attribute of wilderness:

> I also think it no less crucial for us to recognize and honor nonhuman nature as a world we did not create, a world with its own, independent nonhuman reasons for being as it is. The autonomy of nonhuman nature seems to me an indispensable corrective to human arrogance. Any way of looking at nature that helps us remember—as wilderness also tends to do—that the interests of people are not necessarily identical to those of every other creature or of the earth itself is likely to foster *responsible* behavior.[69]

Abandoning wilderness-centered environmentalism is a disastrous error. The finest moments of environmentalism often involve humans exceeding self-concern and caring for wilderness and other species because of their intrinsic being. To be sure, wilderness was often sold as a balm for harried urban souls and a boon for railroad profits, but one cannot read John Muir, Edward Abbey, Rachel Carson, or Janisse Ray, among others, and not be struck by the love of wilderness for its own sake—the love of something outside of human design. More than love, though, the encounter with wilderness is an encounter with a nonhuman other. When we abandon wilderness we risk losing what Derrida terms "monstrosity," the other that exceeds human sense and economic calculation.[70] We need not decry the loss of the pristine wilderness of the Romantic tradition, with its unfortunate race and class consequences. We do need to salvage wilderness as the excess and otherness that grounds and surrounds us, putting us in our place.

Notes

1. Accounts of the environmental justice movement that are good starting points include Bullard (1990), Gottlieb, (1993), and Schwab (1994).
2. The deconstruction of nature came first and wilderness more recently. For arguments about and accounts of the social construction of nature, see

Collingwood (1945), Evernden (1992), Haraway (1989), and Williams (1980). For the argument that wilderness is also a social construction, see, Nash (1973, p. 132), Cronon (1996), Cronon's edited volume (1996), Oelschlaeger (1991), DeLuca (2001), and DeLuca and Demo (2001). Much of the discussion of wilderness is collected in Callicott and Nelson (1998).

3. Available online at www.epa.gov/fedsite/eo12898.htm.

4. Available online at www.epa.gov/region03/environmental_justice/index.htm.

5. Available online at http://www.lacity.org/ead/EADWeb-AboutEAD/environmental_justice.htm.

6. Gibbs (1993, p. 2). The other quotes from Gibbs and the Center for Health and Environmental Justice (CHEJ) are from the CHEJ website online at www.ejrc.cau.edu.

7. Schweizer (1999).

8. Here I am not considering Native American environmental justice groups. For historical, cultural, and legal reasons, Native American environmental justice groups are markedly different from other environmental justice groups. This difference is perhaps most apparent with respect to attitudes toward nonhuman nature.

9. Environmental Justice Resource Center, www.ejrc.cau.edu

10. Southwest Organizing Project, "The Letter that Shook a Movement," *Sierra*, May/June 1993, 54.

11. Di Chiro (1996, p. 319).

12. Di Chiro (1996, p. 311).

13. Quoted in Di Chiro (1996, p. 312).

14. Environmental justice activist Dana Alston, quoted by Di Chiro (1996, p. 302).

15. Di Chiro (1996, p. 315).

16. Humanism can be defined as "a philosophy centered on man and human values, exalting human free will and superiority to the rest of nature; man is made the measure of all things" (*The Concord Desk Encyclopedia, Presented by TIME*, 1982, p. 604). Humanism arose in contrast to Christianity.

17. The Sierra Club is the example here because of its prominence and enthusiastic adoption of environmental justice principles. Other important environmental groups have made similar moves, including the World Wildlife Fund, the National Wildlife Federation, Earth First!, and Greenpeace.

18. "A Place at the Table: A *Sierra* Roundtable on Race, Justice, and the Environment," *Sierra* (May/June 1993): 51.

19. Available online at www.sierraclub.org/policy/conservation/justice.asp.

20. David Brower, "David Brower opposes the Yosemite Valley Plan," available online at www.yosemitevalley.org/HTML/Articles/2000_11_20.html.

21. Leopold (1949/1968, pp. 109–110).

22. A reviewer alerted me that Andrew Dobson (2003) makes a similar argument with respect to socialism and environmentalism. Dobson argues:

"I have come to the reluctant conclusion that social justice and environmental sustainability are not always compatible objectives.... The differences between them and not merely tactical but strategic: their objectives differ in fundamental ways." (p. 83)

In fact, Dobson makes the strong claim that there is no evidence of such a relation: "The US environmental justice movement is, therefore, simultaneously a site for extravagant claims regarding the compatibility of the justice and environmental agendas and a black hole as far as empirical studies designed to substantiate those claims are concerned" (p. 86).

23. Kate Soper (1996) also makes this argument.

24. Michalowski (1998).

25. Lorraine Johnson, "Sound and Fury," available online at www .canadiangardening.com/sound_fury2.shtml.

26. Available online at www.worldwatch.org. The World Wildlife Fund puts out a Living Planet Report available online at www.panda.org/news_facts/publications/general/livingplanet/index.cfm.

27. For an accounting of attacks on environmental activists, see Helvarg (1994, p. 130).

28. Leopold (1949/1968, pp. 129–130).

29. Spence (1999) and Darnovsky (1991).

30. Quoted in Fahn (2004, p. 138).

31. *Sierra* (1993).

32. Cronon (1996, 69, 79). See note 2, above, for citations on the wilderness debate.

33. DeLuca (1999, pp. 217–246), DeLuca (2001), and DeLuca and Demo (2001).

34. There are many good accounts of postmodernism. Besides Lyotard's (1984) seminal account, *The Postmodern Condition*, useful summaries are provided by Calinescu (1987) and Harvey (1989).

35. Foucault (1973, p. 386–387).

36. Derrida (1976, p. 158).

37. Cronon (1996, p. 69).

38. Cronon (1996, p. 73).

39. Cronon (1996, pp. 81, 88).

40. Available online at www.lib.duke.edu/forest/lecture99.html.

41. The dead Greek I am thinking of and defacing here is Protagoras: "Man is the measure of all things."

42. Thoreau, (1906, p. 205).

43. Marx (1975, p. 328).

44. Muir (1888/1976, p. 202); Muir (1901, p. 3).

45. Horkheimer and Adorno (1972, pp. 3, 26, 54).

46. Leopold (1949/1968, pp. 188, 200, 204).

47. Foreman (1991, p. 27).

48. Butterfly's ubiquitous presence in multiple media is one testament to her effectiveness. Besides her international presence in outlets from Europe to Japan, she has appeared repeatedly in every major newspaper in the United States, including the *New York Times*, the *Washington Post*, the *San Francisco Chronicle*, the *Los Angeles Times*, and *USA Today*, as well as news weeklies such as *Time* and *Newsweek*. She has been featured in women's magazines ranging from *Family Circle* to *Ms*. She has been interviewed on many Internet sites and radio stations. She has appeared on major television news programs, including an extended segment on *NBC Dateline*. In environmental circles she has become something of a folk hero and spokesperson, as well as the subject of several independent documentaries.

49. I attained the transcripts of these two online interviews at Julia Butterfly Hill's tree-sit website, www.lunaturu.org. Another current site of information about her activities is www.circleoflifefoundation.org.

50. For a fuller treatment of Butterfly's tree-sit, see DeLuca (2003).

51. Quoted in Singer (2004).

52. Singer (2004).

53. Gray (2003).

54. Gray (2003).

55. Singer (2004).

56. Singer (2004).

57. Hitt (2003).

58. Hitt (2003).

59. Online at http://wildaid.org.

60. Singer (2004).

61. Singer (2004).

62. Schweizer (1999).

63. Foreman (1991, p. 19).

64. Schweizer (1999).

65. Foreman (1991, pp. 26, 32).

66. Grunwald (2003, p. A3). For a more thorough account of the role of images in the debate over the Arctic National Wildlife Refuge, see Check (2005).

67. Tyler (2004).

68. Foreman and Wolke (1989, p. 24).

69. Cronon (1996, p. 87).

70. Derrida (1976, p. 5) is referring to the future as a monstrosity, but I think wilderness must be conceptualized in similar terms: "The future can only be anticipated in the form of an absolute danger. It is that which breaks absolutely with constituted normality and can only be proclaimed, *presented*, as a sort of monstrosity... which will have put into question the values of sign, word, and writing."

References

Brice, A., *The Devil's Dictionary* (New York: Dover, 1993).

Bullard, R., *Dumping in Dixie: Race, Class, and Environmental Quality* (Boulder, Colo.: Westview Press, 1990).

Calinescu, M., *Five Faces of Modernity* (Durham, N. C.: Duke University Press, 1987).

Callicott, B., and Nelson, M. P., *The Great New Wilderness Debate* (Athens: University of Georgia Press, 1998).

Check, T., "Visual Enthymemes of Alaskan Wilderness: Television News Coverage of the Arctic National Wildlife Refuge." Presented at the 8th Conference on Communication and the Environment, June 24–27, 2005, Jeckyll Island, GA.

Collingwood, R. G., *The Idea of Nature* (Oxford: Clarendon, 1945).

The Concord Desk Reference, presented by *TIME* (New York: Concord Reference Books, 1982).

Cronon, W. ed., *Uncommon Ground: Rethinking the Human Place in Nature* (New York: W. W. Norton and Company, 1996).

Cronon, W., "The Trouble with Wilderness, or Getting Back to the Wrong Nature," *Environmental History* (January 1996): 69–90.

Darnovsky, M., "Stories Less Told: Histories of U.S. Environmentalism," *Socialist Review* 22 (1991): 11–54.

DeLuca, K., "Meeting in a Redwood: Wilderness on the Public Screen," *Situation Analysis: A Forum for Critical Thought & International Current Affairs* (spring 2003): 32–45.

DeLuca, K., "Trains in the Wilderness: The Corporate Roots of Environmentalism," *Rhetoric and Public Affairs* 4, no. 4 (winter 2001): 633–652.

DeLuca, K., "In the Shadow of Whiteness: The Consequences of Constructions of Nature in Environmental Politics," in T. Nakayamo and J. Martin, eds., *Whiteness* (Thousand Oaks, CA: Sage, 1999), 217–246.

DeLuca, K., and Demo, A., "Imagining Nature and Erasing Class and Race: Carleton Watkins, John Muir, and the Construction of Wilderness" *Environmental History* (2001): 541–560.

Derrida, J., *Of Grammatology* (Baltimore: John Hopkins University Press, 1976).

Di Chiro, G., "Nature as Community: The Convergence of Environment and Social Justice," in W. Cronon, ed., *Uncommon Ground* (New York: W.W. Norton, 1996), 298–320, 527–531.

Dobson, A. "Social Justice and Environmental Sustainability: Ne'er the Twain Shall Meet?" in J. Agyeman, R. Bullard, and B. Evans, eds., *Just sustainabilities* (Oxford: Oxford University Press, 2003), 83–95.

Evernden, N., *The Social Creation of Nature* (Baltimore: John Hopkins University Press, 1992).

Fahn, J. D., *A Land on Fire* (Chiang Mai: Silkworm Books, 2004).

Foreman, D., *Confessions of an Eco-Warrior* (New York: Harmony, 1991).

Foreman, D., and Wolke, H. *The Big Outside* (Tucson: Ned Ludd Books, 1989).

Foucault, M., *The Order of Things* (New York: Vintage, 1973).

Gibbs, L., "Celebrating Ten Years of Triumph," *Everyone's Backyard* 11, no. 2 (1993): 2.

Gottlieb, R., *Forcing the Spring* (Washington, D.C.: Island Press, 1993).

Gray, D., "Consuming Exotic Animals," *Associated Press* (January 1, 2003), available online at http://wildaid.org/index.asp?CID=8&PID=331&SUBID=&TERID=14.

Grunwald, M., "Some Facts Clear in the War of Spin over Arctic Refuge," *Washington Post* (March 6, 2003): A3.

Haraway, D., *Primate Visions: Gender, Race, and Nature in the World of Modern Science* (New York: Routledge, Chapman, & Hall, 1989).

Harvey, D., *The Condition of Postmodernity* (Cambridge, Mass.: Basil Blackwell, 1989).

Helvarg, D., *The War against the Greens* (San Francisco: Sierra Club Books, 1994).

Hitt, J., "The Eco-Mercenaries," *New York Times* (August 4, 2003), available online at http://wildaid.org/index.asp?CID=8&PID=331&SUBID=&TERID=18.

Horkheimer, M., and Adorno, T., *Dialectic of Enlightenment* (New York: Herder, 1972).

Marx, K., "Economic and Philosophical Manuscripts," in Q. Hoare, ed., *Karl Marx: Early Writings* (New York: Vintage, 1975), 279–400.

Leopold, A., *A Sand County Almanac* (New York: Oxford, 1949/1968).

Lyotard, J.-F., *The Postmodern Condition* (Minneapolis: University of Minnesota Press, 1984).

Michalowski, J., "Letter to Adrian Alvarez and the Association of Latin American Gardeners of Los Angeles," (1998), available online at www.nonoise.org/quietnet/cqs/polphil.htm.

Muir, J., *West of the Rocky Mountains* (Philadelphia: Running, 1888/1976).

Muir, J., *Our National Parks*, (Boston: Houghton Mifflin, 1901).

Nash, R., *Wilderness and the American Mind*, rev. ed. (Binghamton, N.Y.: Vail-Ballou, 1973).

Oelschlaeger, M., *The Idea of Wilderness* (New Haven, Conn.: Yale University Press, 1991).

Schwab, J., *Deeper Shades of Green: The Rise of Blue-Collar and Minority Environmentalism in America* (San Francisco: Sierra Club Books, 1994).

Schweizer, E., "Environmental Justice: An Interview with Robert Bullard," *Earth First! Journal* (July 1999), available online at www.ejnet.org/ej/bullard.html.

Sierra, "A Place at the Table: A *Sierra* Roundtable on Race, Justice, and the Environment," *Sierra* (May/June 1993): 51.

Singer, N., "See the Last Clouded Leopard. See the Last Clouded Leopard Die. See the Last Clouded Leopard Skin on the Black Market. See a Pattern Here?" *Outside Magazine* (May 2004), available online at http://outside.away.com/outside/features/200405/clouded_leopard_wildlife_conservation_l.html

Snyder, G., *The Practice of the Wild* (San Francisco: North Point Press, 1990).

Soper, K., "Nature/'nature'" in G. Robertson, M. Marsh, L. Tickner, J. Bird, B. Curtis, and T. Putnam, eds., *Future/Natural* (New York: Routledge, 1996), 22–34.

Southwest Organizing Project, "The Letter that Shook a Movement," *Sierra*, (May/June 1993), 54.

Spence, M. D., *Dispossessing the Wilderness* (New York: Oxford University Press, 1999).

Thoreau, D. H., "Walking," in *Excursions and Poems* (Boston: Houghton Mifflin, 1906), 205–248.

Tyler, P. E., "Peace Prize Goes to Environmentalist in Kenya," *New York Times* (October 9, 2004): A1.

Williams, R., "Ideas of Nature," in *Problems in Materialism and Culture* (London: Verso, 1980), 67–85.

2

Does Environmentalism Promote Injustice for the Poor?

Peter Wenz

The environmental movement sometimes has been accused of promoting injustice to human beings, especially poor people and people of color, both in industrial and developing countries. In this chapter I argue that there are no inherent conflicts between the goals of environmentalism and environmental justice (justice related to environmental decision making) for the poor. Conflicts commonly exist among worthy goals, and there are some cases of genuine conflict in practice between environmentalism and environmental justice. Most cases of apparent conflict at both the theoretical and practical levels, however, result from faulty analyses and correctable errors in environmental policies. For the most part, environmentalism today and in the foreseeable future can promote justice for people and justice for people can promote environmental goals.

I begin by reviewing seven reasons for suspecting that environmentalism promotes injustice. I next present considerations that suggest a general tendency for convergence between the goals of environmentalism and justice. Finally, I respond to the seven reasons for thinking that environmentalism and justice are in conflict.

The Appearance of Conflict

Justice is a contested concept. Some people claim, as does libertarian Robert Nozick, for example, that justice requires absolute respect for property rights, even if this results in great inequality between rich and poor.[1] Others, such as the liberal contractarian John Rawls, believe, to the contrary, that justice requires maximum equality compatible with individual incentives needed to promote economic growth.[2] Still others, including the communitarian Amitai Etzioni, think that justice rests on community solidarity or traditional moral values.[3] It is possible, however, to sidestep the relative merits of such competing conceptions of justice by relying on an uncontroversial principle: justice increases when the benefits and burdens of social cooperation are born more equally, except when moral considerations or other values justify greater inequality. This principle is uncontroversial because it basically restates the principle of the equal consideration of interests, championed often by Ronald Dworkin and explained well by Will Kymlicka, which rests on the uncontroversial claim that all human beings are of equal moral considerability.[4] Unequal treatment of human beings (some reaping extra benefits or bearing extra burdens related to social cooperation) must therefore be justified, and such justification requires recourse to moral considerations or other values. Environmentalism is often accused of promoting injustice in this sense: without sufficient justification, environmental policies increase inequality between rich and poor. They tend also to increase racial inequalities. In this chapter, however, I focus on differences of class, not race.

Anthropocentric environmentalism centers on the belief that industrial societies are destroying natural resources and processes upon which human flourishing depends. Environmentalists want to preserve and restore these resources and processes. Particular concerns include climate change, species extinction, degradation of agricultural land, preservation of wilderness areas, and protection of such public goods as clean air and water. Nonanthropocentric environmentalists believe additionally that, even when human welfare is unaffected, people should protect species from extinction, ecosystems from degradation, and nonhuman animals from cruelty. The charge that environmentalism caters to the wants and needs of wealthy people and harms the poor has been made against both anthropocentric and nonanthropocentric environmentalism. The following examples, it is claimed, substantiate that charge.

Claim 1: Attempts to curb *global warming* harm the poor.
Environmentalists want to fight global warming. Some give only anthropocentric reasons (to avoid problems associated with flooding, cropland losses, social disruption, and the spread of tropical diseases), whereas others add a nonanthropocentric desire to avoid species extinction regardless

of human benefit. Some environmentalists want to combat global warming by taxing gasoline in the United States as in Europe where, primarily because of taxation, people pay nearly three times as much for gas.[5] But in many places in the United States, there are no viable alternatives to using a car. Tripling the price of gas would hurt poor people who must use their cars to get to work and meet other needs.

This is just one example of a general tendency, critics claim, of environmental policies harming the poor. Norman Faramelli wrote in 1970,

Most of the solutions suggested for environmental quality will have, directly or indirectly, adverse effects on the poor and lower income groups. . . . If the cost of pollution control is passed directly on to the consumer on all items, low-income families will be affected disproportionately. If new technologies cannot solve the environmental crisis and a slowdown in material production is demanded, the low income families will again bear the brunt of it, as more and more of them will join the ranks of the unemployed.[6]

Another environmentalist proposal to combat global warming is permanently to deny China, India, and other Third World countries the right to burn fossil fuels as many First World countries do. But this would seem to deny poor countries the means already used by rich countries to improve their material welfare. The burden of fighting global warming would again fall most heavily on the poor.[7]

Claim 2: Attempts to combat *overpopulation* harm the poor.
Overpopulation is another environmentalist concern that can be either anthropocentric or nonanthropocentric. In "Lifeboat Ethics" environmental economist Garrett Hardin claims, much like Malthus, that people tend to overpopulate when they have enough food to eat. This explains the twentieth century's enormous population growth, which threatens environmental ruin. Hardin's solution is to deprive poor people in overpopulated Third World countries of food by refusing to send them food, refusing to allow them to move to countries where food is plentiful, and refusing to transfer agricultural technologies to them so they can grow their own food.[8]

Claim 3: Environmentalist opposition to *agribusiness* harms the poor.
Environmentalists oppose many aspects of agribusiness. They object to the massive use of insecticides and herbicides, worrying about the

contamination of groundwater used by people and animals. They object to irrigation in the American West, worrying about the salination of soil and the depletion of aquifers.[9] They object to the massive use of artificial fertilizer, worrying about soil erosion and the creation of dead zones in the sea, such as in the Gulf of Mexico. Most recently, they object to genetically modified organisms in our food, worrying about possible adverse environmental and health effects.

Agribusiness, however, is the mainstay of modern agriculture, and it has reduced the price of nutritious food for the American people. Technologies promoted by agribusiness have also helped Third World people obtain food. A critic of environmentalism, Bjorn Lomborg, writes, "Although there are twice as many of us as there were in 1961, each of us has *more* to eat, in both developed and developing countries. Fewer people are starving. . . . While in 1971 almost 920 million people were starving, the total fell below 792 million in 1997."[10] Through opposition to technologies that have helped the poor obtain food, environmentalism seems opposed to the vital interests of the poor both at home and abroad.

Claim 4: Environmentalist opposition to *free trade* harms the poor.
Free trade is often promoted as the best way for the world's poor to obtain the material advantages common in rich countries, yet environmentalists often oppose free trade. Peter Singer, who is guardedly optimistic about it, puts the argument for free trade this way:

[Freed trade] should be particularly good for countries with low labor costs, because they should be able to produce goods more cheaply than countries with high labor costs. Hence we can expect the demand for labor in those countries to rise, and once the supply of labor begins to tighten, wages should rise too. Thus a free market should have the effect not only of making the world as a whole more prosperous, but more specifically, of assisting the poorest nations.[11]

U.S. President George W. Bush shares this view and told the World Bank, "Those who protest free trade are no friends of the poor. Those who protest free trade seek to deny them their best hope for escaping poverty."[12]

The World Trade Organization (WTO) facilitates free trade by enforcing uniform rules of trade that mostly disallow state policies that would inhibit trade, such as taxes on foreign goods or regulations that tend to disadvantage imports. Many environmentalists oppose decisions of the WTO, thereby threatening the growth of trade that promises to help the poor. For example, the European Union (EU) disallowed the importation of American beef that had been given artificial growth hormones. Without convincing evidence, the EU claimed that eating beef treated with these hormones may harm human health. The WTO protected free trade, deciding the case in favor of the United States and requiring the EU to either allow the importation of this beef or suffer retaliatory duties. They chose the latter course. Most environmentalists sided with the EU, arguing against free trade.[13]

In another case, the United States wanted to exclude tuna caught in nets that kill many dolphins but decided that WTO rules disallowed this exclusion as an unacceptable restraint of trade. In two other cases, fear of successful challenge before the WTO deterred Europe from prohibiting importation of furs from countries that allow animals to be caught in steel-jaw leghold traps and cosmetics that had been tested on animals. In all of these cases, nonanthropocentric environmentalists opposed free trade to promote animal welfare.[14] The result of environmentalist victory, free-trade advocates claim, would have been more expensive beef, tuna, fur, and cosmetics. High prices generally harm the poor most.

Claim 5: Environmentalist attempts to protect *public goods* harm the poor.

Cost-benefit analysis (CBA) is a tool favored by many environmentalists to protect such public goods as clean air and water. For example, if automotive exhaust fumes pollute the air, the free market will not protect air quality because few automobile owners will voluntarily spend their own money to install pollution-control devices on their cars. The individual benefit from each device is less than its cost. Therefore, few car owners will install pollution-control devices and air quality will degenerate. In this type of situation, the maintenance or restoration of clean air requires state intervention. Because a primary goal of modern states is to promote economic growth and increase national wealth, environmentalists can advance their goal of fighting pollution by showing that pollution reduces national wealth. They show this by performing CBA. CBAs simulate private markets by assigning dollar values to all inputs and outcomes to indicate the policy that maximizes national wealth. The monetary benefits of cleaner air include less money spent on healthcare, fewer health-related absences from work, and increased property values in formerly smoggy areas. The state attempting to maximize total wealth will require pollution-control devices on all new cars if the consequent improvement in air quality is worth more money than the total expenditures needed to produce this result. Many environmentalists, especially those in government regulatory agencies, endorse using CBA in those contexts.

The problem is that CBA tends to promote injustice. Dollar values of all items relevant to the calculation—cars, clear air, good health, pollution-control devices—are determined in CBA, as in private markets, by people's willingness to pay for things. Rich people can be willing to pay more than poor people, so their desires have more influence on the determination of values in CBA, and this can lead to unjust results. For example, if two geologically suitable sites were available for the disposal of toxic waste, one near a poor city of 20,000 people and one near an up-market town of 5,000 people, CBA would probably recommend locating the waste near the larger number of poor people rather than near the smaller number of rich people. Even if the waste facility poses no danger to human health, its location near a town will lower property values. The total loss of property values is likely to be less in the town of 20,000 because values there are already low. By this logic, total national wealth is maximized by locating the waste facility near poor people rather than near rich people. If justice generally requires helping the poor, CBA, a common environmentalist tool, tends to recommend unjust policies.[15]

Claim 6: Environmentalist attempts to protect *endangered species* and *wilderness areas* harm the poor.
Projects designed to save endangered species from extinction are typically more harmful to poor people than to rich people. Many logging jobs were jeopardized or lost in the Pacific Northwest, critics claim, by attempts to save the northern spotted owl.[16] Saving the snail darter jeopardized completion of the Tennessee Valley Authority's Tellico Dam. The TVA supplies inexpensive electricity to poor communities.[17]

Similar problems beset projects to establish wilderness areas and protect endangered species in the Third World. Holmes Rolston III argues, for example, that poor indigenous people should be removed from the area of their traditional habitation in India to protect endangered tigers.[18] Similarly, attempts to save elephants in Africa often deprive poor people of the livelihood of selling ivory and subject local inhabitants to the depredations of overpopulated elephant herds.[19] In addition, poor people are often expelled from newly established national parks even though the park's resources, such as wood and fruit, are integral to their sustenance. Dan Brockington gives a detailed illustration in *Fortress Conservation: The Preservation of the Mkomazi Game Reserve, Tanzania.* He writes,

> The preservation of Mkomazi has hurt its neighbors. Until the evictions the Reserve's resources had been used by a large number of people for a long time. They derived benefits from that use and built their livelihoods upon it. Exclusion has impeded their use of gathered wild resources, reduced household herd size and performance, damaged the local livestock economy, and caused serious hardship to thousands of people. . . .
>
> The human costs of saving this wilderness have not yet been carefully considered yet at the same time Mkomazi's preservation after eviction has been hailed as a success. The omission and oversight has come at a time when conservation rhetoric in Africa is dominated by concern for "community conservation"; for setting up partnerships between people and protected areas; for providing benefits to the rural poor from wildlife. The story of conservation at Mkomazi challenges the ideals of community conservation.[20]

Claim 7: Environmentalist attempts to promote *animal welfare* harm the poor.

Peter Carruthers claims that nonanthropocentric concern for the welfare of individual nonhuman animals harms people by diverting attention and resources from efforts to alleviate human misery:

> The cost of increasing concern with animal welfare is to distract attention from the needs of those who certainly do have moral standing—namely, human beings. We live on a planet where millions of our fellow humans starve, or are near starving, and where many millions more are undernourished.[21]

Carruthers believes that if people were to cease the current practice of using time, energy, and money to improve the lot of nonhuman animals, they would have more time, energy, and money available to improve the welfare of human beings. If people use these newly available resources appropriately, instead of environmentalist attempts to promote animal welfare, we will have more programs that benefit human beings, especially the poorest and most deprived among us. This will advance the cause of justice among human beings, which is unquestionably a morally appropriate goal, he claims, because human beings are undoubtedly of moral importance. The moral standing of nonhuman animals, by contrast, can be questioned.

These seven ways that environmentalism allegedly harms the poor are representative, not exhaustive, but suggest why some people think that environmentalism promotes injustice.

Environmentalism and Justice Are Mutually Supportive

Some people who consider themselves environmentalists, such as Hardin and possibly Rolston, embrace the view that poor people must (sometimes) suffer uncompensated losses to preserve the environment. In reality, cases of genuine conflict between environmentalism and the welfare of poor people are rare. In general, and in contrast with the concerns outlined above, I contend that achieving environmental goals generally helps poor people most.

Here is one general argument to that effect. People flourish when they can get what they want and need from the environment, such as raw materials, waste sinks, recreation, aesthetic pleasure, and inspiration. Because the earth's resources are limited, efficiency is needed to serve people best. Efficiency is a measure of inputs and outputs. The greater the desired output from a given input of scarce resources, the greater the efficiency of the system. Environmentalists generally favor improved efficiency so that people can get what they want with less environmental disruption.

Improving efficiency typically helps poor people most. Poor people have less access to the earth's resources than rich people, so when those resources are used most efficiently to serve human needs, poor people are likely to gain most. Similarly, policies designed to help the poor tend to be environmentally friendly. Often the most practical way to help the poor is through more efficient uses of the earth's resources and such efficiency permits human fulfillment with less environmental disruption. Reconsidering the seven ways that environmentalism allegedly harms the poor from this efficiency perspective reveals that environmentalism typically helps, rather than harms the poor.

Response 1: Fighting *global warming* helps the poor.
Because current modes of *transportation* use a lot of fossil fuel energy that contributes to global warming, environmentalists favor efficient transportation, and this generally helps the poor most. The goal of transportation is for people to get where they need and want to go. Public transportation is more efficient than the massive use of private vehicles. A train can carry as many people intercity as sixteen lanes of highway designed for automobiles, thereby saving land.[22] It uses less power to transport people and produces less air pollution.[23] It is eighteen times safer than driving a car.[24] It contributes less to global warming. It requires less land use for parking at each end. Similar efficiencies attend light rail within a city. Finally, when such public transportation is fully developed, it is convenient (because it departs and arrives frequently at many locations) and fast (compared to being stuck in rush hour traffic). Such efficiencies are reflected in studies showing that government expenditures on public transportation improve worker productivity and regional economic performance.[25] Thus, public transportation is more efficient and environmentally friendly than the use of private automobiles.

The U.S. government currently subsidizes enormously the automotive and oil industries through tax breaks, road-building programs, health expenditures, and more. Jane Holtz Kay, architecture critic for *The Nation*, writes, "The suburban commuter pays only 25 percent of the costs of travel to the central district by car."[26] She explains,

Things we rarely consider bear a dollar sign: from parking facilities to police protection, from land consumed in sprawl to registry operations, environmental damage to uncompensated accidents. . . . According to one estimate, exactions from U.S. cars and trucks carry three-quarters of a trillion dollars in hidden costs each year.[27]

Military expenditures are a major form of subsidy for automotive over public transportation. Public transportation uses less fuel, reducing our country's dependence on foreign sources of oil. With reduced vulnerability to oil shortages, the U.S. military presence in the Middle East, which currently functions largely to ensure a continuous flow of oil from that region, could be cut back. The military build-up for the Gulf War in 1991, for example, cost the equivalent of 40 cents per gallon of gasoline imported that year.[28] Expenses continued during the 1990s and then ballooned with the second Iraq war in 2003.

If these subsidies gradually were transferred to various forms of public transportation, a public transportation infrastructure could be established, giving everyone convenient, inexpensive alternatives to traveling by car. This would help poor people most for three reasons. First, poor people tend to live where automotive traffic produces the worst health-impairing air pollution. This situation is made worse in the United States by the fact that many poor people have inferior access to decent health care to deal with pollution-related illness. Second, owning and running a car takes a larger percentage of poor people's meager budgets and the cars they own, being older and of poorer quality, tend to break down, jeopardizing poor people's income stream when they cannot get to work.[29] Finally, improving energy security without recourse to war disproportionately benefits the relatively poor because they are overrepresented among those who enlist in the armed forces and are in the line of fire.

In sum, efficient transportation both combats global warming and helps poor people, thereby making environmentalism and justice mutually supportive on this matter.

Environmentalist *energy policies* designed to combat global warming also help the poor most. Such policies favor Amory Lovins's soft energy path of dispersed renewable sources of energy—such as wind, solar, geothermal, and biomass (fuels from crops)—along with energy savings through efficient use—such as home insulation and energy-saving lighting with fluorescent instead of incandescent bulbs. Ross Gelbspan claims that the soft path creates more jobs than the carbon-intensive alternative:

According to some calculations, for every million dollars spent on oil and gas exploration, only 1.5 jobs are created; for every million on coal mining, 4.4 jobs. But for every million spent on making and installing solar water heaters, 14 jobs are created. For manufacturing solar electricity panels, 17 jobs. For electricity from biomass and waste, 23 jobs.[30]

Saving energy through efficient use also creates jobs for some of society's poorer members. Programs of insulating old houses, for example, can provide many jobs throughout the country to people who lack university training. The decline in home heating costs resulting from better insulation also benefits poor people most because they can least afford high bills for heating and cooling.

Mainstream environmentalists easily can justify government subsidy of such programs because society benefits monetarily when energy use is more efficient. Even ignoring the issue of climate change, energy use in the United States typically produces health-impairing pollution (which, again, harms poor people most). When oil is used for heating, inefficiency increases trade deficits and creates dependence on foreign sources of energy that motivates expensive military expenditures and activities. A Harvard University study in the 1970s concluded that, if the public paid for home insulation through tax rebates, the rebates would amount to 60 percent of the cost of insulation improvements.[31] In turn, the money the government would need to subsidize the rebates could come from eliminating the current, enormous tax benefits given to the nuclear power and oil industries, thereby transferring wealth from large corporations to small entrepreneurs and poor families.

If more money were needed for programs promoting energy savings and renewable sources of energy, the federal government also could transfer some of its military savings related to changes from reliance on automobiles to greater use of public transportation. Further, if even that fails, federal income taxes could be used. Middle- and upper-income people currently pay the bulk of these taxes, so the poor would still be prime beneficiaries. Again, helping the poor and fighting global warming could be mutually supportive goals.

Environmentalist attempts to curb emissions of greenhouse gases to fight global warming can also benefit poor people in the Third World. Environmentalists advocate new energy technologies being applied in the Third World, where energy-wasting infrastructures do not yet exist. Such countries can leapfrog over developed economies. For example, the United States has many centralized coal-fired power plants that produce nothing but electricity. These convert about 33 percent of the coal's energy into electrical energy. By contrast, power plants that are site-specific and produce heating and cooling along with electricity can convert as much as 91 percent of the coal's energy to useful purposes.[32] It is less expensive for a developing country to install such plants and gain related efficiencies where they need new power than it is for the United States to replace its existing infrastructure. In this scenario, energy efficiency translates into monetary savings for the poor country.

When environmentalists advocate transferring new coal, wind, solar, and other technologies to Third World countries so they can have improved standards of living without increasing their contribution to global warming, programs for Third World prosperity and for climate stabilization can be mutually reinforcing.[33]

Response 2: Fighting *overpopulation* helps the poor.
Hardin's "Lifeboat Ethics" is based on a faulty Malthusian analysis of population growth. He believes that the only way to prevent increases in the human population is to allow poor people to starve because, if they have enough to eat, they will increase their numbers up to the point of exhausting the planet's capacity to produce food. He is wrong. Human beings with plenty of food have often avoided population increase. Western Europe was doing so when Hardin wrote in the 1970s.

Experience teaches us that empowering women (teaching them to read and giving them access to property and employment outside the home) is a reliable means of stemming population growth. Danielle Nierenberg writes for the Worldwatch Institute,

When women's education, opportunities, and status begin to approach those of men, their economic and health conditions improve. As a result (assuming good access to family planning services), they have fewer children, and the children arrive later in the mothers' lives.

A major contributor to later pregnancies and lower fertility is at least six or seven years of schooling. When girls manage to stay in school this long, what they learn about basic health, sexuality, and their own prospects in the world tends to encourage them to marry and become pregnant later in life and to have smaller families. In Egypt, for example, only 5 percent of women who stayed in school past the primary level had children while still in their teens, while over half of women with no schooling became teenage mothers. In high-fertility countries, women who have some secondary education typically have two, three, or four children fewer in their lifetimes than otherwise similar women who have never been to school.[34]

In sum, to stem the tide of overpopulation, women should be given more power, education, and access to health care and family planning services. Promoting justice, in this case for women, coheres with the environmentalist goal of protecting the earth's environment from human overpopulation.[35]

Another method of combating overpopulation, retaining traditional ways of life in ecosystems that supply free services, also helps the poor most. Partha Dasgupta, an economics professor at Cambridge University, claims that disrupting such ecosystems and traditional life patterns gives poor people an incentive to have more children:

Third World countries are, for the most part, subsistence economies. The rural folk eke out a living by using products gleaned directly from plants and animals. Much labor is needed. . . . In semiarid and arid regions the water supply may not even be nearby. Nor is fuelwood at hand when [due to environmental degradation] the forests recede. . . . Members of a household may have to spend as much as five to six hours a day fetching water and collecting fodder and wood.

Children, then, are needed as workers even when their parents are in their prime. . . . In parts of India, children between 10 and 15 years have been observed to work as much as one and a half times the number of hours that adult males do. By the age of six, children in rural India tend domestic animals and care for younger siblings, fetch water and collect firewood, dung and fodder.[36]

When the local environment retains its integrity, life is easier for people who are poor. Food and fuel are closer and much of it is free, so they have less need for additional children to help with daily tasks. The environmentalist goals of retaining rich ecosystems and reducing overpopulation cohere with the humanitarian goals of helping Third World poor people live fulfilling, traditional lives. (An exception, as noted above, is any tradition that disempowers women, because these are unjust to women and promote overpopulation.)

Response 3: Opposition to *agribusiness* helps the poor.

As with the oil and automotive industries, the government subsidizes agribusiness. Farmers in California, for example, pay only a fraction of the commercial value of the water they use.[37] Herders using federal lands pay only a fraction of the commercial cost of grazing cattle.[38]

In this matter environmentalists who oppose these subsidies are again on the side of the poor. For example, water and grazing subsidies that make meat inexpensive encourage the inefficient inclusion of animals in the human food chain. When humans eat lower on the biotic pyramid, they use much less land to feed themselves because the animal cycle leaves to people only between one-fourth and one-tenth of the land's food-producing capacity. In general, more humans can be fed when people eat what the land produces instead of feeding it to livestock. Improving the availability of food for people helps poor people most, because they are most likely to be harmed if food shortages cause the price of food to rise.

In addition, current agribusiness practices are unsustainable because of the erosion of soil[39] and depletion of aquifers.[40] This means that prices will eventually rise greatly as the food-producing capacity of the land diminishes because of current misuse. Again, the poor will be hit hardest when this occurs.

Many poor people in the United States are already harmed by agribusiness. Federal agricultural subsidies have tended to favor rich over poor farmers. Worldwatch's David Roodman explains:

Most payments are based on how much food farmers grow, not on how small their farms are. Not surprisingly, the number of U.S. farms fell by two-thirds between 1930 and 1990, even as grain elevators bulged with millions of tons of surplus food. As a result of this concentration of ownership, 58 percent of the agricultural support payments . . . went to the top 15 percent of farms in 1991, those grossing over $100,000 per year.[41]

The best way to help poor people in rural areas farm profitably and sustainably is for the government to subsidize labor-intensive conservation measures, such as the reintroduction of hedge rows, the planting of trees as windbreaks, crop rotation, and the use of integrated pest management that uses predator insects to control destructive insects. Rural America has some of the country's poorest communities, and such measures as these promise needed revitalization.

Of course, our current unsustainable and highly subsidized agricultural practices make most food very inexpensive in the United States, and this helps the urban poor. If sustainably grown food is more expensive than most food that is currently available, the government should increase subsidies that help poor people buy sustainably grown food. This requirement of justice does not run afoul of any environmentalist agenda.

Current agricultural subsidies harm poor people in the Third World as well as at home. These subsidies harm the world's poor by flooding Third World food markets with cheap imported food, driving Third World farmers out of business and making Third World countries dependent on imported food. This dependency often justifies programs in poor countries that harm the environment, because those countries must gain hard currency to pay for food and other items. They must use their resources to produce what rich countries want, which may include hardwoods from ancient forests, goods manufactured with few pollution controls, and beef grazed in fields where rainforests recently stood. By opposing current agricultural subsidies in the First World, environmentalists are on the side of the world's poor.[42]

In addition, environmentalists generally favor traditional, diversified agriculture in poor countries, which is agriculture for local consumption, not export. Agriculture for local consumption tends to be more environmentally sound because it uses crop varieties that are adapted to local soils, insects, and climate. Such agriculture uses fewer artificial chemicals and is more sustainable. Vandana Shiva, physicist and director of the Research Foundation for Science, Technology, and Natural Resources writes,

Indigenous varieties, or land races, are resistant to locally occurring pests and diseases. Even if certain diseases occur, some of the strains may be susceptible, while others will have the resistance to survive. Crop rotations also help in pest control. Since many pests are specific to particular plants, planting crops in different seasons and different years causes large reductions in pest populations.[43]

Such agriculture helps poor people, as well. First, it tends to be more labor intensive, thereby providing more jobs for poor people. Also, it tends to be more varied, providing local people with a more nutritionally complete diet.[44] Agriculture for export, by contrast, tends to concentrate on those few crops that can be grown locally at a cost that enables it to compete on the world market. Commercial agriculture for export tends to ignore the needs of poor people in the local area. This is because its point is to make as much money as possible, which cannot be done by meeting the needs of the very poor. For example, Chile uses some of its limited agricultural resources to grow ornamental flowers for export. Such agricultural trade seldom helps the world's poor. In opposing it, environmentalists support policies that promote justice.

Environmentalists also defend traditional Third World agriculture against monocultures of crop varieties scientifically designed to help Third World countries feed themselves. According to Shiva, the so-called Green Revolution provides a cautionary tale. Norman Borlaug received the Nobel Peace Prize in 1970 for developing high-yield varieties (HYVs) of wheat and rice in the 1950s. These were supposed to help poor countries attain self-sufficiency in food because they yield significantly greater quantities of grain per hectare than traditional varieties. However, Shiva notes, HYVs need more water than traditional varieties, and pumping this water lowered the water table in India. Only relatively wealthy farmers could afford to dig deeper wells, so the poorest farmers had to sell out to richer neighbors because they could no longer reach water.

HYVs also need fertilizer. Because this is a purchased input, it again favored richer farmers. Worse yet, the fertilizer turned a native plant that grows wild, bathua, into a weedy competitor of rice, so herbicides, another purchased input, were required to control it. Wild bathua, however, was the major source of vitamin A for poor people because it is available free. Killing bathua deprived poor people of this source of an essential vitamin. Shiva writes, "40,000 children in India go blind each year for lack of vitamin A, and herbicides contribute to this tragedy by destroying the freely available sources of vitamin A." What is more, the herbicides needed to grow HYVs kill wild reeds and grasses that "thousands of rural women who make their living by basket and mat making" need for their livelihood.[45]

Most environmentalists are skeptical of current attempts to help poor people and Third World countries through introduction of genetically engineered crops. First, the experience with the Green Revolution suggests that traditional agriculture is both more environmentally friendly and more helpful to poor people. Second, crops genetically engineered to be resistant to insect pests will not retain resistance for many years, because of the evolution of insect varieties. Third, such crops depend on purchasing seeds each year, which poor people can ill afford, and are not designed to meet the needs of the poor. This is no accident. Agribusiness currently controls almost all genetic engineering and tries to maximize profit. This way of doing business cannot be done by meeting the needs of the world's poorest people. Genetically engineered crops of genuine value to poor people are mostly matters of speculation with uncertain prospects.

In sum, the agricultural policies favored by most environmentalists are those likely to help poor people most, and the agricultural policies likely to help poor people are those employing the kind of ecological diversity that environmentalists favor.

Response 4: Opposition to *free trade* helps the poor.
First World people enjoy many material advantages unavailable to most people in the Third World. Why not work toward worldwide prosperity that will enable everyone to live like people in the United States? Advocates of free trade claim it eventually will enable affluence throughout the world. *New York Times* journalist Thomas Friedman extols the benefits of free trade:

Countries ... can now increasingly choose to be prosperous. They don't have to be prisoners of their natural resources, geography or history. In a world where a country can plug into the Internet and import knowledge, in a world where a country can find shareholders from any other country to invest in its infrastructure ..., where a country can import the technology to be an auto producer or a computer maker even if it has no raw materials, a country can more than ever before opt for prosperity or poverty, depending on the policies it pursues.[46]

Development economist David Korten disagrees; the earth cannot sustain billions of affluent consumers. He writes,

If the earth's sustainable natural output were shared equally among the earth's present population, the needs of all could be met. But it is ... clear that it is a physical impossibility, even with the most optimistic assumptions about the potential of new technologies, for the world to consume at levels even approximating those in North America, Europe, and Japan.[47]

What is more, current efforts to create Third World economies in the First World image tend to harm poor people. Korten gives the example of a Japanese company's development efforts in the Philippines. To reduce pollution in Japan from the smelting of copper, the Japanese financed the Philippine Associated Smelting and Refining Corporation (PASAR).

The plant occupies 400 acres of land expropriated by the Philippine government from local residents at give-away prices. Gas and wastewater emissions from the plant contain high concentrations of boron, arsenic, heavy metals, and sulfur compounds that have contaminated local water supplies, reduced fishing and rice yields, damaged the forests, and increased the occurrence of upper-respiratory diseases among local residents. Local people . . . are now largely dependent on the occasional part-time or contractual employment they are offered to do the plant's most dangerous and dirtiest jobs.

The company has prospered. The local economy has grown. . . . The Philippine government is repaying the foreign aid loan from Japan that financed the construction of supporting infrastructure for the plant. And the Japanese are congratulating themselves for . . . their generous assistance to the poor of the Philippines.[48]

Korten maintains that such impoverished dependence is the typical result of development efforts that attempt to integrate Third World economies into the industrial world.

Rapid economic growth in low-income countries brings modern airports, television, express highways, and air-conditioned shopping malls . . . for the fortunate few. It rarely improves living conditions for the many. This kind of growth requires gearing the economy toward exports to earn the foreign exchange to buy the things that wealthy people desire. Thus, the lands of the poor are appropriated for export crops. The former tillers of these lands find themselves subsisting in urban slums on starvation wages paid by sweatshops producing for export. Families are broken up, the social fabric is strained to the breaking point, and violence becomes endemic.[49]

One indication of family breakdown is increased child prostitution. Freelance writer Germaine Shames writes, "Kham Suk, a delicate girl with fathomless eyes, hovers in the doorway of a Bangkok brothel in Thailand. Three months ago, on her 12th birthday, her mother walked her across the border from Myanmar (Burma), and sold her to a pimp."[50] Worldwatch Institute's Aaron Sachs provides these numbers from 1994:

Brazil alone has between 250,000 and 500,000 children involved in the sex trade, and a recent study conducted by the Bogota Chamber of Commerce concluded that the number of child prostitutes in the Colombian capital had nearly trebled over the past three years. Similar increases have occurred in countries as geographically and culturally disparate as Russia and Benin. But the center of the child sex industry is in Asia: . . . about 60,000 child prostitutes in the Philippines, about 400,000 in India, and about 800,000 in Thailand. Most of the children are under 16 and most are girls.[51]

Selling a child into prostitution is a desperate measure and makes sense only when the alternative is starvation. Peasants around the world traditionally work the land to feed themselves and their children. When the land was taken from them to produce products for export and they cannot find work, they must sell whatever commands a decent price. Often this is a daughter.

Even free-trade proponent Friedman acknowledges that so far globalization has increased gaps between the world's rich and poor:

> According to the 1998 United Nations Human Development Report, in 1960 the 20 percent of the world's people who live in the richest countries had 30 times the income of the poorest 20 percent. By 1995, the richest 20 percent had 82 times as much income.... Today the wealthiest one-fifth of the world's people consume 58 percent of total energy, while the poorest fifth consume less than 4 percent.[52]

In sum, poor people in the Third World do better when they are permitted to retain intact ecosystems that permit continuation of their traditional, sustainable way of life. The environmentalist agenda of protecting ecosystems from the depredations of a global economy coheres with the best prospects for the world's poor.

Environmentalist opposition to free trade helps the relatively poor in the First World as well. Environmentalists generally object to the exclusion of environmental and nonanthropocentric concerns from the calculations of the WTO. Including these concerns would help poor people in industrial countries by making trade fairer between rich and poor countries. Poor workers in rich countries would not be competing with workers in poor countries whose work product is kept artificially inexpensive through industrial practices that degrade environmental public goods, such as clean air and water. Such changes will also help poor people in the Third World by reducing environmental pollution in their midst.

Response 5: Environmentalists are not wedded to CBA to protect *public goods.*

Environmentalists use CBAs to justify internalizing the monetary cost of environmental degradation so that consumers pay the full cost of products. This exposes previously hidden inefficiencies, which is good, but maximizing the monetary worth of society's goods and services, the goal of CBA, does not supply a reasonable criterion for all public policies because maximum wealth only maximizes what money can buy. Everyone

knows that money cannot buy happiness, or the feeling of accomplish-
ment in personal achievement (the cabinet you made yourself, your
mastery of a foreign language or a musical instrument), or a loving relationship, or the health of your children, or peace of mind. We also know
that attempting to maximize income can interfere with attainment of
these other goods. It is no surprise, then, that maximizing social wealth
can interfere also with attaining social justice.

In situations of conflict, we do not always prefer maximum wealth. In
the United States, for example, few people want to legalize prostitution
to maximize economic growth. Similarly, environmentalists, like most
other people, support policies that serve nonmonetary values. In Mark
Sagoff's terms, environmentalists and others act as citizens, not just as
consumers, when they support justice for the poor and such goals as
energy efficiency, pollution abatement, and biodiversity.[53]

Response 6: Protection of *endangered species* and *wilderness areas* need not harm the poor.

The loss of jobs in the Pacific Northwest was due mostly to the movement of wood mills from the United States to Japan. Restrictions on
logging to protect the northern spotted owl were inappropriately blamed
by logging interests looking for a scapegoat. The logging jobs and way
of life were soon to be terminated anyway because 90 percent of old-
growth forests had been logged before the spotted owl controversy
erupted. The best chance for working class people in the region is to base
their economy on the forest's potential to attract ecotourism, and much
of this is now being done.[54] The electricity produced by the Tellico Dam
whose completion was jeopardized by attempts to save the endangered
snail darter would not be needed by people, rich or poor, if conservation
measures were put in place that would help the poor more than the rich,
as indicated in the section on energy policy above.

As environmentalist support for "community conservation" in the
Third World indicates, most environmentalists do not want to sacrifice
the welfare of the Third World poor to protect species diversity in nature
reserves. These environmentalists recognize that desperately poor people
tend to degrade their environments. When people lack food and the fuel
needed to cook it, they will kill wildlife regardless of its endangered

status; they will strip hillsides bare of trees and then try to farm on steep slopes, impairing species diversity and precipitating devastating erosion. Environmentalists know this, so they are eager to spare people desperate poverty for environmental as well as humanitarian reasons. Accordingly, most plans for species preservation in Third World nature reserves include provision for poor people in the area to benefit from the reserve, such as through ecotourism. This is "community conservation."

Brockington's criticism of Tanzania's Mkomazi Game Reserve does not contradict this view. He maintains merely that the analysis in Tanzania of what needed to be done to preserve species diversity may have been flawed from the start[55] and that promising alternatives to the path taken at the Mkomazi Reserve exist, such as the CAMPFIRE program used in Zimbabwe.[56] Better planning, he maintains, could have averted conflicts between the twin goals of preserving species and helping local people.

As for the tigers in India, if the real problem comes from development restricting the tigers' range so that they now need the area inhabited by indigenous people, justice suggests that the people who caused and continue to benefit from the problem, people involved in economic development, incur the loss. They, not indigenous people, should withdraw to make room for tigers.[57]

Considerations of environmental integrity reinforce these considerations of justice. Environmentalists generally support the survival of indigenous people and their cultures because they tend to be environment friendly, notwithstanding controversies about some of their current hunting methods. Alan Durning points out that when indigenous people are left undisturbed by cultural intrusions, the lands they inhabit

provide important ecological services: they regulate hydrological cycles, maintain local and global climatic stability, and harbor a wealth of biological and genetic diversity. . . . Supporting indigenous survival is an objective necessity, dominant cultures cannot sustain the earth's ecological health—a requisite of human advancement—without the aid of the world's endangered cultures. Biological diversity is inextricably linked to cultural diversity.[58]

There is "a remarkable correspondence between indigenous land use and the survival of natural areas."[59] Yet again, environmentalism and environmental justice coincide.

Response 7: *Animal welfare* does not harm the poor.

Neither Carruthers nor anyone else has evidence showing that concern about animal welfare consumes time, energy, psychological commitment, or money that would otherwise be used to help poor people. In fact, animal welfare advocates promote vegetarianism to reduce animal suffering on factory farms. Because, as noted earlier, eating meat is an inefficient use of the earth's food-producing capacity, vegetarianism provides more people nutritious diets. This can only benefit the "millions of our fellow humans [who] starve, or are near starving." In addition, people concerned about animal welfare often oppose experiments on animals to test new medications for people, but these new medications are expensive and therefore available, for the most part, only to the wealthiest 10 or 20 percent of the human population. The billions of dollars spent on animal experiments could help the poorest people more if applied directly to programs designed for that purpose, such as programs to supply clean water to people in poor countries.

History suggests a psychological connection between concern for animal welfare and concern for subordinated human beings. In the nineteenth century, major advocates of women's suffrage were among the founders of the vegetarian society. More recently, ecofeminists have argued that the master mentality that privileges people over animals also privileges men over women and therefore contributes to the subordination and suffering of millions of people.[60]

Conclusion

Environmentalists are seldom in a position to ensure that government entities or private corporations follow their policy recommendations, but that is not the issue here. The issue rather is whether environmentalist goals and policy recommendations work against justice for poor people. I conclude that true conflicts between environmentalism and justice for the poor are rare and seldom appear in environmentalists' practical recommendations. In most cases the goals of environmentalism can be achieved in ways that do not compromise, but in fact promote, justice. Of course, even worthwhile goals and values can come into conflict from time to time. For example, telling the truth and honoring parents are both good, but they conflict when parents request their children to lie. So situations may arise where serving justice conflicts with typical environmental goals. Nothing I have said precludes this possibility. I claim only that it would be an odd situation that indicates no general tendency of environmentalism to promote injustice.[61] In most cases and under most circumstances there are ways of promoting the goals of environmentalism that do not require compromising justice.

Notes

1. Nozick (1974).

2. Rawls (1971).

3 Etzioni (1993).

4 Kymlicka (2002, pp. 3–4).

5. See Flavin and Lenssen (1994, pp. 300–302), for the view that even European energy taxes should be raised.

6. Faramelli (1973, pp. 188, 198).

7. Gelbspan (1998, p. 127).

8. Hardin (1996).

9. Postel (1999).

10. Lomborg (2001, pp. 60–61).

11. Singer (2002, p. 56).

12. Bruni and Sanger (2001), quoted in Singer (2002, p. 77).

13. Singer (2002, p. 61).

14. Singer (2002, pp. 60–62).

15. Wenz (2001, pp. 47–53).

16. Newton and Dillingham (1994, pp. 107–133).

17. See *T.V.A. v. Hill* 437 U.S. 153 (1978).

18. Rolston (1996).

19. Sugal (1997).

20. Brockington (2002, p. 117).

21. Carruthers (1992, p. 168).

22. Lowe (1994, p. 7).

23. Lowe (1994, p. 6).

24. Lowe (1994, p. 16).

25. Lowe (1994, pp. 41–42).

26. Kay (1997, p. 119).

27. Kay (1997, pp. 120–121).

28. Gordon (1991, pp. 41–42).

29. Kunstler (1993, p. 183).

30. Gelbspan (1998, p. 191). See also Sawin (2004), especially pp. 15–16 and 30.

31. Barbour et al. (1982, pp. 110–111).

32. Casten (1998, pp. 4–5).

33. Hawken, Lovins, and Lovins (1999, especially pp. 247–255).

34. Nierenberg (2002, p. 16).

35. Chen et al. (1995, p. 4). See also Newton and Dillingham (2002, pp. 38–39).

36. Dasgupta (1998, p. 407).

37. Roodman (1996, p. 6).

38. Roodman (1996, p. 18).

39. Gardner (1996, pp. 7, 26).

40. Reisner (1993, p. 10) and Blatz (1991, pp. 11–12).

41. Roodman (1996, p. 28).

42. In fall 2003, meetings at Cancun, Mexico, designed to further integrate world markets foundered when some Third World countries refused to lower barriers to imports from the First World until First World countries agreed to reduce agricultural subsidies.

43. Shiva (1991, p. 93).

44. Halweil (2002, pp. 28–30).

45. Shiva (1991, p. 206).

46. Friedman (1999, p. 167). See also Lomborg (2001).

47. Korten (1995, p. 35).

48. Korten (1995, pp. 31–32).

49. Korten (1995, p. 42).

50. Shames (1994, p. 229).

51. Sachs (1994, p. 26).

52. Friedman (1999, p. 259).

53. Sagoff (1988).

54. Renner (2000, pp. 37–38).

55. Brockington (2002, p. 12).

56. Sugal (1997, p. 22).

57. Guha (1997, pp. 16–17).

58. Durning (1993, pp. 80–81).

59. Ayres (2003, p. 30).

60. Adams (1991).

61. A second caveat is that I write only about the present and foreseeable future. The farther future may be so different from the present that someday there will be a general tendency of environmentalism to promote injustice. I really cannot imagine this, but I do not want to identify the limit of my imagination with the limit of possibility.

References

Adams, C., *The Sexual Politics of Meat: A Feminist Vegetarian Critical Theory* (New York: Continuum, 1991).

Ayres, E., "Mapping Diversity," *WorldWatch* 16, no. 2 (March/April 2003): 30–32.

Barbour, I., H. Brooks, S. Lakoff, and J. Opie, *Energy and American Values* (New York: Praeger, 1982).

Blatz, C. V., "General Introduction," in *Ethics and Agriculture* (Caldwell, University of Idaho Press, 1991).

Brockington, C., *Fortress Conservation: The Preservation of the Mkomazi Game Reserve, Tanzania* (Bloomington: Indiana University Press, 2002).

Bruni, F., and Sanger, D., "Bush Urges Shift to Direct Grants for Poor Nations," *New York Times* (July 18, 2001): A1.

Carruthers, P., *The Animals Issue* (New York: Cambridge University Press, 1992).

Casten, T. R., *Turning Off the Heat* (New York: Prometheus Books, 1998).

Chen, L. C., W. M. Fitzgerald, and L. Bates, "Women, Politics and Global Management," *Environment* (January/February, 1995), p 4.

Durning, A. T., "Supporting Indigenous Peoples," in *State of the World 1993* (New York: W. W. Norton, 1993): pp. 80–100.

Dasgupta, P. S., "Population, Poverty and the Local Environment," in D. Van de Veer and C. Pierce, eds., *Environmental Ethics and Policy Book* (London: Wadsworth, 1998), 404–409.

Etzioni, A., *The Spirit of Community: Rights, Responsibilities, and the Communitarian Agenda* (New York: Crown Publishers, 1993).

Faramelli, N. T., "Ecological Responsibility and Economic Justice," in J. Barbour, ed., *Western Man and Environmental Ethics* (Reading, MA: Addison-Wesley, 1973).

Flavin, C., and N. Lenssen, *Power Surge: Guide to the Coming Energy Revolution* (New York: W. W. Norton, 1994).

Friedman, T. L., *The Lexus and the Olive Tree* (New York: Farrar, Straus and Giroux, 1999).

Gardner, G., "Shrinking Fields: Cropland Loss in a World of Eight Billion," *WorldWatch Paper* no. 131 (Washington, D.C. 1996).

Gelbspan, R., *The Heat Is On,* exp. ed. (New York: Perseus Books, 1998).

Gordon, G., *Steering a New Course: Transportation, Energy, and the Environment* (Washington, D.C.: Island Press, 1991).

Guha, R., "The Authoritarian Biologist and the Arrogance of Anti-Humanism: Wildlife Conservation in the Third World," *Ecologist* 27, no. 1 (January/ February 1997): 14–20.

Halweil, B., "Home Grown: The Case for Local Food in a Global Market," *WorldWatch Paper* no. 163 (Washington, D.C. 2002).

Hardin, G., "Lifeboat Ethics," in W. Aiken, and H. La Follette, eds., *World Hunger and Morality* (New York: Prentice Hall, 1996), pp. 5–15.

Hawken, P., A. Lovins, and L. H. Lovins, *Natural Capitalism: Creating the Next Industrial Revolution* (New York: Little, Brown and Company, 1999).

Kay, J. H., *Asphalt Nation: How the Automobile Took over America and How We Can Take It Back* (Berkeley: University of California Press, 1997).

Korten, D. C., *When Corporations Rule the World* (Bloomfield, CT: Kumarian Press, 1995).

Kunstler, J. H., *The Geography of Nowhere* (New York: Simon and Schuster, 1993).

Kymlicka, W., *Contemporary Political Philosophy: An Introduction,* 2d ed. (New York: Oxford University Press, 2002).

Lomborg, B., *The Skeptical Environmentalist: Measuring the Real State of the World* (New York: Cambridge University Press, 2001).

Lowe, M. D., "Back on Track: The Global Rail Revival," *WorldWatch Paper* no. 118 (Washington, D.C. 1994).

Newton, L. H., and C. K. Dillingham, *Watersheds: Classic Cases in Environmental Ethics* (Belmont, CA: Wadsworth, 1994).

Newton, L. H., and C. K. Dillingham, *Watersheds 3: Ten Cases in Environmental Ethics* (Belmont, CA: Wadsworth, 2002).

Nierenberg, D., "Correcting Gender Myopia: Gender Equity, Women's Welfare, and the Environment," *WorldWatch Paper* no. 161 (Washington, D.C. 2002).

Nozick, R., *Anarchy, State, and Utopia* (New York: Basic Books, 1974).

Postel, S., *Pillar of Sand: Can the Irrigation Miracle Last?* (New York: W.W. Norton, 1999).

Rawls, J., *A Theory of Justice* (Cambridge, Mass.: Harvard University Press, 1971).

Reisner, M., *Cadillac Desert: The American West and Its Disappearing Water* (Caldwell: University of Idaho Press, 1993).

Renner, M., "Working for the Environment: A Growing Source of Jobs," *WorldWatch Paper* no. 152 (Washington, D.C. 2000).

Rolston, III, H., "Feeding People versus Saving Nature?" in W. Aiken and H. LaFollette, eds., *World Hunger and Morality*, 2nd ed. (New York: Prentice Hall, 1996), 248–267.

Roodman, D. M., "Paying the Piper: Subsidies, Politics, and the Environment," *WorldWatch Paper* no. 133 (Washington, D.C. 1996).

Sachs, A., "The Last Commodity: Child Prostitution in the Developing World," *World Watch* 7, no. 4 (July/August 1994): 24–30.

Sagoff, M., *The Economy of the Earth* (New York: Cambridge University Press, 1988).

Sawin, J. L., "Mainstreaming Renewable Energy in the 21st Century," *WorldWatch Paper* no. 169 (Washington, D.C. 2004).

Singer, P., *One World: The Ethics of Globalization* (New Haven, Conn.: Yale University Press, 2002).

Shames, G. W., "The World's Throw-Away Children," *Global Issues 94/95* (Dushkin, 1994): 229–232.

Shiva, V., *The Violence of the Green Revolution* (London: Zed Books, 1991).

Sugal, C., "The Price of Habitat," *WorldWatch* 10, no. 5 (May/June 1997): 18–27.

Wenz, P., *Environmental Ethics Today* (New York: Oxford University Press, 2001).

3

Justice: The Heart of Environmentalism

Dale Jamieson

Asking people what environmentalism is elicits diverse answers. Some people think of it as the practice of engaging in various activities from recycling to hunting. Others think of it as supporting pressure groups ranging from the National Wildlife Federation to the Earth Liberation Front. For many of my students, environmentalism implies activism. Even those who are vegetarian backpackers are often reluctant to call themselves environmentalists, for they see themselves as lazy or lacking commitment. Yet, according to surveys, most Americans are willing to identify themselves publicly as environmentalists or environmentally concerned,[1] even those who vote for environmentally abusive candidates. I remember how surprised I was when I moved from Colorado to Minnesota to discover that Minnesota "greens" held more or less the same views as Colorado "browns." In Minnesota, members of the "bait and bullet" crowd are considered environmentalists, whereas in Colorado they are the "wise use" antienvironmentalists.

Asking this question internationally produces an even wider array of answers. Some who claim to speak for the developing world will tell you that environmentalism is a meaningless concept where they come from, because people do not distinguish themselves from nature, or (alternatively and inconsistently) they sometimes say that people in the developing world see nature as a resource. In many European countries "greens" have replaced "reds" on the left of the political spectrum. Once I asked a European friend of mine about the background of his country's new environment minister. "He was an ultra-left terrorist before he was a green," my friend said, exaggerating only slightly.

In this chapter I am not going to address the entire heterogeneous domain of environmentalism. My target will be American environmentalism. I will suggest that it has two distinct sources and that this accounts for some of the uneasiness one finds in the movement. A focus on justice, I claim, can reconcile these perspectives across a broad range of issues. In this respect it can be said that justice is both conceptually and historically at the heart of environmentalism. Justice also gives environmentalism a heart in the sense of motivating people to make change and taming the movement's tendency toward misanthropy and pessimism. The heart is not the whole of an organism, however, and justice does not exhaust environmentalism. There are unruly features of the human relationship to nature that express themselves in both environmentally friendly and environmentally destructive ways. Any attempt to provide even a partial map of American environmentalism must also acknowledge these features.

Think Globally, Act Locally

The American environmental movement can be seen as having two distinct dimensions. One has its source in nineteenth-century movements for community beautification and public hygiene; the other has its source in global concerns about conservation and preservation. The former tradition evolved from a focus on public health to a broader concern with ecological identity and a sense of place. It finds its expression in the work of writers such as Edward Abbey and Wendell Berry. Its signature issues include Love Canal and the construction of the Glen Canyon Dam. The latter tradition came to prominence in the 1970s with the publication of such books as *The Limits to Growth*. Its heroes are scientists such as Paul Ehrlich and E. O. Wilson, and it sees climate change and biodiversity loss as the central environmental issues.

These traditions express very different attitudes toward authority and democratic participation. Those whose environmentalism is motivated by a sense of place tend to be mistrustful of science and management. They see environmental problems as largely caused by failed attempts to manage complex systems and are skeptical of the idea that even more intensive management is the solution to these failures. Those who focus on global change issues as the most serious threats tend to put their faith in science. They point out that it is scientists who have alerted us to climate change and the biodiversity crisis, and it is they who are most credible when it comes to solutions.

These perspectives are not only distinct; they are in some ways quite antithetical. For place-based environmentalists the turn to scientific management, rather than being a solution, is another iteration of the same problem. As Berry writes, "Properly speaking, global thinking is not possible." Those who have claimed to think globally, he writes, have imposed "simplifications too extreme and oppressive to merit the name of thought."[2] Partisans of the global perspective, on the other hand, say that what is needed to protect nature are objective scientific managers who take the long view and are insulated from the emotional storms of local politics that often result in myopic and selfish policies. We can dramatize these differences by saying that those who focus on the global are modernist progressives who valorize science, whereas those who act from place-based concerns are antimodernists, deeply mistrustful of science, and generally pessimistic about the prospects for rational management.

Although this division is deep and profound, it is easy to overlook, because many environmentalists drink from both wells. Indeed, the most important environmental writers, such as Aldo Leopold and Rachel Carson, can reasonably be claimed by both sides. Both Leopold and Carson were trained as scientists, and their writing reflected the abstract, generalized concerns of scientific thinking. At the same time, however, both were in love with particular places that they wrote about with great passion and power.

These two dimensions of environmentalism mingle almost completely when it comes to opposing environmentally destructive initiatives. Greens of various shades can unite in their opposition to nuclear power, sprawl, and the opening up of wilderness areas to development, because they can be seen as either characteristic expressions of science and technology or perverted expressions of them distorted by political corruption and human irrationality. This unity in opposition can obscure the fact that environmentalists share very little by way of positive images of how humans should relate to nature. Far from visionary, environmentalists are better at opposition and obstruction than at creating and articulating positive views.

A ruling vision sourced in an idea of justice can help bring these perspectives together. Consider, for example, how their different views of scientific authority might be treated. Rather than viewing science as the whole of the problem or the entirety of the solution, a perspective that centers on justice would see it as another active participant in the negotiating process. A vision informed by considerations of justice would help us to see science as an institutional agent with important powers and capacities, but also its own interests. Once we see things in this way, science can be spared the full credit or full blame for epistemological closure or conflict. Rather than causing the lack of consensus about environmental policy, the fissures in science will themselves be seen as part and product of larger normative conflicts (Jamieson 1996).

The Environmental Justice Movement

The idea of environmental justice burst into the American consciousness in 1982, when there were more than 500 arrests in the largely African-American community of Afton, North Carolina, during a campaign of nonviolent civil disobedience directed toward preventing the disposal of PCB-laced soil in the Warren County landfill. Among those arrested was Congressman Walter Fauntroy, who subsequently asked the United States General Accounting Office (GAO) to study the racial demographics of hazardous waste siting. Both the GAO study and a larger research effort mounted by the United Church of Christ came to the conclusion that people of color and the poor disproportionately bear the environmental costs of a highly consumptive, affluent society.[3]

Since these events, a growing academic literature on these questions has developed, but in America the idea of environmental justice has come to be identified with the social movement that protests toxic waste siting, excessive pesticide use, and contamination of air and water on Indian reservations, among Latino farm-workers, and in poor white and African-American communities. By the early 1990s, the environmental justice movement had become so influential that President Clinton established an office of environmental justice as part of the Environmental Protection Agency, and on February 11, 1994, he signed

Executive Order 12898, "Federal Actions to Address Environmental Justice in Minority Populations and Low-Income Populations."

From the beginning, there were concerns about the appropriation of the language of environmental justice on behalf of a social movement directed toward promoting the interests of minority groups in America. For most philosophers and theorists, justice involves impartiality and universality and thus moves in the direction of a global perspective. Particular groups may struggle to be treated justly, but this is not the same as struggling to implement a conception of justice. In recent years important elements of the environmental justice movement have begun to organize around broader issues with global import,[4] but constructing a full account of environmental justice very much remains a work in progress.

Dimensions of Environmental Justice

Some may find the very idea of environmental justice strange, for they may think of the environment as a kind of amenity that one may purchase more or less of, depending on one's preferences and resources. On this view environmental quality is like cultural institutions or sports facilities; its allocation is a matter of discretion, not of justice.

Contrary to this view, at least thirty-three nations and twelve American states now recognize a constitutional right to environmental quality.[5] Environmental preservation is increasingly seen as central to human flourishing, and in some cases a matter of life and death. It is also becoming clear that the overconsumption of the earth's resources by some condemns others to poverty. When seen in this way, it seems undeniable that many environmental concerns involve questions of justice.

But what exactly is environmental justice? Aristotle distinguished two types of justice: distributive justice and corrective justice. Distributive justice concerns how various benefits and burdens should be distributed; corrective justice is about punishment and compensation. Although it is plausible to suppose that some instances of environmental justice involve corrective justice,[6] the larger temptation is to think of environmental justice as primarily a kind of distributive justice.[7] On this view the environment is a resource whose distribution should be governed by principles of justice. Because many aspects of the environment cannot physically be transferred from one community to another, this view is more precisely thought of as advocating the distribution of the benefits and costs of environmental resources according to principles of justice. From this perspective environmental resources are in principle no different from money, food, health care, or other distributive goods over which people have claims of justice. It is an open question as to how exactly environmental resources are defined, how benefits and costs are assessed, what principles of justice are appropriate for governing their distribution, and who are the subjects and beneficiaries of these duties.

The idea that duties of environmental justice are global in scope has been around since the 1970s. At the United Nations Conference on the Human Environment in Stockholm in 1972, the notion of global environmental justice was introduced as the developing world's answer to the industrialized world's growing concern to preserve pure environmental goods such as species and ecosystems, many of which exist primarily in developing countries.[8] The idea began to gain traction in 1991 with the publication of *Global Warming in an Unequal World: A Case of Environmental Colonialism* by the Indian environmentalists, Anil Agarwal and Sunita Narain.

Poor countries often argue that rich countries committed various environmental injustices in the process of their development and continue to commit injustices by appropriating more than their share of the earth's resources. For example, they point out that, not only is the United States the world's largest emitter of greenhouse gases, but its annual increases since 1990 have been greater than those of any other country except China. On a per capita basis Americans emit twenty-two times as much carbon dioxide as Indians, eleven times as much as Brazilians, and eight times as much as Chinese.[9]

Viewing global environmental issues from the perspective of distributive justice can certainly be a useful analytical approach, as the case of greenhouse gas emissions illustrates. The Framework Convention on Climate Change, which now has been ratified by 189 countries, including the United States, commits the parties to the goal of stabilizing "greenhouse gas concentrations in the atmosphere at a level that would prevent dangerous anthropogenic interference with the climate system."

There are many ways of reaching this objective, but any successful attempt would impose costs in foregone development opportunities and in economic and social restructuring. Different regimes would distribute these costs differently. One approach would be to establish an annual global ceiling on greenhouse gas emissions, allocate permissions to emit, and then allow unlimited emissions trading. This approach would be highly efficient, but whether it would be just would depend to a great extent on how permissions to emit are initially allocated.[10] Viewing this as a problem of distributive justice is a useful analytical approach because it invites discussion of the issues that matter most, rather than shunting them off into a technical dead end. Although ordinary people are excluded from abstract discussions of atmospheric physics and chemistry, the language of justice implicated in discussions of the distribution of greenhouse gas emissions is one with which everyone can identify.

However useful and intuitive it may be to see global environmental problems in this way, it is also clear that the idea of environmental justice is not exhausted by the notion of distributive justice. In an insightful early article on the American environmental justice movement, Iris Marion Young argued that it was participatory justice, not distributive justice that was the primary demand of communities such as Afton, North Carolina.[11] People objected not only to the fact that they were being subjected to risks, but also to exposure without their consent and without institutional mechanisms that would allow them to articulate their opposition. This was also the case in the late 1970s at Love Canal in New York state, when white working-class homeowners became so frustrated by the lack of governmental responsiveness to their concerns that they detained officials from the United States Environmental Protection Agency who had come to allay their fears about the fact that their community was built on top of a toxic waste dump.[12]

The centrality of participatory justice to environmental justice is also indicated by the fact that the "Principles of Environmental Justice" (appendix A), adopted by the First National People of Color Environmental Leadership Summit in 1991, emphasized self-determination and respect for diverse cultural perspectives rather than distributive justice. Indeed, distributive justice is mentioned in only two of the seventeen principles adopted by the summit.[13]

Participatory justice is also important at the global level. Those who suffer most from environmental insults are often not at the table. For example, rising sea levels caused in part by climate change are likely to destroy completely such countries as Sao Tome and Principe, Kiribati, Maldives, and Tuvalu. Because their land mass will be underwater, these countries may literally cease to exist.[14] Other small countries in the Caribbean and elsewhere will be ravaged by more intense, and perhaps more frequent, storms and hurricanes. Seventy million farmers and their families in Bangladesh will lose their livelihoods when their rice paddies are inundated by seawater. Yet despite the vast number of people around the world who will suffer from climate change, most of them are not included when decisions are made. Indeed, to a great extent, the United States has set the world on this course through its own unilateral action.

Poor people and those who live on the margins are effectively voiceless in many environmental debates. In some cases participation is denied not because of institutional or political failure, but because those in question are not recognized as in the domain of justice. Historically, at various times and places, slaves and women have been denied justice not only in the sense that they have borne disproportionate burdens or that their voices have been muted, but also in that they have not been regarded as the proper subjects of justice. This explains why so much of the rhetoric of the American civil rights movement centered on asserting the "human-ness" (or "manhood") of African Americans. African Americans were not only denied their fair share, but were also excluded from the community over which justice was supposed to prevail.

Poor people and those at the margins are not alone in being disen-franchised. Future generations are not at the table to defend their inter-ests, and the use of standard decision-theoretic tools such as the discount rate is often used to effectively dismiss even their most important inter-ests. Again, this can be seen clearly in the case of climate change. It is rich people currently alive who reap the greatest share of the benefits of emit-ting greenhouse gases. It is poor people who will live in the second half of this century and beyond who will bear most of the burdens. It is dif-ficult to believe that we would behave so irresponsibly if we had to defend our actions directly to those who will suffer from them.[15]

Some of those who speak of global environmental justice also believe that we owe duties of justice to other entities that cannot speak for themselves: individual plants, individual animals, populations, species, ecosystems, geological formations, or even planets. Various cases are made for including such entities in the domain of justice, but they typically appeal to criteria of inclusion such as naturalness, wildness, teleological organization, and sentience.[16] Although there are many difficult and controversial issues here, it seems clear that the case for recognizing duties of justice to some non-human animals is as strong as the case for recognizing such duties to some human animals. The other great apes, for example, have complex social systems and lives that can go better or worse in a way that matters to them. The same reasons that we have for recognizing duties of justice to some humans apply to them as well. Once this point is recognized it becomes clear that many other nonhuman animals also qualify as beneficiaries of duties of justice.[17]

I have claimed that a clear and consistent concern with duties of environmental justice will go beyond the confines of our domestic communities and encompass the globe. It will also project from the present into the future, and include posterity. Finally, it will encompass a great deal of the "more than human world."[18] Having said this, however, I also believe that the bounds of justice will not exhaust our relationship to nature.

Beyond Justice

Justice is at the center of environmentalism, but there are two ubiquitous attitudes toward nature that cannot perspicuously be taken up in the language of justice. The first sees nature as "radically other"; the second sees humans as "part of nature." Both of these attitudes are ancient and remain influential.

The attitude that sees nature as "radically other" is expressed in various spiritual traditions as well as in some Greek philosophical schools. One memorable statement of it may be found in chapter 5 of the *Tao Te Ching*, attributed to the Taoist sage Lao-Tse: "Heaven and Earth are impartial; they treat all of creation as straw dogs." In ancient Chinese rituals, straw dogs were burned as sacrifices in place of living dogs. What is being asserted here is that the forces that govern the world are as indifferent to human welfare as humans are to the fate of the straw dogs used in ritual sacrifice.

From this perspective, nature is seen as amoral: in no way does it provide us with moral concepts. Moral concepts arise either from divine commandment, as in the case in the Hebrew Bible, or they are artificial human constructions laboriously created and maintained to provide us with a refuge in an otherwise heartless world, as in the story told by the sixteenth-century philosopher Thomas Hobbes. Both versions of this story see nature as immensely powerful and humanity as weak, vulnerable, and in need of protection. From this perspective the idea that moral concepts such as justice would apply to nature seems bizarre.

Although this perspective does not support any idea of environmental justice, other important attitudes toward nature do arise. One attitude provides a rationale for human attempts to conquer and dominate nature. If humanity and its projects are to survive and thrive in this amoral world, nature must be subdued and kept at bay. On this view nature, by indifference if not by intention, should be seen as an enemy of humanity

A second attitude that may arise from this perspective involves a profound appreciation of nature. This thought is powerfully developed in Edmund Burke's 1757 treatise, *A Philosophical Enquiry into the Origin of Our Ideas of the Sublime and Beautiful*. The human experience of the sublime is, according to Burke, a "delight" and one of the most powerful human emotions. Yet, perhaps paradoxically, the experience of the sublime involves such "negative" emotions as fear, dread, pain, and terror and can occur when we experience deprivation, darkness, solitude, silence, or vacuity. The experience of the sublime arises when we feel we are in danger, but are not actually in danger. Immensity, infinity, magnitude, and grandeur can cause this experience of unimagined eloquence, greatness, significance, and power. The sublime is often associated with experiences of mountains or oceans. Such experiences may occasion wonder, awe, astonishment, admiration, reverence, or respect. In its fullest extent, the experience of the sublime may cause total astonishment.

The idea of the sublime was profoundly influential on nineteenth-century American culture, notably through nineteenth-century painters such as Thomas Cole and Frederic Church. It has gone on to be an important influence on American environmentalism through the writings of John Muir and, more recently, Jack Turner (1996) and other advocates for "the big outside" (Foreman 1992). Indeed, the case for wilderness preservation is often made in the language of the sublime. Although it is easy to see why concern for the possibility of such experiences can be an important motivation for some committed environmentalists, it is obvious that this concern engages different considerations than the language of justice.

The second ubiquitous attitude, the one that sees humans as part of nature, can be characterized by contrasting it directly with concerns about justice. Viewing nature as an object of or as implicated in duties of justice rests on certain presuppositions. Although these presuppositions may be true, there are ways of viewing nature in which they do not apply. For an entity to be in the domain of justice, it must be conceived as distinct from what owes it justice and it must also be viewed as worthy of respect. If there were only a single entity in the world, no question of justice would arise. For example, if Robinson Crusoe were alone in the world, he would not owe himself duties of justice. Nor would duties of justice arise in Crusoe's world in virtue of adding a stone, for stones are not (in the usual sense) worthy of respect.

We are now in a position to see why some dimensions of nature, viewed from a certain perspective, are not in the domain of justice. The claim that nature *simpliciter* is within the domain of justice fails the first condition. This is because, from this perspective, we are not separate from nature. Nature is inside of us and we are part of nature. Our skin is a permeable membrane that is itself part of the natural world. Thus, the separation between ourselves and nature that is required for duties of justice to obtain cannot plausibly be maintained from this point of view.

When people say things that are similar to what I have just claimed, I confess that I often find myself quite irritated. This is because such claims sound either trivial or false, pernicious or mystical. In one sense such claims seem trivial, at least for a naturalist. Of course we are part of nature. What else is there for us to be part of? Yet in another sense it is clear that we do distinguish people from nature in much the same way that we distinguish artifacts from natural objects. Someone who cannot make such distinctions, at least in the ordinary case, either does not know how to speak the language, or has some serious psychological deficiency or disorder. The claim that we are part of nature can also seem pernicious, because it seems to imply that there is no moral difference between a human being who is killed by an earthquake and one who is killed by another human. Of course those who claim that humans are part of nature typically want to deny this implication, but this is where the mysticism sets in.

My claim that humans are part of nature is more straightforward. Think of it this way. We can take many different perspectives on the relationship between ourselves and nature. For example, we can see nature as a set of cycles, and from within this single perspective there are multiple views. From the point of view of biogeochemistry, nature is the carbon cycle, the nitrogen cycle, and so on. On this view we, like other natural objects, are instances of these cycles. At another level of analysis we can say that breathing and respiration are instances of the same cycles that govern the atmosphere; our circulatory system, as well as various cellular processes, are instances of the hydrological cycle; digestion and metabolism recapitulate the soil cycle; and we are as subject the laws of thermodynamics as any planet or star.[19] We could go on acknowledging other perspectives and various points of view within them. From these perspectives we are not separate from nature. Nature not only has brought us into existence and sustains us, but also constitutes our identity. Because justice requires distinction, and there is no distinction between us and nature, our relation to nature cannot be constituted by relations of justice.

This may seem hopelessly abstract or romantic, but it is because of these perspectives from which we see ourselves as part of nature that we cannot fully reduce nature to competing baskets of distributable goods, at least not without radically changing our own self-understandings. We are hesitant about markets in kidneys, and more than hesitant about markets in brains, in part because these organs are seen as partly constitutive of who we are. Even if we allow such markets, we will not be tempted to think that everything that is important about a kidney or a brain is expressed by its market value. It would be strange for someone to perform a cost-benefit analysis of a brain as if its value in a shadow market were its most important feature. The same sort of strangeness attaches to attempts to assess in market terms "the value of the world's ecosystem services and natural capital."[20] A residue remains of our relation to nature that cannot be fully expressed in the language of justice or economics. This dimension is primordial and expressed in various traditions around the world. It cannot easily be dismissed.[21]

Conclusion

In this chapter I have attempted to maintain a delicate balance. I have claimed that a concern with justice is at the heart of environmentalism but that identifying oneself with nature, and viewing nature as "radically other," also figure in the narratives of American environmentalism. For those who are unimpressed with Whitman's adage "I am large, I contain multitudes," this may seem inconsistent, for each of these attitudes toward nature involves quite different presuppositions. As I have already claimed, however, we live with multiple perspectives, and our stances toward the world and ourselves are simultaneously plural. But just in case this point needs to be made more compelling, I will close by discussing two examples.

Consider first the attitudes that we take toward our fellow humans. We are almost never single-minded about them, nor are our attitudes serial or linear. We live with multiple views and perspectives, often held simultaneously, sometimes with quite different valences. Imagine a colleague who is excellent at his work, narcissistic in his behavior, an emotional abuser of women, but a charming and intelligent social companion. I might give him a paper for review, but I would not introduce him to a female friend. I might enjoy going to the movies with him, but I would not open my heart in a conversation over dinner. Rather than plunging me into inconsistency, I would say that such complexity in human relationships is the stuff of everyday life.

Our relationships to nature are no less complex. Consider my relationship to the Needles District of Canyonlands National Park, part of the American wilderness system. I have hiked and camped there, experiencing the sublimity of Druid Arch and the luminescence of the full moon over Elephant Canyon. In searching for water I have felt myself to be part of the natural system that orders and supports life in this desert. I am irate about proposals to open this area to off-road vehicles. Such a policy would be unjust to backpackers and wilderness adventurers, who would lose the silence and solitude that makes their preferred wilderness experiences possible. I also mourn for the wildlife that would be destroyed or driven away by such a policy. I find the idea of people treating this place as if it were some desert speedway both vulgar and disrespectful. In short, my attitudes toward this area embody all of the perspectives that I have discussed in this chapter: a recognition that my identity is part constituted by my relationship to this place; a desire for the experience of the sublime that it affords; and most of all, a passion that those who love and inhabit this place be treated justly. The moral psychology of my attitudes is complex, but it should not be surprising that our attitudes toward nature can be as complex as our attitudes toward our con-specifics.

In this chapter I have claimed that justice is the heart of environmentalism and that the idea of environmental justice is multidimensional. It concerns the distribution of the benefits and burdens of our interactions with the environment, the need for participation in decisions that concern the environment, and the importance of expanding our conception of who is within the domain of justice. Viewing environmental conflicts in this light provides an opportunity for transforming environmentalism from a collection of views and prejudices united mainly by their opposition to various policies and projects into a set of positive visions that can guide us into the future. Putting justice at the center also gives environmentalism a motivational heart that it often seems to lack.

What I have not claimed is that our complex relationships to nature are fully exhausted by locating nature in a nexus of relationships governed by concepts of justice. We are nature and nature is us, and just as my relationship to myself cannot be exhausted by duties of justice, so my relationship to nature cannot be so exhausted. Yet in other respects we are so alien from nature that it is beyond the reach of concepts such as justice. These perspectives must be acknowledged. Environmentalism can and should be remade with justice at its heart, but it must also respect what it cannot fully capture.[22]

Notes

1. According to the Gallup Organization, "Public anxiety [in the United States] about the environment has held relatively steady since 2002—the percentage

who worry a great deal or fair amount has fluctuated between 62% and 68%" (Gallup Organization, 2005).

2. Thiele (1999, p. 131).

3. United States General Accounting Office (1983); and United Church of Christ Commission for Racial Justice (1987).

4. Robert Bullard, for example, has begun to work against climate change. See http://www.ejcc.org/index.html (accessed June 26, 2005).

5. See, for a review, Rodger Schlickeisen, "Protecting Biodiversity for Future Generations: An Argument for a Constitutional Amendment," available online at http://www.defenders.org/bio-co06.html (accessed June 26, 2005).

6. For example, insofar as some have caused harm to others by appropriating what is rightfully theirs (for example, resources from a global commons, or perhaps habitat in the case of wild animals), duties of corrective justice may be owed.

7. This is how Peter Wenz (1988) thought about environmental justice in one of the first systematic works on the subject.

8. For more on the development of the idea of global environmental justice see Jamieson (1994, 2002).

9. Calculated from data collated by the World Resources Institute, available online at http://earthtrends.wri.org/datatables/index.cfm?theme=3 (accessed June 26, 2005).

10. For more on this topic see Jamieson (2000, pp. 287–307).

11. Young (1983).

12. Gibbs and Levine (1981).

13. The importance of participatory justice as a dimension of environmental justice is argued in Figueroa and Mills (2001) and Figueroa (1999).

14. In the case of Sao Tome and Principe, a small volcanic peak might survive.

15. For an excellent discussion of these issues see Gardiner (2003).

16. For samples of these views see Agar (2001), Callicott (1989), Regan, (1983), Rolston (1988), Taylor (1986), Varner (1998).

17. For further discussion, see Jamieson (2002). The most influential opponents of such views are those who claim that justice concerns mutual advantage rather than impartiality. For further discussion, see Barry (1995).

18. I take the expression, "more than human world," from Abram (1996).

19. These themes are suggested by Suzuki and McConnell (1997).

20. This is the title of Constanza et al. (1997). According to the authors, the value in question is in the range of $16–54 trillion per year. For a critical discussion, see Mark Sagoff, "Can We Put a Price on Nature's Services?" available online at http://www.puaf.umd.edu/IPPP/content.htm.

21. Sagoff (1991) and Dworkin (1993, chap. 3) argue points that are similar to this—Sagoff when he distinguishes nature from the environment, and Dworkin when he talks about species as sacred.

22. Earlier versions of some of this material were presented at two meetings sponsored by the Carnegie Council on Ethics and International Affairs in New York, and in a lecture at the Suzhau Institute of Science and Technology in Suzhau, China. I am grateful to all who participated in those discussions. I also thank Phaedra C. Pezzullo and Ronald Sandler for their comments on an earlier draft.

References

Abram, D., *The Spell of the Sensuous: Perception and Language in a More-Than-Human World* (New York: Pantheon Books, 1996).

Agar, N., *Life's Intrinsic Value* (New York: Columbia University Press, 2001).

Agarwal, A., and S. Narain, *Global Warming in an Unequal World: A Case of Environmental Colonialism* (New Delhi: Center for Science and Environment, 1991).

Barry, B., *Justice as Impartiality* (New York: Oxford University Press, 1995).

Callicott, J. B., *In Defense of the Land Ethic: Essays in Environmental Philosophy* (Albany: State University of New York Press, 1989).

Costanza, R., et al., "The Value of the World's Ecosystem Services and Natural Capital," *Nature* 387 (May 15, 1997): 253–260.

Dworkin, R., *Life's Dominion: An Argument about Abortion, Euthanasia, and Individual Freedom* (New York: Alfred A. Knopf, 1993).

Figueroa, R., *Debating the Paradigms of Justice: The Bivalence of Environmental Justice*, Ph. D. dissertation, University of Colorado, Boulder, 1999.

Figueroa, R., and C. Mills, "Environmental Justice," in Dale Jamieson, ed., *A Companion to Environmental Justice* (Oxford: Blackwell, 2001), 426–438.

Foreman, D. *The Big Outside: A Descriptive Inventory of the Big Wilderness Areas of the United States*, rev. ed. (New York: Three Rivers Press, 1992).

Gardiner, S., "The Pure Intergenerational Problem," *The Monist: Special Issue on Moral Distance*, 86, no. 3 (July 2003): 481–500.

Gallup Organization, "Public's Environmental Outlook Grows More Negative But No Increase in Public Worry about Environment Quality" (April 21, 2005).

Gibbs, L. M., and M. Levine, *The Love Canal: My Story* (Albany: State University of New York Press, 1981).

Jamieson, D., *Morality's Progress: Essays on Humans, Other Animals, and the Rest of Nature* (Oxford: Oxford University Press, 2002).

Jamieson, D., "Climate Change and Global Environmental Justice," in P. Edwards and C. Miller, eds., *Changing the Atmosphere: Expert Knowledge and Global Environmental Governance* (Cambridge, Mass.: MIT Press, 2000), 287–308.

Jamieson, D., "Scientific Uncertainty and the Political Process," *The Annals of the American Academy of Political and Social Sciences* 545 (May 1996), 35–43.

Jamieson, D., "Global Environmental Justice," in R. Attfield and A. Belsey, eds., *Philosophy and the Natural Environment* (Cambridge: Cambridge University Press, 1994), 199–210.

Regan, T., *The Case for Animal Rights* (Berkeley: University of California Press, 1983).

Rolston III, H., *Environmental Ethics: Values in and Duties to the Natural World* (Philadelphia: Temple University Press, 1988).

Sagoff, M., "Nature Versus the Environment," *Report from the Institute for Philosophy and Public Policy* 11, no. 3 (summer 1991).

Suzuki, D., and A. McConnell, *The Sacred Balance: Rediscovering our Place in Nature* (Vancouver: Greystone Books, 1997).

Taylor, P., *Respect for Nature* (Princeton, N.J.: Princeton University Press, 1986).

Thiele, L. P., *Environmentalism for a New Millennium* (New York: Oxford University Press, 1999).

Turner, J., *The Abstract Wild* (Tucson: University of Arizona Press, 1996).

United Church of Christ Commission for Racial Justice, *Toxic Wastes and Race in the United States: A National Report on the Racial and Socio-Economic Characteristics of Communities with Hazardous Waste Sites* (New York: Public Data Access, 1987).

United States General Accounting Office, *Siting of Hazardous Waste Landfills and Their Correlation with Racial and Economic Status Surrounding Communities*, GAO/RCED-83-168 (1983).

Varner, G., *In Nature's Interests? Animal Rights and Environmental Ethics* (New York: Oxford University Press, 1998).

Wenz, P., *Environmental Justice* (Albany: SUNY Press, 1988).

Young, I. M., "Justice and Hazardous Waste," *The Applied Turn in Contemporary Philosophy: Bowling Green Studies in Applied Philosophy*, 5 (1983): 171–183.

II

U.S. Environments

4

Becoming an Environmental Justice Activist

Kim Allen, Vinci Daro, and Dorothy C. Holland

The people who hug trees don't usually hug people. That is another environmental problem.
—George Garrsion, environmental justice activist

Do I belong in a dump ground? Am I trash too?
—Dollie Burwell, environmental justice activist

White people can be environmentalists and racists at the same time.
—Pastor Wilson, environmental justice activist

We, along with other members of a research team, recently completed a multiyear project that combined ethnographic research on local environmental activism in North Carolina and on the Delmarva peninsula with a national survey. The study, which included observation of twenty local environmental groups, in addition to the sixteen reported upon in this chapter, and a collection of 163 environmental and political biographical and identity interviews from members of these groups, is one of the largest ethnographic studies of local environmental groups to date.[1]

In this chapter, we present an analysis of the interviews and the participant observation research that we did with North Carolina environmental justice activists and groups in the late 1990s.[2] We offer a theoretical perspective and an analysis of the qualitative data on how people become active in the environmental justice movement. To explain environmental action, we emphasize the significance of identities— durable subjectivities and self-understandings, both collective and individual—that develop through cultural activities within "figured worlds" of environmental justice and environmentalism and through dialogues with people and groups both inside and outside the movement. A figured world is a socially and culturally constructed realm of interpretation and signification—a horizon of meaning—in which particular characters and actors are recognized, significance is assigned to certain acts, and particular outcomes are valued over others (Holland et al. 1998, p. 52). An identity forms as one grows into a figured world, participating in meaningful action in that world, and over time developing dispositions, sentiments, and sensitivities relevant to that world.

Against models that attribute the causes of collective mobilization to knowledge, beliefs, and values (e.g., Stern et al. 1999) and models that postulate a threshold of tolerance for resource deprivation or economic conflict beyond which material or structural conditions will provoke collective mobilization (e.g., Skocpol 1979; for a related analysis see Flacks 1988), our framework theorizes the importance of identity and the commensurability of identity and action that emerges in the context of a figured world. Activities, events, practices, personalities, and material and semiotic artifacts are interpreted against the horizons of meaning of these "as if" worlds. Although figured worlds are not prescriptive sets of rules that people are supposed to follow, they mediate behavior: they inform outlooks that become salient and more durable for individuals over time with continued participation in them (Holland et al. 1998, p. 52).[3] They structure the orchestration of social discourses and practices that become resources for the crafting of identity and action, including responses defined, in part, by the standpoints of others in a figured world (Holland et al. 1998, p. 272; Holland and Lachicotte, forthcoming).

Insofar as environmental justice proponents are dialogically engaged— directly and indirectly—with self-identified environmentalists, we consider environmental justice to be a form of environmentalism. Amid the dialogic tensions and bridges between these figured worlds, in which different histories are salient, different social divisions are prominent, different cultural activities are relevant, and different forms of organization are valued, the cultural production of new narratives of blame and responsibility and new conceptions of both "the environment" and environmental*ism* are ongoing. Although at the time of our study dialogues between these figured worlds were generated with more intensity within environmental justice communities than in mainstream or dominant environmental groups, dialogue may be evolving to a more two-sided, or multisided, conversation through which mainstream environmental discourse and agendas are being refigured by environmental justice concerns. As is clear from our study, the process of environmentalist identity formation for individual environmental justice activists has been problematic; the expressed ambivalence, contradictory experiences, and internal struggles around whether to consider oneself an environmentalist are evidence of the contested boundaries of environmentalism. The perception expressed by many participants in our study that environmentalism is "occupied"—or already determined—by the concerns of white environmentalists and the interests of wealthy people affects the development of both environmental justice and mainstream environmentalism. In our ethnographic work, we trace the meaning making that shapes the dynamic boundaries between these two environmentalisms, with a focus on how events and activities are made meaningful within the figured worlds of each.

As we emphasize, local groups are conceptual spaces in which identities and actions are shaped and woven into situated practice in connection with the particularities of these figured worlds. For example, environmental justice groups have been organized with a more grassroots, local, and horizontally networked approach than many large national, membership-based, environmental organizations. In addition, race, class and other social divisions figure much more prominently in the narratives and activities of environmental justice than in many other forms of environmentalism. Also distinctive is the influential role that histories of environmental justice efforts play in the development of both collective and individual identities—and in guiding the cultural activities that are valued—in the figured world of environmental justice.

What an "environmentalist" is within these different contexts is contested in many ways, and part of the cultural production of these figured worlds is in response to the stereotypes and negative images of environmentalists that circulate in public discourse. People in our larger study reported encountering, and in some cases concurring with, many negative descriptions of environmentalists before they became active in environmental work, for example: "radicals," "crazies," "starry-eyed," and people who "had the idea they were doing something right but they really didn't know their ass from a hole in the ground." Answering to stereotypes and negative images of environmentalists such as these was an integral part of developing an environmentalist identity for many of those we interviewed. People who become involved in environmental justice work, too, are often familiar with stereotypes of environmentalists and must answer to these potential identities, additionally complicated by inflections of race and class, as they negotiate new understandings of who they are. In this chapter we explore the identities that are cultivated within the figured world of environmental justice. We show how local environmental justice groups are spaces where people struggle—personally and collectively—to refigure themselves and their actions as meaningful within the figured worlds of both environmental justice and environmentalism.

Figuring the World of Environmental Justice

The environmental justice movement has emerged from more than twenty-five years of collective struggle. Here, in our brief telling of its emergence, we highlight the development of racialized and ecological discourses and recount the significance of meetings of activists and researchers and of legislation and research findings. We identify them not to provide an ostensibly accurate historical account of the movement, but rather to introduce the events that our research participants told us in accounting for redefinitions of cultural meanings of the "environment" and their changing ecological awareness and self understandings in the worlds in which they "live, work and play."

We concur with Cole and Foster (2001), who contend that the environmental justice movement is composed of tributaries of which the civil rights movement is one, the antitoxins movement is another, and Native American struggles, the labor movement, traditional environmentalism, and the findings of academics are others. Yet, unlike these authors, who liken the movement to a river, we treat the movement as a figured world to highlight the contingent and often contentious processes of meaning creation that make it possible to think, imagine, and act as environmental justice activists. For us, the environmental justice movement continues to produce a collective, meaningful world of environmental action— a horizon of meaning against which experiences are interpreted, plans are made and actions are taken.

Environmental justice activists have reshaped environmental politics by producing distinct discourses and practices. For instance, in one well-known version of the movement's origin—the 1982 Warren County protests—activists refigured cultural meanings of the taken-for-granted concepts of racism and environment. In this origin story protestors invented a new phrase to describe their historical experiences of racism—one that connected civil rights era antiracist protests with the governor's decision to bury soil laced with toxic PCBs (polychlorinated biphenyls) in their community, a county with the highest percentage of blacks and one of the lowest median family incomes. That expression, "environmental racism," reflected an ecological dimension to black people's enduring struggle against racial oppression. Coined in the midst of collective action, it since has become a shorthand reference to racial discrimination in environmental decision-making processes.[4]

What is not highlighted in this often told story is the contingent nature of the collective work that went into figuring a world of meaningful action. During the protests, concepts like racism and images of barking dogs and billy club–waving police that circulated in the public sphere were drawn in, translated, and made meaningful as people struggled to have their concerns addressed. It was not inevitable that the new phrase "environmental racism" would emerge, much less that it would find resonance in struggles since. Yet the Warren County protests and the phrase became seminal in the figuring of the incident.[5]

One of our research participants, activist Glenice Baker, describes the 1991 National People of Color Environmental Leadership Summit (Summit I) as another watershed event in the history of the movement. Baker, among others of our research participants, told us how hundreds of Blacks, Native Americans, Latinos, Asian Americans and other people of color spent days developing what became the Principles of Environmental Justice (Appendix A). Before Summit I, she noted that dozens of local groups scattered across the country struggled in isolation. Like many in our study, Baker credits the gathering with firmly establishing environmental justice as a movement and with refiguring the environment. According to her, until then,

the word "environment" had been more or less co-opted by the environmentalists. But people [racial minorities] began to see their environment completely differently. And the idea that the environment was, in the holistic sense, you saw it in terms not of wilderness, and not of whales, but the air over your head and the asthma patient down the block and the kid who died, or the old person who died.

Movement leaders defined and solidified several trends at, or soon after, Summit I. For one, environmental justice activists made an explicit decision to organize along a network structure; local campaigns would receive support from regional network organizations rather than a national organization. Using these networks, proponents established the Environmental Justice Fund in 1995, which connects six regional environmental justice networks with a goal of supporting grassroots environmental justice organizing. Some of these networks, such as the Northeast Environmental Justice Network (NEEJN), were created specifically to address environmental justice issues. Formed in 1992, NEEJN is a Boston-based multiracial organization composed of veteran organizers and environmental justice advocates and member organizations. In contrast, other networks like the Atlanta-based Southern Organizing Committee for Economic and Social Justice have over a twenty-five-year old history of social justice work that predates environmental justice activism in the area. Through the efforts of these organizations, as well as statewide and race-based networks such as the North Carolina Environmental Justice Network (NCEJN) and the African American Environmental Justice Action Network, proponents have organized the movement horizontally, rather than reproduced the hierarchical structures of other types of environmental organizations. The movement continues to devote a good part of its effort to developing local grassroots groups through community organizing and to developing networks among them through such events as summits. Because of its rootedness in community and everyday life, the movement has developed what one of our research participants, Conrad Ratcliffe, calls a "homegrown flavor." In his estimation, this local focus is necessary: "Organizations at a state level could not provide the man-hours and those day-to-day grind routine things that we all hope would be taking place in the community or would save us from the industries inside of the communities."

Notably, since the 1982 Warren County protests and Summit I, government actions and legislation, though sometimes characterized by activists as environmentally racist, have shaped the figured world of environmental justice. Particularly helpful federal legislation includes the Environmental Justice Act, reintroduced in 1993 by Georgia Congressman John Lewis and Montana Senator Max Baucus, and the 1998 Florida Environmental Equity and Justice Act. Also significant have been local proclamations, such as those issued in North Carolina in 1998 for Environmental Justice Awareness Week and Environmental Justice Awareness Month. Moreover, legal precedents utilized in the movement include Title VI of the 1964 Civil Rights Act and the 1979 *Bean v. Southwestern Waste* legal decision. The history of the movement is conveyed through these precedents, even though they were not identified with environmental justice when initially issued.

The figured world of environmental justice also incorporates government agencies and bodies, including the EPA's Office of Environmental Justice, formerly the Office of Environmental Equity, and the National Environmental Justice Advisory Council (NEJAC). In addition, environmental justice leaders have drafted position papers for government officials and served as advisors to presidential teams,[6] administrations, and other public officials who, pressured by activists, publish reports such as the EPA's "Environmental Equity: Reducing Risk of All Communities," which was one of the first comprehensive government reports to examine disparities in the siting of environmental hazards. Amid the critical and essential work of local communities' struggles, commitments from a sympathetic Clinton-Gore administration, for example, helped push forward a national environmental justice agenda.

Environmental justice has become further institutionalized both as a concept and a social movement through new forms of state governance. Through public/private partnerships, for example, governments and private foundations have made funds and personnel available to carry out work *in the name of* environmental justice. These contributions have been used to extend the figured world of environmental justice in time and space. For example, the Concerned Citizens of Thornton secured grant money to hire a health educator to travel the county to conduct health education workshops and to teach residents about environmental racism—drawing people into the figured world of environmental justice by encouraging them to reframe health issues as environmental justice issues.

Legislation and funding resulting from environmental justice campaigns have come to populate the public domain, becoming available for environmental justice proponents to recall and refer to as they figure themselves and their worlds. They cite these precedents, as well as previous antiracist struggles, as they conceptualize environmental justice as a distinct world of environmental action. For example, when some in our study compared their 1990s campaign against expansion of the Westchester St. (a pseudonym)[7] landfill in Fayetteville to the 1968 Memphis sanitation workers strike led by Martin Luther King, Jr., and cited Executive Order 12898, they were actively (re)figuring themselves, contemporary events, and their campaign as they constructed interpretations of the movement and its history.

Other inputs into the figuring of environmental justice have come from scholars studying the movement and transnational connections. When researchers like us cite the participation of environmental justice activists in major world forums such as the 1999 World Trade Organization protests in Seattle, the United Nations sponsored 2001 World Conference against Racism, and the 2002 Rio+10 Earth Summit, we author versions of the movement's history that point to how it has become international and pluralistic. Through such gatherings, according to these histories, the movement addresses an array of class, multiethnic and racial concerns within alternative framings of struggle that go beyond the problem of racism. Interpretations built in these transnational relationships build commonalities. For instance, for South African environmental justice activists, environmental justice is explicitly related to the antiapartheid movement and critiques of the country's spatially segregated and unequal development of capitalism. Despite differences in the histories and trajectories of environmental justice movements in South Africa and the United States, activists simultaneously articulate concerns for social justice *and* the environment; for them, the environment is both social and ecological (Checker 2002).

People of Color Relate Differently to the Environment: Naming the Difference

As will become clear later, individual activists' accounts of their paths to environmental justice tend to include personal issues around themes that are or have been worked out collectively. One of these recurring themes concerns how race is relevant to environmentalism. The now-famous 1987 United Church of Christ commissioned study authored by Charles Lee has become an important cultural resource that highlights a racial dimension to the environmental question. "Toxic Wastes and Race in the United States" was the first national study to correlate waste facility siting with race. It determined that "race" is "the most significant among variables tested in association with the location of commercial hazardous waste facilities." An earlier 1983 study, "Siting of Hazardous Landfills and Their Correlation with Racial and Economic Status of Surrounding Communities," authored by the U.S. General Accounting Office, substantiated this claim by finding that three-fourths of the off-site commercial hazardous waste facilities in EPA Region IV were located in African American communities, although African Americans made up just one-fifth of the region's population. Regardless of whether these and other studies prove racism,[8] research participant Glenice Baker speaks to the significance of them for aiding individuals in figuring new cultural worlds:

For the first time, people of color began to see the environmental question as their own and a really fantastic redefinition of the meaning of environmentalism took place.

In our interview, Baker recounted an incident that illustrates how environmental justice was forming in dialogue with what she might call "wilderness" or "wild blue yonder environmentalism."

I remember a Native American, in particular, getting up at a breakout session . . . at the Environmental Justice Conference where a scientist had been talking for hours, and he [the Native American] just got up and said, "You know, your knowledge isn't superior to ours. Because your knowledge only depends on human beings, and ours includes the trees and the animals." And there was dead silence. You almost have to experience [things like this] to see how different it is from previous movements. . . . [Before the environmental justice movement] there were very, very few people of color, with any of the national environmental groups, until this movement started. And now, they're rushing like crazy to hire people of color. . . . Because it's like [the environmental] movement was way out there in the wild blue yonder before this, and now, it's right at the center of the city.

Criticisms like these highlight differences that the African American environmental justice activists in our research noted between the environmentalism of people of color and that of what they see as the mainstream or dominant form of environmentalism. The apprehension of this difference also stimulated environmental justice activists to initiate dialogues between the two environmentalisms. For example, the 1990 letters to the Group of Ten called for discussions of how environmental issues affect communities of color and an increase in hiring minorities and their assignment on their governing boards.[9] Several of the national environmental organizations responded positively. For example, the Sierra Club's National Environmental Justice Grassroots Organizing Program, formed in 2000, provides organizing assistance, empowerment training, seed grants, and paid staff to work in low-income communities and communities of color. Though contentious, these conversations and ensuing developments illustrate how the movement has developed in productive tension with more hegemonic forms of environmentalism.

Emerging Racialized Identities

Race matters not only in how environmental justice activists have come to understand environmental problems, but also in how they understand themselves in relation to those problems. According to Pulido and Peña (Pulido 1996, 1998. Pulido and Peña 1998), race affects individuals' access to and participation in the environmental movement, with the environmental justice movement being one site where the "people of color" racial identity has gained currency. Although Pulido rightly notes that the people of color racial identity is a collective identity around which many environmental justice activists organize, her work does not fully explore the processes important to making this a salient identity for movement proponents. Several incidents from our research illustrate important exclusionary practices directed at whites. While attending the 2002 Second National People of Color Environmental Leadership Summit (Summit II), one of us (Allen) observed, for example, an incident that occurred during a session planned by the organizers to build solidarity and multicultural organizing.[10] The idea was to engage candid discussions of perceived barriers and conflicts that, according to them, prevented the movement from being a "more cohesive force." Although it did not appear that session organizers had planned to ask white people to leave, this growing sentiment came from those who wanted only people of color to be present so that, according to them, they could speak frankly about intraracial tensions in the movement. They were adamant that white people representing mainstream environmental organizations should not be privy to such conversations, though a black man who represented the World Wildlife Federation was allowed to stay. As the situation grew tense, Allen watched as many of the white people reluctantly exited; presumably those who remained represented environmental justice, not mainstream groups. Incidents such as these, interpreted from our approach, are part of the unifying but exclusionary process of generating racially marked environmental identities and building racial solidarity.

During our interview, Glenice Baker recounted a similar process of exclusion that occurred at Summit I. It likewise demonstrates the changing understandings of race that are developing in the environmental arena. She recalled how white people, mostly representatives of mainstream environmental groups, were not allowed to participate in the portion of the Summit devoted to drawing up what became the Principles of Environmental Justice. Baker maintains that "there was no hostility toward white people" but that, for people of color, "there was a sense of sort of being chosen almost." She comments further:

And to me it was very, very different... because these people who were involved in this, people of color thing, were Black, Native American, Asian American and Hispanic; a completely new dynamic developed. You know, the whole issue of Black and White has been fought with such tension—every word, so to speak, is a very sensitive word. But this group of people of color had never really worked together, and they were coming together under these new circumstances of a new definition. It was just amazing. . . . A very different dynamic from when you have other people who have had no history of working together. . . . And if you think about it in that sense, you really begin to get some idea, first of all how grassroots it was, and how [differently] people began to relate to one another.

It is during events like Summit I and II that racial identities such as the "people of color" identity and the exclusionary practices that accompany their making became salient to the environmental justice movement's broader identity. In building the movement, people have come together to establish principles and build solidarity on the basis of being a person of color, in the name of environmentalism. Through these cultural processes and practices, the social identity of "environmental justice activist" has been created and claimed by people of color, at least at this historical juncture.

The environmental justice movement is similar to other social movements in that it is composed of what Lave and Wenger (1991) refer to as "communities of practice." Communities of practice are associations and networks of people who carry out activities and engage in practices that they interpret against the evolving, dynamic, and often contested horizons of meaning or figured worlds that emerge in processes of the types we have just recounted (Holland et al. 1998, p. 60). As communities of practice, local environmental groups offer more social immediacy to their members than is available to those individuals whose environmentalism forms primarily in the public sphere, where environmental images and narratives are often fragmented, incoherent, and disconnected from specific actions. Communities of practice are sources of cultural production where general public discourses are interwoven with local particularities and developing bodies of practice. In them, inchoate sentiments are linked with specific actions and become marked by race, class, gender, and other social divisions.[11] Persons involved in communities of environmental practice are often engaged in overt contention locally, and through this collective engagement they develop not only a culturally coherent understanding of a specific environmental problem, but also a coherent understanding of themselves as actors in relation to that problem.

Pathways to Environmental Activism

By sharing how he became involved with a group of environmental justice advocates and learned to experience the environment in a new way, research participant Conrad Ratcliffe provides a sense of how individuals are drawn into the figured world of environmental justice. Like many Northampton County residents in eastern North Carolina, Ratcliffe had grown accustomed to the noxious smells of sulfuric acid from the nearby Champion International Paper Mill. Although he and others suspected that their health was suffering as a result of living near and working in the paper mill, they had grown "desensitized to the mill's stench" and indifferent to operations at the mill that, according to Ratcliffe, were "killing them." Yet through his employment with the North Carolina Student Rural Health Coalition, an organization that works to improve poor people's access to health care, his resignation changed. The coalition collects and disseminates health statistics on county residents and, with them, validates many of their suspicions. As a paid community organizer for the coalition, Ratcliffe became aware of the "staggering numbers of early deaths in the area," which many residents attributed to the mill. At public meetings and other forums hosted by the coalition, residents aired health problems that beforehand were discussed only privately. A lay minister, Ratcliffe likens his environmental justice work with that of a religious zealot: "It's like carrying the good news, like carrying gospel."

Through his work with the community of practice organized by the coalition, Ratcliffe was introduced to a new explanation for the numbing paper mill stench; he refigured his understanding of the mill to be a case of environmental racism.[12] At meetings, rallies and workshops held across the state he had frequent contact with activists who worked with hog waste, poor sewage, antilandfill expansion and cleanup, and lead abatement, and he credits the coalition and the 1999 summit, organized by the NCEJN, for the opportunity to establish and build relationships with environmental justice activists from across the state. In his meetings and travels, Ratcliffe had seen evidence that for him proved that communities like his suffer from "environmental racism." The movement, through the work of local networks, validates peoples' suspicions in ways that, according to Ratcliffe, made sense: environmental racism is not only the cause of people's poor health but also the reason why Blacks who have suffered from many sources of inequality have heretofore been resigned and inactive about the mill's stench. His ongoing participation in these communities of practice has developed and kept meaningful the figured world of environmental justice, gathering him and others in meetings and summits, and helping shape them as "environmental justice activists" as their lives intersect with this developing figured world.

Dollie Burwell's Path to Environmentalism: Redefining "Environment"[13]

Dollie Burwell's case and the others described in this chapter reveal people undergoing personal struggles over, and changing awareness of, themselves as environmentalists. Their efforts are one of the forces leading to the changing collective identity of the environmental movement and the development of environmental justice activists as a social identity familiar to people within and outside the movement.

Burwell recalls that she neither readily nor initially saw herself or her community's struggle as contributing to the environmental movement. Although at the time of the initial Warren County protests Burwell acknowledged an ecological dimension to environmental racism, she refused to be identified as an environmentalist. In an interview with Allen, Burwell tells of her refusal to be involved with the Audubon Society's magazine. She declined an Audubon interview because, she says, "I didn't have a clear understanding. . . . I didn't want them to, I thought they saw me as an environmentalist and I didn't see myself as an environmentalist. I saw myself as an activist for justice rather than an activist for the environment."

Only years after the 1982 protests, at the 1991 summit, was Burwell able to resolve the long-standing dilemmas she had with being labeled an environmentalist.

After the 1991 People of Color Summit where I met with many people . . . Native Americans, Hispanics, and Black people all working on different issues. Some was housing, toxic waste issues, and seeing the passion that people brought to whatever their respective issue was and being a person who sat through those meetings and hammered out the term of environment . . . where we worked, where we played, where we lived. That came out of the People of Color Summit in 1991 and that was the turning point for me understanding. That definition allowed me to consider myself an environmentalist, with that definition where you work, where you play, and where you live. That encompassed those justice issues that were near and dear to me.

After Summit I, Burwell was more comfortable calling herself an environmentalist. Yet these changes did not happen solely on the intimate terrain of self-authoring. They were the result of her ongoing involvement in communities of practice, first the Warren County Concerned Citizens Against PCBs and then later in work sessions at the summit. It was in the Warren County group that she learned alongside fellow members about the dangers of PCBs to human health *and* ground water, plants, and wildlife. It was during her participation in the summit that she and others "hammered out" the Principles of Environmental Justice. Instead of wildlife and "nature," the environment came to mean, *"where we live, work, and play."* Up to that point, environmentalists were not people like herself, but, "traditionally white males or some wealthier kind of people who can afford to take two or three months and go overseas and protest."

George Garrison's Desire to Remain Distinct from Environmentalists

Our "identity trajectory" interviews began with two structured questions. The first asked the interviewee to respond to the question "Who am I?" The second asked whether the interviewee considered himself or herself to be an environmentalist. Many of the interviewees in both the larger study and the companion environmental justice study spontaneously revealed personal dilemmas in their relationship to the movement. Fully one-third had difficulties with identifying with environmentalism because they feared being considered a "radical." Many other research participants were uncomfortable with claiming to be environmentalists because they felt their level of activism and/or their compliance with their standards of environmentally friendly behavior was too low. Others, especially environmental justice activists, had a different sort of problem with the question of whether they considered themselves to be environmentalists. Along with activists from some of the other streams of the contemporary environmental movement, environmental justice activists face the challenge of being at odds with the popular and media images of "the environmentalist" and environmentalism. They recognized that their views and sentiments set them apart from the mainstream movement and that they either did not wish to, or could not, even if they wanted to, occupy the space of the imaginary environmentalist.[14]

Local environmental justice groups serve as "spaces of authoring" where people can re-figure themselves and their actions as part of the cultural world of environmentalism, but not without effort. Environmental justice communities of practice are not only spaces in which people develop coherent understandings of environmental problems and solutions, but are also spaces in which individuals can work through their differences with the images of environmentalists they have previously formed. We earlier described Burwell's nine-year effort to come to terms with thinking of herself as an "environmentalist." George Garrison, another research participant, answered the question about whether he considered himself to be an environmentalist in this way:

I guess I would say I never considered myself as being labeled an environmentalist. I have never in the traditional sense of the definition of an environmentalist.... I have never enjoyed the killing of animals even as a child and watching full forests being cut down or trees being destroyed needlessly.... I think that we all have some environmental tendencies. [But] I would not have labeled myself an environmentalist and I still don't because I still see environmentalists as tree huggers, go save the whales! And that kind of a definition for an environmentalist. If we look at environment as holistically, then yes, I am an environmentalist because holistically we are talking about people. My basic theory is that if you say people then you say everything else. [Would you say that you are a strong environmentalist?] No, meaning that I would not be going out to save a whale. I wouldn't be protesting the fishing of whales even if they are about to be extinct. So I wouldn't say. No. [Even with your redefinition of what the environment is?] With my redefinition of what the environment is, I would be a strong environmentalist.

Environmental justice first pays attention to people, and the environment is "what is around" them. Garrison is clear again in a later part of the interview that he does not want to be mistaken for the stereotypical environmentalist. He does not want to be labeled an environmentalist, "Because they [other people] think you are hugging trees.... [It's a problem] to be thought of as hugging trees and not people. The people who hug trees don't usually hug people." He then told a story about several environmentalists who had tried to stop his community organization from cutting down some trees to build a health clinic. When their efforts failed, the environmentalists became distraught. In Garrison's eyes, they were willing, at least temporarily, to deny health care to local poor people simply because it would mean several trees would have to be cut. Moreover, he found their intense emotional reaction to the tree cutting unfathomable.

Primarily because they focused on people as victims of environmental degradation, most of the environmental justice activists in our study did not identify with, and did not want others to identify them with, the more biocentric stances of environmentalism. This does not mean, however, that environmental justice advocates are unaware of, or discourage all of the practices of, what they distinguish as the mainstream movement. They recycle and support the avoidance of environmentally harmful products in their homes and businesses. These practices do not demand forfeiting core environmental justice positions and may be recognized as things that black people and poor people have been doing for a long time. As Garrison put it, "Black people and poor people have been recycling a long time because that is the only way we could have made it." Working in alliances with mainstream environmentalism, environmental justice activists sometimes try to accommodate the sensitivities of mainstream environmentalists, as in the following account:

At the first Hog Round Table some real environmentalists came to the meeting we prepared for them. We had Styrofoam cups to drink out of. We noticed people going outside and coming back in with their mugs. They never said a word but that was enough. From that time on we found paper cups or gave enough mugs.

Still, the differences in the meanings assigned to such issues are quite deep.

S.H.I.T. versus H.E.L.P: Awareness of Inequality and Injustice

In 1992 a local group started an environmental justice project in Halifax County. They wanted to prevent more hog factories from locating in the area. Uncharacteristically for protest efforts there, the group included good numbers of both African Americans and European Americans. According to the humorous account given by Garrison, Help Environmental Loss Prevention (H.E.L.P.) was the name suggested for the group by one of the white members. The black people wanted to call it Swine Habitat Is Terrible (S.H.I.T.), a reminder that hogs produce an amazing amount of feces.

The African American members saw the group as helping people because large-scale hog operations negatively affect people, but the whites wanted to communicate the purpose as one of saving the environment. Actually, Garrison thought the radio announcements for S.H.I.T. and its activities would be funny. But, regardless of the humor, the point that whites often have different perspectives on environmental problems than African Americans is a familiar one. Pulido (1996) and Pulido and Peña (1998), for example, make the point that a person's environmentalism is likely to be closely linked to his or her social position. They emphasize the different life conditions that racially and ethnically marked people typically face and thus the aspects of the environment likely to concern them. As Ratcliffe said, "It [the issue of environmental justice] is about life and death for the black person, not just a geographical [environmental] problem." Or as Garrison said, in speaking about the threat posed by hog factories, "Most of the whites are concerned about the surface waters because *it is recreation for them.* And those of us who live in rural communities [and have old and shallow wells] are more concerned about the ground water because *it is life for us* and the potential contamination of that from the chloroform that comes out of lagoons" [emphases added].

Most of the environmental justice activists we talked with originally had come to environmental justice from a focus on social and racial justice. Older activists had been involved in the civil rights movement.[15] As already discussed, for activists with a focus on social and racial justice, environmental justice is figured as one among *many* injustices. Ratcliffe had lots to say on the topic:

> With regards to environmental issues with Black folks, it parallels and is deeply connected to other injustices. . . . It is not the first injustice against them. It is deeply connected and rooted with the rest of the injustices. . . . But, more so than anything else, injustices on top of injustices is what Black people are dealing with.

Ratcliffe went on to paint a larger picture. Black peoples' actions and inactions are rooted in their experiences of not having the political position to affect decisions that profoundly affect their lives, being treated like objects by doctors and many other professionals who minister to their needs, and having to fit into institutions that provide no respect for their cultural traditions or life experiences. "How the injustice with regards to the environment takes place as a whole [is] because they don't have a fair representation in saying what is going to take place in their county." For example, he pointed out that their water quality standards are low because the decisions are left up to people who do not have to drink the water.

These are the social and cultural milieus in which African American and other people of color develop identities as environmentalists (or not). As Ratcliffe sums it up, "[W]hen we talk about environment from an activist standpoint, then we talk about [social] conditions, not just the trees, river, and streams, but the people and the system that they deal with and they live in, so it is a different ball game." The interviews underscore three defining aspects of environmental justice. First, the meaning of "environment" and "environmentalist" has been captured by, and is associated with being white. Second, environmentalism, for African Americans in the environmental justice movement, must be embedded within or combined with the recognition that people of color live in a world that is pervaded by racism and racist structures. Thus, a central part of environmental justice activist work is organizing people and raising consciousness about social and material conditions on people's *home ground*. As mentioned earlier, the environmental justice movement, at least in the southeastern United States, with its focuses on racism and helping people learn to stand up to racism, has so far eschewed an emphasis on national level organizing and instead focused on local empowerment and regional organizing. The third distinctive feature of environmental justice concerns the ways that environment is experienced—as a source of danger.

An Environmentalism of Ever-Present Danger

The environmental activism of environmental justice activists addresses real and perceived threats faced in everyday living, working, and playing situations. Referring to this type of environmentalism as an "environmentalism of everyday life," Pulido characterizes environmental justice struggles as principally about economic issues. This environmentalism, she maintains, is a "material and political struggle" mobilized on the basis of collective identity (Pulido 1998, p. 30). Similar to Pulido, we maintain that social position guides people's actions in the environmental justice arena and that it is used in the interpretation and mobilization of collective action on issues of health and well-being that activists are most concerned about. Yet social position does not fully determine what, if any, actions or activities individuals will undertake. Rather, the *meanings* that people *collectively make of* structural positions are aspects of their identities, and those meanings are developed in social action. For environmental justice activists, their activism reflects their concern with everyday living and dying in their environments: environmental degradation reacts upon their bodies and the bodies of others and is experienced as a threat to the body and to the self in the social context of struggling with others.

All environmental activists come into contact with the environment. Their encounters, however, are mediated through cultural activities that tend to vary from one environmental group to the next. For example, for members of the Audubon Society, bird watching, a principle activity of the group, brings them into contact with a variety of plant and wildlife in the outdoors and models the environment as something to be respectfully observed. In stark contrast, for environmental justice activists, key activities that relate one to the environment are living, working, and playing in dangerous, contaminated places. As illustrated by the contrasting images used in the cultural materials of each type of group—for example, of people engaged in bird watching, recycling, "buying green," hiking, on the one hand, and of children playing in the shadow of smokestacks on the other, many of the activities and concerns of environmental justice activists and more typical environmentalists are not shared. In all of these images people are active in the environment, but what the environment is (fragile ecosystem to be protected versus a place of dangerous threat) and what activities develop one's sensitivities to it (leisure activities versus everyday life) differ dramatically.

Several of our ethnographic cases illustrate environmental justice activists' concern with the social and physical consequences of environmental degradation in everyday life. Dollie Burwell, for example, is saddened and outraged that Warren County residents view themselves negatively because they live in a place made infamous for housing a hazardous waste landfill. According to her, many residents have internalized these negative associations, asking, "Do I belong in a dump ground?" and "Am I trash too?" Burwell tells the crowd at an antilandfill rally that the site has to be detoxified so that her children and other county residents can be proud, not ashamed, to live in Warren County. She fears that they will not be able to shed the internalized image of a dump until the state of North Carolina fulfills its promise to detoxify the contaminated soil and residents are able to transform the site into a recreational center and consign the episode to history by commemorating Warren County as the birthplace of the environmental justice movement.[16] For many environmental justice activists, landfills symbolize the demise of community through death and abandonment and evoke a sense of being disregarded.

A downtown rally sponsored by the Westchester St. antilandfill group in Fayetteville captured the sense of an environmentalism of ever-present danger. Jackie Savin, the group's spokesperson, dressed herself in itchy tan burlap bags and draped a black lace veil about her head and face. She wore the homemade dress, she told Allen later, to "show how poor we was down there." Marchers held up signs that read: "Snakes on Westchester St.—Snakes in City Hall," "Your Trash Is in My Backyard," and "Living on Westchester St. Is Living on Death Row." At the mock funeral, a placard perched against a van windshield listed the names of twenty-eight people who had died in the neighborhood. The funeral march organized by Savin was a time for mourning both the loss of a once vibrant community and the deaths of many people who, according to Savin, have "dropped like flies."

The Story of Pastor Wilson: Continuing Developments

Pastor Lawrence Wilson was among those who brought key people and institutions together in the events that developed into the Warren County protests of 1982. His story shows both the latitude that is possible in self-authoring within the environmental justice movement and the constraints imposed on people of color who would act on any nonenvironmental justice identities they might form.

Recounting for Allen his trajectory through the period of the Warren County protests, Pastor Wilson expressed doubt that he would have become involved if the injustice of the landfill had happened to others: "I went down there because I felt like dumping on those Black folk was an injustice. If they want to dump on those rich White folk in Raleigh I probably would never have become an environmentalist." From those sentiments Pastor Wilson had moved over the years to the point of describing himself as a "lover of nature." He gave this description as an answer to the "who am I?" question posed at the beginning of the interview. At the end, Allen returned to the theme of whether he considered himself an environmentalist. He replied, "Yes, when I say I am a lover of nature, it is an identity, I have empathy with those things."

Pastor Wilson attributed his transformation to reading a passage from the bible while he was "moving into the reality" of the Warren County struggle:

As I became involved in the struggle marching all the way from Warren County landfill through Warrenton to Raleigh to the state capitol. . . . In Jeremiah 30 . . . all of a sudden this struggle is about the salvation of the earth. [How did that happen?] Just a leap that is called empathy. This struggle is not really about a Black community that is being dumped on. Warren County is a predominantly Black community. Warren County is all [about] being polluted. That chapter that I was reading, it shows off what slavery was about. . . . [I]t really was about the economics of it. What ended up being used are people and the earth. The earth was not supposed to be used [it is supposed] to be related to. But you understand that God so loved the world that God gave his son. Paul goes a lot into that. The earth . . . it really is about justice for the earth because if you don't have justice for the earth, you are not going to have justice for people because everything becomes a thing to be used rather than a part of it.

In addition to preaching about justice for the earth as well as people, Pastor Wilson approached organizations working to save the earth. These efforts lead to revelations about the multiple ways in which environmentalism is entangled with race. He tried to join the well-known Riverkeepers group in New Bern, North Carolina, which monitors and advocates for the Nevse River. Yet he gradually concluded that it would be very difficult for him to make the contributions to caring for the river that he wanted to make because the other members persisted in treating him as though his concerns were limited to those of environmental justice. Eventually he lost interest in white-dominated environmental groups and concluded that the best opportunity for Blacks to contribute is through the environmental justice movement.[17]

Let me tell you why. The environmentalist movement in this nation has no room for Black folk. [What do you mean?] The Sierra Club is dominated by White [people]. It has not really had a Black agenda. The Riverkeepers in New Bern is a White-dominated environmentalist movement. I have wanted to be a part of it because I really thought I had a contribution to make. It has the blessings of the state to deal with those issues and White folk don't really need Black folk. . . . [You are saying that environmental racism is an opportunity for Black people to participate in the environment?] In the total environmental issue because . . . [those issues] have not yet been dominated by the White power structure. Trust me they are not going to get to it. They will touch it, but they are not going to get to it. That is a legitimate role, to become a spokesperson for the environmental racism issue. From where I was, real conversion comes about when you discover the way the earth and the environment have been treated—the issue of injustice. It is a great opportunity. [For a black person to come to that kind of awareness?] Come to the awareness because if they come to that awareness they have the whole. White people can be environmentalists and racists at the same time. If they see the environment being hurt they may not be able to transpose that to see the injustice in racism.

Here Pastor Wilson points out a key way in which he considers environmental justice to differ from mainstream environmentalism. In his view, for the latter there is no inconsistency between a person who takes care to be environmentally friendly and fights fiercely to save the earth, yet at the same time participates in and even promotes racism. In other words, concerns about damage to the environment have no relationship to concerns about the damage caused by systems of racial privilege. But in Pastor Wilson's revelation, these two kinds of injustice flow from the same source.

Possibilities?

The environmental justice movement is now several decades old. Several of those interviewed in our study participated in the original Warren County protests, which figures in movement and academic narratives as the birthplace of environmental justice (for example, Kaplan 1997). Interviews with them and others who entered the movement later, together with additional ethnographic research, shed light on the ways in which the environmental justice movement has developed and continues to develop and transform through the understandings and campaigns of activists and through the events, institutions and networks that are being established. In this chapter we have looked at similarities and differences between environmental justice and other environmental activists through a social practice theory of identity formation, with special attention to the cultural or figured world developed by the movement and to the paths that environmental justice activists have taken in locating themselves within that world.

The history and trajectory of the environmental justice movement as developed by African Americans and other people of color is distinctive within the broad range of environmentalisms that comprise the environmental movement. The cultural activities that mediate environmental sensibilities, as practiced by the full range of local environmental groups we studied, included birding, hiking, and backpacking. These activities provided ways of experiencing the environment that are quite different from those of environmental justice. Within the figured world of environmental justice, the environment is associated with the daily smells and sights of blight, along with an awareness of ever-present danger and insult to one's body and to the community. Accompanying these threats are the experiences of other forms of injustice and disregard. It is not surprising that the environmental justice movement sees the empowerment of environmentally stressed communities as equally important to the removal of environmental threats. The work of the movement simultaneously addresses people's concerns *and* helps them change oppressive systems under which they live. For these reasons, activists continue to emphasize local and regional organizing instead of concentrating only on building national level organizations.

These differences in salient aspects of the environment and in organizational preferences are intensified by the distance of environmental justice from popular images of environmentalists and by the marking of environmental justice by race and class. Environmental justice activists in our study did not constitute the prototypical environmentalist, nor did they occupy the imaginary space of the environmentalist. Instead, their struggles to define themselves as environmentalists involved accepting the label of environmentalist in spite of their own sense of distance from the concerns and social positions they attribute to "real" environmentalists. In a sense, white people owned the environmental movement. Or, to put it in the words of a person we interviewed, "White people, and their issues, dominate the environmental movement."

In thinking about possibilities for rapprochement between environmental justice and the other strands of the environmental movement, our theoretical approach counsels consideration of opportunities for merging figured worlds. From the vantage point of our research with environmental justice activists, efforts toward transcending the differences are difficult and sometimes asymmetrical. Dialogues, imagined and actual, with "real" environmentalists have driven many of the conceptual developments of the environmental justice movement, including the reworking of the central concept of "environment." As a conceptual touchstone for activists, the modified definitions of environment give a broad scope for projects that address social injustices.

At the time of our research in the late 1990s, environmental justice was not well known within the broader environmental movement in the sense that its ideas had not been widely circulated either in the mainstream movement or in the public sphere. Few of the people in the twenty other local environmental groups that we studied in our larger project were conversant with the concepts and contributions of the environmental justice movement. In several cases, we witnessed leaders making overtures to environmental justice activists, but not necessarily progressing in the formation of alliances. Environmental justice was even more unfamiliar to those who knew the environmental movement only peripherally through avenues such as mailings, environmental programs on public television, and media coverage of spectacular protests against, for example, the cutting of old-growth forests or declining habitats of favorite wild species.

We did note some alliances among environmental justice activists and other environmentalists. This was true in our research, despite complaints by environmental justice activists that the mainstream environmental movement, including the issues it addresses, marginalizes environmental justice concerns. Local people threatened by large-scale hog factories or leaking landfills were willing to team up across color lines, despite histories of racial tension. For example, two longtime participants in the Warren County struggle are white. Another of the environmental justice groups we studied had both black and white participants and, in fact, was significantly shaped by members' participation in a statewide environmental justice summit organized by George Garrison, among others. These alliances are potential places where more encompassing figured worlds could develop. Pastor Wilson, for example, directed attention to the similarities of people and nature and the injustice that arises when either is treated not as beings deserving respect in their own right but as objects to be exploited. Another of our interviewees came to the conclusion that justice is owed to both people *and* nature from a position critical of capitalism: "Capitalists are hellbent on raising capital with no regard to life or limb."

And, then, there is the Styrofoam cup. Garrison described a change in practice that came about when the members of his group recognized the aversion of "real" environmentalists to the cups. This small, but tangible marker of different sensibilities played a role in a number of other interviews in the study. Seemingly a small thing, recognition of aversion to

Styrofoam on the parts of others can sometimes function as a wedge issue or a disruption of a taken-for-granted indifference. As people take part in the figured world of any environmentalism, they can learn about new ways to care about the consequences of their actions and to care about evaluations of themselves by others in this figured world. Identification as any sort of environmentalist involves investing one's self, taking responsibility, being answerable for one's actions while gaining practical knowledge, and becoming familiar with the social relations and activities of environmental work as it is defined in the communities of practice of which one becomes a part. Alliances provide at least a temporary community of practice where different environmentalisms can be learned and where new forms can be created. This is the most likely positive path for the future. The question is how long the process will take.

Postscript

The ethnographic research that we have summarized here was carried out primarily from 1996 to 2000. During that period national environmental organizations, especially the Sierra Club, had begun to publicize environmental justice movement issues. Academic interest in the environmental justice movement has accelerated as well, producing books (for example, Adams, Evans, and Stein 2002; Bullard, Johnson, and Torres 2004; Camacho 1998; Cole and Foster 2001; Faber 1998; Gottlieb 2001; Stein 2004) to augment the early work of Bullard (1983) and others. Films and videos, including those made by environmental justice groups, have become more available, and churches such as the Episcopal Church in Raleigh, North Carolina, have taken on environmental justice projects. These resources make it possible for students and others to become familiar with environmental justice issues and concepts. New research would tell us whether this broader circulation of the perspective of environmental justice is being incorporated into local environmental groups that have heretofore focused primarily on mainstream activities and concerns. What we saw in our research on individual and local level environmentalism was primarily a one-way conversation. At that time, local environmental justice activists were the ones struggling to understand and modify the relationship between environmental justice and other forms of environmentalism. There were few local environmental groups of other sorts that seemed aware of environmental justice issues and none that were engaged with expanding their vision to accommodate environmental justice issues. Today, should we study local environmental groups, we might see more of a two-way conversation.

Notes

1. We gratefully acknowledge the help of the many people who made this project possible, not the least of which were the local environmental groups that permitted our participation and the individuals whom we interviewed. Kim Allen conducted the research on environmental justice groups and activists in North Carolina and in Washington, D.C., at the 2002 summit. We draw this chapter primarily from her participant observation and interviews, but the additional researchers deserve commendation for the work they did with the twenty other groups and 159 activists that constitute an important basis for our comparison of environmental justice activists with other sorts of environmentalists. The research was sponsored by grants SBR-9615505 and SBR-9602016 from the National Science Foundation (NSF), for which Dorothy C. Holland and Willett Kempton were the principal investigators. Kim Allen first became involved in environmental justice research through an REU (research experience for undergraduates) grant from NSF. And, last but not least, Phaedra C. Pezzullo, Ronald Sandler, and Gretchen Fox made very helpful comments on earlier drafts of the chapter.

2. Of the twenty-nine interviews in the environmental justice component of the larger study, twelve were environmental, political biography, and identity interviews, and seventeen were key informant interviews. The sixteen groups were all of the groups in North Carolina that we were able to learn about through snowball sampling and through attending conferences that brought environmental justice groups together. We consider the study to be a statewide investigation of the environmental justice movement in the late 1990s. As is clear from the dynamic, localized processes of the movement, we do not necessarily expect the *content* of the movement to be the same from region to region. Nonetheless, even though we were unable to fund a companion study of environmental justice groups in the Delmarva region, we were fortunate in having the larger study for comparison of the mainstream groups in the two regions.

In contrast, we do expect the identity formation *processes*, arrived at through analytic induction and described elsewhere (Holland et al. 1998; see subsequent footnote regarding Kempton and Holland 2003) to be common. Davies (1999) reviews the past thirty years of important developments in ethnographic research in anthropology and explains the conditions under which ethnographic research is considered to produce generalizable results.

3. A survey instrument was devised from the ethnographic research with the local environmental groups and their members and administered to three

national samples. Consistent with a social practice theory of identity, Holland, Lachicotte, and Kempton (in prep.) report strong, statistically significant relationships between strength of environmental identities and environmental action. Moreover, indications of an environmental identity turned out to be better predictors of reported action than environmental knowledge, beliefs, and values.

4. For a more detailed account of the Warren County protests, see Pezzullo (2001).

5. In still other versions of the movement's history, but not in those of the people we interviewed, the 1978 antitoxins struggle led by Lois Gibbs at Love Canal is cited as the key event that ushered in the movement (Fletcher 2003). Developments such as those cited here do not merge inevitably as streams coming together to form the environmental justice movement; rather, individuals and groups actively figure the movement by highlighting some aspects and historical events and ignoring others as significant to it.

6. For example, Benjamin Chavis and Robert Bullard were appointed to the Clinton-Gore presidential transition team in the natural resources cluster and Deeohn Ferris coordinated a national campaign that drafted the "Environmental Justice Position Paper" submitted to the Clinton-Gore transition team.

7. Allen promised anonymity to those interviewed and groups studied. Unless otherwise indicated, names are pseudonyms.

8. Subsequent studies have sought to discredit findings from reports such as these, including a 1994 University of Massachusetts study funded by Waste Management, Inc.

9. Moore and Head (1994).

10. Allen is African American; Daro and Holland are European Americans.

11. It is noteworthy that many, if not a majority, of the leaders of environmental justice groups are women, see for example Krauss (1992) and Kaplan (2001). In our interviews and related participant observation research, gender issues and differences did not receive spontaneous attention. When specifically asked about differences, however, people linked women's passion for activism against environmental health hazards to their frequent roles as guardians of their family's health.

12. Kempton and Holland (2003) describe general individual identity processes characteristic of members of all of the environmental groups in the larger study. "Reformulations," where the individual begins to understand environmental conditions and the social and political sources of these conditions in new ways, are an important aspect of most trajectories of identity formation.

13. Burwell's name is used with her permission.

14. Holland (2003) describes another group from the larger study, one composed of hunters and their supporters, that faced somewhat similar dilemmas with the dominant image of environmentalists.

15. Again, we are focusing on environmental justice as conceived by the African American activists we interviewed and the African American communities of

practice we studied. White people, albeit in the minority, do participate in environmental justice projects and groups, and, as described in the first part of the chapter, do attend summit meetings and conferences. We lack the space here to describe their perspectives that were often quite different from those of their black colleagues.

16. Since the time of this interview, the Warren County PCB landfill has been remediated. Whether the clean up will bring about the results Burwell had hoped for is yet to be seen.

17. Albeit few, there were some African American participants in the mainstream groups of the larger study. At least one, a middle-class woman in the Delmarva Peninsula area, did not describe her experience as one of being automatically assigned to environmental justice issues.

References

Adams, J., M. M. Evans, and R. Stein, eds., *The Environmental Justice Reader: Politics, Poetics, and Pedagogy* (Tucson: University of Arizona Press, 2002).

Bullard, R. D., G. S. Johnson, and A. O. Torres, eds., *Highway Robbery: Transportation, Racism and New Routes to Equity* (Cambridge, Mass.: South End Press, 2003).

Bullard, R. D., ed., *Confronting Environmental Racism: Voices from the Grassroots* (Boston: South End Press, 1993).

Camacho, D., ed., *Environmental Injustices, Political Struggles: Race, Class, and the Environment* (Durham, N.C.: Duke University Press, 1998).

Checker, M., "'It's in the Air': Redefining the Environment as a New Metaphor for Old Social Justice Struggles," *Human Organization* 10, no. 1 (2002): 94–105.

Cole, L., and S. Foster, *From the Ground Up: Environmental Racism and the Rise of the Environmental Justice Movement* (New York: NYU Press, 2001).

Davies, C. A., *Reflexive Ethnography: A Guide to Researching Selves and Others* (London: Routledge, 1999).

Faber, D., ed., *The Struggle For Ecological Democracy: Environmental Justice Movements in the United States* (New York: Guilford Press, 1998).

Flacks, R., *Making History: The American Left and the American Mind* (New York: Columbia University Press, 1988).

Fletcher, T., *From Love Canal to Environmental Justice: The Politics of Hazardous Waste on the Canada-U.S. Border* (Peterborough, Ont.: Broadview Press, 2003).

Gottlieb, R., *Environmentalism Unbound: Exploring New Pathways for Change* (Cambridge, Mass.: MIT Press, 2001).

Holland, D., "Multiple Identities in Practice: On the Dilemmas of Being a Hunter and an Environmentalist in the USA," *European Journal of Anthropology*, 42 (2003): 23–41.

Holland, D., W. Lachicotte Jr., D. Skinner, and C. Cain, *Identity and Agency in Cultural Worlds* (Cambridge, Mass.: Harvard University Press, 1998).

Holland, D., and W. Lachicotte, Jr., "Vygotsky, Mead and the New Sociocultural Studies of Identity," in H. Daniels, M. Cole, and J. Wertsch, eds., *Vygotsky: Modern Masters Series* (New York: Cambridge University Press, forthcoming).

Holland, D., W. Lachicotte, Jr., and W. Kempton, "Environmental Identity as a Mediator of Environmental Action: The Importance of Investing One's Self" (in prep.).

Kaplan, T., "When It Rains, I Get Mad and Scared: Women and Environmental Racism," in T. Kaplan, ed., *Crazy for Democracy: Women in Grassroots Movements* (New York: Routledge, 1997): 47–71.

Kempton, W., and D. Holland, "Identity and Sustained Environmental Practice," in S. Liayton and S. Opotone, eds., *Identity and the Natural Environment: The Psychological Significance of Nature* (Cambridge, Mass.: MIT Press, 2003): 317–341.

Krauss, C., "Women and Toxic Waste Protests: Race, Class and Gender as Resources of Resistance," *Qualitative Sociology* 16, no. 3 (1992): 247–261.

Lave, J., and E. Wenger, *Situated Learning: Legitimate Peripheral Participation* (Cambridge: Cambridge University Press, 1991).

Moore, R., and L. Head, "Building a Net That Works: SWOP," in R. Bullard, ed., *Unequal Protection: Environmental Justice and Communities of Color* (San Francisco: Sierra Club books, 1994): 191–206.

Peña, D., *Chicano Culture, Ecology, Politics: Subversive Kin* (Tucson: University of Arizona Press, 1998).

Pezzullo, P. C., "Performing Critical Interruptions: Rhetorical Invention and Narratives of the Environmental Justice Movement," *Western Journal of Communication* 64, no. 1 (2001): 1–25.

Pulido, L., "Development of the 'People of Color' Identity in the Environmental Justice Movement of the Southwestern United States," *Socialist Review* 26, nos. 3–4 (1998): 145–180.

Pulido, L., *Environmentalism and Economic Justice: Two Chicano Struggles in the Southwest* (Tucson: University of Arizona Press, 1996).

Pulido, L., and D. Peña, "Environmentalism and Positionality: The Early Pesticide Campaign of the United Farm Workers' Organizing Committee, 1965-71," *Race, Gender & Class* 6, no. 1 (1998): 33–50.

Skocpol, Theda, *States and Social Revolutions: A Comparative Analysis of France, Russia and China* (Cambridge: Cambridge University Press, 1979).

Stein, R., ed., *New Perspectives on Environmental Justice: Gender, Sexuality and Activism* (New Brunswick, N. J.: Rutgers University Press, 2004).

Stern, P. C., T. Dietz, T. Abel, G. A. Guagnano, and L. Kalof, "A Value-Belief-Norm Theory of Support for Social Movements: The Case of Environmentalism," *Human Ecology Review* 6, no. 2 (1999): 81–97.

5

A More "Productive" Environmental Justice Politics: Movement Alliances in Massachusetts for Clean Production and Regional Equity

Daniel Faber

The self-defined environmental justice movement first emerged in the 1980s, as hundreds of grassroots organizations began to address the disparate social and ecological problems impacting their communities. Plaguing people of color where they "work, live, and play,"[1] unequal exposure to ecological hazards assumed the form of (1) higher concentrations of destructive mining operations, polluting industrial facilities and power plants; (2) greater presence of toxic waste sites and disposal/treatment facilities, including landfills, incinerators, and trash transfer stations; (3) severe occupational and residential health risks from pesticides, lead paint, radiation waste, and other dangerous substances; and (4) lower rates of clean-up and environmental enforcement of existing laws.[2] In the movement's earliest stages of development, environmental justice organizations were largely isolated or loosely connected to one another and focused on local issues. With the 1991 National People of Color Environmental Leadership Summit (Summit I), however, recognition developed of the need to build stronger institutional linkages between these local community-based groups. As a result, a number of strategic regionally based networks, as well as national constituency-based and issue-based networks for environmental justice, were created and consolidated during the 1990s.

In the new century, as environmental justice activists confront what are (perhaps) their most difficult set of challenges, a third stage of development is being initiated. With a number of new organizational entities, such as the National Environmental Justice Advisory Council (NEJAC) to the Environmental Protection Agency (EPA), and the consolidation of the regional and national constituency–based networks, the environmental justice movement is attempting to develop a new infrastructure for building internetwork collaboration and coordinated programmatic initiatives that can take the work beyond the local level to have a broader policy impact at the state, national, and international levels. As witnessed by the closing of the Washington Office on Environmental Justice in the late 1990s, as well as the profound tensions between different sectors of the movement present at the 2002 National People of Color Environmental Leadership Summit (Summit II) and the subsequent disbanding of the Environmental Justice Fund (EJF),[3] however, it is clear that this will be no easy task. More than ten years after Executive Order 12898, the EPA has failed to consistently implement its mandate to integrate environmental justice into its day-to-day operations.[4] Furthermore, the U.S. Supreme Court's ruling in *Alexander vs. Sandoval* (April 24, 2001) that demonstrating a racially discriminatory *effect* (as opposed to the discriminatory *intent*) of an action is not sufficient to win a Title VI Civil Rights action has proven to be a major legal setback for the environmental justice movement.

Significant organizational problems, political conflicts, and growing pains also plague the movement. To some degree, this is characteristic of any large social movement, particularly one as young and underfunded as the environmental justice movement. Nevertheless, the challenges of winning significant improvements at the federal level—a situation that will likely persist at least until the end of President George W. Bush's term in office—are compelling activists to focus their attention on more local and state-based strategies (some of these initiatives are part of larger nationally oriented campaigns and alliances). These local and state-based strategies include a return to more collaborative approaches with government agencies, as well as more traditional environmental organizations.[5]

Massachusetts is an example of a state where such a collaboration is taking place. In fact, these collaborations and coalitions have produced exemplary approaches to solving problems of "distributive environmental justice" (approaches aimed at reducing the unequal distribution of ecological hazards), "productive environmental justice" (approaches aimed at reducing the production of ecological hazards at the source), and "transformative environmental justice" (approaches aimed at bridging the urban/suburban divide to produce greater equality in regional planning). In short, Massachusetts is providing new and exciting models of what can be accomplished when mainstream environmentalists and environmental justice activists join forces to bring about change.

Environmental Injustices in the Commonwealth of Massachusetts

Since World War II, Massachusetts has witnessed both a dramatic growth in suburban development and a severe socioeconomic decline of the inner cities and older manufacturing centers. As industry and white, middle-class citizens left for the residential outer rings, once-thriving city neighborhoods were left to poorer working-class whites and people of color. As the tax base, schools, property values, and public services in the cities eroded with the exodus, the urban landscape became riddled with vacant lots, abandoned buildings, and brownfields. The concentration of poverty in the inner cities also became more severe. In greater Boston, explicit racial lending policies, known as redlining, further concentrated people of color in the inner city.[6] From a peak population of just more than 800,000 in 1950 (when the city was only 5 percent nonwhite), the city of Boston decreased to just over 560,000 in 1980, a loss of almost 240,000 people. However, the number of poorer racial minorities who moved into the city greatly offset the exodus of middle-class whites. In the most recent 2000 census, people of color have become the majority of Boston's current population of 580,000 residents for the first time in history.[7]

Over the past four decades, neglected inner-city neighborhoods have become the target for unwanted and noxious land uses, such as trash transfer stations, junkyards, truck and bus depots, incinerators, and auto body shops. Decrepit housing and schools contribute to indoor environmental hazards such as lead paint, asbestos, and mold. The cumulative impact of these relatively smaller and more disperse sources of pollution contribute to and further exacerbate poor health conditions. Residents must also deal daily with hazards from illegal dumping of chemical wastes on vacant lots, toxic air and water pollution from the old "dirty" industries that do remain behind, as well as a lack of greenspace and parks, and inadequate public transportation systems. This dual process of inner-city decline and environmental injustice is well illustrated by the case of Roxbury, a low-income neighborhood of color in Boston.[8]

In Roxbury, divestment and relocation of the manufacturing sector resulted in a decline of the industrial job base from more than 20,000 in 1947 to 4,000 by 1981 (the percentage of jobs in the manufacturing sector in greater Boston declined from 32 percent in 1950 to 17 percent in 1990).[9] Along with this, the number of businesses in the heart of the community around the Dudley Street area declined from 129 in 1950 to only 26 in 1980.[10] Along with the economic decline came the flight of white residents. Redlining denied home loans to people of color, while "block busting" by realtors scared whites into leaving. Arson became an increasingly common means for residents to "escape" the neighborhood. In 1987, the elevated Orange Line discontinued service, cutting off the heart of Roxbury from the region's rapid transit system and the higher-paying jobs in the growth areas of greater Boston. Thus, a once predominantly white immigrant neighborhood was quickly transformed into a low-income community of color.

By 1996, residents found more than a thousand vacant lots in their 1.5-square-mile area. Noxious and polluting land uses filled the void. In 1999, the Boston Office of Environmental Health found that more than 64 percent of Boston's seventy-nine trash transfer stations, dumpster storage lots, and junkyards were located in Roxbury and adjoining North Dorchester. A 1997 survey by the Roxbury-based Alternatives for Community and Environment (ACE) found that there were more than fifteen bus and truck depots within 1.5 miles of Dudley Square that were used by more than a thousand diesel vehicles (including one half of the public transit bus fleet). Overall, Roxbury now ranks as the eighth most environmentally overburdened community in the state, with an average of forty-eight hazardous waste sites per square mile. Roxbury residents have also been exposed to more than 37,000 pounds of chemical emissions per square mile from large industries between 1990 and 1998.[11] The prevalence of environmental pollutants such as these are largely responsible for asthma hospitalization rates in Roxbury being more than five and a half times the state average.[12]

These conditions are not unique to Roxbury and Boston alone. Across Massachusetts, environmentally hazardous facilities and sites—ranging from toxic waste dumps to polluting industrial plants, incinerators, power plants, and landfills—are disproportionately located in communities of color and lower-income communities.[13] Residents in Chelsea, Lawrence, Lowell, New Bedford, and many other urban areas must deal daily with hazards from midnight dumping of chemical wastes on vacant lots, toxic industrial emissions into the air and water, substandard housing contaminated with lead paint, traffic congestion and inadequate mass transportation systems, few parks or recreational spaces, unsightly trash, and a variety of unwanted land uses. As a result, residents of these communities live each day with substantially greater risk of exposure to environmental health hazards than the general citizenry.

Statewide there are more than 21,000 hazardous waste sites. More than 3,380 of these sites are considered by the Department of Environmental Protection (DEP) to pose serious environmental or human health threats. For instance, elevated rates of leukemia (especially among children) have been linked to the industrial chemical trichloroethylene found in the town of Woburn's drinking water, as well as tetrachloroethylene in drinking water on Upper Cape Cod.[14]

But not all Massachusetts residents are in the same danger: communities of color average an incredible twenty-seven hazardous waste sites per square mile (psm) and low-income communities average fourteen waste sites psm. In contrast, middle-to-upper income white communities average only three sites psm.[15]

White working-class communities and communities of color also bear a significantly greater portion of the pollution emitted by large industrial facilities. According to data collected under the Massachusetts Toxics Use Reduction Act (TURA) program, from 1990 to 1998 some 1,029 of the largest industrial facilities statewide produced 164,385,598 pounds of chemical waste byproduct (pollution) that was *released* on site directly into the environment (discharged into the air, ground, underground, or adjacent bodies of water in the communities in which they were located). This is an amount equivalent to the weight of the *Titanic*. Low-income communities (average household median income of less than $30,000) received an average of some 73,061 total pounds of chemical emissions psm. This contrasts sharply in comparison to higher income communities (average household median income of $40,000–49,999 or more), which averaged 10,937–12,502 pounds of chemical emissions psm. Communities of color, on the other hand, averaged 110,718–123,770 pounds of chemical emissions psm, compared to 22,735 pounds of chemical emissions psm for "low-minority" communities.

White working-class communities and communities of color are also disproportionately affected by incinerators, landfills, trash transfer stations, power plants, and other environmentally hazardous sites and facilities. In fact, "high-minority" communities face a cumulative exposure rate to all of these environmentally hazardous facilities and sites (including pollution industrial facilities and toxic waste dumps) that is nearly nine times greater than "low-minority" communities. There is a consistently sharp increase in the cumulative exposure rate to these hazardous facilities/sites, which directly corresponds to increases in the size of the minority population in all communities. Likewise, low-income communities face a cumulative exposure rate to environmentally hazardous facilities and sites that is 3.13–4.04 times greater than all other communities in the state. Fourteen of the fifteen most intensively environmentally overburdened towns in Massachusetts are of lower-income status, and nine of the fifteen most environmentally overburdened towns in the state are minority communities. This is significant given that there are only twenty communities of color of the 368 communities in the entire state: nearly half are among the worse fifteen. If you live in a community of color in Massachusetts, the chances are nineteen times higher that you live in one of the twenty-five most environmentally overburdened communities in the state.

A New Coalition in Support of "Distributive" Environmental Justice Policy: An Act to Promote Environmental Justice in the Commonwealth

For environmental justice activists, the most immediate mission is to dismantle the mechanisms by which capital and the state disproportionately displace social and ecological burdens onto people of color and working-class families. Although the tactics for attacking environmental inequities are varied, one common political demand of these movements is for greater democratic participation in the governmental decision-making processes affecting their communities. By gaining greater access to policy makers and agencies, environmental justice activists hope to initiate better governmental regulation of the discriminatory manner in which the market and policy makers distribute environmental risks. At the national level, this has led important segments of the environmental justice movement to draw upon liberal-democratic strategies aimed at reforming the EPA's "institutional focus," particularly the manner by which the agency drafts and enforces environmental policy.[16] This effort resulted in President Clinton signing the Executive Order on Environmental Justice, ordering all federal agencies to begin initiatives aimed at reducing environmental inequities, and creating NEJAC as a formal federal advisory committee to the administrator of the EPA.

In the early part of 2000, Robert Durand, the secretary for the Executive Office of Environmental Affairs (EOEA) under Governors Paul Cellucci and Jane Swift, created a similar advisory body at the state level called the Massachusetts Environmental Justice Advisory Committee (MEJAC). All state environmental agencies in Massachusetts come under the oversight of EOEA. The purpose of MEJAC was to assist the secretary "in the development of a broad-range environmental justice policy that would steer the environmental justice agenda for all of the Commonwealth's environmental agencies for the first time with cohesion and formality."[17] In the words of Veronica Eady, former director of environmental justice and brownfields at the EOEA,

MEJAC coordinated all public outreach, held public meetings, conducted neighborhood tours and coordinated presentations by activists across the state in order to expose state policy-makers to the diverse world of environmental justice and communities at risk in Massachusetts. The MEJAC guided the development of the state's philosophical environmental justice policy and made recommendations for implementation. In the second phase of policy-making, the state working group was charged with developing an implementation strategy based on that philosophical policy.[18]

The initial push for adoption of the EOEA policy came from the Environmental League of Massachusetts (ELM), which filed the first piece of environmental justice legislation in 1998. ELM policy efforts were supplemented by years of community organizing efforts and public pressure led by environmental justice groups across the eastern half of the state. Fusing the struggles for civil rights, social justice, and a healthy environment, these community-based movements for environmental justice were committed to reversing the processes by which business and the government disproportionately displaces ecological and economic burdens onto working-class families and communities of color. In Boston, organizations such as ACE and the Greater Boston Environmental Justice Network (GBEJN) took up the cause.[19]

Once the draft environmental justice policy was released for public comment, however, more mainstream environmental organizations such as the Toxics Action Center joined hands with ELM and the environmental justice movement to demand a more comprehensive policy by the EOEA that would be applicable to state agencies across the board (not just environmental agencies). In October 2002, Secretary Durand signed an improved policy that includes detailed definitions and directives for state environmental agencies to use in addressing the issue; however, because the policy failed to provide enforcement provisions, and remained limited to environmental agencies only, the coalition was concerned and began casting about for ways to win further improvements.

Although mainstream environmentalists and environmental justice activists adopted different tactics, both chose to support one another in a larger strategy to win these improvements. As an environmental organization with a long track record, and high comfort level, working within the machinery of the Massachusetts policy system, ELM took the lead in lobbying for the passage of additional environmental justice legislation. ACE and GBEJN, as environmental justice organizations committed to changing the system of power, took the lead in mobilizing significant external public pressure on the legislature in support of ELM advocacy efforts (including generating large turnouts of supporters at legislative hearings). Despite the existence of some very profound differences and problems (including a lack of funder support for ELM to undertake environmental justice work), the more moderate "insider" tactics of ELM and the more radical "outsider" methods of ACE proved to be highly complementary and enabled the committed leadership of both organizations (and movements) to work in close collaboration.[20]

The collaboration also allowed for the inclusion of religious and faith-based organizations, college students groups, and public health associations in the organizing and lobbying efforts aimed at the Massachusetts State House, further increasing the range of movement sectors working to transform the state's environmental justice policy into stronger law.

The sought after legislation—termed An Act to Promote Environmental Justice in the Commonwealth—was deemed necessary to protect the policy from potential assault by future governors. The current policy is not binding upon the executive branch, whereas a law would be. If it were to be adopted, this bill would be among the most comprehensive and far-reaching pieces of environmental justice legislation adopted by any state in the nation. The bill is a necessary antidote to the indifference of the EPA and other federal agencies under the control of the Bush Administration to environmental justice concerns and directs the state EOEA to develop statewide regulations that give communities much greater protection from pollution.

The environmental justice bill now includes a number of innovative and significant measures for enhancing the education, notification, and participation of environmental justice community residents in state-based environmental problem solving. Furthermore, among the important aims of this environmental/environmental justice collaboration are to assist communities in determining whether they qualify for consideration under the law; to establish an environmental justice advisory committee to the director of environmental justice and brownfields redevelopment in the office of the secretary; to develop and maintain a list of alternative information outlets that service environmental justice populations for the purpose of seeking public comments or publishing public notices; and to direct agencies to develop and implement a formal strategy to enhance public participation and input to agency decision making that potentially affects environmental justice communities.

A potential model for other states to emulate (a draft formed the basis for similar efforts in Alabama, led by the Alabama Environmental Council), the environmental justice bill would (1) increase public participation and outreach through environmental justice training programs for government staff (including greater language accessibility); (2) minimize risk by targeting compliance, enforcement, and technical assistance to environmental justice populations and enhancing Massachusetts Environmental Policy Act (MEPA) review of new or expanding large sources of air emissions and regional waste facilities in environmental justice neighborhoods; (3) encourage investments by expediting MEPA review of brownfields redevelopment projects that offer opportunities to clean up contaminated sites and bring them into clean productive use; (4) expand existing brownfields efforts to support the development of an inventory of underutilized commercial/industrial properties in the commonwealth, incorporating environmental justice as a criterion for awarding technical assistance, grants, audits, and toxic waste site investigations in environmental justice populations, and targeting open space resources to more effectively create, restore, and maintain open spaces located in environmental justice neighborhoods; and (5) promote cleaner development by encouraging economic development projects that incorporate state-of-the-art pollution control technology, and alternatives to hazardous chemicals in neighborhoods where environmental justice populations reside.[21]

While ELM leads the charge on the legislative front, ACE is working to see that the existing policy is used to its fullest extent by affected communities and also generating general awareness and support for environmental justice issues through community organizing. Together, ACE and ELM have developed a participatory game, "Pass the Bill," which is used to educate new partners about the legislative process and highlight the importance of building coalitions to promote bills. In the current political-economic environment in Massachusetts, industry opposition to new environmental regulations is staunch. To make progress, environmentalists and environmental justice activists are finding it advantageous to work together. Each movement brings a different set of political skills, experiences, and constituencies that, when combined, can be far more effective than when the groups work in isolation. Time will tell whether this unique coalition will prove successful. There are also limitations. For instance, as a white-led mainstream environmental organization, ELM receives no foundation support for its work to promote environmental justice (in spite of dedicating significant staff time to the effort for more than three years). Furthermore, ACE and other environmental justice organizations may have more pressing and immediate concerns in their own communities and also face significant resource constraints. Nevertheless, if such a coalition can continue to overcome differences and develop a constructive method for resolving tensions and growing the collaboration, the prospects are bright that Massachusetts may soon adopt the most comprehensive environmental justice legislation of any state in the nation.

A New Collaboration for "Productive" Environmental Justice and the Precautionary Principle: The Alliance for a Healthy Tomorrow

An environmental justice policy and politics aimed at eliminating the discriminatory or unequal distribution of ecological hazards is an essential step in the right direction, but alone it is not sufficient. In this respect, although the proposed environmental justice legislation would provide important environmental safeguards often denied to poorer communities of color, this is just one piece in a larger puzzle. Defensive strategies aimed at arresting disproportionate impact can inadvertently result in environmental hazards being shifted out of the poorer communities of color and into other communities, running the risk of turning potential allies into adversaries and thus being political self-defeating.[22] In Massachusetts, there is a sophisticated understanding among the Environmental League of Massachusetts, ACE, and other organizations working on behalf of the environmental justice legislation that the overall struggle for environmental justice is not just about more fairly distributing pollution risks "so that all people are harmed equally." Rather, the need is for a more "productive" environmental justice politics with an orientation toward preventing environmental risks from being produced in the first place, "so that no one is harmed at all." A movement for environmental justice is of limited efficacy if the end result is to have all residents poisoned to the same perilous degree, regardless of race, color, or class. The struggle for environmental justice must be about the politics of production per se and the elimination of the ecological threat, not just the "fair" distribution of ecological hazards via better government regulation of inequities in the marketplace.

Any attempt to rectify distributional inequities without attacking the fundamental processes that produce the problems in the first place focuses on symptoms rather than causes and is therefore only a partial, temporary, and necessarily incomplete and insufficient solution. What is needed is a politics for procedural equity that emphasizes democratic participation in capital investment decisions through which environmental burdens are produced and then distributed. As Michael Heiman has observed, "If we settle for liberal procedural and distributional equity, relying upon negotiation, mitigation, and fair-share allocation to address some sort of disproportional impact, we merely perpetuate the current production system that by its very structure is discriminatory and non-sustainable."[23] It is precisely this distinction between distributional justice and productive justice that many in the environmental justice and environmental movements in Massachusetts are beginning to address. The transition to clean production and use of the precautionary principle are key components of this more "productive" environmental justice politics.

Formation of the Alliance
Under the leadership of Lee Ketelsen, director of New England Clean Water Action, a statewide coalition was created and now includes more than 150 environmental, labor, consumer product safety, health affected groups (breast cancer, asthma, learning and behavioral disabilities, and others), scientific and public health associations, religious and faith-based organizations, student groups, and community-based environmental justice organizations. Joining hands under the umbrella of the Alliance for a Healthy Tomorrow (AHT), the coalition's goal is to help forge a more precautionary and preventive approach to environmental policy in the Bay State. More than thirty-two national and statewide organizations are among the members. Policy and strategy is established by nearly thirty elected organizational and six individual board members (with the input of the full membership), and includes Clean Water Action, Massachusetts Breast Cancer Coalition, Boston Urban Asthma Coalition, Environmental League of Massachusetts, and the Toxics Action Center, among others. Social and environmental justice group members of the governing board include the Coalition for Social Justice/Coalition Against Poverty and the Dorchester Environmental Health Coalition. Labor groups on the governing board include the Massachusetts Coalition for Occupational Safety and Health, as well as IUE-CWA (International Union of Electronic, Electrical, Salaried, Machine, and Furniture Workers–Communications Workers of America) Local 201. A scientific advisory committee consisting of forty-two scientists specializing in environmental health and chemicals policy provides coalition members with technical information and expertise. For instance, Joel Tickner of the University of Massachusetts—Lowell's

Center for Sustainable Production has been an international leader on the application of the precautionary principle and substitution principle and plays a lead role in advising the coalition.

In addition to inadequately preventing environmental and community health problems outside of the factory, the current regulatory regime also fails to prevent serious health and safety problems from affecting Bay State workers inside the factory. An estimated 800 workers died from occupational disease, another 1,866 were newly diagnosed with cancer caused by workplace exposures, and 50,000 more were seriously injured in the year 2003.[24] To fully incorporate labor into this larger environmental health coalition, the AHT governing board also created an official labor advisory committee. Made up of AHT board members, member labor groups, and other interested labor union participants, the committee works to strengthen the long-term alliance between labor and AHT through discussions, trainings, sharing information, mutual solidarity work, recruiting labor to the AHT and by soliciting the perspectives and input of labor on AHT goals and strategies.

Tactics and Strategies

Current regulations in Massachusetts do not adequately protect human health and the environment from toxins. Like most federal environmental regulations, such as the Clean Air Act and the Clean Water Act, state policy is aimed at cleaning up existing pollution and limiting the quantity released into the environment. Regulations are not aimed at eliminating the production of the harmful pollutant altogether, as in a clean-production approach. As a result, ineffectual pollution control measures that aim to limit public exposure to "tolerable levels" of industrial toxins are emphasized over pollution prevention measures that deter whole families of dangerous pollutants from being produced in the first place. Most environmental policy is predicated on the use of "risk assessment" to determine whether a substance or practice should be regulated; however, the scientific standards of proof for demonstrating the vast array of potential health impacts of a chemical are very difficult to demonstrate conclusively. More than 70 percent of the 3,000 high-production-volume (HPV) chemicals produced by industry (HPV chemicals are produced in quantities of one million pounds or more annually) have not undergone even the simplest health and safety testing.[25] In cases where there is a strong potential for adverse health effects from an activity, but not yet "definitive proof," more and more environmentalists are calling for the adoption of a precautionary approach. According to the Wingspread Statement on the Precautionary Principle,

When an activity raises threats of harm to the environment or human health, precautionary measures should be taken even if some cause and effect relationships are not fully established scientifically.

The AHT is working for the adoption of proactive, prevention-oriented policies that make use of a precautionary approach (the precautionary principle) to toxic hazards, call for the adoption of safer alternatives (the substitution principle), and provide a transition blueprint to a greener economy that is beneficial for workers and environmental justice communities (clean production principle). All three principles are key to the formation of a more "productive" environmental justice politics. In this light, member organizations throughout the coalition are educating and mobilizing their constituencies to assist in the design and adoption of model legislation that is mutually beneficial to all the groups. As part of these efforts, grassroots and professional advocacy organizations alike are being called upon to place both external and internal public pressure upon legislators in their own districts to support a package of key bills in the state legislature and help prepare a set of policy proposals for state agencies that will be packaged as an executive order. These organizing and lobbying efforts were first initiated in 2003 and will take a sustained effort to win passage.

One focus of the effort so far, and an example of the comprehensive and integrated nature of the approach, has been the proposed Act for a Healthy Massachusetts: Safer Alternatives to Toxic Chemicals. This bill aims to create a model for the gradual replacement of toxic chemicals with safer alternatives. It initially targets ten toxic substances used by industry to be replaced with safer alternatives. It does this by laying out a careful process for examining all available evidence to identify safer alternatives and manufacturing processes that will benefit the health of workers, customers, children, the environment, and the economy. The proposed program would also stimulate research and development on new technologies and solutions when a safer alternative is not economically viable or technically feasible. In addition, it would create programs to assist workers and businesses in the transition to the safest available alternatives, with funding provided through a fee on toxic chemicals.

A number of other legislative initiatives also supported by the AHT are designed to push the state toward the adoption of a more "productive" environmental justice politics. An Act to Promote Sustainable Agriculture and the Use of Non-Toxic Pest Management would remove the sales tax exemption from toxic pesticides and fertilizers and dedicate those dollars to a nontoxic pest management fund. In addition, 30 percent of existing revenues raised from pesticide registration fees and licenses and from certain fines would also be placed directly into the nontoxic pest management fund. This bill complements An Act to Prevent Use of the Most Dangerous Pesticides. Spearheaded by the Environmental League of Massachusetts, this bill will require the Department of Public Health to compile a list of pesticides known to be carcinogenic, mutagenic, or toxic to development or reproduction and prohibit their use by the state, municipal governments, schools, day-care centers, hospitals, health-care facilities, or public housing officials.

AHT has also organized the legislation and pushed for the adoption of An Act to Reduce Asthma and Other Health Threats from Cleaning Products. This legislation would require that no cleaning product may be used in schools, hospitals, and other health-care facilities, day-care centers, public building, and public housing unless the product is included on the "Healthy Cleaning Products" list established annually by the commissioner of the Department of Public Health (DPH).[26] The bill has enlisted the support of labor unions representing janitors and cleaning workers, as well as environmental health advocates. In addition, An Act Relating to Mercury Reduction and Education supports a regional strategy, set by all New England governors, to reduce mercury emissions 75 percent by 2010 (and for eventual zero mercury emissions in New England). Mercury is a powerful neurotoxin linked to the development of learning disabilities in children. The proposed legislation would (1) require producer take-back, whereby manufacturers of mercury-added production would be financially responsible for collection and recycling of the products; (2) require labeling that reveals the mercury content of the product and advising the purchaser on proper disposal;

and (3) prohibit the knowing collection and disposal of mercury-containing products by solid waste haulers for landfills or incinerators.

The AHT is working for the creation and adoption of a number of these and other far-reaching bills. If adopted, such policies will only be carried out well if the governor and the agencies he controls are supportive. Therefore, AHT will have greater ability to make fundamental change if advocacy is directed at both the executive and the legislature. For these reasons, AHT is also seeking an executive order from current Governor Mitt Romney. Although the state legislature gives authority, mandates, duties, and funds to state agencies, the governor is typically given great leeway and general powers in directing the actions of state agencies. In fact, most existing laws grant environmental and public health agencies in Massachusetts greater power to protect public health from toxic chemicals than they are currently utilizing.

The executive order AHT is seeking would follow the same theme of the legislative campaign around the replacement of toxic chemicals with safer alternatives, rather than permitting supposedly "safe allowable levels" of pollution. The executive order would include very specific directions and implementation plans to specific state agencies, and would direct the state to require the use of the safest feasible alternatives to toxic chemicals in its own activities and through its regulatory powers for private toxic chemical users. Based upon independent scientific information and evidence indicating that a toxic chemical is causing harm to human health, the state government should act, whenever feasible, to require the implementation of safer alternatives. This approach would be included in the permitting process and would target some thirty-five chemicals that the TURA science advisory board selected as the worst chemicals used by Massachusetts industry. Environmental justice communities would enjoy some of the biggest improvements in environmental quality in such a program.

The EOEA would publicize the list of chemicals to be replaced and give notice to companies that these are targeted. DEP would revise regulations regarding its permitting process to require safer alternatives analysis and substitutions be demonstrated in applications and require the use of safer available substitutes by applicants prior to permitting any emissions or discharges of the high-concern chemicals. The Toxics

Use Reduction Institute would provide analysis of safer alternatives and take into account potential effects upon jobs and worker health and safety, environmental health concerns, consumer product safety, and business operations. The executive order would also direct the DPH to take regulatory action to protect consumers from toxic chemicals in consumer products by using its general mandate to protect public health. Such power would include the authority to ban the sale of products containing hazardous substances that are accessible to children or intended for household use. The authority to ban a product is triggered where the DPH finds that a product contains hazardous substances and that labeling cannot adequately protect health. DPH would also analyze the availability of safer alternatives for the product of concern, and ascertain that consumers would have the ability to purchase safer products that meet the same use before the regulatory action takes effect.

Finally, the proposed executive order would direct all agencies to use the safest cleaning chemicals in all buildings owned and managed by the commonwealth (similar to the proposed legislation, it would utilize the list of products screened by the state's Environmental Preferable Purchasing Program). It would also require that all state agencies develop and implement plans to avoid the use of toxic pesticides. The advantage of the executive order campaign is that it establishes a clear goal and target for educating and mobilizing the various constituencies of the organizations (and general public) that make up the alliance. It gives the movement a clear way to measure "success" and take advantage of the political competition between a Republican governor and Democratic legislature to promote comprehensive environmental reforms. It also has the advantage of being potentially winnable, but still aggressive with far-reaching, short-term demands.

Expanding the Constituencies

Another interesting component of AHT is the manner in which new constituencies of citizens are recruited to join environmentalists and environmental justice activists in their movement-building work. For instance, Faith in Action: The Greater Boston Interfaith Environmental Justice Project is part of the broader AHT-inspired strategy to build a popular movement to reduce toxic pollution in Massachusetts. Spearheaded by the Massachusetts Council of Churches, Clean Water Fund, and the Episcopal Divinity School, this subcollaboration brings together the decades of antioppression work of church leaders and communities of faith with the grassroots organizing capabilities of the environmental justice movement and the effective advocacy campaigns of AHT.[27] The theme "Making Connections between Poverty, Health, Racism and the Environment" reflects the aim of the collaborators: to expand the diversity and number of people of faith from communities of color taking action on issues of racism, environmental health, and justice. By placing "Fellows" in six to eight congregations of color within greater Boston and providing them with training, peer group support, mentorship, education tools, and advocacy action resources, Faith in Action will also expand environmental justice and interfaith leadership and participation in the AHT coalition and campaigns.

Making antioppression/antiracism work and health protection the primary focuses for Faith in Action appeals to faith organizations that do not prioritize "environmental" issues. Racial justice, children's development, and the protection of community health are issues with strong appeal to faith communities. By funneling resources into leadership development and congregation-based social ministry in communities of color, Faith in Action will enable and empower community leaders to be partners in the safer-alternatives movement. Rather than expecting leaders in overburdened communities to take time from any pressing needs to add another "issue" to their agenda, the AHT has raised funds to support leadership and funnel resources into communities of color to build capacity. By increasing awareness and leadership development among people of faith from communities of color, the project hopes to build partnerships between diverse communities of faith and the AHT's large coalition of secular organizations, and create a stronger movement. By grounding their outreach and mobilization in participatory education, antiracism and antioppression training, leadership development, and religious values and principles, the project promises to create new models for integrating environmental health work into social and environmental justice organizing. With the support of the Massachusetts Council of Churches' seventeen member communions, including interest in expanding the project to other communities of color beyond greater Boston, the Faith in Action initiative holds the potential to mobilize faith-based communities to become part of the struggle for a more "productive" environmental justice politics in Massachusetts.

A More Comprehensive Approach to Achieving Social and Environmental Justice: Action for Regional Equity

New environmental coalitions aimed at eliminating both the production and inequitable distribution of ecological hazards are gaining force in Massachusetts and creating exemplary strategies and policies for activists in other parts of the country, but there is an additional component to achieving healthy, livable, and sustainable communities that includes the creation of safe, family-supporting jobs in clean industries; healthy and affordable homes; accessible and efficient public transportation; zoning and land-use planning that accentuates the cultural, economic, social, and natural assets of a community; sufficient public parks, greenfields, and recreational spaces; good schools, libraries, health clinics and hospitals, child care, and other essential social services; racial equality and economic justice; and a profound respect for cultural diversity. The potential benefits of an environmental justice policy are limited if the choices for a marginalized community are to reject construction of a polluting industrial facility that may pose significant health hazards, on the one hand, versus community acceptance of such a facility because of the greater job opportunities and tax revenues it affords, on the other. Unless movements for environmental justice can address the larger political and economic forces that compel communities to make such trade-offs, their ability to achieve significant improvements will remain limited. And while increased participatory democracy by citizens in environmental policy making and local community planning is desirable (if not essential) and should be supported, it is, in and of itself, insufficient. What is needed is a more holistic strategy for achieving social and environmental justice, one that involves moving from locally reactive actions to more regionally proactive approaches to community planning and economic development. To do so requires crossing profound racial and ethnic boundaries and bridging the divides between the white middle-class of suburbia and poorer people of color and working-class whites in the inner cities.

This is no easy task in Massachusetts. During the 1990s, the Boston metropolitan area grew by 262,000 people, or 6.4 percent. Eighty percent of this population increase occurred in the suburbs surrounding Boston and was fueled by "white flight" from the inner city. In all, more than 47,000 whites left the city of Boston, while suburban communities such as Franklin, Mansfield, Plymouth, and Taunton gained about 90,000 whites. As the whites moved out of neighborhoods such as East Boston, nearly 62,000 residents of color (especially recent Asian and Latino immigrants) moved in to replace them. As a result, whites dropped sharply from 59 percent of the city's population in 1990 to 49.5 percent in 2000.[28] Although Boston neighborhoods are becoming more multiethnic, the economic segregation of people of color continues. According to the Metro Boston Equity Initiative of the Civil Rights Project at Harvard University, poor residents of color are twice as likely to live in high-poverty neighborhoods (where more than 20 percent of residents are poor) and three times as likely to live in severely distressed neighborhoods than are poor whites. In fact, African-American and Latino households with incomes higher than $50,000 are more likely to live in high-poverty neighborhoods than are white households with incomes less than $20,000. As a result, racial segregation in metropolitan Boston is far more intense than income differences would produce. As identified by the Harvard Civil Rights Project, much of the problem lies with the differential treatment people of color receive in the mortgage market.[29]

There is a disturbing pattern of mortgage lending in Massachusetts that reproduces highly segregated patterns of residential location by race and ethnicity. Just a handful of town and cities—typically the most polluted and environmental degraded communities in the Bay State—account for the majority of loans given to African Americans and Latinos. For instance, just four communities (Brockton, Randolph, Lynn, and Lowell) typically receive more than half of all home-purchase loans to African Americans, whereas five other communities (Lawrence, Lynn, Chelsea, Brockton, and Revere) receive more than half of all home-purchase loans to Latinos.[30] Five of these seven towns (the exceptions being Randolph and Revere) are ranked among the twenty-five most environmentally overburdened communities in Massachusetts.[31] In addition, African Americans and Latinos at all income levels are more than twice as likely to be rejected for a home-purchase mortgage loan than are white applicants at the same income levels.[32] Racial discrimination of this sort has severely restricted home-ownership opportunities for people of color—opportunities that have facilitated large-scale class and geographic mobility for most white Americans.[33] More than two-thirds (67.8 percent) of the housing units in the city of Boston are rental units (rather than owner-occupied), with home ownership rates for Latinos only one-third those of whites (21.7 percent versus 65.8 percent). For African Americans, ownership rates (31.5 percent) are half those of whites.[34]

A major contradiction now confronting environmental justice activists is that movement victories that result in the substantial environmental cleanup of a community often result in dramatic increases in property values, promote gentrification, and inadvertently displace the (primarily poorer people of color) renter population from the neighborhood. Between 1998 and 2003, the costs of Boston's rental housing increased 60 percent. By 2003 the National Low Income Housing Coalition ranked Massachusetts the least affordable state in the country for residential rents.[35] High rents create a number of economic hardships for poor residents and the underemployed (between 1992 and 2002 the total number of manufacturing jobs in the state declined by 20 percent).[36] More than 25 percent of Massachusetts workers have low-wage jobs that pay less than $8.84 per hour, or $18,387 per year, working full-time. It is generally accepted that people should strive to spend no more than one-third of their income on rent or mortgage payments. In Massachusetts more than three-quarters of low-wage working families spend more than one-third of their income on housing. As a result, under the Massachusetts Family Economic Self-Sufficiency Standard—a measure of the real income needed to meet the basic housing, health care, child care, food, and transportation needs of different types of families in specific regions—25 percent of all families in the state (and nearly 50 percent of all urban families) did not earn enough to meet their basic needs in 1998.[37]

The high costs of housing is driving families to search for suburban homes increasingly further from Boston and other cities, as well as places of employment. This contributes to suburban sprawl, which is consuming an ever-larger amount of precious forests, wetlands, farms, and open space for commercial and residential development. According to the Commonwealth of Massachusetts Executive Office of Environmental Affairs, between 1950 and 1990, the state's population increased by 28 percent, while the amount of developed land increased by 188 percent.[38] Sprawl also requires significant capital investments in public facilities, roads, and infrastructure, creates traffic congestion and travel time, underuses significant public investments in urban infrastructure, and diminishes the overall quality of life. The Massachusetts Institute for a New Commonwealth has found that the number of residents who spend at least ninety minutes commuting each day increased from 11 percent to 18 percent between 1980 and 2000. Well over half a million workers fall into this unenviable category.[39]

To address the social, economic, and environmental dislocations caused by sprawl and other policies in both urban and suburban areas of eastern Massachusetts, another unique alliance of traditional conservation groups, labor, environmental justice organizations, housing advocates, and community-based movements for social justice have recently come together to create Action for Regional Equity (or Action!).[40] The primary mission of the coalition is to launch a movement for a more advanced form of smart growth that would reverse the inequitable patterns of development that have concentrated poverty, segregated communities, and limited opportunities for lower-income residents in the region.

The Action! coalition's vision for achieving equity in the greater Boston region is guided by four underlying principles: (1) environmental justice and social equity must be central components of regional development; (2) public transit, affordable housing, workforce development, and open space issues are closely linked and require integrated solutions at the regional level; (3) displacement of low-income residents should be avoided through local and regional mechanisms that connect low-income communities to opportunities and resources; and (4) equitable development is guided by policies that promote balanced land-use decisions across jurisdictions. These principles imply the adoption of an integrated, multiissue approach to issues of affordable housing, transportation equity, economic investment and development, and environmental justice, whereby formally divided social movements (environmentalists, housing advocates, labor unions, environmental justice activists, and community advocates) in both urban and suburban communities come together to develop a common agenda for dealing with the various aspects of what are the same problems.

Action for Regional Equity has prioritized key policy goals to advance regional equity in greater Boston. The membership and constituencies of their own individual organizations are educated around the issues and mobilized to come together as a coalition to work with government agencies and pressure elected officials to enact appropriate policies. As stated by Dwayne Marsh of PolicyLink, the policies should "enable communities to cooperate across jurisdictions, share fairly in the benefits of development, build a diverse housing stock, ensure accessible green space, create efficient transit systems, and maintain bustling commercial services."[41] As part of this effort, Action for Regional Equity has endorsed An Act to Promote Environmental Justice in the Commonwealth and An Act for a Healthy Massachusetts.

Conclusion

For too long, mainstream environmentalism has failed to fight against ecological inequities and social injustice. In so doing, far too many mainstream environmental organizations neglect the central social and environmental issues of poor people of color and working-class Americans and are often insufficiently accountable to their own membership as well. In many parts of the country, however, this relationship is beginning to change. In Massachusetts, innovative collaborations between environmentalists and environmental justice activists are emerging to create new and more powerful coalitions for social change. The growth of such coalitions of grassroots environmental and environmental justice organizations committed to genuine base building and community organizing in alliance with more traditional advocacy oriented environmental groups is a reaction to the new challenges posed by the hegemony of neoliberal politics at both the national and state levels. As we have seen, these coalitions in the Bay State are pushing for comprehensive and progressive approaches to environmental problem solving, such as the adoption of the precautionary principle over risk assessment; source reduction and pollution prevention over pollution control strategies; and regional equity initiatives that address the broader social, economic, and ecological disparities that exist between suburbia and the inner city.

The new environmental and environmental justice coalitions described in this chapter offer enormous potential for revitalizing the environmental movement in a number of ways. First, these coalitions promise (as seen in the environmental justice policy initiative) to bring new constituencies into environmental activism, particularly in terms of oppressed peoples of color, the working poor, and other populations who bear the greatest ecological burden. This can also be seen in the integral involvement of the labor movement, faith-based communities, health professionals, and health activists in the Alliance for a Healthy Tomorrow and the campaign for pollution prevention and clean production, as well as the coordinated work between housing advocates, preservationist and green space activists, labor, community organizers, environmentalists, and environmental justice proponents on issues of sprawl and regional equity.

Second, each of these coalitions is working to broaden and deepen traditional understandings of ecological impacts, particularly in terms of linking issues to larger structures of state and corporate power. These coalitions are also using traditional forms of professional environmental advocacy that are informed and reinforced by community organizing and grassroots base-building strategies. As a result, the coalitions are developing new organizational models designed to maximize the democratic participation of community residents and organizational members in decision-making processes of both the coalitions and government policy-making bodies. Few coalition organizational structures afford the opportunity for true democratic participation by member groups in the strategic planning of a movement as is provided by the AHT model. In this respect, the environmental justice policy initiatives of ELM and ACE, the safer-substitution policy initiatives of the AHT, and the regional planning efforts of Action for Regional Equity all serve to connect local grassroots and state-level layers of environmental/environmental justice activism.

The multilayered nature of these coalitions create new pressure points for policy change and help span community boundaries by crossing difficult racial, class, gender-based, and ideological divides that weaken and fragment communities. Because the environmental and environmental justice coalitions described here take a multiissue approach, they function as community capacity builders to organize campaigns that address the common links between various social and environmental problems (in contrast to isolated single-issue-oriented groups, which treat problems as distinct). Such a multiissue perspective facilitates much more innovative and comprehensive approaches to environmental problem solving and often brings additional social movements into the effort as important allies.

Should the environmental and environmental justice coalitions in Massachusetts continue to build upon the early but already impressive organizing successes and find ways to collaborate with the broad array of other social movements (such as labor), we will witness the birth of a more broadly based, democratic, and effective ecology movement capable of addressing the root causes of the ecological crisis. If such coalitions fail, and retreat back to more traditional forms of environmentalism that conceive of the ecological crisis as a collection of unrelated problems, it is possible that some combination of regulations, incentives, and technical innovations can keep pollution and resource destruction at "tolerable" levels for many people of higher socioeconomic status. Poorer working-class communities and communities of color that lack the political and economic resources to defend themselves, however, will continue to suffer the worst abuses. If the interdependency of issues is emphasized so that environmental devastation, ecological racism, poverty, crime, and social despair are all seen as aspects of a multidimensional web rooted in a larger structural crisis, then a transformative ecology movement can be invented, more diverse people will join the campaigns, and many more victories can be achieved. This is the promise of the new environmental activism in Massachusetts.

Notes

1. Alston, Summit I.

2. Bullard (1994) and Faber (1998).

3. Established in 1995, the Environmental Justice Fund is a collaboration of the regional and national networks. It initiated the Strategic Assessment Project in coordination with the Environmental and Economic Justice Project and pursued workplace fundraising strategies as a supplemental means of financing the movement. The fund also served as the lead anchor organization for Summit II, and its meetings provided one of the few venues for strategic face-to-face collaboration among the networks around a variety of initiatives. After the conflicts surrounding the organization of Summit II, as well as the determination that workplace giving was not an option, the fund essentially ceased functioning in 2003.

4. Office of the Inspector General (2004).

5. Zoll and Boyce (2003) and Fleming and Hanks (2004).

6. Medhoff and Sklar (1994, pp. 24–25).

7. Bluestone and Stevenson (2000, p. 16).

8. According to the 1990 census, 94 percent of Roxbury's 60,000 residents are people of color. Roxbury is also among the poorest communities in the entire state, with a household median income of only $20,518. Some 30 percent of the population lives in poverty, as do 45 percent of all children, including 62 percent of all Latino children (Faber, Loh, and Jennings, 2002, pp. 109–132.)

9. Bluestone and Stevenson (2000).

10. Medoff and Sklar (1994).

11. Faber and Krieg (2001).

12. Massachusetts Division of Health Care Finance and Policy (1997).

13. Faber and Krieg (2002).

14. Cutler, Parker, Rosen, Prenney, Healey, and Caldwell, (1986); Lagakos, Wessen, and Zelen (1986); and Aschengrau, Ozonoff, Paulu, Coogan, Vezina, Heeren, and Zhang (1993).

15. According to the 1990 census, higher-income communities, where the household median income is $30,000 or greater, average 3.1 to 4.1 hazardous waste sites per square mile. In contrast, "high-minority" communities, where 25% or more of the population are made up of people of color, average 27.2 hazardous waste sites per square mile. "Low-minority" (5 percent or more minority) communities average 2.9 hazardous waste sites per square mile. As a result, "high-minority" communities average more than nine times the number of hazardous waste sites per square mile than "low-minority" communities (Faber and Krieg 2001).

16. Ferris (1994, pp. 298–319).

17. Eady (2003, p. 170).

18. Eady (2003, p. 170).

19. ACE's primary constituency is made up of lower-income communities and communities of color in greater Boston, with a focus on their home neighborhood of Roxbury. ACE also provided staff to the Greater Boston Environmental Justice Network, which brings together thirty neighborhood groups and is the New England coordinator for the NEJN.

20. Many of the constituents from the environmental justice movement found the process disconnected from more immediate issues confronting their lives, and experienced difficulty in supporting a fairly abstract principle (the environmental justice bill). Thus, integration of outside environmental justice communities into an essentially "insider" process proved unrewarding to some environmental justice activists.

21. The bill has gone through a number of iterations in various legislative sessions in 1999, 2001, 2003, and 2005. At two legislative hearings on the bill, leaders in communities of color, representatives of public health organizations and affected communities, high school students, and academicians all lined up to make the case for the bill. In a tribute to the breadth of the collaboration, legislators received letters from groups ranging from the Surfrider Foundation and the Essex County Greenbelt Association to Nuestras Raices and the Massachusetts Public Health Association. For two legislative sessions, the bill has passed the Senate by unanimous vote but failed to reach the House floor for debate. Passage of the bill may take years.

22. Faber, Loh, and Jennings (2002, pp. 121–123).

23. Heiman (1996, p. 120).

24. Massachusetts AFL-CIO, Mass COSH, and Western Mass COSH (2004, p. ii).

25. Environmental Defense Fund (1997).

26. Healthy cleaning products on the list are defined as products that: do not contain chemicals that cause or trigger asthma, as determined by DPH; are on the environmentally preferable products contract list; and are fragrance-free. The legislation requires manufacturers of cleaning products to submit information to DPH that details the ingredients contained in their products and to require worker training and testing (to be paid for by a fee on the manufacturers of cleaning products).

27. Members in this subproject also include Janitors for Justice; No Ordinary Time; Boston Theological Institute and its nine member seminaries; Harvard Divinity School; sixteen member denominations of the Massachusetts Council of Churches; Massachusetts Conference of Catholic Bishops; Leadership Council of Women Religious; and Jewish Community Relations Council of Greater Boston.

28. Blacks comprise roughly a quarter of Boston residents (the largest minority group) and are highly concentrated in the city neighborhoods of Roxbury, Mattapan, South Dorchester, and Hyde Park. Roughly a quarter of the city's population is foreign born (27 percent). Some 14 percent are immigrants who came to Boston in the last decade. Latinos now make up 39 percent of the population in East Boston (McArdle, 2003, p.1).

29. Campen (2004).

30. Campen (2004, pp. 3–8).

31. Faber and Krieg (2001, pp. 36–37).

32. Campen (2004, p. 3).

33. Oliver and Shapiro (1995).

34. Campen (2004, pp. 9–18).

35. Boyle, Feinberg, and Liebowitz (2004, pp. 5–11).

36. Vinson and Singh (2003, p. 1).

37. The real cost of living in Massachusetts has gone up 17–35 percent in regions across the state between 1998 and 2003, as low-wage working families faced severe job losses and stagnant wages. As a result, it is likely that more than 25 percent of Massachusetts families now earn less than the income needed to meet their basic needs without public or private supports (Boyle, Feinberg and Liebowitz, 2004, pp. 5–11).

38. Cited in Marsh (2003, p. 25).

39. The average commute in Massachusetts in 2000 was 27 minutes each way, the ninth longest of any state (up from 21.4 minutes in 1980), which translates into twenty-five workdays lost in transit each year. People are moving further away from Boston in search of affordable homes. Sprawling residential and commercial development is largely to blame for the lengthening commute times, affecting the time that people have to spend with their families and participate in civil life or have a social life (Greenberger 2004; Goodman, Ansel, and Nakosteen 2004).

40. Key participants include Alternatives for Community and the Environment; Asian Community Development Corporation; Boston Tenant Coalition; Citizens' Housing and Planning Association; Chelsea Human Services Collaborative; City Life/Vida Urbana; Conservation Law Foundation; Environmental League of Massachusetts; Essex County Greenbelt Association; Greater Four Corners Action Coalition; Lexington Fair Housing Committee; Massachusetts AFL-CIO; Massachusetts Affordable Housing Association; Massachusetts Association of Community Development Corporations; Somerville Community Development Corporation; Tri-City Community Action Program; and Waltham Alliance to Create Housing.

41. Marsh (2003, p. 4).

References

Aschengrau, A., Ozonoff, D., Paulu, C., Coogan, P., Vezina, R., Heeren, T., Zhang, Y., "Cancer Risk and Tetrachloroethylene-Contaminated Drinking Water in Massachusetts," *Archives of Environmental Health* 48, no. 5 (1993): 284–292.

Bluestone, B., and M. H. Stevenson, *The Boston Renaissance: Race, Space, and Economic Change in an American Metropolis* (New York: Russell Sage Foundation, 2000).

Boyle, H. B., S. A. Feinberg, and M. Liebowitz, *Investing in Massachusetts Working Families: A Framework for Economic Prosperity* (Boston: The Women's Union, 2004).

Bullard, R. D., *Unequal Protection: Environmental Justice & Communities of Color* (San Francisco: Sierra Club Books, 1994).

Campen, J., "The Color of Money in Greater Boston: Patterns of Mortgage Lending and Residential Segregation at the Beginning of the New Century," Prepared for the Metro Boston Equity Initiative of the Harvard Civil Rights Project (January 2004).

Cutler, J. J., G. S. Parker, S. Rosen, B. Prenney, R. Healy, and G. G. Caldwell, "Childhood Leukemia in Woburn, Massachusetts," *Public Health Reports* 101, no. 2 (1986): 201–205.

Eady, V., "Environmental Justice in State Policy Decision," in J. Agyeman, R. D. Bullard, and B. Evans, eds., *Just Sustainabilities: Development in an Unequal World* (London: Earthscan Publications, 2003), 168–186.

Environmental Defense Fund, *Toxic Ignorance: The Continuing Absence of Basic Health Testing for Top-Selling Chemicals in the United States* (Washington, D.C.: Environmental Defense Fund, 1997).

Faber, D. R., P. Loh, and J. Jennings, "Solving Environmental Injustices in Massachusetts: Forging Greater Community Participation in the Planning Process," *Projections: The MIT Journal of Planning* 3 (2002): 109–132.

Faber, D., and E. Krieg, "Unequal Exposure to Ecological Hazards: Environmental Injustices in the Commonwealth of Massachusetts." A report prepared by the Philanthropy and Environmental Justice Research Project, Northeastern University, 2001.

Faber, D., and E. Kreig, "Unequal Exposure to Ecological Hazards: Environmental Injustices in the Commonwealth of Massachusetts," in "Advancing Environmental Justice through Community-Based Participatory Research," a special issue of *Environmental Health Perspectives* 11 (supplement 2) (April 2002): 277–288.

Faber, D., ed., *The Struggle for Ecological Democracy: Environmental Justice Movements in the United States* (New York: Guilford Press, 1998).

Ferris, D., "A Call for Justice and Equal Environmental Protection," in R. Bullard, ed., *Unequal Protection: Environmental Justice and Communities of Color* (San Francisco: Sierra Club Books, 1994), 298–319.

Fleming, C., and K. Hanks, "Not Business as Usual: Using Collaborative Partnerships to Address Environmental Justice Issues." A report by the International City/County Management Association, 2004.

Goodman, M., D. Ansel, and R. Nakosteen, "MASScommuting," A report by the Massachusetts Institute for a New Commonwealth and the University of Massachusetts Donahue Institute, October 2004.

Greenberger, S., "Commuting Troubles Get Worse in Mass.," *Boston Globe* (October 17, 2004): A1, A12.

Heiman, M. K., "Race, Waste, and Class: New Perspectives on Environmental Justice," *Antipode* 28, no. 2 (1996): 111–121.

Lagakos, S. W., B. J. Wessen, and M. Zelen, "An Analysis of Contaminated Well Water and Health Effects in Woburn, Massachusetts," *Journal of the American Statistical Association* 81 (1986): 583–614.

Marsh, D. S., "Promise and Challenge: Achieving Regional Equity in Greater Boston." A Report by PolicyLink, May 2003.

Massachusetts AFL-CIO, MassCOSH, and Western MassCOSH, "Dying for Work in Massachusetts: The Loss of Life and Limb in Massachusetts Workplaces," April 28, 2004.

Massachusetts Division of Health Care Finance and Policy, *State of Massachusetts Asthma Preventable Hospitalizations FY 1996–1997* (Boston: Executive Office of Health and Human Services, 1997).

McArdle, N., "Race, Place, and Opportunity: Racial Change and Segregation in the Boston Metropolitan Area: 1990-2000." Prepared for the Harvard University Civil Rights Project, April 2003.

Medhoff, P., and H. Sklar, *Streets of Hope: The Fall and Rise of an Urban Neighborhood* (Boston: South End Press, 1994).

Office of the Inspector General, "EPA Needs to Consistently Implement the Intent of the Executive Order on Environmental Justice: Evaluation Report," (Washington, D.C.: Environmental Protection Agency, March 1, 2004).

Oliver, M. L., and T. A. Shapiro, *Black Wealth/White Wealth: A New Perspective on Racial Inequality* (New York: Routledge, 1995).

Vinson, R., and N. Singh, *Manufacturing: Losses and Gains* (Boston: Commonwealth Corporation, 2003).

Zoll, M. H., and J. K. Boyce, "The New Environmental Activists: Fighting Pollution, Poverty, and Racism by Building Natural Assets." A report by the Political Economy Institute, University of Massachusetts at Amherst, 2003.

6

The Silences and Possibilities of Asbestos Activism: Stories from Libby and Beyond

Steve Schwarze

On May 9, 2002, I traveled to Libby, Montana, a small community in the northwest corner of the state that has put asbestos back on the environmental and public health agenda in the United States. That night, the Environmental Protection Agency (EPA) was expected to declare a public health emergency in Libby. Such a declaration was long overdue. For most of the twentieth century, the Zonolite and W. R. Grace companies operated a vermiculite mine and processing facility just outside the town, in spite of the fact that mine managers and government officials knew that the vermiculite was contaminated with tremolite asbestos.[1] As early as 1956, they had evidence of dangerous levels of asbestos exposure and high rates of asbestos-related illness and deaths among the mine's workers. Nonetheless, the mine operated until 1990, and vermiculite products and mine tailings were distributed for use throughout the community and beyond. The effects in Libby are stunning. Approximately 18 percent of the adult population have signs of asbestos-related lung abnormalities resulting from occupational and environmental exposures to tremolite, and there have been more than 200 deaths already documented. Unknown numbers of people may yet get sick because of the decades-long latency period of asbestos diseases. Declaration of a public health emergency would be a fitting response to these circumstances. It would help provide long-term health care for Libby's residents and heighten public awareness about the potential dangers of consumer products containing Libby vermiculite. In addition, it would allow EPA to remove one of those products, Zonolite attic insulation, from homes in Libby.

The announcement that night fell far short of expectations. The EPA did not declare a public health emergency in Libby, thereby denying potential federal health resources to a county that has the highest unemployment rate in the state of Montana, with approximately 50 percent of its population lacking health insurance. Nor did the announcement make any reference to the national scope of the hazard posed by Zonolite insulation, which is estimated to be in 15–35 million homes in the United States. This particular omission is striking, because the announcement did authorize removal of Zonolite from homes in Libby. In spite of the Zonolite hazard, the EPA did not issue any public warning about Zonolite until a year later, on May 8, 2003. That warning received little media attention, overshadowed by a bigger story from the EPA earlier that day: Christine Whitman resigned as administrator.

From one angle, these events can be seen as yet another story of how environmental health hazards are downplayed in contemporary public discourse. As investigative journalists Andrew Schneider and David McCumber have shown, the Office of Management and Budget (OMB) was involved actively in the wording of the 2002 announcement in Libby and appears to have downplayed both the health effects specific to tremolite asbestos and the national scope of the Zonolite problem. If a public health emergency were declared in Libby, it would have set a precedent for citizens across the country to demand that EPA remove Zonolite from their residences at a cost of tens of billions of dollars. As one EPA memo put it, "[T]he national ramifications are enormous."[2]

From another angle, this story points to the connections between a local instance of environmental injustice and the global circulation of an environmental hazard, for the environmental injustice perpetrated in Libby has led journalists to remind readers of the pervasiveness of asbestos contamination: from the hundreds of facilities around the United States that processed Libby vermiculite to the hundreds of thousands of buildings (such as the World Trade Center towers) that were sprayed with Monokote (a fireproofing product made from Libby vermiculite) to the millions of homes containing Zonolite insulation throughout the world. In this regard, the events in Libby recall previous chapters of the asbestos story. For decades, industry and government agencies had evidence about the hazards of asbestos but hid that knowledge through silence and deception. These silences not only prolonged dangerous exposures to workers and communities, but also allowed asbestos-containing products to flood the national marketplace. And even as the production of asbestos in the United States has waned in the past three decades, increased distribution to developing countries portends yet another wave of asbestos-related disease.

Because of the global reach of asbestos and its intense localized effects, the elimination of the asbestos hazard is an issue on which mainstream environmental organizations and environmental justice groups should be able to find common ground; however, this has so far not been the case. This chapter provides an interpretation of the silences of mainstream environmentalists and environmental justice activists in relation to Libby, while at the same time highlighting the productive possibilities offered by these two movements for struggles in Libby and beyond.

In the first section, I provide a brief overview of events in Libby that illustrates how the story of Libby gains its power as much from fundamental matters of human justice as from its depiction of narrow environmental concerns. Second, I discuss how the story that the environmental justice movement has told thus far about mainstream environmentalism provides a limited set of resources for interpreting the rhetorical obstacles faced in Libby. In particular, I emphasize how silences about material constraints, institutional inertia, and corporate cover-up played critical roles in enabling the asbestos hazard to remain unaddressed for decades. In the third section, I explore how local activists generated knowledge about the hazard and broke the silence about it in ways that mirror antitoxic struggles elsewhere. I find that neither mainstream environmentalism nor an environmental justice perspective has taken hold in Libby nor is either currently poised to become a significant social force in the foreseeable future. Yet, the situation of Libby and the larger environmental problem of asbestos present a significant opportunity for productive interaction between mainstream environmentalists and environmental justice advocates. The final section of the chapter, then, describes this opportunity in the context of ongoing problems and struggles over asbestos, ranging from the post–September 11 controversies over asbestos contamination in New York City to the growing concentration of asbestos-related industries in India. These struggles serve as a reminder of the work that remains in order to forge a mode of environmentalism that is truly engaged with questions of social justice.

The Story of Libby

That the events in Libby already have spawned three books, two documentaries, and dozens of articles in popular magazines testifies to the compelling human-interest angle of the story. It should, therefore, serve as a reminder to mainstream environmentalists that the human component of environmental degradation and fundamental questions of morality and justice can help establish powerful frames for understanding environmental problems. The stories told about Libby often fall into a pattern that I call "environmental melodrama," a rhetorical frame that employs highly moral and emotional appeals to stage social conflict between polarized actors. To the extent that melodrama creates a space for acknowledging the moral and emotional dimensions of environmental controversies, it arguably provides a fitting response to technical and scientific discourses that often dominate the rhetorical landscape of those conflicts. In addition, melodrama places into sharper relief the social conflicts connected to environmental problems, providing an effective means for engaging the environmental justice assumption that humans are an important part of their environments. Indeed, the power of the story of Libby lies less in its depiction of the environment than in how it tells a story about the way that human beings treat one another.

The story of Libby is filled with sins of commission and omission. As early as 1956, state industrial hygiene inspectors were sounding the alarm to the Zonolite Company about the "considerable toxicity" of asbestos dust in the mine's processing facility. These reports, however, were circulated only among the managers, not the workers, and because of weak occupational safety laws the state had virtually no power to force changes in production practices. The mine was purchased by W. R. Grace in 1963, and, knowing of the "dust problem," the managers contracted with local doctors to perform annual X-ray studies of the workers. Depositions of mine officials and workers suggest that the results of these studies were not communicated to the workers. Moreover, internal W. R. Grace memos reveal that the company was tracking the correlation between incidence of lung disease among miners and time on the job and that company officials discussed the financial ramifications of disclosing information about asbestos that might threaten product sales or increase liability.

In spite of this knowledge, the company's actions and the silence of the state of Montana allowed asbestos exposure to continue for decades—and reach well beyond the mine. Former miners report that mine managers told them the dust they experienced on the job was merely a "nuisance dust" that they would cough out. W. R. Grace also dragged its feet in building changing rooms and showers for the workers so that, for decades, this so-called nuisance dust was brought home, exposing workers' families. The company had open piles of asbestos-contaminated vermiculite at a processing facility next to the Little League ball fields, where children would play on them. They also let community residents take vermiculite home to use as a soil conditioner and attic insulation and allowed vermiculite to be used as fill in the high school running track, a skating rink, and other community projects. This indiscriminate circulation of tremolite and tremolite-contaminated vermiculite, enabled by the public silence of state and corporate officials about the known hazards of exposure, led to the deaths and physical impairment of hundreds of their fellow citizens.

For many, W. R. Grace's villainy has been underscored by its actions after closure of the mine. Although the company settled many civil cases out of court, its lawyers have earned a reputation for callousness in cases that have gone to trial, berating sick victims and blaming them for their disease. Its initial cleanup efforts did not meet EPA standards, and then it fought the EPA in court over a $54 million assessment for cleanup costs. The medical program that it sponsors for some Libby victims has had a spotty track record, denying benefits and coverage for unexplained reasons. And like many other companies with asbestos liabilities, W. R. Grace declared bankruptcy in April 2001. This move stayed all legal action against the company, halting hundreds of claims related to exposure to Libby asbestos. The ire of many in Libby was exacerbated when allegations surfaced that W. R. Grace had engaged in fraudulent transfers to shield billions of dollars in assets from claims that would be made in the bankruptcy proceedings. As of February 2005, seven former and current W. R. Grace executives had been indicted on federal criminal charges related to operation of the mine.

This brief narrative barely scratches the surface of the asbestos problem in Libby, but it suggests that this environmental problem, like so many others, is deeply embedded within a set of unjust social relations and practices. It is the all-too-human aspects of these events that make the story of Libby a compelling environmental melodrama. Andrew Schneider's first article on Libby puts it well: "The story of Libby, Mont., is the story of the monumental, even unforgivable, failure of government at all levels to protect its people from corporate misdeeds that at best were neglectful and insensitive and at worst were dishonest, immoral and criminal."[3] While this story is far from over, it is already apparent that the story of Libby intersects with the broader stories that are told about environmentalism and environmental justice.

Silences

The concept of silence provides one point of intersection between the story of Libby and broader discussions of mainstream environmentalism and the environmental justice movement. Although the strategic use of silence can serve as a tool of both domination and empowerment,[4] in many situations it serves the ends of domination. Through silence, privileged groups encourage public reliance on taken-for-granted beliefs and assumptions.[5] To the extent that these beliefs and assumptions undergird the status quo, silence can serve to sustain privilege and normalize existing patterns of injustice. And, as Robert Scott notes, this kind of silence is likely to be accompanied by a reassuring voice: "Ironically, the most powerful rhetoric for maintaining an existing scheme of privilege will be silent. The voice that covers the silence will tend to sound beneficent."[6] These dynamics of silence and voice provide a useful point of departure for thinking about not only the silences surrounding asbestos, but also the relationship between mainstream environmentalism and environmental justice.

The environmental justice movement is constituted in part by the story that it tells about mainstream environmentalism's silence.[7] According to this story, the mainstream movement has pursued a narrow political agenda focused on public land preservation and species protection that is rooted in a false dichotomy between humans and nature. As a consequence of these tendencies, mainstream environmentalism has developed a significant silence regarding issues that it perceives as insufficiently "environmental" in character. Participants in the environmental justice movement claim that mainstream environmentalism is stuck within a tradition of defending white, male, middle- and upper-class interests and has been unable to articulate how environmental degradation often is connected to the dynamics of privilege and exploitation as they pertain to race, class, and gender. More broadly, the dominance of these privileged interests within mainstream environmentalism has made it difficult to envision a political agenda that poses any significant challenges to the environmental degradations of capitalism. Instead, the discursive formation built around a human/nature dichotomy positions the mainstream movement to be saviors of "pristine nature" and wilderness, the sublime object of environmentalism.[8] Insofar as mainstream environmentalism's message is focused on this rather narrow definition of what counts as the environment, attention is directed away from workplace, domestic, and other mundane environments in which humans are more explicitly integrated. Environmental justice activists point out that this silence is a strategic problem for the mainstream environmental movement, because it leaves them vulnerable to the charge that their version of environmentalism is opposed to jobs and progress and hinders the mainstream's ability to reach a broader constituency.

In several ways, this story line could explain why environmentalists failed to confront the problem of asbestos in Libby. To the extent that environmental activism focused on wilderness preservation and river protection, mining-related environmental issues were construed in relatively narrow terms. Environmental concerns focused on protecting pristine public lands and waterways from the by-products of mining. Private domains—in particular, workplace and domestic arenas—where humans are central characters did not become a concern among environmentalists. In Libby, the material consequences of the human/nature dichotomy and the subsequent obsession with pristine nature are painfully apparent. During the emergency phase of cleanup and medical screening of area residents, EPA and Agency for Toxic Substances and Disease Registration (ATSDR) researchers identified no less than twenty-nine asbestos exposure pathways in the community, including the ball fields and gardens mentioned above. Consistent with the environmental justice critique of mainstream environmentalism, one might argue that construal of the environment as "pristine nature" helps explain why the workplace environment at the mine never became an object of concern for environmentalists and why widespread community contamination was largely unaddressed.

Yet in the case of Libby, the silence of mainstream environmentalists cannot be reduced to the standard environmental justice critique. On the most basic level, there is the material problem that asbestos is invisible to the naked eye. Asbestos fibers are measured in microns, and one million fibrils can be lined up in one inch. In addition, the latency period of asbestos-related disease can run as long as forty years. As a result, the signs of asbestos contamination and exposure can remain invisible for decades. Thus, silence is not simply an effect of pure ideological blindness. The microscopic size of asbestos and the long latency of its effects also obscure recognition of the asbestos hazard.[9]

Further, the silence of the asbestos industry and government agencies exceeds material constraints. Their silence regarding the health hazards of asbestos has been documented copiously.[10] As early as the 1930s, asbestos manufacturers and their insurers were dealing with liability claims from workers who had asbestos-related diseases, but their silence kept the asbestos hazard unaddressed, enabling the industry to maintain production for most of the twentieth century, such that asbestos is now woven into the fabric of everyday life.

In Libby, there is ample evidence of the deliberate industrial and governmental silence about the asbestos content of dust in the workplace and of the incidence of workers with lung abnormalities.[11] In 1956, Benjamin Wake, industrial hygiene officer for the state of Montana, reported the existence of asbestos in the dust at the Zonolite processing facility, and in subsequent inspections throughout the 1960s and 1970s he and other officials regularly reported amounts of asbestos that exceeded permissible exposure limits. These reports, however, were confidential and circulated only among mine administrators. Also, managers knew from the company's X-ray program that significant percentages of its workers had lung abnormalities, and they were receiving reports that workers at other processing sites were getting sick from diseases related to asbestos exposure.[12]

Silence was not only a matter of keeping study results private, but also keeping public discourse free of the word "asbestos." It is notable that, after producing report after report on dust levels at the Libby mine, Wake contributed a chapter on air pollution to the 1972 volume "Environmental Pollution in Montana." The chapter discusses smelters, refineries and pulp mills in several Montana communities but has just one line devoted to the vermiculite operation, which states that "the Zonolite Company in Libby is constructing an essentially new plant." The report's subsequent paragraph on Lincoln County describes air pollution problems, but it obscures the connection between the Zonolite facility and specific types of pollution. Wake claims that "the suspended particulate loading of the air in this area [is] extremely high and have shown an increase of nearly 70% over the past ten years. Dust fall and suspended sulfates are also high." No mention is made of the fact that asbestos is one of the pollutants from the Libby facility. It is a glaring omission, because the report expresses concern that the Libby Valley's air quality is in "imminent danger of further degradation" unless "stringent control measures" are put into place. Also, a chart at the end of the chapter shows that Zonolite received a variance from the state's emission regulations but that installation of new pollution control equipment will stretch more than two years beyond that variance—a longer time period than any other company on the chart. In short, Wake's report characterizes Libby's air pollution as among the worst in Montana, notes that Zonolite is a significant polluter in the area, and shows Zonolite as potentially operating in violation of state law for two years, but it says nothing about the pollutants that he himself had investigated at Zonolite.

Public silence on asbestos problems in Libby continued through the 1970s and 1980s, despite increasing attention to asbestos issues nationally and federal investigations of asbestos-contaminated vermiculite.

In 1978, the horticultural company O. M. Scott & Sons—a big user of Libby vermiculite—reported to EPA that several workers in its Marysville, Ohio, plant were exhibiting lung diseases that they suspected were related to asbestos exposure. This report prompted EPA to issue several decision papers and study the risks associated with asbestos-contaminated vermiculite. But in 1983 the scope of these studies was drastically attenuated. The agency claimed that asbestos-contaminated vermiculite was "a lower priority" than asbestos in schools and commercial asbestos. Some suspect that this study and a proposed occupational health study of Libby mine workers were cut short due to the influence of J. Peter Grace, chief executive officer of W. R. Grace, who was appointed chairman of a commission to reduce government inefficiency by President Reagan.[13] Regardless of the cause, the foreclosure of these studies effectively maintained public silence about the asbestos hazard emanating from Libby, despite concerns within multiple federal agencies. Moreover, during this same period W. R. Grace sponsored, but never disclosed, a study of the effects of tremolite on hamsters.[14] The lack of disclosure is not surprising, because all the hamsters in the experimental groups developed lung fibrosis. Thus, as public concern over asbestos grew, multiple silences about the specific problems of tremolite asbestos from Libby kept the public spotlight away from the mine and its products, allowing the mine to continue operating until 1990.

I offer this evidence to suggest that the failure of the environmental movement to respond to an environmental problem or injustice is not simply the product of ideological misrecognition. Although ideological factors may have kept environmentalists (as well as workers and community members) from seeing the problem, the material characteristics of asbestos and its related diseases arguably delayed recognition of the scope of the problem. Moreover, a stunning web of silence among industry and agency officials constricted the circulation of knowledge claims about occupational and environmental conditions in Libby. As such, Libby points to the limits of the environmental justice critique of mainstream environmentalism. The stories of the environmental justice movement may rely on the mainstream environmental movement's ideological silence as the key point of dissociation between the movements, but ideologically driven silence may not be the sole or central explanatory principle for the failure of environmentalists to recognize environmental injustice.

On Breaking and Transforming Silences in Libby

Nonetheless, the story of Libby does confirm other compelling arguments made by environmental justice scholars. For starters, it illustrates how contemporary mainstream environmentalism largely has failed to generate support among rural and working-class communities. Consequently, Libby underscores a more fundamental environmental justice criticism: that mainstream environmental voices have failed to articulate a persuasive alternative to dominant discourses about the relationship between economic well-being and environmental regulation.

Mainstream environmentalism's inability to capture the imagination of many rural and working-class citizens is clearly exemplified in Libby.[15] Historically, the community has been heavily dependent on the timber industry, and thus it is no surprise that environmentalism has been seen as a threat to the very livelihood of area residents. In addition, Libby's size and remoteness has contributed to insularity. To the extent that environmentalists are perceived as outsiders, coming from coastal urban centers or from the university town of Missoula a few hours south, their stances often are viewed with suspicion. Libby's mayor, Tony Berget, articulated this perspective in one of the first articles about the town's asbestos problem: "The environmental politics of the nation don't always go over well in small towns . . . The environmental laws have hurt the logging industry, and that has cost us a lot of jobs. Add that to Grace closing the vermiculite mine and it's been a rough 10 years for a lot of our people. Our unemployment is between 14 and 16 percent."[16]

Berget's perspective on the economic impact of environmentalism lends credence to Robert Bullard's argument about mainstream environmentalism's inadequate engagement with related economic issues: "Unless an environmental movement emerges that is capable of addressing these economic concerns, people of color and poor white workers are likely to end up siding with corporate managers in key conflicts concerning the environment."[17] The twist in Libby is that workers sided with corporate managers to such a degree that conflicts concerning the environment never even emerged. The same factors that blocked affiliation with environmentalists likely contributed to local acquiescence to workplace and environmental conditions.[18] Libby has had limited work opportunities outside the timber industry, and its isolation made it difficult to commute to larger communities where jobs were more plentiful. Retrospective accounts by Libby residents allude to the perception that job openings at the vermiculite mine were rare and coveted. In a cruel irony, jobs at the mine were considered to be among the best in the area, compared to many of the back-breaking tasks involved in logging. At the mine, the pay was good, the camaraderie was high, and the company gave back to the community in the form of monetary donations and public service. As Zonolite and W. R. Grace capitalized on this situation, they virtually eliminated the possibility of oppositional politics. Andrea Peacock contrasts Montana's contentious copper town, Butte, with the more unitary social milieu in Libby: "The town and its industries were of one mind. They were, so far as the citizens were concerned, all on the same team."[19]

It was not until residents began to observe health problems beyond the miners that this team mentality began to break down and the silence about asbestos was broken. In this way, the development of knowledge and emergence of activism surrounding the asbestos hazard in Libby mirrors other antitoxics and environmental justice struggles. For example, knowledge about the hazard was generated through layperson observations of family and community health. Gayla Benefield, the most prominent victims' advocate in Libby, is a feisty miner's daughter who first became concerned with asbestos exposure when her mother was hospitalized routinely with diagnoses of pneumonia. Knowing that her father had died from lung disease attributed to what they called "the dust," she wondered whether that same dust had contributed to her mother's illness. Over time, she received several phone calls from wives and children of miners who also were sick, and these lay person observations led her to conclude that this "dust disease" was not merely pneumonia and was not confined to miners. Ultimately, Benefield and her sister won a wrongful death suit against W. R. Grace on behalf of their mother, and she continued to speak with others who sought medical help or were pursuing civil suits against the company.

In addition, like many antitoxics and environmental justice activists, Benefield is reluctant to embrace the label "environmentalist." Yet it was a more traditional "environmental" concern—inadequate reclamation at the mine site—that motivated Benefield to reengage the issue on a political level. In the summer of 1999, Benefield drove up Rainy Creek Road to the old mine site and discovered a large tailings pile of asbestos and a relatively barren landscape that was supposed to have been reclaimed after closure of the mine in 1990. A few weeks later, Benefield saw a public notice in the local newspaper describing how the state was planning to return the remaining $67,000 of the reclamation bond to the current owners of the mine site. It boiled her blood. "When I drove up to Rainy Creek and saw that [I said] OK, that's my focus. This is our environment, I'm not an environmentalist but this is our environment, this is not right."[20] Her trajectory of involvement, typical of antitoxic and environmental justice advocacy, shows how concern for family and community can be motivating forces behind environmental awareness.

Benefield's subsequent pursuit of this issue with state officials, along with the investigative reporting of Schneider and several reporters for Montana newspapers, ultimately drew the attention of multiple federal and state agencies. By December 1999, EPA and ATSDR had established a presence in Libby and began environmental studies and health screenings that ultimately demonstrated the scope and the effects of asbestos contamination in the community. These studies, along with persistent advocacy by the Community Advisory Group, persuaded Governor Judy Martz to endorse a fast-track designation of the town to the National Priorities List under the Comprehensive Environmental Response Compensation and Liability Act (CERCLA).

In many ways, then, the recent activism in Libby appears to reflect patterns that are similar to some other antitoxics and environmental justice struggles—a lone working-class woman, seeing the signs of a health problem in her family and her community, takes the lead in fighting to eliminate an environmental hazard despite her skepticism of "environmentalism as usual." But activism in Libby has remained local. Although advocates pursue remedies at the state and national level, the advocacy is largely focused on the immediate problems of the community. In this regard, activism in Libby reinforces the distinction that Giovanna Di

Chiro makes between antitoxics groups and the environmental justice movement. Activists in Libby are not "forging coalitions among diverse disenfranchised communities and engaging in discursive politics," nor are they developing "an explicit critique of capitalism" or characterizing themselves as "descendants of the civil rights, workers' rights, and indigenous rights movements of the past."[21] Let me be clear: this is not a criticism of their activism. The Libby community has a massive set of immediate and long-term local problems that need to be addressed, and few resources with which to address them. It is understandable that their efforts have been focused more on dealing with these problems than engaging in cultural politics or starting a social movement.

In other words, although Libby is a clear example of environmental injustice, activist discourse has not proceeded from the usual environmental justice frame. What does the absence of a typical environmental justice framing mean for the environmental justice movement, and environmentalism more generally? In light of the environmental justice movement's resistance to top-down, hierarchical modes of organizing, we would not expect participants in the movement to impose themselves on Libby. And indeed, in their adherence to this principle, the environmental justice movement has done as little for Libby as mainstream environmentalism has. Yet if Libby is such a clear example of environmental injustice, and if Libby has indeed "uncovered a national scandal," as the title of Schneider and McCumber's book claims, the question must be posed: to what extent does environmentalism of any type have the resources to adequately appreciate, frame, and address the asbestos hazard?

The lack of significant support for Libby from both mainstream environmental groups and environmental justice groups, and their relative silence on asbestos issues nationally, does not portend a very positive answer for any strand of environmentalism. Journalist Ray Ring comes to a similar conclusion in an article that uses the Libby situation to test the arguments of Michael Schellenberger and Ted Nordhaus' polemic "The Death of Environmentalism."[22] In Ring's view, "The environmental movement as a whole failed in the Libby disaster."[23] But, as I suggested at the beginning of this chapter, there is hardly a better issue on which mainstream and environmental justice movements could find common cause than the asbestos hazard. The remainder of this chapter, then, depicts the full scope of the asbestos hazard to suggest both the scale of work that remains in addressing it, as well as the opportunities for collaboration between the two movements within the effort to do so.

Beyond Libby

Because asbestos is woven into the fabric of everyday life, localized grassroots activism is necessary but not sufficient to adequately address the asbestos hazard. The pervasiveness of asbestos demands that mainstream, policy-oriented environmental organizations complement the work of grassroots groups engaged in local struggles. Public policy initiatives at the national and international levels are needed to raise public awareness of potential exposure pathways, to challenge the "double-standards" in occupational and environmental health that allow hazards to concentrate in less-developed countries and among less-protected populations in developed countries and ultimately to implement bans on asbestos.

Statistical projections bring the scope of the asbestos hazard into sharp relief. The Environmental Working Group has estimated that more than 10,000 asbestos-related deaths will occur each year during the next decade in the United States alone. Worldwide, the International Labor Organization estimates that anywhere from 100,000 to 140,000 workers may die annually from asbestos-related cancers. (These estimates are likely to be conservative, in light of their extrapolation from historical data that likely underreport the incidence of disease). When one takes into account historical exposure trends and the typical latency period of asbestos-related disease (upwards of forty years), these studies also anticipate that the peak of asbestos mortality will not be reached at least for another decade.[24]

Even though peak exposures to asbestos in the United States took place decades ago, exposure is hardly a thing of the past. If anything, in the United States the asbestos hazard is as much an issue of environmental exposure as it is of occupational exposure. First of all, significant amounts of asbestos are currently in the U.S. environment. At the height of concern over asbestos in buildings, the EPA estimated that 733,000 public and commercial buildings had friable asbestos-containing material and that twice that many had asbestos-containing floor tiles.[25] Also, as mentioned earlier, the number of U.S. homes containing Zonolite insulation is estimated in the tens of millions. Renovation and deterioration of these buildings presents the potential for ongoing exposures.

Recently, for example, residents of northeast Minneapolis have begun to raise awareness of how asbestos was spread in their community by their own hands. The Western Mineral Products plant in Minneapolis was one of more than 200 sites around the United States where raw Libby vermiculite was shipped for processing. In the 1970s and 1980s, children and homeowners would play with and take vermiculite from piles outside the Western Mineral Products plant, where a sign read: "Free Crushed Rock." Now, "federal and state agencies [that] are trying to track down the millions of tons of vermiculite shipped from Libby over the mine's 65-plus years of operation" have discovered that this community and many others were exposed to potentially dangerous levels of asbestos.[26]

In addition to hazards from past uses of asbestos, it should be noted that significant amounts of asbestos continue to be introduced into the U.S. environment. A recent United States Geological Survey (USGS) study estimates that more than 29 million pounds of asbestos were imported into the United States in 2001 and more than $200 million of asbestos-containing products were imported in 2002.[27] Even as homes in Libby are being cleaned of asbestos-containing material, current laws and regulations still allow importation and use of raw asbestos and some asbestos-containing products.

For most citizens, though, these statistics about the asbestos hazard are far less meaningful than the images of the dust clouds rolling down the streets of New York City in the aftermath of the September 11, 2001, attacks on the World Trade Center. The collapse of the towers sent hundreds, and perhaps thousands, of tons of asbestos—including asbestos that contaminated W. R. Grace products made from Libby vermiculite—into the environment. Yet several reports, including that of the EPA inspector general, show that the agency's public discourse offered misleading reassurances about the safety of lower Manhattan.[28] Announcements claiming that there were no significant levels of asbestos repeatedly contradicted the agency's long-standing foundation of asbestos policy: that there is no safe level of asbestos exposure. These announcements relied on standards that were developed as detection limits and were widely recognized within the agency as not protective of public health.[29] Thus, EPA Administrator Whitman's assertion that the air was "safe to breathe" was not supported by the available evidence.[30] Such a claim is even more egregious in light of a significant percentage of test results that exceeded actionable levels of asbestos contamination.[31] In addition, there is some evidence that, as in the case of the public health emergency declaration in Libby, an executive agency—in this case, the Council on Environmental Quality—actively intervened to revise EPA statements to suggest that there were no environmental concerns.[32] As a result, thousands of people—rescue workers, firefighters, police, cleanup workers, and ordinary citizens—were actively misled about the occupational and environmental health hazards to which they were being exposed.

The scope of these problems, and the deception and injustice that inevitably accompany them, should lead both mainstream and environmental justice groups in the United States to undertake a common effort to deal with the asbestos hazard. This effort could attempt to reimplement a ban on asbestos in the United States. For mainstream groups, the manipulation of environmental regulations as evidenced in the World Trade Center controversy should provide ample reason to get involved in such efforts. To the extent that these groups are experienced in holding agencies accountable to well-established scientific findings, their advocacy could play a central role in generating support for an asbestos ban. For environmental justice groups, the disproportionate health burden faced by workers—construction workers and tradespersons, brake mechanics, abatement workers, and so forth—is something that has been a central environmental justice concern.

The World Trade Center controversy shows there is potential for such a common effort. Groups such as the New York Environmental Law and Justice Project and the New York Committee on Occupational Health and Safety have collaborated with the Sierra Club to draw attention to the range of problems associated with the September 11 attacks, but there is room for more work and broader advocacy. The Sierra Club's report, for example, is an exhaustive document with a stinging indictment of the Bush administration, but its recommendations stay within the orbit of reform-oriented, "better government" suggestions about how to prevent a repeat of these problems. Even as they highlight the importance of the precautionary principle in the context of government risk communication, the Sierra Club does not apply that principle to the actual use and import of asbestos—a known carcinogen—occurring in the United States. Support of an asbestos ban would fulfill the promise of that principle.

A collective effort to establish an asbestos ban in the United States could take shape along the lines of the "toxics use reduction" approach identified by Robert Gottlieb as a promising strategy for linking social movements in a common cause. Such a strategy "suggests a common focus for workplace groups concerned with occupational issues, consumer movements focused on product hazards, and environmental groups dealing with community hazards or with problems in the natural environment."[33] Linkages between these groups could strengthen the political leverage needed to accomplish a ban on asbestos. Moreover, such linkages could promote further discussion and development of "safe substitutes" for asbestos and alternatives to asbestos-containing products. Examples of effective discussions along these lines can be found in efforts to use safer processes and products in the dry cleaning and janitorial trades.[34] This component—the opportunities inherent in an asbestos ban—is at present a very small part of asbestos advocacy in the United States. Greater attention to it would provide a positive dimension to that advocacy, as well as bring together mainstream environmentalists and environmental justice activists under a unifying theme.

Looking beyond U.S. borders forces us to consider the inequitable distribution of the asbestos hazard on a global scale. As Barry Castleman has shown, regulatory and liability concerns have motivated several asbestos companies to move their operations to developing countries.[35] By doing so, these companies reap the benefits of weak or nonexistent labor and pollution regulations. Under these conditions, exporting industry means exporting disease. In Joseph LaDou's words, "In developing countries, where protection of workers and communities is scant or nonexistent, the asbestos cancer epidemic may be even more devastating than it has been in developed countries."[36] Indeed, the concentration of asbestos production and consumption should give pause to environmentalists of all stripes. Antti Tossavainen reports that, "over 70% of the world's production is used in Eastern Europe and Asia. The highest per-capita consumption occurs in Russia, Kazakhstan, Belorussia, Kyrgysztan, and Thailand (more than 2.0 kilogram/capita/year), whereas less than 0.1 kilogram/capita/year is still used in Western Europe or North America."[37]

India provides a particularly powerful illustration of these consequences, and one that brings several of the issues discussed in this chapter to full circle. There, the asbestos industry has boomed as a consequence of reduced tariffs on asbestos imports, and the concentration of shipbreaking in the state of Gujurat has put tens of thousands of workers at significant risk.[38] Just as shipyard workers and miners in the United States took asbestos dust home to their families, shipbreakers in India now expose their families. India serves as a mirror to the United States in more ways than one, though. In 2002, Greenpeace India reported that at least 30,000 tons of scrap steel from the World Trade Center wreckage had been exported India, raising concerns over potential toxic exposure of workers who handle the scrap. And of the 37,500 metric tons of asbestos that are mined in India, nearly all of it (35,000 tons) is tremolite asbestos—the same extremely toxic form of asbestos that contaminated the vermiculite in Libby, Montana.[39]

Thus, the work of mainstream and environmental justice activists must stretch beyond national borders to eliminate the asbestos hazard. Again, there are already hopeful signs pointing in this direction. The Global Asbestos Congress meets biennially to discuss ongoing efforts by workers, asbestos victims, trade unionists, health care professionals, civil servants, scientists, and environmentalists that address all dimensions of asbestos. The International Ban Asbestos Secretariat takes a leading role in this congress and serves as a clearinghouse for information from several national-level advocacy and victims' rights groups. Yet even here, many of these groups are single-issue groups, and there is little support from major national or global environmental organizations.

A Cause for Collaboration

On local, national, and global levels, there is much work yet to be done to eliminate the asbestos hazard. But it can be done. As of July 2004, twenty-eight countries have implemented bans on asbestos.[40] The scientific evidence about the hazards of asbestos is overwhelming. The compelling human dramas have been told. The instances of silence and deception are numerous. The images of asbestos' effects are breathtaking.[41] In short, there are ample rhetorical resources that can be deployed to take on the asbestos hazard, but those resources can be deployed effectively, for the common good, only by organized groups with a commitment to the overarching goal of sustaining a clean and healthful environment for all living beings. Mainstream environmentalism and environmental justice groups agree on that goal. Asbestos should be among the many issues on which they seek collaboratively to achieve it.

Notes

1. Asbestos is the common name for several types of naturally occurring, fibrous minerals. Because of its resistance to heat and its exceptional tensile strength, asbestos has been added to thousands of consumer products, from insulation to small appliances to vehicle brake shoes. Most of this asbestos is of the chrysotile type; however, other forms of asbestos, such as the tremolite found in Libby, contaminate minerals like vermiculite and talc. Consequently, exposure to products made with these minerals can generate potentially hazardous exposures to asbestos.

2. Schneider and McCumber (2004, p. 369).

3. *Seattle Post-Intelligencer* (1999).

4. Scott (1993) and Clair (1997).

5. Crenshaw (1997).

6. Scott (1993, p. 10).

7. Versions of this story can be found Hofrichter (1993, introduction), Di Chiro (1998, pp. 105–107), and Dowie (1996).

8. Deluca and Demo (2000, p. 243).

9. For a discussion of how invisibility constrains public response to environmental hazards, see Vyner (1988).

10. See, for example, Brodeur (1985) and Castleman (1996).

11. See Peacock (2003), and Schneider and McCumber (2004). Schneider's initial reports that broke the story to a national audience and provide the basis for their book can be found at http://seattlepi.nwsource.com/uncivilaction.

12. For a more detailed explanation and original sources see Schwarze (2003, pp. 313–314).

13. See the comments of former mine worker Bob Wilkins and EPA emergency coordinator Paul Peronard in Peacock (2003, pp. 137–145).

14. Peacock (2003, pp. 108–109).

15. See Ring (2005, p. 8).

16. Schneider (1999).

17. Bullard (1993, p. 23).

18. The dynamics of power in Libby is not unlike that described in Gaventa (1980).

19. Peacock (2003, p. 131).

20. Interview with author, June 2002.

21. Di Chiro (1998, p. 118).

22. Available on line at http://www.thebreakthrough.org/images/Death_of_Environmentalism.pdf.

23. Ring (2005, p. 11).

24. The claims in this paragraph are taken from the Environmental Working Group website online at http://www.ewg.org/reports/asbestos/facts/fact1.php.

25. Global Environment and Technology Foundation (2003).

26. Johnson (2004, p. 23).

27. Schneider (2003).

28. Office of the Inspector General, EPA (2003); Gonzalez (2002); Kupferman (2003); Mattei (2004).

29. Mattei (2004, pp. 24–31).

30. Inspector General, EPA (2003, p. 7).

31. Mattei (2004, p. 31).

32. Inspector General, EPA (2003, pp. 14–16).

33. Gottlieb (1993, p. 303).

34. Gottlieb (2001).

35. Castleman (1996, chap. 11).

36. La Dou (2004, p. 285).

37. Tossavainen (2004, p. 22).

38. Braun et al. (2003, p. 197).

39. Information available online at http://www.indiatogether.org/environment/articles/asbtos1.htm.

40. Laurie Kazan-Allen, "Current Asbestos Bans and Restrictions," available online at http://www.ibas.btinternet.co.uk/Frames/f_lka_alpha_asb_ban_280704.htm.

41. See portions of "Breath Taken: The Landscape and Biography of Asbestos," an exhibition by Bill Ravanesi, available online at http://www.bumc.bu.edu/SPH/Gallery/Intror.html.

References

Braun, L., A. Greene, M. Manseau, R. Singhal, S. Kisting, and N. Jacobs, "Scientific Controversy and Asbestos," *International Journal of Occupational and Environmental Health* 9, no. 3 (2003): 194–205.

Brodeur, P., *Outrageous Misconduct: The Asbestos Industry on Trial* (New York: Pantheon, 1985).

Bullard, R., *Confronting Environmental Racism: Voices from the Grassroots* (Boston: South End Press, 1993).

Castleman, B., *Asbestos: Medical and Legal Aspects*, 4th ed. (New York: Aspen Law and Business, 1996).

Clair, R. P., "Organizing Silence: Silence as Voice and Voice as Silence in the Narrative Exploration of the Treaty of New Echota," *Western Journal of Communication* 61, no. 3 (summer 1997): 315–348.

Crenshaw, C., "Resisting Whiteness' Rhetorical Silence," *Western Journal of Communication* 61, no. 3 (summer 1997): 253–279.

DeLuca, K. M., and A. T. Demo, "Imaging Nature: Watkins, Yosemite, and the Birth of Environmentalism," *Critical Studies in Media Communication* 17, no. 3 (September 2000): 241–260.

Di Chiro, G., "Environmental Justice from the Grassroots: Reflections on History, Gender, and Expertise," in D. Faber, ed., *The Struggle for Ecological Democracy: Environmental Justice Movements in the United States* (New York: Guilford Press, 1998), 104–136.

Dowie, M., *Losing Ground: American Environmentalism at the Close of the Twentieth Century* (Cambridge, Mass.: MIT Press, 1996).

Gaventa, J., *Power and Powerlessness: Quiescence and Rebellion in an Appalachian Valley* (Urbana: University of Illinois Press, 1980).

Global Environment and Technology Foundation, "Asbestos Strategies: Lessons Learned about Management and Use of Asbestos" (May 16, 2003).

Gonzalez, J., *Fallout: The Environmental Consequences of the World Trade Center Collapse* (New York: New Press, 2002).

Gottlieb, R., *Environmentalism Unbound: Exploring New Pathways for Change* (Cambridge, Mass.: MIT Press, 2001).

Gottlieb, R., *Forcing the Spring: The Transformation of the American Environmental Movement* (Washington, D.C.: Island Press, 1993).

Hofrichter, R., ed., *Toxic Struggles: The Theory and Practice of Environmental Justice* (Gabriola Island, B.C.: New Society Publishers, 1993).

Johnson, D., "Hot Rocks: Minneapolis' 'Free' Gravel Contaminated Asbestos," *E Magazine* (September/October 2004): 23–25.

Kupferman, J., "The Public Health Fallout from September 11: Official Deception and Long-Term Damage," in C. Brown, ed., *Lost Liberties: Ashcroft and the Assault of Personal Freedom* (New York: New Press, 2003), 184–206.

LaDou, J., "The Asbestos Cancer Epidemic," *Environmental Health Perspectives* 112, no. 3 (March 2004): 285–290.

Mattei, S., *Pollution and Deception at Ground Zero: How the Bush Administration's Reckless Disregard of 9/11 Toxic Hazards Poses Long-Term Threats for New York City and the Nation* (San Francisco: Sierra Club, 2004).

Office of Inspector General, EPA, "EPA's Response to the World Trade Center Collapse: Challenges, Successes, and Areas for Improvement," Report No. 2003-P-00012 (August 21, 2003).

Peacock, A., *Libby, Montana: Asbestos and the Deadly Silence of an American Corporation* (Boulder, Colo.: Johnson Books, 2003).

Ring, R., "Where Were the Environmentalists when Libby Needed Them Most?" *High Country News* 37, no. 3 (February 21, 2005): 8–13, 19.

Schneider, A., and D. McCumber, *An Air that Kills: How the Asbestos Poisoning of Libby, Montana Uncovered a National Scandal* (New York: Putnam, 2004).

Schneider, A., "U.S. Imports of Asbestos Brake Material Are on Rise," *St. Louis Post-Dispatch* (October 26, 2003): A14.

Schneider, A., "A Town Left to Die," *Seattle Post-Intelligencer* (November 18, 1999), available online at http://seattlepi.nwsource.com/uncivilaction/lib18.shtml.

Schwarze, S., "Melodrama: A Frame for Rhetorical Theory and Environmental Controversy," *Quarterly Journal of Speech* 92, no. 3 (2006).

Schwarze, S., "Juxtaposition in Environmental Health Rhetoric: Exposing Asbestos Contamination in Libby, Montana," *Rhetoric & Public Affairs* 6, no. 2 (2003): 313–336.

Scott, R., "Dialectical Tension of Speaking and Silence," *Quarterly Journal of Speech* 79, no. 1 (February 1993): 1–18.

Seattle Post-Intelligence, "A Town Left to Die," *Seattle Post-Intelligencer* (November 18, 1999), available online at http://seattlepi.nwsource.com/uncivilaction.

Tossavainen, A., "Global Use of Asbestos and the Incidence of Mesothelioma," *International Journal of Occupational and Environmental Health* 10, no. 1 (2004): 22–25.

Vyner, H., *Invisible Trauma: The Psychosocial Effects of Invisible Environmental Contaminants* (Lanham, Md.: Lexington Books, 1988).

Wake, B. F., "Air Pollution in Montana," in R. Bigart, ed., *Environmental Pollution in Montana* (Missoula, Mt.: Mountain Press Publishing, 1972), 23–38.

7

Moving toward Sustainability: Integrating Social Practice and Material Process

M. Nils Peterson, Markus J. Peterson, and Tarla Rai Peterson

We ground this chapter on the assumption that the tradition of identifying human society and the natural environment as mutually exclusive is the most fundamental conceptual challenge facing both the environmental and social justice movements.[1] Human society cannot achieve environmental sustainability without understanding the relationship between material processes and sociopolitical practices and then applying that understanding in the policy arena. Such an understanding, let alone its application, is impossible when nature itself divides human communities through environmental injustice. Environmental injustice blocks attempts toward environmental sustainability by rendering the materiality of nature a wedge between social elites and the disenfranchised. Sustainability and social equity can only develop when humans begin to understand nature as a fundamental material for crafting what Aldo Leopold described as an expanding community of ethical responsibility, rather than a socioeconomic wedge.[2] As we will illustrate, the concept of sustainable development offers potential for environmental movements and environmental justice movements to work together in an alliance toward common goals.[3] Achieving this potential, however, requires "movement fusion," or thoughtful integration of physical processes typically stressed by environmental movements with social practices stressed by environmental justice movements.[4]

Both unsustainable development and environmental injustice are chronically acute on borders between comparatively affluent and poor nations (for example, United States/Mexico, Costa Rica/Nicaragua, South Korea/North Korea), where long-time residents and mushrooming immigrant populations are prone to differential treatment, differential access to political systems, and differential conceptions of justice. This context has growing implications in a globalizing world where communication, transportation, and associated technologies facilitate existence of borderlands between countries without physical contiguity (for example, Singapore/Indonesia) by altering the trajectories of permeability between nations. Further, communities must share common-pool resources that influence environmental quality.[5] Because such resources and their impacts often travel great distances, this condition does not necessarily mandate physical adjacency of communities.

In this chapter we explore the potential nexus of environmental justice and environmentalism in the context of borderland development using a mixed-method case study among border residents of Cameron and Hidalgo counties, Texas (United States). In this region immigration is driving development initiatives, which, in turn, shape environmental justice and environmental conditions. This region is familiar with explosive population growth, transnational disputes over common-pool natural resources, and environmental degradation. For decades, it has faced a divide between those who would implement Garrett Hardin's lifeboat ethics by keeping out, or at least isolating poor immigrants, and those who are struggling to build a more inclusive and sustainable community.[6]

As a critical case study of environmental justice and environmentalism on the southern border of the United States, this chapter begins to identify possibilities and constraints for fostering sustainable community development. The first step is to identify subjectivities of local people and how those subjectivities articulate with material processes such as degradation of air and water quality. This chapter, therefore, uses an emic perspective to elicit environmental issues crucial to local residents and imposes an etic bioscience perspective to examine their articulation with material processes. We use space (that is, the relationship between households and both perceived and scientifically verified environmental problems) to link these social practices and material processes. Although we are aware of the political and economic barriers to justice described earlier in this volume, our focus is on the logics behind the life choices made by those assumed to be the victims of environmental injustice.

First we discuss potential points of convergence between sustainability and the environmental justice movement within a liberal-democratic context. Second, we describe the methods used for data collection and analysis. Third, we share results of our analysis, using spatial relationships to demonstrate connections between social practices and material processes. Finally, we discuss what these border residents taught us about the promises and problems involved in drawing from both the environmental justice movement and environmental movement to develop sustainable communities in borderlands and beyond.

Sustainable Development: Panacea or Pandora's Box

No concept associated with environmental protection has enjoyed more widespread public legitimacy than sustainable development, something conservation biologists have long advocated in an attempt to encourage careful use of natural resources.[7] During the last decade of the twentieth century, virtually everyone supported it. With the publication of *Our Common Future*, the idea was internalized into the popular lexicon. An explosion in publications using the term soon followed.[8] The concept became a centerpiece for global development policy following the 1992 United Nations Conference on Environment and Development in Rio de Janeiro and the 2002 World Summit on Sustainable Development in Johannesburg.[9] This social shift was legitimized by science and capitalized on the residual uncertainty inherent to the World Commission's definition of development as that meeting "the needs of the present without compromising the ability of future generations to meet their own needs."[10]

The definition's greatest strength and weakness is that, although communities embracing sustainable development must subscribe to a direct link between sustainability and development, as well as intergenerational and international equity, those communities also create their own terms of implementation, including operational definitions.[11] For example, some advocates for indigenous groups use sustainable development to argue that, because such groups have always used their natural resources, they should not be denied access to them by those who would protect wilderness, whereas others use the same concept to argue that such groups should not be denied the right to protect natural resources from those who would spur economic development.[12] Julian Agyeman, Robert Bullard, and Bob Evans have suggested a modified definition of sustainable development that includes the clause "in a just and equitable manner," but this definition has yet to attain popular currency among sustainable development proponents.[13]

The conflicting values and beliefs associated with the confusing array of perspectives toward sustainable development should surprise no one. Given a definition that "allows proponents to simultaneously endorse both environmental protection and economic development, governments, private industry, natural resource agencies, conflict resolution professionals, and many environmental advocacy groups wholeheartedly embraced sustainable development."[14] Multiple meanings evolved as sustainability advocates rooted the concept in their personal moral sentiments without making the values and politics associated with those sentiments explicit.[15] Powerful business interests joined in the attempt to co-opt the meaning and use of the term.[16] For example, business interests have colonized sustainable development for use in marketing campaigns designed to convince the public that purchasing certain high-end brands of building materials, food, toiletries, and other products will eliminate environmental problems associated with the consumer society epitomized by the United States.[17]

Many advocates of sustainable development discarded the concept when they discovered sustainable development was "code for perpetual growth ... force-fed to the world community by the global corporate-political-media network."[18] Deep ecologists eventually rejected the World Commission's definition for its implicit anthropocentrism, and many environmental ethicists rejected sustainable development in favor of "ecosystem sustainability."[19] When the competing views of sustainable development and its failure to meet the expectations of its advocates became apparent, "it fell from grace among ecologists nearly as rapidly as it had become popular."[20] Critical evaluation of sustainable development as a conceptual framework for environmental management can be summed up in the claim that, at best, it is an unproven concept and, at worst, it has failed to slow the inexorable degradation of environments needed to preserve environmental health for humans and other species.

What Is Environmental Justice and Who Gets to Decide?

Connections between sustainable development and environmental justice have only recently begun to develop.[21] Our review of the environmental justice movement, particularly as it applies to sustainability within democratic political contexts, suggests the need to clarify what environmental justice is and who participates in shaping it. Even tentative answers to these issues would contribute to our ability to evaluate the degree to which environmental justice is achieved in specific situations and how it contributes to sustainability.

Critics of the environmental justice movement claim it has no basis in scientific fact, but rather is a mask for efforts of minorities and other disenfranchised groups to gain political power.[22] They note that, although poor and minority communities often are located in or near environmentally degraded areas, few if any studies have demonstrated a causal relationship between decisions to locate a polluting facility and either the income or ethnicity of local residents.[23] In other words, it is difficult to document a phase of decision process during which managers explicitly state, "Let's dispose of our toxic waste in this neighborhood because it is inhabited by minority and/or poor people."

Claims that the environmental justice movement is grounded in political goals, rather than scientific fact, ironically reveal the epistemological fragility of the critics' argument. The Environmental Protection Agency's (EPA) definition of environmental justice mandates "fair treatment" and "meaningful involvement" of all potentially impacted groups.[24] If minorities and those from lower income brackets must struggle to gain political power in the environmental decision-making arena, they probably find their current involvement insufficiently meaningful. Moreover, the EPA version of environmental justice defines "fair" as equal (that is, no group receives a disproportionate share of negative environmental consequences). Data from numerous studies demonstrate that different socioeconomic groups bear differential shares of negative environmental impacts.

Agyeman, Bullard, and Evans note equal treatment is necessary but insufficient for environmental justice, adding that "access to the decision-making and policy-making processes" also is required.[25] Even institutional access is insufficient within liberal democratic contexts where both equality and liberty are valued.[26] If, as Agyeman argues, democracy is critical to the development of sustainable communities, both equality and liberty must be taken into account.[27] But protection of individual liberty maintains differences in decisions that influence exposure to environmental hazards and the ability to act on those decisions. For example, I may prefer to live far from a toxic waste dump, yet my income may be insufficient for me to obtain housing anywhere other than near the dump. Although it may be physically possible for me to take a second job that augments my income sufficiently to enable purchase of a home far from the dump, I may choose not to do so. For example, two participants in the study we describe below chose to live in homes without indoor plumbing or adequate outdoor drainage yet they purchased flat screen televisions so large they had to be placed at an angle to fit into the living rooms. Still others chose to exchange air conditioning, indoor plumbing, and/or electric lights for the pleasures of country living. These respondents said it was unhealthy to be crowded into the towns, and they liked sharing the native brush with wildlife.

Michael Walzer's categorization scheme of free exchange, need, and desert is a widely used approach to distribution that is directly relevant to environmental justice.[28] For instance, if all people received an equal level of environmental quality for a given investment of time or money, free exchange justice would exist. This version of environmental justice might preclude disparities rooted in ethnicity, but not income. It would be "just" for all poor humans to live in pressboard shacks, with open sewers, in the shadow of landfills filled with toxic waste from plants producing luxuries for wealthier humans. In contrast, environmental justice rooted in the need version of justice would mandate expending exceptional efforts for those living in degraded environments. Wealthy communities would be expected to provide the revenue needed to supply indoor plumbing with hot and cold running water for their poor neighbors. The third option, rooted in the merit system, might require residents to earn the right to protection from exposure to toxic waste (regardless of who benefits from that waste) by contributing a predetermined amount of money and/or time to, for example, the local sheriff's reelection campaign. We learned that all these options have been implemented in our study area to some degree, with varying results. Although it should be clear that none of these versions of justice is adequate in all circumstances or cultures, and each version has different implications for environmental justice, they provide a useful starting point in the attempt to move beyond mandated equality in the distribution of harm.

Although critics have failed to trivialize the material significance of the environmental justice movement, they unwittingly have pointed out an inordinate focus on the results of environmental injustice as compared to the physical processes and social practices that create it. Environmental justice studies have tended to focus on the spatial relationship between pollution sources and disenfranchised people.[29] Some studies are beginning to identify the everyday cultural politics leading to environmental injustices, but few delve into the practices that exclude disenfranchised voices from the environmental decision-making process itself.[30] Another need is the exploration of appropriate responses to current injustices.[31] Agyeman, Bullard, and Evans note the paucity of research addressing potential solutions, which suggests it may stem from the relative ease of reactive, as opposed to proactive behavior.[32] Further, to have political weight, those solutions must integrate social practice with physical process.[33] This requires us to grapple with differences among those who focus on conceptualizing justice, as well as differences between those who focus on achieving social justice and those who focus on preserving biodiversity.

To address environmental degradation associated with environmental injustice, we must explore the sociopolitical practices of those living in degraded environments, understand how different sociocultural groups define environmental justice, and discover how the material that constitutes bodies and habitats interacts with these political practices. People who live along borders regularly make development choices others also eventually must make. The Spanish translation for "the border" is "*la frontera*," a term whose ordinary language significance best captures this phenomenon. Those who live in *la frontera* between relatively affluent and poor nations are the vanguard of global justice and sustainability. They face the reality of environmental degradation on a daily basis and have much to teach the rest of us about issues that currently stymie efforts to create sustainable communities. This study among those living in the United States, yet along the far southeastern border between the United States and Mexico, explores how minorities and the poor are excluded from environmental decision-making processes and invites them to share their interpretations of environmental justice and sustainable development.

Research Methods

We capitalized on the benefits of methodological heterodoxy by combining a personally administered survey with open- and closed-ended questions, conducting informant-directed interviews, living within the social situation, and taking field notes.[34] We collected all data in a spatially explicit fashion. This approach allowed us to use the advantages of grounded theory to identify previously unimagined reasons for public participation and conceptions of environmental justice among border residents. We promoted design validity by utilizing prolonged on-site engagement, peer debriefing, triangulation, and member checking.[35] Time in the field enabled us to develop an intimate knowledge of the people, region, and context.[36] Practical constraints limited the time we were able to spend living on the border, and we relied on advisors who grew up in the Lower Rio Grande Valley to provide additional contextual insight. We used peer debriefing to address potential biases of "native" researchers and identify biases in interviewing approaches. We achieved triangulation by combining individual interview notes, field notes taken while living within the social situation, and summaries of historical accounts. Our member checking took two forms: including clarification questions in the interview and asking those who became informants to critique conclusions from past and current analyses of the situation.

Survey Preparation, Administration, and Evaluation
Survey questions asked (1) for perspectives toward environmental justice, pollution, and environmental issues in general; (2) whether respon-

dents had participated in any public process to address an environmental problem; and (3) basic demographic information, including household size, education, political affiliation, ethnicity, and income. We employed bilingual translators to conduct a forward (English to Spanish) and backward (Spanish to English) translation process to improve comparability between English and Spanish surveys.[37] We employed one translator whose first language was English and another whose first language was Spanish. The Spanish-first translator was native to the region of Texas along the U.S.-Mexico border. Each translator worked individually first and then consulted with other translators and the authors to resolve discrepancies.

To achieve our objectives, we studied a population of rural residents of the U.S.-Mexican border. Although we had arranged to obtain a sampling frame for the survey from county tax roles, we soon discovered that, regardless of whether they were legal residents, many people we sought lived off the grid. We therefore designed a sampling approach that avoided potential errors associated with traditional sampling frames. Rather than questioning a random sample of county taxpayers, we questioned a purposive sample of residents along the Military Highway (the southern-most transportation corridor along the U.S. border), between Hidalgo/McAllen and Brownsville, Texas. This gave us access to Texas residents living along approximately fifty-two miles of the farthest southeastern border between the United States and Mexico. We included all homes that fronted directly on the highway, as well as subdivisions, or *colonias*, connected to the highway. The term *colonia* simply means neighborhood for Spanish speakers in this region, but the Texas Secretary of State defines *colonia* as "a residential area along the Texas-Mexico border that may lack some of the most basic living necessities, such as potable water and sewer systems, electricity, paved roads, and safe and sanitary housing."[38] With one exception, neighborhoods in our study area were *colonias* by either definition.

Within this framework, we attempted to administer a survey to the person who answered the door of every fifth dwelling while moving northeast to southwest along the border. When no one was home we noted the address and returned daily until the interview was completed.

If the person answering the door chose to defer to another member of the household—usually someone with more education—we did not remonstrate. When the person claimed to be too busy, we asked whether we could leave the survey with them and pick it up later. Although we introduced ourselves first in English, we also noted the availability of Spanish translations of the survey. Because only one of the authors was comfortable conversing in Spanish, when potential respondents preferred to use a Spanish version, we had to ask them to wait a few minutes until that author was available. No one responded to this situation by refusing to let us return. Some respondents asked us to read the survey questions, explaining that, although they spoke Spanish, they were not comfortable reading it. They usually nodded encouragingly whenever we stumbled and helpfully corrected pronunciation as needed. Most respondents seemed to enjoy the role of teacher. In some households, a second resident invited the English-only researchers to sit down and engage in a conversation conducted from mixed fragments of English and Spanish. We stumbled upon one wealthy neighborhood, built around an elaborately landscaped *resaca* (an oxbow lake or abandoned river meander). Our response rate was slightly lower in this neighborhood and people were less likely to invite us back for further conversation.

All spatial analyses were conducted in ArcView 3.2 (Environmental Systems Research Institute, Redlands, California). We used landmarks (for example, canals, levies, forests) and road intersections as references to mark the general locations of interview households on a paper map (scale 1:16,800). We then used individual homestead attributes (for example, lawn shape, roof type, house shape, topography, driveway shape and type) to identify and enter the location of each house on a digital aerial photograph. Because image resolution was sufficiently fine to locate the actual interview households, spatial precision of interview household locations was better than ten meters. All descriptive and inferential statistics were calculated using Statistica 6.1 (StatSoft, Tulsa, Oklahoma, United States). We used either t tests or one-way analysis of variance (ANOVA) to determine whether differences in response variables of interest occurred by categories (.05 level of significance). If ANOVA was significant, we used Duncan's range test to evaluate differences among means (.05 level of significance).

Informant-Directed Interviews

We followed Peterson's approach to conducting informant-directed interviews.[39] We gave informants every opportunity to discuss any aspect of environmental quality and development but never required them to do so. This process allowed informants to lead the discussion and talk about issues they found important, thereby reducing the constraints that accompany highly structured interview protocols, as well as increasing the amount of information we gained. Informants were drawn primarily from survey respondents, with some supplementation from additional individuals involved in human health, environmental preservation, and development issues.

After respondents had completed the survey, we encouraged them to become informants, talking further about the survey questions, concerns the experience of filling out the survey had prompted, or anything else about the relationship between environmental quality and sustainability. We encouraged all informants, as well as other residents of their households, to participate in informal conversations with us. Thus, survey administration evolved into conversations, or informant-directed interviews, as residents began to accept researcher questions as the result of curiosity and a desire for understanding. The role of informants who preferred to speak Spanish evolved smoothly from language tutor to cultural tutor. Some who chose to take the survey in Spanish switched to English for the less-structured conversations because they no longer felt threatened by the interview context. We did not use a tape recorder during interviews that evolved from survey responses. We took notes as unobtrusively as possible and then filled in details, as well as added comments regarding affect, immediately following the interviews. We used a tape recorder during interviews with individuals who had not responded to the survey. We spent postsurvey time conversing with most of our survey respondents. Although we produced field notes from all conversations, we did not consider them interviews unless the conversation lasted at least twenty minutes after the survey was completed. Depending on the informants' needs and desires, most interviews lasted between twenty and sixty minutes. Within these parameters, we engaged in informant-directed interviews with sixty survey respondents as well as additional informants drawn from the health professions, biological sciences, and environmental management.

As the conversations evolved, our informants became increasingly willing to explain their perspectives and statements. We gained significant understanding of what it meant to live on *la frontera* as they guided the interviews into issues we may not have considered, as well as clarified previously vague concepts and verified or refuted our interpretations of events. Outside of the formal survey procedure, residents told stories, drew family members and friends into the conversation, and often contradicted statements they had made when answering the survey. In the case of apparent contradictions, we asked them for further clarification but did not change any survey responses. Detailed field notes of all interviews enhanced our reflexivity by enabling us to make frequent comparisons between statements informants made in various settings and our own experiences living in the area. Within this chapter, we use first-name pseudonyms for all informants, and we use interview number parenthetically to identify informants.

Living On-Site

Living on the border was critical to our ability to design an appropriate sampling frame. We arranged to live in a camp-trailer at the Santa Ana National Wildlife Refuge from mid-May through mid-August 2005. Established in 1943 for the protection of migratory birds, the 2,000-acre refuge is home to nearly 400 different species of birds and myriad other wildlife, including the indigo snake, malachite butterfly, and the endangered ocelot.[40] Both people and wildlife traversing the U.S./Mexico border use the area extensively. Refuge personnel informed us that they stopped providing trail maps for visitors because immigrants and smugglers were using them to navigate the dense thorn-scrub vegetation. Now humans passing through the refuge face the same navigational challenges as wildlife. The refuge is bounded on the north by the Military Highway and on the south by the Rio Grande River and Tamaulipas, Mexico. As mentioned earlier, we had intended to use a random sample drawn from county tax roles for our survey. The wisdom of that plan was called into question as soon as we arrived. We discovered immediately that society was divided into legal and illegal residents and that both often bypassed common identifying markers. As we got our bearings, we learned that multiple households often lived in several buildings but on one property owned by a family patriarch or matriarch. Utilities were occasionally shared by means of electric cords run from one home to another, and some either used an outdoor privy or borrowed the neighbors' facilities. We also learned that the largest *colonias* were developing along Military Highway. We revised our sampling frame to take advantage of this transportation corridor, sampling from a population that lived on the border of a wildlife corridor, on the border between urban and rural, and within sight of the border between Mexico and the United States.

Results

Our survey compliance rate was 92.8% (402 of 432). Our sample was slightly more Hispanic and more female than the populations of Cameron and Hidalgo counties: 57.6% of respondents were female (51.5%, 2000 census), and 94.2% were Hispanic (86.3%, 2000 census). The average age of respondents was 42 years (SD = 16.4 years). Median annual household income fell between $15,000 and $24,999. The most frequent annual household income category was less than $15,000 (42.6%), and 87.2% reported annual household incomes less than $50,000. Average household size was 4.4 (SD = 1.9). Most respondents had either not completed high school (40.0%) or had completed their education at the high school level (31.1%, includes GED). Only 9.6% of respondents had received a junior college or university education. The most common sources of income for our respondents were service (16.6%), retired (12.1%), retail sales (9.3%), hourly physical labor (8.6%), public schools (8.6%), construction (7.2%), disability (6.9%), health care (5.5%), and self-employed (5.5%).

When respondents were asked about their political affiliation, the most common response was that they did not vote (43.5%), while 34.8, 13.8, and 7.4% reported being Democrats, Independents, and Republicans, respectively. We had not designated the phrase "do not vote" as an option on the paper survey but added it to our analysis because it was the most common response. Within our study area, being a Democrat was an act of cultural acquiescence more than a political action. For example, when members of the Gonzalez family appeared confused by the "what is your political affiliation" question, Pablo explained why the question was not relevant for his family saying, "[W]e live on the river; we sure as hell ain't Republican" (137). Several times, eavesdropping family members informed older respondents that they were Democrats when they expressed the same confusion over the political affiliation question.

The high incidence of respondents who viewed not voting as their political affiliation probably related to the noncitizen status of some respondents, but most who felt compelled to explain their answers expressed disillusionment with government. For example, "I don't even want to vote because the parties just fight. They don't do anything for the community. The politicians don't do anything for the community, they just do it for themselves" (47); "It's the nature of people to do what's in their own best interest instead of the public" (203); "I won't vote because they do what they want anyway" (385); and, most commonly, "Poor people don't believe in that" (100). Disillusionment with local government was probably fueled by personal experience. After making the shift from respondent to informant, Ricardo told us, "I work at the county jail and he [the county sheriff] would have us all over at his house for a barbeque and then try to get us to vote for him" (321). The sheriff in question and several deputies were implicated in crimes ranging from running drugs and guns to sexual misconduct with inmates. This sheriff was being held in jail during our field study because other local law enforcement officers were afraid he would run to Mexico where he had a second family. Another informant said, "[O]ff the record, . . . the sheriff was working with the mafia to sell drugs and guns and when he went before the judge the judge said 'we're only human' but when I went in for a DWI they said, '[Y]ou messed up and you're going to pay,' and they told me not to say anything or you'll get more time. I'm not going to say anything about the sheriff though because he's got friends in law, but he's got more friends in the mafia, and if they find out they will come and burn my house" (104).

Social Perceptions of the Environment and Justice

Environmental Problems   The vast majority of our respondents (82.4%) thought there were important environmental problems along *la frontera* and identified a diverse array of examples. Although no single problem was implicated by the majority of respondents, illegal dumping, water pollution, problems with drainage and mosquitoes, and various air pollution issues were cited most commonly (34.7, 15.3, 10.5, and 10.5% of respondents, respectively). When asked to rank acceptability of exposure to pollution on a scale of 1 to 9, with 1 representing a completely unacceptable risk and 9 the most acceptable risk, the average score was 5.7 (SD = 2.3). Female respondents found pollution exposure levels less acceptable than did male respondents ($t = 2.14$; $p = .033$). Those who had graduated with associate's, bachelor's, or graduate/professional degrees found pollution exposure less acceptable than other respondents ($t = 2.36$; $p = .019$). Political affiliation also was related to the acceptability of pollution exposure ($F = 3.07$; $p = .028$), with Independents finding pollution exposure levels less acceptable than Republicans and those who reported they did not vote. Democrats could not be distinguished statistically from Republicans, Independents, or those who did not vote. The acceptability of pollution exposure levels was not related statistically to ethnicity, source of income, or household income ($p = .121 - .333$).

Illegal dumping was a pervasive problem throughout our study area. The Texas Natural Resource Conservation Commission suggested in 1997 that the more than 20,000 illegal dumping sites on the Texas/Mexico border would require more than $20 million to clean up.[41] The estimate of sites and cost has undoubtedly increased since that time. This problem plagued the most rural areas of our study site because surveillance was minimal there. One informant, who was employed by the U.S. Department of Transportation, expressed the problem in these words: "People dump old tires, furniture, mattresses in the ditches that are supposed to be for drainage.... [W]hen it rains the trash clogs the ditches and you get drainage problems, and people complain and say, '[O]h now my house is flooding.' Well you filled up the drainage ditches" (176). We saw evidence to corroborate the claims of informants who often directed us to the local "dump," which was a street, dried pond, or canal used for garbage disposal. A young woman described how a class from a local university changed her perspective: "[W]e need to be careful about disposal of our wastes and recycling." She regretted losing a local *resaca* because of the combined actions of her extended family and the Hidalgo County Water Control and Improvement District: "[T]he government dammed up the lake and after it dried out we [neighborhood] used it for our garbage" (27). Many residents attempted to solve the trash problem by burning their garbage. Unfortunately, this practice simply converted one problem (trash) into another (air pollution). In fact, fire and smoke associated with trash burning was identified by 5.5 percent of our respondents as the most important environmental problem in the area.

When we asked respondents to describe water pollution, they typically referred to tap water. With rare exceptions, such as the disabled military veteran who said, "[S]ometimes bad water comes out, sometimes its yellowish, I drink it because I got used to bad water in the military" (100), even those making less than $2,000 a year purchased bottled water for drinking. They said, "We have to get bottled water because tap water feels weird and has a smell" (295), "we don't drink it anyway because they say its *venenoso* [poisonous]" (326), and "I would rather be thirsty when it [bottled water] runs out than drink it from the tap" (142). One informant warned us, "[W]ater around here, no one drinks the water. It smells and tastes okay. You can take a bath with it, but if you drink it, give it about one half hour and it turns your stomach. You can ask anyone around here. Nobody drinks the water" (164). Residents were sure their neighbors knew the dangers of drinking tap water saying, "[B]etween here and Laredo nobody drinks the water. Everybody drinks bottled water" (254). Although few people considered drinking tap water an option, they were concerned about their clothing and pets, because "we get dirt out of the faucet and there is an oily film on top of the water" (48), "the water... stinks your clothes. You can't even wash with it" (343), and "some people give it to dogs and cats and it can make them sick" (157).

Residents saw poor drainage and mosquito infestations as different manifestations of the same problem. Drainage problems had two causes: trash and inadequate infrastructure. Some trash items (for example, washers, tires, sheet metal, propane tanks) led to mosquito problems by holding water, while others (such as sofas, mattresses, bags) led to mosquito problems by clogging drains and drainage ditches. While pointing to an adjacent yard full of old tires, automobiles, and appliances, Anita explained, "[T]he problem is trash in lots, makes mosquitoes, it's bad for kids" (47). In a nearby *colonia*, Andres described what happened when the drains clogged: "The drainage ditch behind my house gets trash and standing water, mosquitoes. It turns green color" (50).

Even without trash clogging drains and holding water, residents of *colonias* in our study area faced serious drainage problems. Many were built on land that was unsuitable for other purposes because of poor soils and inadequate drainage. According to John, "the farmer who owned the land [where the *colonia* was built] was supposed to put in drainage and fill to bring it up to code, but he didn't really do it, and so the water stays and there are mosquitoes" (357). John did, however, gratefully acknowledge that the county sometimes brought pumps to drain the *colonia* after heavy rains. Bluetown, a *colonia* developed in the 1960s, had received its first drainage system two years prior to our study, but the system held standing water. One resident we met walking down the street told us, "[T]hey didn't use any kind of machine, they just eye-balled it, and you see how well that worked!" (field notes). An informant from the neighborhood explained why some homes were separated from the street by a ditch: "They just started putting street drains in and made people on the street pay for the materials like the concrete pipes. If you didn't pay you didn't get a drain, and they left a ditch in front of your house" (87).

Overspray from crop dusters and smoke from burning sugarcane were considered serious problems by 7.1 percent and 4.2 percent of respondents, respectively. Several people suggested agrochemicals were a necessary evil because people needed food, so Anna was more upset that, once people became sick from chemicals, they had no medical care: "People get sick from asthma and breathing problems from the spraying of fields. They go to get [medical] help and its not there" (163). Several respondents considered sugarcane a bigger problem than trash burning. This feeling, however, may have resulted from frustration at watching hundreds of acres of cane burn while they were fined for burning trash in a barrel. Javier expressed this concern, saying, "The county cops come to our door as soon as we burn a little trash, but the cane farmers can burn that entire field and its fine. It should be fair. Tell us something, should tell them too. Have it straight" (61).

Although only 3.7 percent of our respondents identified *maquiladoras* as an important environmental issue, the *maquiladoras* evoked strong and bitter emotions in some informants. Lando (figure 7.2, point 4) shared the gristly details of his friend's experience working in one: "He dipped electrical boards into some kind of resin you know, and had his hands get mutilated so he couldn't work. . . . He lost much of his vision from that chemical . . . they gave him gloves but it ran in still. . . . It was an American company, and they give him a little money because he can't work anymore, but they don't have to give you much in Mexico" (29). Juan, a disabled oil rig worker broke down in frustration and anger while telling us about his eight-year-old grandson, who "has lung cancer, and they had to move him to San Antonio to get help. They have a lot of *maquiladoras* in Mexico and they don't give a fuck! All that shit blows over here and maybe that hurt him when the wind was blowing. It came out in the paper two or three years ago about the wind. The plants in Reynosa and Matamoros—and it might hit you when [pause] maybe five or ten years. [pause] I hope I don't get sick" (366). Juan (figure 7.2, point 9) was directly downwind from the *maquiladoras* in Matamoros (figure 7.1).

Political Engagement in Environmental Issues   Only 10.0 percent ($n = 40$) of our respondents had ever participated in political processes designed to address environmental problems. Most saw such engagement as futile. Marcos described his reasons for not participating.

I worked in John Deere and Barge factories for about 20 years and they didn't give a damn. They just threw it in the bay. The Coast Guard caught them and gave them a $100,000 fine and they tried to blame me. They ordered me to throw it in the water. I was working in one of those big tanks. I don't know if you have seen those tanks, but they have a big door on the bottom. They told me to open that manhole, and they paid me so I did it, and all the oil drained into the water. They tried to say I didn't know what I was doing and I messed up, but I said I'd tell them the truth, so they were like, "No, no, no, we'll pay." That all went in the Brownsville Channel. Then I had to move, and went to the Mississippi to work for John Deere. They threw all their stuff into the Mississippi and everything. There were other tractor factories on the other side. When I went fishing, all the fish I caught smelled like oil. They can break the law, but I can't because I'm no good. I'm a poor man. They will pay money and say shut up. That's the way of life man. (171)

Of the 10 percent of our respondents who did participate in environmental politics, the most common modes were contacting governmental agency personnel to obtain information or make a complaint ($n = 16$; 43.2%), voting for or against a political candidate based on her or his position on the environment ($n = 14$; 37.8%), attending a public meeting or hearing about environment issues (n = 12; 32.4%), and contributing either time or money to conservation groups (n = 6; 16.2%). The most common approach, contacting an agency to make a complaint, involved creative use of a phone tree: "We call the county and they say it's not easy because they have too many places to spray mosquitoes. Our neighbors, we all get together and call. I call my neighbor and they call their neighbor and we all call on one day. That's what it takes to get them to come" (345).

Hispanic respondents were more likely than whites to have participated in environmental politics (t = 3.02; p = .003). Education also was related to whether respondents participated in environmental politics (F = 3.72; p = .001), with those who graduated from a four-year college or university more likely to participate than those who had not graduated from high school, high school graduates, and those with associate's degrees. Respondents with graduate or professional degrees also were more likely to participate than high school graduates. Put another way, those who had obtained associate's, bachelor's, or graduate/professional degrees, collectively, were much more likely to participate in environmental politics than those without the benefit of either a college or university education (t = −3.48; p < .001). Similarly, household income was related to whether respondents participated in environmental politics (F = 3.12; p = .005). Those reporting annual household incomes between $75,000 and $99,999 (2.7% of respondents) were more likely to participate in environmental politics than those whose incomes ranged from less than $15,000 to $49,999 (87.2%). Respondents living in households earning at least $100,000 annually (2.9% of respondents) also were more likely to participate in environmental politics than those reporting incomes of less than $15,000 to $24,999, or $35,000 to $49,999 (72.6%). Whether respondents participated in environmental politics was not related statistically to gender, source of income, or political affiliation (p = .126 − .329).

Linking the Material and Social

Environmental Problems   Although there was a prominent spatial pattern in concern about illegal dumping, it was not related to a material aspect of dumping location or its impact on the environment. Rather, the distribution of concern about illegal dumping was related to political boundaries. Only 17.5 percent of Hidalgo County respondents saw illegal dumping as a problem, as compared to 36.8 percent of Cameron County respondents. No public trash service in rural areas existed in Cameron or Hidalgo counties prior to our study. Private companies offered service. However, because most residents lived on incomes far below the poverty level, a monthly $20 trash service was relatively low on their list of priorities. Cameron County began a mandatory rural trash service during the last two weeks of our study. On July 28, 2005, Red River Service Corporation (the rural trash service contract bid winner) began unloading trash bins at our respondents' homes. A brochure taped to the bin notified residents of the mandatory service, described billing (it was included in their water bill), and provided service information. Only 23.5 percent of respondents interviewed after trash bin delivery began ($n = 98$) were aware of the mandatory trash service before cans were dropped of at their homes. Many residents in our study area discovered other county residents considered illegal dumping a serious problem only after the trash bins arrived, but they did not change their views on environmental problems. Only 33.9 percent considered dumping a serious problem after the cans arrived as compared to 34.9 percent prior to their arrival.

As with illegal dumping, the spatial distribution of water pollution and concern about water pollution (15.3%) were mediated more by sociopolitical than material factors. The Military Highway Water Supply Corporation provided water to most households in our study area, so large wells and water treatment facilities filtered both the water and the relationship between point source water pollution and pollution of water at individual households. Although residents did not tie water pollution to point sources in the environment, they did tie it to the Rio Grande River. John told us, "[T]he water in the river is no good. It used to be good and people used to fish in it" (324). According to Ted, "[T]he other side, they throw shit in the river. When I was a kid you could drink out of it [made hand scooping water to mouth gesture], but now there are Pampers floating by" (374). One common theme was that water treatment was inadequate to clean the river. Joanne explained that "the water in the river is kinda green. They say they clean it and shit, but I know a guy at the water place, and he says, '[H]ey I urinate in a cup and I don't care how many tests you give to it, its still going to be urine.' We used to have wells that went down real deep, but they came to us and said that water is poison and we need to get city water. Now they just use big wells from the farmers. We're still in the same boat" (121). Sal was "worried about air and water because they burn everything and dump shit in the water and don't care in Mexico and you can't stop it from coming here" (137). Mercedes claimed, "You can't filtrate it enough. The river is dead; it foams. How can you filtrate that?" (209).

There was a clear spatial link between perceived environmental threats from agriculture (11.3 percent of informants), including overspray from crop dusters and smoke from sugarcane burning, and point sources of agricultural pollution. Of the respondents concerned about agricultural pollution, 88.0 percent lived directly adjacent to an agricultural field that was currently being farmed (51.5 percent of all respondents did). Twenty-seven respondents (7.1 percent) objected to overspray of agricultural chemicals, primarily from crop dusters. From this group, 88.9 percent lived directly adjacent to an actively farmed field. This immediate adjacency is critical because when a crop duster attempts to spray to the edge of a field, overspray only hits houses directly adjacent to the field and those a mere fifty meters inside a *colonia* are spared. Respondents cited damage to yard plants as evidence that defoliants were occasionally missing their intended targets: "[W]e have a crop duster right there and sometimes he throws chemicals to kill the cotton and sometimes he spills on us and we know it because all our neighbors' trees were killed. A lot of people went to complain to him but he doesn't give a darn. A lot of children play in the street and it can fall on their head and become a serious problem" (100). Another informant living adjacent to a cotton field said, "[T]he public is the one that will be hurt if they use too much and throw it around. The public should be like 'hey, you endangered this kid's life with that'" (333).

Concern about sugarcane burning also was spatially related to the environmental problem. Of the fifteen respondents listing cane burning as an environmental problem, thirteen lived adjacent to an actively farmed field, eleven lived adjacent to a field planted in sugarcane when the interview took place, and three lived in homes completely surrounded by sugarcane fields. One person living adjacent to a sugarcane field warned that the smoke was "deathly ill to some people. It doesn't seem fair that no one does anything" (18). Another described the burning, saying, "[T]hose little things they plant and burn [sugarcane], yah, little black things falling from the sky. You can see it coming in the sky" (305). Because these people lived next to cane fields, the long range effects (smoke, particulate matter, and ash) were less important to them than the local (that is, the edge of the field) effects. Our informants expressed far more concern about the grisly scene unfolding in the fields than about the resulting air quality. One afternoon we approached several men sitting on the porch of an old wooden shack bordering a cane field, and fighting off the heat with a cooler of beer. One tough-looking man with calloused hands and skin creased from scars and the sun grew so angry and indignant his eyes welled up with tears when describing a burn: "They burn half the creatures. . . . They get pissed off when I say it, but like they say, the truth hurts better than a lie. They need to stop the burning of sugarcane and killing the creatures. I would like to do something about all the animals I see burned. I would like you to come here when they burn and see . . . [what] I seen burned; they come burning out of the fields. Sometimes they are burning when they come out. And you see them burned lying by the edge. Sometimes they run out of the fire and run right back in" (91). A wealthier resident of the Progresso Lakes community was so distraught by the scene that he bought a small lot and left it wooded as a hiding place for animals fleeing the burns (18). This sentiment was shared by one sugarcane farmer we interviewed. He hated to see the "raccoons, possums, and rabbits lying burned in the ditches" but was most upset by the panicked and burned coyotes that "would run out of the fire and then run right back in" (106).

Concern about air pollution (from trash burning and factories) was spatially related to point sources, but respondents generally did not know or mention the source. Prevailing winds from the southeast characterize the Lower Rio Grande Valley, so the Brownsville/Matamoros region is the only urban area upwind of any portion of our study area.[42] Every respondent who was alarmed about air pollution lived within the area that was downwind of the urban region 90 percent of the time, and 87 percent lived within the much narrower area that was downwind of the urban region 60 percent of the time (figure 7.1). Respondents con-

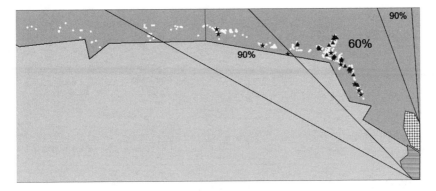

Figure 7.1.
Area downwind of Brownsville (checkered polygon) and Matamoros (striped polygon) 60% of the time and 90% of the time. Black stars represent informants concerned with air pollution, black triangles represent informants concerned with smoke from trash burning, and white circles represent all other informants interviewed.

cerned about trash burning (*n* = 17) also were clustered closer to the urban area than those disturbed about air pollution in general. Trash burning was more prevalent in the fringe near urban areas, where burning bans were enforced, and larger particulate matter no doubt fell out more quickly in these areas because they were closer to where trash burning occurred (figure 7.1).

Only 14 (3.7 percent) of our respondents mentioned *maquiladoras* as environmental problems. Two of these individuals lived in Los Indios, the only *colonia* in our study site with an active *maquiladora* (figure 7.2, points 4 and 5). One of them (figure 7.2, point 5) charged that, "[W]hen the Free Trade Bridge was built, the *maquiladora* came and dumped crap from toilets, or something, and it killed all the fish and birds in that pond. We used to fish there, but now there's nothing there" (137). Another respondent had recently moved from Reynosa, where several *maquiladoras* operate, to a rural farming area across the river from those *maquiladoras* (figure 7.2, points 1–3). While the remaining respondents were more isolated from *maquiladoras* spatially, they were socially tied through tragic losses or employment (figure 7.2, points 6–14).

Environmental Justice Perceptions of justice in the distribution of environmental problems were different from perceptions of the problems'

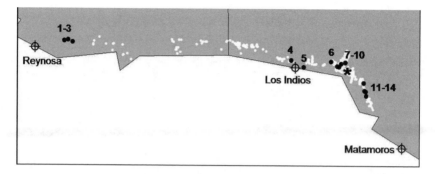

Figure 7.2.
Study area with maquiladoras (target), people expressing concern about them (numbered black points), Alejandra (asterisk), and all other informants interviewed (white circles).

existence. Most of our respondents lived below the poverty level in substandard housing, used water from a river carrying agricultural, human, industrial, and nuclear wastes, and breathed smoke-laden air—and knew it. Yet they saw other people as the victims of environmental injustice. Although most identified serious environmental problems (82.4%), only 37.7 percent (n = 149) felt any group of people was exposed to more environmental pollution than another. Whether respondents thought one group of people was exposed to more environmental pollution than other groups was not related statistically to any of our demographic variables (p = .151–.926). Of respondents who maintained that some people were exposed to more pollution than others, virtually all found the situation unjust (89.5%). Respondents who found this fair (9.8%) typically explained that people chose to live in polluted environments for economic or other reasons: "People in big cities are exposed to more [pollution], but that's the life they choose to live" (201). Perceived fairness was not related statistically to any of our demographic variables (p = .094–.923).

Concern over agrochemical exposure was the only case where a spatial link between pollution and environmental justice emerged. Nine of the eleven respondents who thought people living adjacent to farm fields suffered environmental injustice lived adjacent to farm fields. One crop duster we interviewed corroborated the concerns of these respondents.

He was standing on the top of a rickety step ladder tinkering with engine parts of the plane he had just crashed in an adjacent field while we conducted the interview, and we were occasionally interrupted when he dropped his wrench and one of us retrieved it from the ground. He used his most recent crash (one of eight he had survived) to describe the risk associated with living near farm fields:

Well, the other crop dusters would be mad for me telling you this, and wouldn't want to go on record, but the applicators and people living by the fields definitely have higher exposure to chemicals, so the potential is there for harm. But there would have to be an occurrence for a problem. It's like having a loaded gun in the house. We still use methyl-parathion, which is quite deadly. It has the potential of causing death. Usually I get a little too much, but not this year. If this engine went out on me in the north end of that field instead of the south end, I'd have landed in that *colonia* (pointing with his wrench) with a load of poison. The wind is always out of the southwest and that *colonia* is on the north end of the field. We are careful and try to spray early in the morning when the wind is low—and we go in before and tell them to stay inside, and we've never had a complaint—but to consider the risk factor, they are more at risk than people in downtown Harlingen. (155)

Respondents who thought environmental injustice was a problem identified the poor ($n = 23$; 16.9%) and people living in cities ($n = 22$; 16.2%) as the groups most often experiencing environmental injustice. None of our respondents lived in cities, but most would be classified by an outsider as poor. The respondents, however, were referring to others as the "poor" in the context of environmental justice. Eva, a woman whose household of three survives on an annual household income of considerably less than $15,000, told us, "[P]oor people get pollution. Those people would like to live more clean, but they don't have the money to live better" (294). The poor people to whom she referred were not her own family. Alan differentiated between himself and the poor that suffer environmental injustice: "We're poor people, but those poor people live like chickens, like animals" (403). Another respondent ironically referred to the mandatory rural trash service as environmental injustice, saying, "[S]ome people here don't work and it's hard for them. They would use that $18 to buy food or milk for the baby" (317). Concern for the other also was illustrated by respondents who thought that children ($n = 12$; 8.8%) and people in *colonias* ($n = 11$; 8.1%) suffered the brunt of environmental injustice. Although most of our respondents lived in *colonias*, only three of the twelve who considered *colonia* residents victims of environmental injustice lived in a *colonia*. Further, two of the three respondents living in *colonias* were referring specifically to residents of Cameron Park, an urban *colonia* in Brownsville. Alejandra (247) exemplified the tendency to see environmental injustice as the plight of others when she expressed gratitude that she had been able to move from her previous home of Buttonwillow, California, where a close friend had given birth to a child with a neural tube defect. "We used to live just five miles from a factory with chemical wastes and a lot of kids were being born without brains. They said it was the burning of chemicals," she told us. "Of course the people didn't win. They even had people picketing and stuff."

Learning from the People of *la Frontera*

Our results paint a dire picture for sustainability on *la frontera*. The poor, uneducated, and patriarchal communities we surveyed lacked virtually all characteristics typically considered critical to effective identification and remediation of environmental problems. Women and people with higher education levels were more likely to identify the existence of a problem, but education levels were low and these women lacked formalized power. Further, informants with higher education and income were more likely to become politically engaged in addressing a problem, but were spatially or economically, or both, (for example, bottled water, health care) distanced from environmental problems. We saw the lands and people of *la frontera* locked into a positive feedback loop of degradation catalyzed by infusion of the global society's discards. In this sacrifice zone, the earth could not protect or provide for its inhabitants, and the humans drawn to them for economic and social reasons lacked resources to protect or provide for the earth.

Our results support Haraway's argument that "socio-techno-bio bodies" shape our world.[43] Social (happiness, economics, health, power), technical (water filtration, crop dusters, factories), and material (human bodies, nonhuman animal bodies, ash, chemicals) dimensions were linked in what our respondents perceived as environmental problems. The likelihood that people would identify a specific environmental issue, and act on that identification, was directly linked to its material presence as it affected their own bodies. For example, based on predictor variables, such as household income and education, whites should have been more likely to have participated in environmental politics. Hispanics, however, were significantly more likely to have done so, probably because those who self-identified as white lived far (or upwind or upstream) from the primary sources of air and water pollution.

Our respondents supported much of the discourse of the environmental justice movement by demonstrating awareness of the existence of environmental pollution, the location of the pollution, and its potential threat. Yet they challenged that discourse by adamantly refusing to designate themselves as victims of injustice. For our informants, human health was the central issue, not race, ethnicity, civil rights, or distributional justice. Most did not describe the socio-techno-material configurations shaping their lives as unjust. The few who identified injustice, described a generic "other" as the victim. Can one cry environmental injustice when the "victims" do not self-describe as such? We propose that sustainability demands an affirmative answer to this question. By repudiating certain bodies, and the spaces they inhabit, society has positioned nature as a wedge between social elites and the disenfranchised. The resulting hostilities preclude any opportunity to build sustainable communities.

Although it remains vital to respect the presence of individual choice in the lives of these people, we do not assume they make decisions in a social vacuum, or that they can easily escape environmental degradation. The poor and otherwise disenfranchised flock to *la frontera*, where they can survive on as little as $200 a month. One reason our response rate was so high is that the disabled, the elderly, and the unemployed are home much of the time. The homebound elderly woman who persisted in believing we were county healthcare workers coming to check on her (despite our repeated protestations to the contrary) was notable for her similarity to other respondents rather than her distinctiveness. For these people, escape is nearly impossible. As Alejandra (247) told us, one of the reasons she left her home in Buttonwillow was to escape the horrors of toxic chemicals and brainless babies. Yet, unbeknownst to her, social ties and economic circumstances drew her to another sacrifice zone. Her friend's baby was born and buried in Buttonwillow in 1992, just after a spike in neural tube birth defects in Cameron County, Texas. Both the Buttonwillow and the Cameron County cases drew national attention from human health professionals and the public.[44] Official reports vaguely blamed the outbreaks on individual lifestyle choices such as diet, bemoaned the lack of sufficient data, and found no evidence that the birth defects were related to exposure to industrial wastes such as xylene and toluene.[45] Alejandra currently lives directly downwind from the *maquiladoras* in Matamoros and downstream from those in Reynosa (figures 7.1 and 7.2).

Alejandra and other residents of *la frontera* measure the concentrations of environmental pollution with their bodies. An openly just society can promote sustainability by bridging the gap between the material needs of human bodies (as well as those of other animals, rivers, ecosystems, and so forth) and social practices developed and displayed through culture, economics, law, and politics. We can design and inhabit democratic societies in which people have defensible rights. Similarly, we can design and inhabit societies that are simultaneously just and sustainable. Agyeman suggests the *Just Sustainability Paradigm* as a unifying construct for this effort.[46] Discovery and implementation of sustainable communities, however, requires a far more inclusive discourse than we have thus far invented. Advocates for environmental sustainability can help by discovering how to re-present Earth's voices in language that resonates with human residents of *la frontera*. Environmental justice advocates can help by grappling directly with sociopolitical structures that place humans at odds with other species and by re-presenting spatial scales that currently encourage the material and social to speak past each other.

Notes

1. Leopold (1949); World Commission on Environment and Development (1987); Busch (1996); Agyeman, Bullard, and Evans (2003); Latour (2004).
2. Leopold (1949).
3. Peterson (1997).
4. Agyeman (2005, p. 8).
5. Ostrom (1990).
6. Hardin (1968, 1993); Peterson (1997).

7. Leopold (1949); Allen and Hoekstra (1993).

8. World Commission (1987); Aguirre (2002).

9. Agyeman et al. (2003).

10. World Commission (1987); Peterson, Peterson, and Peterson (2005).

11. Peterson (1997).

12. Nabhan (1995); Amnesty International and Sierra Club (2000).

13. Agyeman et al. (2003, p. 5).

14. Peterson and Franks (2005).

15. Lélé and Norgaard (1996).

16. Aguirre (2002); Peterson et al. (2005).

17. Stauber (1994); Woollard and Ostry (2000).

18. Willers (1994, p. 1146).

19. Jacob (1994); Callicott and Mumford (1997).

20. Peterson et al. (2005, p. 264).

21. Waterman (2002); Agyeman et al. (2003).

22. Bowen and Wells (2002).

23. General Accounting Office (1983); Commission for Racial Justice (1987); Bryant and Mohai (1992); Mennis (2002).

24. U.S. Environmental Protection Agency (2005).

25. Agyeman et al. (2003, p. 3).

26. Mouffe (2000).

27. Agyeman (2005, p. 77).

28. Walzer (1983); Dobson (1993).

29. General Accounting Office (1983); Commission for Racial Justice (1987); Bryant and Mohai (1992); Mennis (2002).

30. Maantay (2002); Pezzullo (2003a).

31. Pezzullo (2003b).

32. Agyeman et al. (2003, p. 3).

33. Latour (2004).

34. Newman and Benz (1998); Tashakorie and Teddlie (1998); Strauss and Corbin (1997).

35. Newman and Benz (1998).

36. Creswell (2003).

37. Marín and Marín (1991).

38. Texas Secretary of State (2005); Texas Water Development Board (2005).

39. Peterson (1997).

40. U.S. Fish and Wildlife Service (2005).
41. Texas Natural Resource Conservation Commission (1997, 2005).
42. Texas Department of Environmental Quality (2005).
43. Harroway (1997).
44. Peterson (1997); Cole and Foster (2001).
45. Texas Department of Health (1992); California Birth Defects Monitoring Program (1993).
46. Agyeman (2005).

References

Aguirre, B. E., "Sustainable Development as Collective Surge," *Social Science Quarterly* 83 (2002): 101–118.

Agyeman, J., *Sustainable Communities and the Challenge of Environmental Justice* (New York: NYU Press, 2005).

Agyeman, J., R. D. Bullard, and B. Evans, eds., *Just Sustainabilities: Development in an Unequal World* (Cambridge, Mass.: MIT Press, 2003).

Allen, T. F. H., and T. W. Hoekstra, "Toward a Definition of Sustainability," in W. W. Covington, and L. F. Debano, eds., *Sustainable Ecological Systems: Implementing an Ecological Approach to Land Management* (Fort Collins, Colo.: Rocky Mountain Forest and Range Experiment Station, 1993), 98–107.

Amnesty International and Sierra Club, *Environmentalists under Fire: 10 Urgent Cases of Human Rights Abuses* (2000). Retrieved May 28, 2004, from http://www.sierraclub.org/human-rights/amnesty/report.pdf.

Bowen, W. M., and M. V. Wells, "The Politics and Reality of Environmental Justice: A History and Considerations for Public Administrators and Policy makers," *Public Administration Review* 62 (2002): 688–698.

Bryant, B., and P. Mohai, eds., *Race and the Incidence of Environmental Hazards: A Time for Discourse* (Boulder, Colo.: Westview Press, 1992).

Busch, L., "Bringing Nature Back in: Principles for a New Social Science of Nature," *Centennial Review* 40 (1996): 491–501.

California Birth Defects Monitoring Program, *Neural Tube Defects in Kern County: Buttonwillow Area Cluster Investigation* (1993), Retrieved August 20, 2005, from http://www.cbdmp.org/pdf/buttonwillow.pdf.

Callicott, J. B., and K. Mumford, "Ecological Sustainability as a Conservation Concept," *Conservation Biology* 11 (1997): 32–40.

Cole, L. W., and S. R. Foster, "Buttonwillow: Resistance and Disillusion in Rural California," in *From the Ground Up: Environmental Racism and the Rise of the Environmental Justice Movement* (New York: NYU Press, 2001), 80–102.

Commission for Racial Justice, *Toxic Wastes and Race in the United States: A National Report on the Racial and Socio-economic Characteristics of*

Communities with Hazardous Waste Sites (New York: United Church of Christ, 1987).

Creswell, J. W., *Research Design: Qualitative, Quantitative, and Mixed Methods Approaches* (Thousand Oaks, Calif.: Sage, 2003).

Denzin, N. K., and Y. S. Lincoln, *The Sage Handbook of Qualitative Research*, (Thousand Oaks, Calif.: Sage, 2005).

Dobson, A., "Social Justice and Environmental Sustainability: Ne'er the Twain Shall Meet?" in J. Agyeman, R. D. Bullard, and B. Evans, eds., *Just Sustainabilities: Development in an Unequal World* (Cambridge, Mass.: MIT Press, 2003), 83–95.

General Accounting Office, *Siting of Hazardous Waste Landfills and their Correlation with Racial and Economic Status of Surrounding Communities* (Washington, D.C: Government Printing Office, 1983).

Hardin, G., "Tragedy of Commons," *Science* 162 (1968): 1243–1248.

Hardin, G., *Living Within Limits: Ecology, Economics, and Population Taboos* (New York: Oxford University Press, 1993).

Haroway, D., *Modest_Witness@Second_Millenium. Femaleman ©_meets_Onco Mouse™:Feminism and Technoscience* (New York: Routledge, 1997).

Jacob, M., "Sustainable Development and Deep Ecology: An Analysis of Competing Traditions," *Environmental Management* 18 (1994): 477–488.

Latour, B., *Politics of Nature: How to Bring the Sciences into Democracy*, translated by C. Porter (Cambridge, Mass.: Harvard University Press, 2004).

Lélé, S., and R. B. Norgaard, "Sustainability and the Scientist's Burden," *Conservation Biology* 10 (1996): 354–365.

Leopold, A., *Sand County Almanac and Sketches Here and There* (London: Oxford University Press, 1949).

Maantay, J., "Zoning Law, Health, and Environmental Justice: What's the Connection?" *Journal of Law, Medicine & Ethics* 30 (2002): 572–593.

Marín, G., and B. V. Marín, *Research with Hispanic Populations* (Newbury Park, Calif.: Sage, 1991).

Mennis, J., "Using Geographic Information Systems to Create and Analyze Statistical Surfaces of Population and Risk for Environmental Justice Analysis," *Social Science Quarterly* 83 (2002): 281–297.

Mouffe, C., *The Democratic Paradox* (London: Verso, 2000).

Nabhan, G. P., "Cultural Parallax in Viewing North American Habitats," in M. E. Soule, and G. Lease, eds., *Reinventing Nature: Responses to Postmodern Deconstruction* (Washington, D.C.: Island Press, 1995), 87–101.

Newman, I., and C. R. Benz, *Qualitative-Quantitative Research Methodology: Exploring the Interactive Continuum* (Carbondale: Southern Illinois University Press, 1998).

Ostrom, E., *Governing the Commons: The Evolution of Institutions for Collective Action* (New York: Cambridge University Press, 1990).

Peterson, M. N., M. J. Peterson, and T. R. Peterson, "Conservation and the Myth of Consensus," *Conservation Biology* 19 (2005): 762–767.

Peterson, T. R., *Sharing the Earth: The Rhetoric of Sustainable Development* (Columbia: University of South Carolina Press, 1997).

Peterson, T. R., and R. R. Franks, "Environmental Conflict Communication," in J. G. Oetzel and S. Ting-Toomey, eds., *The Sage Handbook of Conflict Communication: Integrating Theory, Research, and Practice* (Thousand Oaks, Calif.: Sage, 2006).

Pezzullo, P. C., "Resisting National Breast Cancer Awareness Month: The Rhetoric of Counterpublics and their Cultural Performances," *Quarterly Journal of Speech* 89 (2003a): 345–365.

Pezzullo, P. C. "Touring Cancer Alley, Louisiana: Performances of Community and Memory for Environmental Justice," *Text and Performance Quarterly* 23 (2003b): 226–252.

Stauber, J. C., "Going . . . going . . . green!" *PR Watch* 1, no. 3 (1994): 1–3.

Strauss, A., and J. Corbin, *Grounded Theory in Practice* (Thousand Oaks, Calif.: Sage, 1997).

Tashakkori, A., and C. Teddlie, *Mixed Methodology: Combining Qualitative and Quantitative Approaches* (Thousand Oaks, Calif.: Sage, 1998).

Texas Department of Environmental Quality, *Wind Roses 1984–1992*, retrieved August 20, 2005, from http://www.tceq.state.tx.us/compliance/monitoring/air/monops/windroses.html

Texas Department of Health, "An Investigation of a Cluster of Neural Tube Defects in Cameron County, Texas," a report prepared by the Texas Department of Health and the Centers for Disease Control (Austin, Tex., and Atlanta, Ga., July 1, 1992).

Texas Natural Resource Conservation Commission, "Illegal Dumping Assessment of Impacts on County Governments in the Texas-Mexico Border Region," AS-138, July 1997.

Texas Natural Resource Conservation Commission, "Border Activities," retrieved August 20, 2005, from http://www.tnrcc.state.tx.us/exec/ba/activities.html.

Texas Secretary of State, "Colonias: Frequently Asked Questions," retrieved August 24, 2005, from http://www.sos.state.tx.us/border/colonias/what_colonia.shtml.

Texas Water Development Board, "Economically Distressed Areas," retrieved August 24, 2005, from http://www.twdb.state.tx.us/colonias/index.asp.

U.S. Environmental Protection Agency, "Environmental Justice," retrieved August 31, 2005, from http://www.epa.gov/compliance/environmentaljustice.

U.S. Fish and Wildlife Service, "Santa Ana National Wildlife Refuge," retrieved July 30, 2005, from http://www.fws.gov/southwest/refuges/texas/santana.html.

Walzer, M., *Spheres of Justice: a Defense of Pluralism and Equality* (New York: Basic Books, 1983).

Waterman, P., "The Call of Social Movements of the Second World Social Forum, Porto Alegre, Brazil, 31 January–5 February, 2002," *Antipode* 34 (2002): 625–632.

Willers, B., "Sustainable Development: a New World Deception," *Conservation Biology* 8 (1994): 1146–1148.

Woollard, R. G., and A. S. Ostry, eds., *Fatal Consumption: Rethinking Sustainable Development* (Vancouver: University of British Columbia Press, 2000).

World Commission on Environment and Development, *Our Common Future* (New York: Oxford University Press, 1987).

III
International Environments

8

Golden Tropes and Democratic Betrayals: Prospects for the Environment and Environmental Justice in Neoliberal "Free Trade" Agreements

J. Robert Cox

Admittedly, there are serious problems of environmental degradation in the Third World. . . . Although growth may initially lead to environmental deterioration, once a nation's per capita income reaches $8,000, growth leads to improved environmental quality.
—Bruce Bartlett, "The High Cost of Turning Green"

Let us beware of this dangerous theory of equilibrium which is supposed to be automatically established. A certain kind of equilibrium, it is true, is reestablished in the long run, but it is after a frightful amount of suffering.
—Simonde de Sismondi, *New Principles of Political Economy*

As World Trade Organization officials struggled to launch new trade negotiations after failed attempts in Seattle (1999), Doha (2001), and Cancun (2003), questions about the impacts of economic globalization on poverty, sweatshop labor, human rights, and the environment continued to haunt trade ministers. In the face of such criticism, U.S. Trade Representative Robert Zoellick responding to reporters' questions at a trade meeting in Mexico City, insisted that "[O]pen trade and growth are not only consistent with good environmental practices, but [are] usually *supportive* of those" (2001, p. 1, emphasis added).

Zoellick's remarks echoed other adherents of "open markets" who cited research purporting to show an inverted U-curve relationship between a nation's economic growth and its environmental quality. That is, as an economy grows, environmental air or water pollution increases, until a point is reached when it begins to decline. In a frequently cited study, Grossman and Krueger, for example, found that "for most indicators [for pollution] . . . economic growth brings an initial phase of deterioration followed by a subsequent phase of improvement" (1995,

p. 369). Drawing on such research, Zoellick testified before the U.S. Senate: "Free trade promotes free markets, economic growth, and higher incomes. And as countries grow wealthier, their citizens demand higher labor and environmental standards" (2002, p. 1).

Similar assurances from free traders came amid growing skepticism of globalization's promises. As large-scale protests occurred in Seattle (1999), Prague (2000), Washington, DC (2000), Quebec City (2001), Genoa (2001), Quito (2002), Porto Alegre (2003), and Cancun (2003), Zoellick and others recharacterized the negative impacts of globalization—pollution of water and air, poor working conditions, and continued poverty—as a temporary, though normal, phase of development. Deployed in debates over restructuring loans as well as trade agreements, this "normal" timeline has been used to reassure developing nations: "Grow now, worry about the poor [or the environment] later" (Gallagher 2001, p.1).

In this chapter, I suggest that it is useful to think of the differing versions of Zoellick's response as a trope—that is, a "turning" or refiguration of our understanding of globalization's impacts.[1] As a trope, such a turning not only reveals a larger contradiction in Neoliberal narratives of globalization, but also rationalizes a weakening of democratic remedies of social and environmental harms. On one hand, despite their insistence on the natural working of the market, U.S. trade officials, economists, and others have had to salvage rhetorically neoliberalism's promises in the face of the problems that have emerged in newly deregulated Third World economies. More important, I contend that, by assuming that the impacts of unregulated markets on environmental quality are always positive, such tropes discipline the "rhetorical space" (Code 1995) of debate and divert attention from profoundly antidemocratic aspects of recent trade and investment agreements.

I develop this argument by identifying neoliberal narratives as an instance of what Beers and Hariman (1996) called a "realist style" and argue that criticism has led its defenders to supplement this style's claim to realism with a critical tropical repair. Second, I illustrate such criticism in a case of environmental injustice in Guadalcazar, Mexico, and describe a "golden" trope of sacrifice/reward that neoliberal defenders use to assure Third World nations that, despite short-term hardships, both economic and environmental benefits will eventually materialize. More important, I argue that such tropical sleights of hand divert attention from the ways in which neoliberal "free trade" undermines the ability of Third World nations to cope with environmental damage. Finally, I identify how, as such impacts become evident, environmentalists and environmental justice activists have begun to work together as allies to protest the exclusions of democratic redress in neoliberal trade and investment agreements.

Narrating Globalization and the Environment

References to "globalization" are increasingly interpolated in a collage of (competing) stories, particularly in narratives that tell of "the system that has replaced the old Cold War" (Friedman 2000, p. ix). In accounts of media ecology, cultural studies, and sociology, globalization gestures to the porousness of borders, the sheer scale of the collapse of space and time by new communication and information technologies, and the diffusion and merger of identities, such as the "Americanization" of cultures (Wallerstein 1991). It also suggests the nature of this interconnectivity, what Rushkoff calls the new global narrative of a "networked being" (2002, p. 56)

On the other hand, many economists and government and corporate leaders invoke the more specific term "neoliberal globalization" for the efficient movement of goods and capital under "liberalized" trade rules (Gills 2000; Gilpin 2001). Indeed, popularized by media coverage of demonstrations at meetings of the World Bank, the World Trade Organization (WTO), and other trade and financial forums, neoliberal globalization has come to identify a specific vision—and critique—of political economy. It is this set of terms and narratives of "growth" that now implicate the peoples and environments of the barrios in Cochabamba, Bolivia, or *las colonias* of Matamoras, Mexico, in ways similar to those in Louisiana's Cancer Alley or the neighborhoods of East Los Angeles.

Neoliberal Economic Globalization

Coalescing around ideas associated with classical economic theory that are variously termed "free-market capitalism," "neoliberal economic globalization," and the "Washington consensus,"[2] the concept of economic globalization generally has been characterized by three conditions:

1. *A set of "liberalized" market conditions for the global expansion of capital.* Narratives of neoliberal globalization assume that economic growth occurs through "liberalization [and] 'freeing up markets,'" including privatization, deregulation, and measures for financial stability that are intended to "create a climate to attract investment" (Stiglitz 2002, p. 67). Such accounts call specifically for reducing state intervention in the economy: deregulation of markets, fiscal discipline and control of inflation, lower corporate taxes, privatization of services, and elimination of tariffs and other restrictions on trade, capital transfers, and direct foreign investment (Pieterse 2000; Scholte 2000).

2. *New multinational arrangements for the security of capital transfers, trade, and investment.* Supplementing the World War II Bretton Woods institutions—the World Bank and International Monetary Fund—new arrangements for trade and investment have linked the push for "deep integration" of global economies with what the first director of the WTO, Peter Sutherland, called a "revolutionary framework for economic, legal and political co-operation" (1994, p. 1). These legal and institutional safeguards were set forth principally in the Uruguay Round trade agreements[3] that established the WTO. These agreements are intended to ensure "market access" and adjudicate trade disputes over such access among member states.

3. *Harmonization of nation states' regulation of capital with the new transnational, institutional rules.* One of the major accomplishments of the Uruguay Round was recognition that social regulation of health, food production, workers' safety, and the environment could constitute "non-tariff barriers"[4] to trade. As the WTO launched its 2001 Doha Round of trade negotiations, the World Bank lamented the "trade-impeding regulations such as environmental and health standards and restrictive rules of origin" that continued to limit the industrial nations' access to markets in developing economies (World Bank 2002). Gills similarly argues that the new Neoliberal institutions have the aim of "re-articulating states to the purposes of facilitating global capital accumulation" (2000, p. 4).

For many critics, the trend toward the deep integration of global economies has been accompanied by a decline of democratic controls and spaces for the participation of civil society. Gills, for example, fears that the exclusion of political subjects in these arrangements serves only to "de-socialize the subject and to insulate the Neoliberal state . . . against the societies over which they preside." Rather than serving social ends, such state/global arrangements exist principally "to serve [capital's] need for self-expansion" (2000, pp. 4, 5). Not surprisingly, advocates of neoliberal economic policy offer a very different story of globalization.

Golden Tropes and "Realist" Narratives

Along with the tenets of "open markets" and new protections for capital, neoliberal adherents also have insisted on a claim to knowledge of how markets "really work." By the early 1990s, proponents of what Richard Falk called the "world picture of 'neo-liberalism'" had succeeded largely in consolidating a coherent narrative of the virtues of free-market economic growth, so much so that "the mainstream rejection of all criticism of markets and their operations by policymakers and the media was commonplace" (1999, pp. 1, 5). Echoed in popular accounts of the post–Cold War era such as Francis Fukuyama's (1990) *The End of History and the Last Man*, the plot of neoliberalism's story acquired a triumphalist tone. *New York Times* columnist Thomas Friedman assured his readers that *The End of History* "contained the most accurate insight about what was new—the triumph of liberalism and free market capitalism as the most effective way to organize a society" (2000, p. xxi).

Affecting a realist epistemology, such narratives told of a new system that had replaced the drama of capitalism *contra* communism, one that "had its own unique logic, rules, pressures and incentives" (Friedman 2000, p. 7). Neoliberal adherents purported to describe an inexorable working of markets and their progressive *telos*—one that told of "freeing up markets" and the growth of national economies. "The more you let market forces rule and the more you open your economy to free trade and competition," Friedman explained in his bestseller *The Lexus and the Olive Tree*, "the more efficient and flourishing your economy will be" (2000, p. 9). Such discipline was not only the "only way" to sustain growth; fiscal and regulatory sacrifice, while harsh at times, was also inevitably benign. Friedman assured his readers that, "when it comes to the question of which system today is the most effective at generating rising standards of living, the historical debate is over. The answer is free-market capitalism. . . . The free market is the only ideological alternative left" (p. 104).

Integral to the neoliberal narrative is the assurance that present circumstances—however dire—can be converted into a more attractive state of affairs. In return for fiscal and regulatory discipline, neoliberal proponents assure nations a payoff in the form of unparalleled growth, rising incomes, and other "social amenities" as they are more deeply integrated into the global economy. Indeed, the acceptance of economic hardship and shrinking of social welfare as consequence of the move to deregulation and open markets is portrayed as a necessary, albeit temporary, condition for eventual growth.

Friedman captures the necessity of such sacrifice: "When your country recognizes . . . the rules of the free market in today's global economy, and decides to abide by them, it puts on what I call the *Golden Straightjacket*. The Golden Straitjacket is the defining political-economic garment of this globalization era" (p. 104). According to globalization's new logic and "to fit into the Golden Straitjacket," Friedman explains,

A country must either adopt, or be seen as moving toward, the following golden rules: making the private sector the primary engine of its economic growth, . . . shrinking the size of its state bureaucracy, maintaining . . . a balanced budget . . ., lowering tariffs . . ., removing restrictions on foreign investment, . . . privatizing state-owned industries . . ., deregulating capital markets . . . [and] its economy. (p. 105)

But those who conform to the neoliberal rules can expect something in return: "As your country puts on the Golden Straitjacket," Friedman explains, "two things tend to happen: your economy grows and your politics shrink. That is, on the economic front the Golden Straitjacket usually fosters more growth and higher incomes—through trade" (pp. 105–106). The choice, however, is quite literally binding. Once a country puts on the trope of the "Golden Straitjacket," "its political choices get reduced to Pepsi or Coke—to slight nuances of . . . policy . . . but never any major deviation from the core golden rules" (p. 106). Nations that try to loosen their self-imposed bindings "will see their investors stampede away, interest rates rise and stock market valuations fall" (p. 106).

Nor can nations delay accepting the neoliberal strictures, lest their own economies slip further behind. Former Australian trade minister Robert McMullan confidently predicted: "It will not be possible to stop what has become an inexorable movement to an ever more deeply integrated world economy, not least because deeper integration brings tremendous potential economic benefits and broader political and social benefits" (1995, p. 9).

Such at least are the claims of the neoliberal "story of itself," as Beer and Hariman (1996) have observed of the realist style more generally. Valorizing empiricism, and rejecting merely verbal ways of knowing, realism purports to describe the workings of the economy as they "really are." Still, such a style often must be augmented with other claims that explain shortcomings in its realist narrative and that "establish it as an account of permanent, ubiquitous, essential conditions" (Beer and Hariman 1996, p. 3). Such supplements occur as realism's story finds itself having to compete for assent in the face of skepticism, contrary facts, or alternative accounts. In accounting for globalization's dark side, neoliberal apologists have increasingly found themselves needing to refigure its social dysfunctions through other tropes of sacrifice and reward.

It Gets Worse before It Gets Better

The Case of Metaclad, Inc.

Residents of Guadalcazar, one of the poorest regions in the state of San Luis Petosi, Mexico, were not buying the neoliberal narrative: "Open your markets, deregulate, and with economic growth the quality of your environment will improve." In 1994, they persuaded the town council to deny a construction permit for the U.S. company Metalclad to build an industrial toxic waste facility near the town. Its proposed location in the La Pedrera valley, approximately seventy kilometers from Guadalcazar, had been the site of a previous waste dump. Metalclad had acquired the abandoned site in 1993 and was preparing to construct and operate its own waste facility.

Neighbors of the proposed waste facility feared that the *Norte Americano* company's plans to reopen the site would cause sickness and possibly contaminate their water supply. The site's previous owners had left more than 20,000 tons of hazardous waste, "lying around, exposed—equal to what had been buried beneath New York's Love Canal" (Moyers 2002, p. 6). Many believed this waste had been making them sick. One resident explained that cancer "began to appear in peoples' bones, cancer in women's wombs, cancer in people's blood.... And we blame it completely on the contamination, which started in the early 1990s and continues to this day" (Moyers 2002, p. 6).

By the early 1990s, Mexico's democracy reform movement had mobilized thousands of supporters in San Luis Petosi, and local opposition to Metalclad's plans to build a toxic waste facility was "intense" (Kass and McCarroll 2000, p. 1). Residents' concerns about the earlier site had forced its Mexican owners to shut down. Now they demanded that Metalclad clean up the waste site before they brought in more waste (Moyers 2002). Metalclad ignored residents' complaints, believing it had the necessary permits from the federal government in Mexico City. The federal operating permit "gave the company five years to clean up the existing waste. But the democratically-elected Guadalcazar town council would not give its permission unless Metalclad agreed that the cleanup would happen first" (Moyers 2002, p. 7). Metalclad refused and began construction without either the required cleanup or a local construction permit.

When ordered by the local town council to stop, Metalclad refused. Company president Grant Kesler, explained, "We felt that the key to the broader political support was not direct to the people.... Every adviser that I had in Mexico told me, if the governor [of San Luis Petosi] supports this project, you don't have to worry about that local community" (Moyers 2002, p. 7). In 1995, at ceremonies to open the facility, protesters blocked access to the site and chanted, "If they want permission, they have to get it from us ... they have to respect the local municipality" (p. 7). The new facility remained closed.

With the democracy reform movement in full bloom, the new governor of San Luis Petosi refused to override the wishes of local voters in Guadalcazar. Earlier Metalclad had appealed for help to the U.S. embassy. The U.S. ambassador, for his part, informed Governor Horacio Sanchez Unzueta that he would place San Luis Petosi on a blacklist of regions in Mexico that investors should avoid: "If this is the way you do business in San Luis Petosi, we're going to tell other businesses in the United States who want to invest in Mexico, you can invest here, but don't invest in San Luis Petosi" (Moyers 2002, p. 7).

Nevertheless, in 1996, the governor "ordered the site closed down after a geological audit showed the facility would contaminate the local water supply... [and] then declared the site part of a 600,000 acre ecological zone" (Greenfield 2000, p. 1). On January 2, 1997, Metalclad sued the government of Mexico under a provision of the North American Free Trade Agreement (NAFTA) that granted sweeping protections to foreign investments. (Under NAFTA, a private corporation, for the first time, may directly sue a sovereign nation.) On August 30, 2000, a NAFTA panel ruled against the actions of local authorities and ordered the Mexican government to pay $16.7 million to Metalclad for "damages" from its lost opportunity to operate a hazardous waste facility (U.S. State Department 2004). The ruling in *Metalclad Corp v. Mexico*[5] was viewed widely as a test of new guarantees of foreign corporate activities under NAFTA's Chapter 11 provisions protecting investment. Environmentalists and human rights groups feared that the ruling sends a chilling message: If local or national authorities interfere with foreign corporate operations, they will pay a burdensome cost in sanctions or financial compensations. A *New York Times* editorial warned that such lawsuits "discourage environmental regulation" in other nations ("The Secret Trade Courts" 2004, p. A30). It cited the case of a U.S. manufacturer of a gasoline additive that filed a Chapter 11 complaint against Canada after that country tried to ban the additive on the basis of health concerns. Under pressure, Canada revoked the ban and paid the U.S. corporation $18 million.

The cases of Guadalcazar and Canada are not isolated. Similar neoliberal guarantees of private corporate "investment" have undermined the ability of many Third World nations to protect environmental quality, health, and, in some cases, human survival itself. Doyle notes, for example, that "there is nothing post-materialistic" about the environment movement in the Philippines to halt the destructive effects of mining. As with other Third World green movements, "activists involve themselves in the struggle to survive—a fight for social and environmental justice" (2005, p. 52). Two looming threats particularly have united environmental, social, and human rights activists in many Third World countries:

1. *Privatization of water*   In Africa and Latin America, many countries in debt to the International Monetary Fund (IMF) and World Bank feel pressure to allow multinational corporations to assume control of public water systems, from communal drinking water to irrigation of farms. For example, local activists and human rights groups cite the uprising in Cochabamba, Bolivia, in 2000 when the bank pressured that country to privatize its water supply. The move resulted in crippling fees for water in poor neighborhoods of many cities (Finnegan 2002). *La Guerra del Aqua* (the Water War) in Cochabamba's barrios became a wider rallying cry against excesses of neoliberal policies of the bank and free trade agreements.[6]

2. *Social and environmental impacts of mining*   The mining of copper, zinc, uranium, and other minerals, as well as drilling for oil, has had devastating consequences on local waterways and farmlands, the clearing of vegetation, and displacement of peoples in places such as Indonesia, the Philippines, Nigeria, and other Third World nations. Weak regulation of oil and mining industries in these countries is often due to neoliberal pressures for "market access" and "the concomitant weakening of national legislation" (Doyle 2005, p. 56). Antimining activist Roger Moody noted that state-owned mining assets "are being offered for sale under 'free market' privatization" and that "under pressure from the IMF and the World Bank, more than 70 countries have changed their mining laws to make them more attractive to foreign investment" (1996, p. 46).

The effects of mining and the drive to privatize water are only two of the consequences of neoliberal "free trade" and investment rules that are bringing together environmental and social justice activists in many parts of the world. Along with the shipment of toxic wastes to Third World nations and the impact of multinational companies on drinking water and sanitation in the *maquiladora* zone along Mexico's border with the United States, the failed promises of "open markets" have prompted new coalitions of resistance. For example, when the WTO attempted to restart negotiations at Cancun, Mexico, in 2003, trade ministers were met in the streets by farmer, environmentalist, human rights, labor, and environmental justice groups that denounced not only the effects of economic globalization, but also the weakening of local and national autonomy by neoliberal restrictions. And it is these criticisms that have led defenders of neoliberal economic globalization's "story of itself" to supplement its claims by a particular "golden" trope.

Kuznets Curves: Refiguring Environmental Impacts

As the "realist" story of Neoliberal globalization confronts skepticism, its defenders have attempted to refigure the negative effects of free trade and investment by assuring nations of an eventual "turn" toward higher environmental quality. The Zoellick trope—"as countries grow wealthier, their citizens demand higher labor and environmental standards"—is drawn from research in developmental economics that is based on a figure known as the "Kuznets curve." The term is named for Simon Kuznets (1955), a Nobel Prize winner who, in studying the effects over time of development on a nation's income equality, hypothesized that the relationship between an inequality in the distribution of a nation's income and the level of income is an inverted U-shaped curve (Stern 2001). Kuznets held that, "while in the initial stages of development inequality increased, later on the trend was reversed (Stiglitz 2002, p. 79; Kuznets 1955).

First developed in the theory of income, the idea of an inverted U-shaped relationship seemed to be an ideal supplement to neoliberal narratives that accounted for the dark side of globalization (poverty, pollution, poor working conditions, and other such conditions). By the early 1990s, some economists and World Bank officials believed that they had found evidence of an "*environmental* Kuznets curve" (EKC). Its hypothesis predicts "an inverted U-shaped relation between various indicators of environmental degradation and income per capita. This has been taken to imply that economic growth will eventually redress the environmental impacts of the early stages of economic development and that growth will lead to further environmental improvements in the developed countries" (Stern 2001, p. 193). Yandle, Vijayaraghavan, and Bhattarai (2002) display the typical environmental Kuznets curve in figure 8.1.

The first evidence of a Kuznets curve relationship for the impacts of open markets on a country's environmental quality came in research in 1991. Grossman and Krueger (1991) examined air pollution data

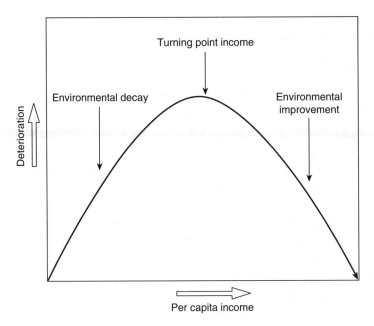

Figure 8.1
Environmental Kuznets Curve

collected by the Global Environmental Monitoring System in forty-two countries for sulfur dioxide (SO_2) and nineteen countries for "dark matter" or fine smoke. They concluded, "[A]mbient levels of both sulfur dioxide and dark matter suspended in the air increase with per capita GDP at low levels of national income, but decrease with per capita GDP at higher levels of income. The turning point comes somewhere between $4,000 and $5,000, measured in 1985 U.S. dollars" (1991, p. 5).[7] In each case, the authors reported "an inverted-U shaped relationship between pollution and national income" (p. 19).

Grossman and Krueger's findings soon found reflection in other studies. Moreover, as Harbaugh, Levinson, and Wilson note, "[F]ar from being an academic curiosity," such studies soon persuaded some policy advocates to conclude that "developing countries will *automatically* become cleaner as their economies grow" (2000, pp. 1–2). Indeed, World Bank and trade officials began to draw on the idea of Kuznets curves to represent the impacts of open markets not only on income growth, but also on human rights, labor, and environmental quality in developing nations. For example, the World Bank's *World Development Report 1992* confidently reported that many forms of air and water pollution "initially worsen but then improve as incomes rise." Echoing Grossman and Krueger's 1991 assumptions, the Bank assured readers that, "as incomes rise, the demand for improvements in environmental quality will increase, as well the resources available for investment" (1992, p. 39).

It is interesting that such use of the Kuznets curve is not an intrinsic feature of the realist rationale for neoliberal globalization. Instead, one finds its deployment precisely at those moments in which neoliberal policy itself comes under criticism. Confronted with skepticism, its apologists cite the predicted outcome of the Kuznets curvature: Despite apparent conditions, the opening of markets and "growth" will inevitably (eventually) yield a benign effect. For example, Bruce Bartlett (1994) admitted that, although there were "serious problems of environmental degradation" in Third World countries, the "evidence suggests that the best way to eliminate them is to increase the rate of economic growth." Citing research by Grossman and Kruger (1994), Bartlett assured critics that "[g]rowth leads to more efficient production *and invariably leads to reduced pollution*" (p. A18; emphasis added). And Daniel Griswold of the Cato Institute insisted, "Expanding trade is not merely compatible with high standards of environmental quality but can lead directly to their improvement (2001, p. 8).

Golden Tropes and Democratic Betrayals

According to neoliberal theory, the residents of Guadalcazar got it backward. Poor nations are supposed to accept environmental deterioration in opening their markets. With rising incomes, citizens of (formerly) poor regions like San Luis Potosi, Mexico, eventually can "afford" such social amenities as clean air and water and will demand that their government protect these. Though seemingly harsh, neoliberals argue, the development curve figured by the EKC provides its own promise of prosperity and (eventually) environmental quality.

But is the Kuznets curve thesis an accurate description of the relationship between neoliberal prescriptions and environmental quality? Or is the Kuznets figure (an inverted U curve) a trope after all—a rhetorical turning from, or simplification of, the contingencies of unregulated markets? And, if the latter, do neoliberal trade rules provide for the democratic means to redress the negative consequences of trade and open markets on the environment?

Kuznets Curves and Globalization's Impacts

Despite the confidence of its proponents, research scrutinizing the Kuznets curve generally—and environmental quality specifically—has found little support for it. Deninger and Squire (1996) report no evidence for the inverted U-shaped effect for development and income equality. And Drazen, summarizing the empirical literature examining the basic Kuznets hypothesis, reports "a largely, though not uniformly, negative finding" (2000, p. 517).

Neoliberal claims of a Kuznets curve for the alleviation of poverty, expected to arrive with "growth," also appear doubtful. Stiglitz (2002), former chief economist at the World Bank, observes that the history of the past fifty years has not supported the Kuznet hypotheses. On the one hand, South Korea, China, Taiwan, and Japan "showed that . . . one could achieve rapid growth without a substantial increase in inequality" (p. 79). On the other hand, Stiglitz reports that, "where governments adopted the Washington Consensus policies, the poor have benefited less from growth. In Latin America, growth has not been accompanied by a reduction in inequality, or even a reduction in poverty" (p. 79; see also Drazen 2000). More bluntly, Malaysian Prime Minister Mahathir bin Mohamed—after defying the IMF's harsh proscriptions for his country—castigated neoliberal policies as a "sacred truth . . . so contrary to the facts" in the experience of the countries of East Asia (Stiglitz 2002, p. 93).[8]

Similarly, research in environmental economics casts doubt on the empirical bases for an environmental Kuznets curve. Gallagher reports that the EKC pattern "has held true for only a few of the pollutants that have been studied" (2001, p. 1). One reason may lie simply in the quality of the data from which the Kuznets curve is drawn. For example, Harbaugh, Levinson, and Wilson reexamined the evidence that the

World Bank (1992) and Grossman and Krueger (1995) used and concluded, "[T]he evidence for an inverted-U is much less robust than previously thought. . . . Merely cleaning up the data, or including newly
available observations, makes the inverse-U shape disappear" (2000,
p. 2). Finally, the research on environmental effects has failed to examine the effects of GDP growth on toxic (airborne) pollutants. World Bank
economists concede that "the underlying scarcity of data has as yet made
it impossible to do more than speculate about the shape of an environmental Kuznets curve for toxics" (Dasgupta, Laplante, Wang and
Wheeler 2002, p. 151).

Still, in some cases, there is evidence of the expected decline in certain
environmental pollutants as incomes rise (World Bank 1992; Selden and
Song 1994; Holtz-Eakin and Selden 1995; Grossman and Krueger 1995;
and Hilton and Levinson 1998). The relevant question becomes, why?
What accounts for the differential impacts of personal income growth on
environmental quality? And, most important, do neoliberal free trade
agreements themselves enable states and local governments like
Gaudalcazar to respond to these contingent developments?

Metonymy's Labor: Kuznets Curves and Democratic Assumptions
Of particular importance to the environmental Kuznets curve hypothesis
is "political demand" and the availability of modes of democratic
redress. In their discussion of their early findings, Grossman and Krueger
(1991) ventured an important assumption to account for the observed
decrease in pollution as income rises. "If trade liberalization generates an
increase in income levels, the body politic may demand a cleaner environment as an expression of their increased national wealth. Thus, *more
stringent pollution standards and stricter enforcement of existing laws
may be a natural political response to economic growth*" (p. 5; emphasis added). Again, after reviewing the sources of pollution abatement,
Grossman and Krueger suggested that "the strongest link between
income . . . and pollution in fact is via an induced policy response. As
nations or regions experience greater prosperity, their citizens demand
that more attention be paid to the noneconomic aspects of their living
conditions" (1995, p. 372). That is, as nations regulate more strictly,
environmental quality rises. Dasgupta et al. conclude that "the available

evidence suggests that *regulation* is the dominant factor in explaining the decline in pollution as countries grow beyond middle-income status" (2002, p. 152; emphasis added; see also Panayotou 1993; and Mani, Hettige, and Wheeler 2000).

This view was quickly adopted by those neoliberal proponents who voiced the idea of a Kuznets curve as a critical supplement to the realist story of globalization. One of its chief public defenders, Columbia University economist and UN special advisor, Jagdish Bhagwati, noted that "the fear is widespread among environmentalists that free trade increases economic growth and that growth harms the environment. That fear," Bhagwati argued, "is misplaced. Growth enables governments to tax and to raise resources for a variety of objectives, including the abatement of pollution and the general protection of the environment" (1993, p. 42).

Relevant to our concerns, then, are the EKC assumptions of (1) a political demand for more stringent environmental standards as personal incomes rise and (2) the availability of democratic mechanisms for translating popular will into state regulatory control of industrial pollutants and other environmental harm. And it is here that we begin to see the specifically metonymic labor of neoliberal narratives that reduce, refigure, or discipline the complexities and assumptions behind claims of a benign telos for market forces.

In a comprehensive review of EKC literature, Stern found that the purported appearance of a Kuznets-type relationship for the environment depended upon the presence or absence of "proximate causes" (e.g., available technologies) and "underlying causes" such as environmental regulation, awareness, and education (2001, p. 193). Similarly, Panayotou (1993) has observed that, although pollution generally increases in the initial stages of economic development, as the Kuznets curve assumes, the outcome at the later stages—whether a decline or rise in environmental degradation—depends upon certain "structural changes toward information-intensive industries and services, coupled with increased environmental awareness, enforcement of environmental regulations, better technology and higher environmental expenditures" (in Stern 2001, p. 193). As a result, Stern (2001) has identified a number of problems with many of the environmental Kuznets curve estimates and interpretations. Depending on whether a study has accounted for the presence of regulatory authority, public demand, "higher environmental expenditures," and so forth the data may not support a figure of an inverse U-shaped curve. In other words, in the absence of factors such as state regulatory and tax authority, environmental pollution may continue to rise or remain constant.[9]

In a study that explores such contingencies, Harbaugh, Levinson, and Wilson (2000) discovered varying shapes of the EKC curve for the relationship between growth and environmental quality. These resulted from the possible variations for specifying which assumptions guide the "reduced form" of the income/environmental quality relationships. For example, does the EKC model include the latest release of pollution date or an index of democratic governance? When different specifications are included in regressions showing the relationship between SO_2 pollution and per capita gross domestic product (GDP), the shape of this relationship changes dramatically. The results range from a lazy U (but not the assumed *inverse* U of the Kuznets thesis) to a J and even a wobbly W. Although Harbaugh et al. note that there is no a priori reason to prefer any one of these outcomes, they conclude that, "the specifications generally show a *U-shaped*, rather than inverted U-shaped relationship between income and sulfur dioxide pollution" (2000, p. 10). As incomes rise, these environmental pollutants initially decline, but then they rise and continue upward. In other words, in the absence of state authority to regulate or enforce standards in response to popular demand, the EKC's predicted decline in environmental pollution is harder to find.

As a consequence, neoliberal arguments for deregulation of the economy, lowering of corporation taxes, and so forth introduce a tension in the use of the environmental Kuznets curve. Whereas favorable EKC models assume the continued ability of governments' regulatory and tax abilities as a response to political "demands" of citizens, trade agreements such as NAFTA prohibit this authority, as "trade-impeding regulations" (World Bank 2002). That such contingencies are routinely passed over by neoliberal apologists suggest the tropical work of the Kuznets curve. Specifically, the EKC reduces relationships of contingency and complexity to a specific figuration—the inverted U curve relationship of trade and its assumed corollary of economic growth and environmental protection. Thus, its adherents are able to characterize the complaints of environmentalists and environmental justice supporters as ignorant of market "laws."

Neoliberal Trade Agreements and Democratic Betrayals

When Metalclad sued the government of Mexico in 1997 under NAFTA, it relied upon new guarantees for noninterference with foreign business operations. NAFTA's Chapter 11 ("Investment") provisions extend protection to "the establishment, acquisition, expansion, management, conduct, operation, and sale or other disposition of investments" by foreign corporations in a host member State (Article 1102).

Chapter 11 grants specific neoliberal safeguards for capital transfers, investment, and, in Metalclad's case, the purchase and profitable operation of a business. In the event a member state interferes with such provisions, an "investor" (private corporation) may seek a remedy. Article 1110 lays the legal foundation for such protections by redefining "expropriation" by governmental authority: "No Party may directly or *indirectly* nationalize or expropriate an investment of an investor of another Party in its territory or take a measure *tantamount* to nationalization or expropriation of such an investment," (emphases added) unless the action is for a "public purpose" and compensation is paid to the business party.

Under NAFTA's assumptions of "indirect" expropriation, regulation of commercial activities that threaten public health or the environment may constitute an action that is "tantamount to...expropriation" (Article 1110) of an investment, including an investor's expected income (profits). Until the Metalclad ruling, however, the meaning of Chapter 11's language had not been tested in a case involving a direct clash over the local regulation of an environmental hazard. Metalclad's claim would be the first to pit investment (capital) directly against popular democratic desires for environmental protection.

After more than three years, NAFTA's private dispute panel ruled that the government of Mexico had violated Chapter 11, specifically citing denial of the permit to operate the waste facility as an action that was "tantamount to expropriation" of a business (Kass and McCarroll 2000, p. 4). Such an expropriation, the panel explained, need not be a formal seizure of property; in this case, it included the "incidental interference with the use of property which has the effect of depriving the owner, in whole or in significant part, of the use or reasonably-to-be-expected economic benefit of property" (quoted in Kass and McCarroll 2000, p. 4).

The citizens of Guadalcazar had persuaded their town council to require Metalclad to clean up the toxic waste left by the previous owner before allowing construction to begin on the site. The existence of such "induced policy response" to citizens' political demand is precisely the condition that a favorable environmental Kuznets curve assumes in predicting a downward turn in pollution after a certain point. It is the assumption that nation-states or local communities have the ability to require performance standards and also the financial resources to enforce environment rules. Yet neoliberal trade rules penalize not only the use of such authority (as in *Metalclad Corp. v. Mexico*), but also such regulatory responses to popular demands threaten an "exit" of direct foreign investment.

In both cases—taxes and regulations—nations face an extralegal threat in addition to the disciplinary power of trade rules. Public choice theorist Jean-Luc Migué (1993) points out that under neoliberal terms of free trade, capital has an incentive to "exit" a country or migrate to other markets when faced with the prospect of regulation, workers' wage demands, or taxes. Such threats to exit minimize what Migué calls political "coercion" (government authority). Differing from the EKC models' assumption of citizen demands for environmental standards once personal incomes rise to a certain level, "exit (mobility) is . . . a substitute for the political process" (p. 31). Friedman similarly warns that corporate investors will "stampede away" (2000, p. 106) if governments loosen their golden straightjacket by reimposing regulations or taxing industry.

In fact, there is evidence that a flight of investment has begun from Mexico as GDP grows and workers' average wage has risen to $4,416 per year (Fleeson 2003, par. 3). Ironically, as Mexican workers' income neared the "turning point" that Grossman and Krueger cited, when "the body politic may demand a cleaner environment" (1991, p. 5), a growing number of foreign companies seem to be fleeing Mexico for lower wages elsewhere—the classic "race to the bottom" that critics have feared. As of 2003, business investment under NAFTA had brought some 1,600 *maquiladoras* to Mexico's border area. But, "in the past two years, more than 500 of those plants have closed, taking with them nearly a quarter million jobs, according to Mexico's official statistics agency" (Fleeson 2003, par. 3).

Conclusion

The residents of Guadalcazar were moved by hopes of democratic reform in Mexico in the early 1990s. Yet, their experience and that of others elsewhere in Mexico, as well as those in places such as the Philippines, Indonesia, Ghana, and Bolivia, betray hopes for environmental justice in neoliberal free trade and investment agreements. The tropes of sacrifice and reward in the story of globalization promise an increase in standards of living and environmental quality (eventually) as national economies grow. I have argued, however, that such "golden" tropes turn attention away from two important questions: (1) Will mechanisms for democratic mediation (performance standards and so forth) of damaged environments be available to citizens under neoliberal trade and investment rules? The early evidence from the decisions of NAFTA tribunals is not encouraging. And (2), assuming the presence of such mechanisms, what is the cost to human health or the environment in the interim—that is, in the period of environmental degradation occurring before the alleged EKC "turn" that discloses a political demand for environmental protection?

The citizens of Gaudalcazar still face left-over toxic waste from the previous site near their community. Whether they will continue to fall ill or their water will become polluted will depend on the answers to the questions just posed. Without the authority of local governments to regulate, even the EKC literature seems to admit that environmental harms will continue or actually worsen. But there is another concern as well. Italian economist Marzio Galeotti (2003) reminds us that in the search for the alleged "turning point" in environmental Kuznets curves that leads to declining pollution, researchers have lost sight of certain concerns. Drawing on the work of Panayotou (2000), Galeotti asks, "[H]ow much damage would have taken place by the time a turning point is reached and can it be reduced? [And] would any ecological thresholds be violated and irreversible damages take place before environmental degradation turns downward?" (2003, p. 14). By focusing solely on the level of per capita growth, Galeotti argues, neoliberal economists have tended to forget that, "for many pollutants, levels of emission and concentrations may be intolerably high even before the turning point...*the accumulated damages in the meanwhile may far exceed the present value of higher growth*" (p. 14; emphasis added).

Such concerns bear directly on prospects for environmental justice and the environment in future trade and investment agreements. The proposed Free Trade Area of the Americas includes similar provisions to NAFTA's Chapter 11 for the preemption of local democratic authority, and World Bank requirements for water privatization, as well as WTO negotiations over trade in "services" (for example, education, drinking water supplies, and health care) suggest similar exclusions of democratic authority. The actions of citizens of Guadalcazar and *la Guerra del Aqua* in the barrios of Cochabamba may simply be the forerunners of struggles for the right of local communities to determine the fates of their environments in the neoliberal global future.

The neoliberal story of how things "really work," however, remains open to retelling and revision. New narratives of globalization are being composed in the streets of Genoa, Porto Alegre, and Cancun and in workshops at World Social Forums, as environmentalists, human rights workers, labor unions, and environmental justice activists increasingly join together as allies to resist neoliberal trade and investment policies. Among the retellings of the story of globalization is the cautionary tale of disembodied theory. In the nineteenth century, the Swiss economist Simonde de Sismondi challenged classical economists' belief that the economy automatically gravitates toward full employment. His warning seems prescient of golden straightjackets, environmental Kuznets curves, and neoliberal assurances that "open markets" are inexorably benign: "Let us beware of this dangerous theory of equilibrium which is supposed to be automatically established. A certain kind of equilibrium, it is true, is reestablished in the long run, but it is after a frightful amount of suffering" (1819, pp. 20–21).

Notes

1. Beyond classical traditions of ornamentation, tropes have figured in theories of discourse as a means for *knowing*, at least since Nietzsche's claim that, "with respect to their meaning, all words are tropes in themselves" (1989, p. 23).

2. According to Robert Gilpin, the term "Washington Consensus" was introduced in 1993 to describe the "broad agreement among public officials in the industrial economies and international institutions on the importance of the neoliberal program for economic development and its emphasis on free markets, trade liberalization, and a greatly reduced role for the state in the economy" (2001, pp. 314–315; see, also, Williamson 1993).

3. The Uruguay Round of trade negotiations, the eighth round conducted under the auspices of the General Agreement on Trade and Tariffs, has been called "the greatest trade agreement in history" (Sutherland 1994). The final act, signed on April 15, 1994, provided a dramatically expanded scope of authority and powers of enforcement to the GATT's successor entity, the World Trade Organization.

4. The term "nontariff barriers" refers to a range of indirect, often technical, governmental actions that impede trade, other than tariffs, quotas, or subsidies. Included are forms of social regulation that may be intended for other, nontrade purposes (for example, health, food safety, or environmental protection) but that, in the view of trade advocates, provide unfair advantage to domestic producers. See the discussion in Dunkley (2000, chap. 4.)

5. Mexico appealed the ruling of the NAFTA panel to the Supreme Court of British Columbia, Canada, on the grounds that the panel had exceeded its jurisdiction. On May 2, 2001, the British Columbia court ultimately found in favor of Metalclad and upheld the major portion of the damage award (Shrybman 2001).

6. See also efforts in West Africa by the Ghana National Coalition against Privatization of Water, at http://ghanacap.org.

7. However, "at income levels over $10,000–15,000, Grossman and Krueger's estimates show increasing levels of all three pollutants" (Stern 2001, p. 197). Similarly, Gallagher (2001) notes, "[I]n some of the cases where pollution eventually decreases, the decline does not begin until an extremely high income level has been reached" (pp. 1–2).

8. For a similarly skeptical view of a Kuznets-type hypothesis for the impacts of economic globalization on human rights and workers, see Hertz (2001, pp. 71–72).

9. Some propose that environmental quality is contingent on nonregulatory factors such as technology transfers (that is, cleaner production methods and/or pollution abatement equipment) and a shift in the composition of industrial activity (nations shift to less-pollution-intensive industries as their GDP rises). This assumption is problematic. Even economists who have found an inverted U-shaped relation note that such downward-sloping patterns, as incomes rise, might *not* be sustained for poor nations, if this result is obtained through the import of pollution-intensive goods from nations with less stringent environmental standards. See Grossman and Krueger (1995) and Stern (2001).

References

Bartlette, B., "The High Cost of Turning Green," *Wall Street Journal* (September 14, 1994): A18.

Beer, F. A., and R. Hariman, eds., *Post-Realism: The Rhetorical Turn in International Relations* (East Lansing: Michigan State University Press, 1996).

Bhagwati, J., "The Case for Free Trade," *Scientific American* (November 1993): 42–49.

Code, L., *Rhetorical Spaces: Essays on Gendered Locations* (London: Routledge, 1995).

Dasgupta, S., B. Laplane, H. Wang, and D. Wheeler, "Confronting the Environmental Kuznets Curve," *Journal of Economic Perspectives* 16 (2002): 147–168.

Deninger, K., and L. Squire, "A New Data Set Measuring Income Inequality," *World Bank Economic Review* 10 (1996): 569–591.

Doyle, T., *Environmental Movements in Majority and Minority Worlds: A Global Perspective* (New Brunswick, N.J.: Rutgers University Press, 2005).

Drazen, A., *Political Economy in Macroeconomics* (Princeton, N.J.: Princeton University Press, 2000).

Dunkley, G., *The Free Trade Adventure: The WTO, the Uruguay Round, and Globalism: A Critique* (London: Zed Books, 2000).

Falk, R., *Predatory Globalization: A Critique* (Malden, Mass.: Polity Press, 1999).

Fleeson, L., "Leaving Lorado," *MotherJones.com* (September 2003), accessed online August 16, 2004, at www.motherjones.com/news/outfront/2003/09/ma_506_01.html.

Finnegan, W., "Leasing the Rain," *New Yorker* (April 8, 2002): 43–53, accessed online June 30, 2005, at www.newyorker.com/fact/content/?020408fa_FACT1.

Friedman, T., *The Lexus and the Olive Tree*, rev. ed. (New York: Anchor Books, 2000).

Fukuyama, F., *The End of History and the Last Man* (New York: Free Press, 1990).

Galeotti, M., "Economic Development and Environmental Quality," Working Paper N. 89.2003 (Milan, Italy: Fondazione Eni Enrico Mattei, 2003).

Gallagher, K., "Have Faith in Free Trade: The Greatest Story Ever Sold," *Foreign Policy in Focus* (June 2001), accessed online March 15, 2005, at www.fpif.org.

Gills, B. K., "Introduction: Globalization and the Politics of Resistance," in B. K. Gills, ed., *Globalization and the Politics of Resistance* (Hampshire: Palgrave, 2000), 3–11.

Gilpin, R., *Global Political Economy: Understanding the International Economic Order* (Princeton, N.J.: Princeton University Press, 2001).

Greenfield, G., *The NAFTA Ruling on Metalclad vs. Mexico: the Broader Context* (September 18, 2000), accessed online August 18, 2004, at www .nadir.org/nadir/initiativ/agp/free/nafta/000918metalclad.htm.

Griswold, D. T., "Trade, Labor, and the Environment: How Blue and Green Sanctions Threatens Higher Standards," *Trade Policy Analysis* 15 (August 2, 2001), accessed online March 15, 2005, at: http://www.freetrade.org/pubs/ pas/pas.html.

Grossman, G. M. and Krueger, A. B., *Environmental Impacts of a North American Free Trade Agreement. NBER Working Paper 3914* (Cambridge, Mass.: National Bureau of Economic Research, November 1991).

Grossman, G. M., and A. B. Krueger, *Economic Growth and the Environment. NBER Working paper W4634* (Cambridge, Mass.: National Bureau of Economic Research, February 1994).

Grossman, G. M., and A. B. Krueger, "Economic Growth and the Environment," *Quarterly Journal of Economics* 110 (1995): 353–377.

Harbaugh, W., A. Levinson, and D. Wilson, *Reexamining the Empirical Evidence for an Environmental Kuznets Curve. NBER Working Paper 7711* (Cambridge, Mass.: National Bureau of Economic Research, May, 2000), accessed online March 15, 2005, at www.nber.org/papers/w771.

Hertz, N., *The Silent Takeover: Global Capitalism and the Death of Democracy* (New York: Free Press, 2001).

Hilton, H., and A. Levinson, "Factoring the Environmental Kuznets Curve: Evidence from Automotive Lead Emissions," *Journal of environmental Economics and Management* 35, no. 2 (1998): 126–141.

Holtz-Eakin, D., and T. Selden, "Stoking the Fires? CO_2 Emissions and Economic Growth," *Journal of Public Economics* 57 (1995): 85–101.

Kass, S. L., and J. M. McCarroll, "The "Metalclad" Decision under NAFTA's Chapter 11," *New York Law Journal/Law.com* (October 27, 2000), accessed online June 15, 2004, at www.clm.com/pubs/pub-990359_1.html.

Kuznets, S., "Economic Growth and Income Equality," *American Economic Review* 45 (1955): 1–28.

International Institute for Sustainable Development and World Wildlife Fund, *Private Rights, Public Problems: A Guide to NAFTA's Controversial Chapter on Investor Rights* (Winnipeg, Manitoba: International Institute for Sustainable Development, 2001).

Mani, M., H. Hettige, and D. Wheeler, "Industrial Pollution in Economic Development: The Environmental Kuznets Curve Revisited," *Journal of Development Economics* 62, 2 (2000): 445–476.

McMullan, R., *Winning Markets: Australia's Future in the Global Economy* (Canberra, Australia: Government of Australia Department of Foreign Affairs and Trade, 1995).

Miqué, J-L., "Federalism and Free Trade." Hobart paper 122. London: Institute of Economic Affairs, 1993.

Moody, R., "Mining the World: The Global Reach of Rio Tinto Zinc," *Ecologist* 26, no. 2 (1996): 46–52.

Moyers, B., "Bill Moyers Reports: Trading Democracy," *NOW with Bill Moyers* (Alexandria, Va.: Public Broadcasting Service, 2002).

Nietzsche, F., "Ancient Rhetoric," in S. L. Gilman, C. Blair, and D. J. Parent, eds. and trans., *Friedrich Nietzsche on Rhetoric and Language* (New York: Oxford University Press, 1989).

North American Free Trade Agreement. Accessed online March 15, 2005, at www.nafta-sec-alena.org/DefaultSite/home/index_e.aspx.

Panayotou, T., *Empirical Tests and Policy Analysis of Environmental Degradation at Different Stages of Economic Development*. Working paper WP238 (Geneva: Technology and Employment Programme of the International Labor Office, 1993).

Panayotou, T., "Economic growth and the environment." CID working paper no. 56 (2000), in K.-G. Mahler and J. Vincent, eds., *Handbook of Environmental Economics* (Amsterdam: North-Holland, forthcoming).

Pieterse, J. N., *Global Futures: Shaping Globalization* (London: Zed Books, 2000).

Rushkoff, D., "Renaissance Now! Media Ecology and the New Global Narrative," *Explorations in Media Ecology: The Journal of the Media Ecology Association* 1, no. 56 (2002): 41–57.

Scholte, J. A., *Globalization: A Critical Introduction* (New York: St. Martin's Press, 2000).

Selden, T. M., and D. Song, "Environmental Quality and Development: Is There a Kuznets Curve for Air Pollution Emissions?" *Journal of Environmental Economics and management* 27 (1994): 147–162.

Shrybman, S., *Mexico v. Metalclad: Reasons for Judgment* (Canadian Union of Public Employees (CUPE), June 10, 2001), accessed August 18, 2004, at www.cupe.ca/www/TradeUpdates/3999.

Simonde de Sismondi, J.-C.-L., *New Principles of Political Economy*, vol. 1 ([1819] New Brunswick, N.J.: Transaction Publishers, 1991).

Stern, D. L., "The Environmental Kuznets Curve: A Review," in C. J. Cleveland, D. I. Stern, and R. Costanza, eds., *The Economics of Nature and the Nature of Economics* (Cheltenham: Edward Elgar, 2001), 193–217.

Stiglitz, J. E., *Globalization and Its Discontents* (New York: W. W. Norton, 2002).

Summit of the Americas. Declaration of Quebec City. Accessed online April 22, 2006, at www.summit-americas.org/eng-2002/quebeccity-summit.htm.

Sutherland, P., "Global Trade: The Next Challenge," *News of the Uruguay Round of Multilateral Trade Negotiations*, NUR 082 (Geneva: GATT, January 28, 1994).

Sutherland, P., *GATT Focus Newsletter*, 107 (Geneva: GATT), 10.

The Secret Trade Courts. [Editorial]. *New York Times*, (2004, September 27): A30.

U.S. State Department. 2004. *Metalclad Corp. v. United Mexican States*, accessed online April 22, 2006, at www.state.gov/s/l/c3752.htm (May 1994).

Wallerstein, I., "The National and the Universal," in A. Kind, ed., *Culture, Globalization, and the World System* (London: Macmillan, 1991), 91–106.

Williamson, J., "Democracy and the 'Washington consensus,'" *World Development* 21 (1993): 1329–1336.

World Bank, *News Release No: 2002/374/S* (June 26, 2002).

World Bank, *World Development Report 1992: Development and the Environment* (New York: Oxford University Press, 1992).

Yandle, B., M. Vijayaraghavan, and M. Bhattarai, "The Environmental Kuznets curve. PERC Research Study 02-1," accessed online March 15, 2005, at www.perc.org (May 2002).

Zoellick, R. B., "Statement of U.S. Trade Representative at Press Conference at the WTO Mini-Ministerial Meeting" (Hotel Presidente, Mexico City, September 1, 2001).

Zoellick, R. B., "Statement of U.S. Trade Representative before the Committee on Finance of the U.S. Senate" (February 6, 2002), accessed online April 22, 2006, at www.ustr.gov/assets/Document_Library/USTR_Zoellick_Testimony/2002/asset_upload_file215_4354.pdf?ht=.

9

Indigenous Peoples and Biocolonialism: Defining the "Science of Environmental Justice" in the Century of the Gene

Giovanna Di Chiro

Call it the new wave of colonialism, the new biotechnology, the bio-revolution, or bio-colonialism, . . . it is an area that we dare not ignore.
—Debra Harry, Northern Paiute[1]

The diverse and interdisciplinary literature of environmental justice offers important critical assessments of the role of modern science in creating many of the social and environmental problems facing the world today (Agyeman 2005; Tickner 2003; Brown 2002; Adamson, Evans, and Stein, 2002; Di Chiro 2004b; Kuletz 1998; Peña 1997; LaDuke 1997; Hofrichter 2000; Shiva 1993). While rigorously critiquing techno-science's less-admirable accomplishments (toxic pollution, nuclear waste, weapons of mass destruction, eugenics), activists and scholars remain optimistic that advancing and professionalizing the practice of "science in the public interest" would make possible a healthier, more peaceful, and more just world. Many environmental justice organizations embrace this double consciousness of both the progressive and destructive powers of technoscience by refusing to dismiss the modern sciences as inevitably entangled with the controlling interests of powerful corporations and national governments. Much like the mainstream U.S. environmental movement's appropriating the ecological and earth sciences to provide scientific evidence for the existence of a worsening environmental crisis and demanding government funding to design energy-efficient and non-polluting technologies to avert it, many environmental justice organizations have shifted their political strategy from the stance of distrusting modern scientific advances to the aim of enrolling them. Forging complex political–scientific alliances, a growing number of environmental justice activists have joined forces with toxicologists, medical doctors, epidemiologists, agroecologists, foresters, and geographic information system (GIS) experts to shape a new "science for the people" that reappropriates the tools and resources of science and technology in the service of human and environmental rights (Heiman 2004; Di Chiro 2004a; Corburn 2005).[2] In so doing, these activists are creating the conditions—epistemological and political—for the development of a new "science of environmental justice."

But, as Native American activist Debra Harry asks, "on whose terms" are such alliances being built? Whose sciences and environmental knowledge systems will comprise the emergent "science of environmental justice"? For many Indigenous organizations, the conditions necessary to produce genuine scientific–environmental partnerships have not yet materialized because the economic and ideological apparati of colonialism continue to thwart Native communities' battles for sovereignty over their ancestral territories and traditional knowledges. Postcoloniality, many Indigenous activists argue, is the precondition for generating a viable science of environmental justice whose objective it is to centrally involve in the problem-solving process those communities who suffer the lion's share of the negative externalities of modern industrial society.

This chapter examines the specificity of the response by Indigenous activists from around the world to new developments in science and technology; in particular I focus on new genetics research initiatives publicly promoted as advancing the goals of social equality and environmental justice. I argue that these responses by Indigenous groups represent a critical postcolonial lens through which activists evaluate the benefits of embracing or opposing particular technosciences and, furthermore, they represent an invitation for dialogue and exchange as "equal partners" among scientists, environmentalists, environmental justice groups, and Indigenous communities to generate essential economic, biomedical, and ecological knowledges for living sustainably in the world.

The Age of Genetics: Whose Revolution?

Until recently, the environmental justice movement, at least in the United States, has not focused much attention on the genetic "revolution," even though many environmental, human rights, and Indigenous activists have challenged attempts by large biotechnology corporations to privatize and commercialize the world's genetic resources in the fields of agriculture, medicine, and pharmaceuticals. This international network of activists asserts that, in the name of curing human diseases, preserving biodiversity, and sharing equally in the economic benefits of scientific research, corporate-driven biotechnology companies have pushed the frontiers of global capitalism into the realm of genetics, a new scientific-industrial complex committed to the commodification of "life itself" (Krimsky and Shorett 2005; Tokar 2001; Shiva 1997). Indigenous activists in particular have resisted the incursion of genetic "advances" into their lives by questioning the scientific and ethical rationales of the "benefits to humankind" that would result from scientific ventures such as the Human Genome Diversity Project,[3] which aims to preserve the potentially valuable DNA of "vanishing" Indigenous populations, or from United Nations initiatives such as the Convention on Biological Diversity, which aims to facilitate access by member states to the world's vast genetic resources, much of which lies within Indigenous peoples' territories.[4]

As acknowledged in the Principles of Environmental Justice, Indigenous Peoples have a "special relationship" to claims for environmental justice owing to their rights to self-determination and to sovereignty over their lands and resources (Appendix A). Although the Principles of Environmental Justice document compiled a comprehensive list of concerns to help focus the movement, it could not foresee the challenges that would arise as the interest in and funding for genetics research increased sharply in the late 1980s and early 1990s. Consequently, the issue of genetics has not, until recently, emerged as an issue of concern for most environmental justice organizations in the United States. In light of the environmental justice movement's recognition of the uniqueness of Indigenous peoples' environmental struggles, can we see opportunities for productive intersectional environmental justice politics among environmental justice organizations, Native communities, and other progressive movements at the dawning of the "century of the gene"?[5]

Although historically the environmental justice movement in the United States has not focused much attention on the media frenzy that followed the declaration of the "golden age" of genetics,[6] a broader recognition of the promises and pitfalls of these new scientific developments has emerged (Sze, Prakash, and Shepard 2003; Shostak 2003; Di Chiro 2004c). With the recent launching by the National Institutes of Health (NIH) of new research initiatives under the rubric of "environmental health genetics" dedicated to uncovering the genetic basis for the environmental illnesses suffered by communities of color, many activists in the environmental justice movement have begun to grapple with the bioethical concerns of introducing genetics and biotechnology into their social and environmental change agendas. The first section of this chapter analyzes this recent activist response by examining a conference attended by both environmental justice and Native American organizers that focused on government-sponsored research initiatives that articulate human genetics research objectives with the rhetoric of environmental justice. The chapter then locates the responses by the Native American conference attendees within the emergence of a global movement of Indigenous peoples against the spread of "biocolonialism," a new strain of colonialism propelled by the genetics revolution that many indigenous activists maintain further imperils their centuries-old fight for self-determination. Identifying the new biocolonialism as an offensive uniquely targeting and threatening the sovereignty of Indigenous communities, activists such as Debra Harry have developed creative tools to educate Indigenous peoples around the world about these new developments. The final section focuses on Harry's film, *The Leech and the Earthworm,* a creative documentary that uses/appropriates modern film, video, and new media technologies to explore Indigenous activists' critical perspectives on genetics research and on the future prospects of life on earth. The film makes the point that, by not seeing the colonialist stance underlying the genetic "revolution" and its implications for Indigenous peoples, otherwise supportive, nonindigenous groups miss an opportunity for finding common purpose with the human rights and environmental justice objectives of many Native organizations. Paying closer attention to the specific resistances by Indigenous activists to the geneticization/colonization of what they consider the most essential sphere of life—the *whakapapa* (genealogy, in Maori)—may create new opportunities for a more expansive definition of environmental justice and for building alliances among many other progressive environmental and social justice movements.

Points of Intersection? The Conference on Human Genetics, Environment, and Communities of Color

At a recent meeting held in New York City and hosted by West Harlem Environmental Action (WE ACT), a prominent New York–based environmental justice organization, hundreds of environmental justice organizers from thirty-four states and Puerto Rico, Native American representatives from several North American tribes, and a group of scientific researchers and government officials convened to explore the significance for communities of color of the ground-breaking developments in genetics research and new genetics technologies. Praised as an "historic event" by many attendees, the "Human Genetics, Environment, and Communities of Color: Ethical and Social Implications" conference and a subsequent symposium, "Human Genetics and Environmental Justice," took place February 4–5, 2002, and represented the first national gathering of environmental justice activists in the United States to focus exclusively on the potential benefits, as well as the social and ethical challenges, raised by new genetics research programs that are devoted to identifying the cause of the "environmental health disparities" found in different racial and ethnic populations. Organized by WE ACT and cosponsored by the National Institute of Environmental Health Sciences (NIEHS), the Mailman School of Public Health at Columbia University, and the Environmental Protection Agency (EPA), the conference aimed to "begin a dialogue among environmental justice advocates regarding their perceptions, concerns, and hopes for the impact of genetic research on environmental health in communities of color" (Sze and Prakash 2004, p. 741).

Environmental Health Genetics and Communities of Color: A Synopsis
The first day of the conference consisted of a series of lectures and panels that explained the technical details of the science of genetics, presented a sampling of the various environmental health genetics research projects underway, and spelled out a set of critical ethical, legal, and

social questions associated with this research. Two major research initiatives launched by the NIH in the late 1990s were introduced to the conference participants by the then director of the NIEHS, Dr. Kenneth Olden. One of these initiatives, the Environmental Genome Project (EGP), was described by Olden as a new and more advanced scientific "tool" that would help us to understand, and ultimately develop cures and treatments for, the environmental illnesses suffered by the "environmental justice populations" in the United States: the primarily low-income, communities of color that exhibit disproportionately higher incidence and mortality rates of environmental illnesses such as cancer, asthma, heart disease, and birth defects.[7]

Geneticists working in the EGP aim to develop a catalogue of all the genetic variations, or "single nucleotide polymorphisms" (SNPs), that exist in human populations and are believed to predispose people to differential susceptibility to environmental illnesses. The specific "susceptibility genes" scientists are targeting are those thought to help mediate between us and the "environmental triggers" to which we may be exposed (including, for example, toxic substances, ultraviolet radiation, and drugs). The genetic catalogue being generated, Olden explained, will create a database of all the possible variations (SNPs) in these "susceptibility genes" that may exist among different groups of people. Researchers in the EGP draw upon the existing "DNA Polymorphism Discovery Resource," created by the National Human Genome Research Institute (NHGRI), which is a set of 450 immortalized cell lines[8] taken from 450 U.S. citizens representing the five racial/ethnic subpopulations in this country—Asian American, African American, Hispanic, Caucasian, and Native American. Olden argues that this path-breaking research will help identify "susceptible subgroups" in the United States and provide more precise information for regulators, such as the Food and Drug Administration and the EPA, to help them develop more scientifically informed disease prevention programs and devise the most cost-effective environmental regulatory policy.[9]

Another NIEHS-sponsored environmental health genetics program introduced to the conference participants was the National Center for Toxicogenomics. The science of toxicogenomics consists of determining at a molecular level exactly how a particular toxic substance damages

DNA. Using new experimental techniques, scientists expose samples of target genes to a carcinogenic chemical such as benzene, for example, to determine exactly how those genes are impaired or altered as a result of exposure. Toxicogenomic research aims to develop computer-assisted genetic assays that may assist the aforementioned federal agencies in developing guidelines to more precisely regulate the exposure rates and concentrations of hazardous substances discharged into the environment (Schmidt 2002).[10]

Genetics Research for Environmental Justice? Women Activists Speak Truth to Power

The underlying message woven through the dazzling array of PowerPoint presentations delivered by government and university researchers at the conference was that, once properly informed of the scientific rationale underlying the studies, the environmental justice activists in the audience would jump on the genetics bandwagon and enthusiastically participate in EGP and toxicogenomic research projects. Even more important, according to Olden, the historically justified yet in recent times unwarranted mistrust of medical researchers by communities of color should not result in activists impeding the research from "mov[ing] forward to completion" (Olden and Wilson 2000, p. 153).

On the second day, the more interactive "Symposium on Human Genetics and Environmental Justice" offered greater opportunities for discussion among the participants, most of whom were women activists from environmental justice organizations from around the country. After having absorbed an enormous quantity of new scientific data, legal information, and bioethics analysis, the participants were prepared to ask questions. For many activists, this conference made clear that it had become necessary to increase their knowledge and scientific expertise on these topics to participate in the debates on genetics research and policy, and many wondered, if the new age of genetics and biotechnology has "already left the station," how can environmental justice activists proactively respond to these new scientific developments?

At the final plenary session of the symposium, several women activists stood up and directed a series of pointed questions to the NIEHS director, who had just delivered his summary remarks exhorting the audience to join in and embrace the "future" of science. One woman worried that, by conducting environmental genetics research on asthma in inner-city kids, her child would be "stigmatized as 'inferior' because he's Black." Another woman inquired, "What are the implications of collecting DNA samples from Native American research subjects and then making genetic inferences about the tribe as a whole?" Irritated at this line of questioning directed at the ethical and biological implications of the research rather than its presumed benefits to humankind, the NIEHS director asserted that the session had deteriorated into an "unproductive conversation" and declared, "I'm a scientist, not a sociologist, I won't talk about race." Nevertheless, a large portion of his audience—women activists newly acquainted in the discourse of genetics—questioned the racialized tenor of the government's research initiatives even if they claimed allegiance to "environmental justice."

In a postconference report, lead organizers Julie Sze and Swati Prakash noted that "the concerns and beliefs expressed at the environmental justice symposium spanned the spectrum from distrust to optimism" (2004, p. 743). Outlining several themes that were presented at the conference (from the re-emergence of a presumed link between race and genetics to the issue of informed consent in government research protocols) and discussing some of the questions, concerns, and recommendations that arose from the more discussion-oriented symposium (including the critique of genetic reductionism, the concern about the rise of a new "eugenics," and the misgivings related to racial/genetic stigmatization and discrimination), the report concluded that, "as this research and its social and policy implications unfold, ongoing dialogue, shared approaches, and a community-driven agenda will be essential for maximizing promised benefits" (p. 744). Keenly aware of the link between the appalling fact that 25 percent of African American and Latino children in upper Manhattan (Harlem and Washington Heights) suffer from asthma, and that 75 percent of the diesel bus depots spewing harmful polycyclic aromatic hydrocarbon–contaminated exhaust[11] are located in these neighborhoods, the environmental justice activists know that "faulty genes" are not the cause of the documented higher rates of environmental illnesses in their communities (Pérez-Peña 2003). While critical about the racist undertones reflected in the EGP's fixation on genetic causes of asthma rather than the obvious environmental ones, some environmental justice activists were willing to continue a conversation about how to increase the possible benefits of genetics research given proper legal protections, transparency in the research process, and genuine community collaboration. In contrast, the group of Native American women sitting in the audience was not so sanguine about the government assurances to protect human subjects or about the underlying assumptions that research on genetic variation was guided by humanitarian and "environmental justice" principles. Activists such as Debra Harry (Northern Paiute) and Brenda LaFrance (Akwesasne Mohawk) stated that nothing at the conference had convinced them that these "new" directions in genetics research, repackaged in the vocabulary of "environmental justice," were anything more that the latest form of biocolonialism.[12]

Biocolonialism and Self-Determination: A New Spelling of Environmental Justice

As affirmed in the Principles of Environmental Justice, the "special relationship" of Indigenous peoples to their territories and to the state (including the state's representatives in government science projects) contributes to a unique understanding and definition of the relationship between environmentalism and social justice. Examining the specificity of the growing collective response by Indigenous activists from around the world to the triumphalist discourse of the "gene age" reveals particular kinds of languages and practices of resistance, as the Native American voices at the New York Conference on Human Genetics and Environmental Justice illustrated.

A significant difference in the language and practices of environmental justice and human rights activism in Indigenous communities living within states is the assertion of their right of self-determination: the recognition of their status as distinct societies with rights of self-governance and control of land and resources that derive, in turn, from their status as original peoples. The central aim of the global movement of Indigenous activists fighting against the onslaught of genetic researchers into their communities is to resist the neocolonial state apparati (in this case represented by government-funded genetic studies) from gaining further access to and exploitation of their bodies, their territories, and their traditional knowledge. As Debra Harry and Le'a Malia Kanehe explain,

Indigenous peoples' struggle for self-determination is occurring on many fronts, globally, nationally, and locally. The corporate hunt for genetic resources within our territories raises new difficulties for those maintaining permanent sovereignty over natural resources that have long been sought after by colonial governments. Intellectual property rights are being used to turn nature and life processes into private property. Once deemed private property, genetic material becomes alienable; that is, it can be bought and sold as a commodity. This, in the eyes of many Indigenous peoples, is an attempt to legalize thievery, a thievery that we recognize as "biocolonialism"—the extension of colonization to the biological resources and knowledge of Indigenous peoples. (2005, p. 15)

The contention that modern science has been deployed as one of the forces of colonialism and the need to resist its continuing offensive into Indigenous peoples' lives reflects a somewhat different stance on the role of science than that taken by many environmental justice communities in the United States. Certainly, African American and Latino environmental justice activists express well-founded misgivings about biomedical research that highlights racialized bodies or that is preoccupied with the concept of genetic variation. This wariness (sometimes characterized by the medical community as "science-phobia") is situated in the context of two notorious historical episodes: the late nineteenth- and early twentieth-century eugenics movement, which, in the name of scientific objectivity and social improvement, aimed to breed out racially and biologically "inferior" segments of the population through sterilization programs and antimiscegenation laws, and the now-infamous Tuskegee syphilis experiment conducted between 1932 and 1972 by the U.S. Public Health Service on unsuspecting, poor, African American men suffering the agonizing symptoms of late-stage syphilis. Used as the quintessential human "guinea pigs," the men were not informed of the experiment by government scientists or given medical attention, all in the interest of tracing the etiology of the disease in the human body to develop better treatments and cures.[13]

In recognition of this checkered history of government-supported scientific research, the NIH has devoted 5 percent of the budget of NHGRI to a program known as ELSI (Ethical, Legal, and Social Implications), whose mandate is to conduct studies to ensure that the rights of human subjects are protected and that informed consent is obtained in all human genetic research. Mindful of the history of racist medical experimentation by government scientists, the ELSI program was established to provide a "new approach to scientific research" that can anticipate potential legal, ethical, and social problems before they actually occur "at the same time that the basic scientific issues are being studied."[14] Although many members of environmental justice communities maintain a critical eye toward the field of genetics, they adopt a stance of "cautious optimism" in the hopes that the NIEHS's rhetoric of melding environmental health genetics with the principles of environmental justice may at long last produce actual beneficial results for those populations who in the past have been either ignored or exploited in medical research studies. Citing the Principles of Environmental Justice, many environmental justice organizations insist that the government agree to "strict enforcement of the principles of informed consent" and invite historically marginalized communities "to participate as equal partners at every level of decision-making" (Sze and Prakash 2004, p. 741). For most Native American communities, the condition of "participating as equal partners" in the research process cannot be met until the U.S. government recognizes their right of self-determination and protects their cultures and territories as distinct and sovereign. In contrast, citing different histories of dispossession and environmental racism, environmental justice activists see themselves as rightful, though marginalized, citizens making demands on the democratic state to fulfill its duty to protect all citizens equally by regulating industrial pollution, mandating corporate accountability, and, most important, assuring that low-income communities of color partake of the benefits that may spring from the latest scientific advances.

Although Indigenous communities also call for equality of access within national states to entitlements such as education, health care, and economic opportunities, the overriding goal to protect their right of self-determination dictates a different relationship to the state, the scientific enterprise, and claims for environmental justice. For the vast majority of Indigenous activists, the EGP and many other modern genetic research projects reflect the emergence of just the newest version of or extension of colonialism—again, what many activists term biocolonialism.

Biocolonialism refers to the process through which scientists representing governments, universities, or research institutes travel the globe functioning as "bioprospectors" to collect samples of genetic materials from
humans, animals, or plants that are deemed to have commercial value for
pharmaceutical, agricultural, or industrial purposes. Furthermore, as
Maori attorney Moana Jackson explains, biocolonialism must be understood as situated within a much longer history of dispossession and
attempts at cultural annihilation:

> I see genetic modification and the whole GE (genetic engineering) debate as sim-
> ply the latest debate in the long process of dispossession and colonization. It's a
> new technology that's being built upon a whole lot of other technologies and atti-
> tudes that impact Maori and other Indigenous peoples. If we go back to the first
> colonization of this country, it was about the tearing down of our forests and the
> rape of the land to introduce the technology of sheep farming. Then it was the
> polluting or damming of the rivers to introduce the technology of hydropower.
> And now it's polluting our spiritual base to introduce genetic modification, so it's
> not new. It's part of a continuum and in each case our people have essentially
> been deemed irrelevant to the process. The only substantive difference now is
> that whereas the other instances were largely driven by the colonizing govern-
> ment, genetic modification is driven by multi-national corporations.[15]

As documented in the *Akwé: Kon* guidelines drafted by the United
Nations Convention on Biological Diversity (CBD), much of the genetic
diversity on the planet is located in Indigenous territories. Therefore, the
newest army of "genetic prospectors" most often target these ancestral
environments looking for Native peoples' traditional knowledge about
biodiversity, agriculture, forestry, fisheries, animal and plant ecology,
medicines, and natural resources.[16] Echoing Jackson, Harry argues that
the "newness" of this era of biocolonialism lies not in the practice of
"gene hunting" itself, for the pursuit of and profiteering from new biological materials taken from food crops, seed stocks, and animal breed-
ing systems have always been a core objective of colonialism (Juma
1989). The new phase of biocolonialism is unique in its marshalling of the
legal mechanisms afforded by developments in intellectual property rights
law, in which it has become possible to obtain patents on genetic materials or on traditional knowledge about these materials (Posey 2000; Riley
2004; Harry 2005). For Harry and many other Indigenous activists,
therefore, the definition of "environmental justice" must take into
account the history of Western property rights, the idea of individual

land ownership, and the concept of the alienability and commodification of land, resources, and genetic materials. These are cultural assumptions that run contrary to the truths held to be self-evident by many Indigenous peoples that all components of the earth—humans, animals, plants, air, water, land—are interrelated, and all bodily materials—hair, blood, skin, genes, and the bodily remains of one's ancestors—are sacred elements that cannot be given away, bought, or sold (Mead 1996; Smith 1999). By granting "intellectual property rights" in the form of a seventeen-to-twenty–year patent to individual scientists or corporations on biological entities such as bacteria, plants, or human DNA sequences and claiming they are a scientist's "invention," the U.S. Patent Office transforms life forms into commodities, making them alienable, and thus available for incorporation into the market (Harry and Kanche 2005). Expressing the central tenet of human-environment interdependence underlying the view of environmental justice held by most Indigenous peoples, Harry asks, "Is the human body a commodity? Is the medicine that we depend on a commodity? Is the food that we need for future sustainability a commodity?"[17]

Long identified by many Indigenous peoples as a growing threat to their cultural integrity, human rights, and self-determination, the dangers of the patenting phase of the new biocolonialism were acknowledged in "Environmental Justice Principles of Working Together" (Appendix C), drafted at Summit II in October 2002, which included the following among its guidelines, "The Principles of Working Together recognize traditional knowledge and uphold the intellectual property rights of all peoples of color and Indigenous Peoples." As the vision of environmental justice expands, specifically addressing the unique perspectives on self-determination put forth by Indigenous peoples, so will the opportunities for "working together" among diverse communities and within social movements fighting for environmental justice.

Beyond Resistance: Postcoloniality and Environmental Justice

At the Conference on Human Genetics and Environmental Justice, one of the strongest voices challenging what she considered the "faulty reasoning" behind the geneticization of environmental health in the name of "equality of access and participation of communities of color" was that of Harry, the executive director of the Indigenous Peoples Council on Biocolonialism (IPCB). In the final sections of this chapter, I focus on the work of Harry and the IPCB in the context of the global movement of Indigenous peoples against biocolonialism and in support of a postbiocolonial movement for living sustainably and respectfully on the earth. I argue that the important lessons embedded in Indigenous activists' critiques of the new trends in genetics and biotechnology derive from particular historically and ecologically grounded cultural perspectives and experiences, not from either a naturalized conception of Native peoples as mystically closer to the earth, nor from a narrow-minded, antimodern or antiscience positionality. Furthermore, I suggest that these lessons are political and scientific/ecological analyses that remain "unheard," or at least underused, not only in the mainstream environmental movement, but also in some branches of the U.S. environmental justice movement. To construct a postcolonial "science of environmental justice," the knowledges and practices developed by many Indigenous communities must be taken seriously and not dismissed as relics of the primitive past or caricatured as stemming from an inherent, intuitive ecological consciousness.

The New "Biowarriors": Protecting "Our Life, Lineage, and Sustenance"

Recognizing that she would not have walked a life path absorbed in the science and policy of genetics and biotechnology had the path not "chosen her," Harry laments the lost opportunities for cultural growth and development that more than 500 years of colonialism has wrought:

Our early ancestors made significant contributions to astronomy, arts, architecture, agriculture, mathematics, ecology, social science, political science, and genetics. . . . How far we would have gone in these areas is unknown because our recent ancestors put them aside as they were forced to contend with colonization.[18]

Putting aside other interests and personal goals to challenge the ongoing legacy of colonialism in Indigenous peoples lives, Harry's political activity ranges from a focus on "nuclear colonialism"—opposing plans to develop a uranium mining industry in Nevada—to her current focus on "biocolonialism" (Muldowney 2001). In the mid-1990s, Harry teamed with the late Dr. Frank Dukepoo, the respected Hopi geneticist, who was one of the early Native American scientific voices questioning the potential dangers to Indigenous peoples of some of the new directions in genetics research. As one of only two American Indian research geneticists at the time, Dukepoo made the decision in the early 1990s, after a thirty-year academic career studying the genetic basis of albinism in the Hopi people, to "put a moratorium on his own research . . . mapping genes and constructing pedigrees" and direct his energies toward educating and advocating for the rights of Native Americans in scientific research.[19]

Pursuing her growing concerns about the impact of genetic colonialism on the lives of Indigenous peoples, in 1999 Harry founded the IPCB and invited Dukepoo to serve on the board of directors. The IPCB adopts an internationalist perspective identifying genetic variation research on "distinct, isolated populations" and genetic prospecting for commercially valuable biological materials and ecological knowledge as a global threat to the self-determination of all Indigenous peoples, but also to the nonindigenous world and to the earth itself. Harry maintains a demanding schedule of presentations, lectures, and expert testimonials and sits on the board of several transnational Indigenous organizations, such as the Call of the Earth and Je Atawha ote Ao: Independent Maori Institute for Environment and Health, and numerous genetics watchdog organizations, including the Council for Responsible Genetics.[20] The IPCB produces educational materials translated into other Native languages (Harry, Howard, and Shelton 2000, 2001) and offers technical support to Indigenous tribes advising them on how to protect their rights by devising culturally appropriate legal frameworks to regulate the research process if tribal members decide to participate in genetics research studies like, for example, the NIH's EGP. One protective measure encourages tribes to enact legal codes that regulate research within tribal jurisdictions. The IPCB developed a model code called the Indigenous Research Protection Act (IRPA). Such a code encourages the development of a community-generated institutional review board (IRB) that clearly lays out guidelines concerning informed consent, use and disposal of bodily materials, individual versus tribal rights, and benefits sharing arrangements regarding any products generated from the research. While the research review laws devised by the Mohawk, Navaho, Hopi, and

Cherokee are some of the best-established community IRBs, Harry cautions that other ethical codes of conduct of guidelines not backed by law are insufficient. She continues,

> The unmet need for tribes who want to interface with genetics research is for enforceable, legal frameworks that regulate this research. What we're missing are *enforceable* policies; we only have *ethical* standards, and that's not enough. We encourage tribal communities who have legal jurisdiction to establish regulatory frameworks for research, such as the IRPA, as an act of *sovereignty* using the human rights frameworks they already possess.[21]

The IPCB also represents Indigenous peoples' concerns about genetics research at international forums including the United Nations Permanent Forum on Indigenous Issues and the United Nations Convention on Biological Diversity (CBD). At the CBD's Seventh Conference of the Parties (COP–7) meeting held in Kuala Lumpur in February 2004, Harry joined with other regional and transnational Indigenous organizations to urge Indigenous communities from around the world to declare their territories "access-free zones for genetic resources" (Harry 2004). This was in response to the COP–7 decision to mandate an "ad hoc open-ended working group on access and benefit-sharing to negotiate the international regime on access and benefit-sharing" that would deliver its recommendations to the next meeting of the CBD, to be held in Brazil in 2006.[22] Because "potentially large sums of money are at stake," the CBD argues that,

> By granting an international company or other organization access to its genetic resources (such as plants that can be used to produce new pharmaceuticals or fragrances), a country or local community will in return receive a fair share of the profits or other benefits.[23]

At the COP-7 Indigenous peoples insisted that in the elaboration and negotiation of the international regime all parties *shall* recognize the rights of Indigenous peoples, with no qualifications. But, the COP-7 decision merely states that, "the international regime *should recognize* and *shall respect* the rights of indigenous and local communities." Without any assurance that the rights of Indigenous peoples would be recognized within the international regime, Harry and other Indigenous representatives at the meeting argued that this decision will neither prevent the impending "biopiracy free-for-all" nor protect Indigenous peoples' most basic rights of self-determination in terms of free access to and control over the "resources and traditional knowledge handed down from the ancestors and necessary for our survival" (Harry 2004). Pointing out that Article 15 in the official CBD text declares that only states have sovereign rights over their natural resources and that "the authority to determine access to genetic resources rests with the *national governments* and is subject to national legislation" (CBD-Article 15; emphasis added), Indigenous representatives object that "our voices and presence are completely disregarded" (Harry 2004). Because Indigenous nations are not recognized as nation-states within UN forums, having only in 2000 won a victory with the establishment of a "permanent forum" on Indigenous issues at the UN, their human rights of self-determination are given scant attention, which suggests that for Indigenous peoples the "post" in postcolonialism has not yet materialized (Niezen 2003).

Rethinking Environmental Justice in the Age of Genetics

Mirroring the opening preamble to the Principles of Environmental Justice, which refers to "our interdependence with the sacredness of Mother Earth," in his keynote address to the CBD meeting in Kuala Lumpur, the Canadian geneticist and environmental advocate David Suzuki reflected on the time-tested ecological knowledge developed by many Indigenous cultures that long predates the advent of the modern environmental sciences:

I believe that we need to go back, to look back and rediscover ancient truths. Aboriginal people around the world refer to the Earth as our mother. They say that we are created by the four sacred elements earth, air, fire and water. This is not meant to be a poetic or metaphoric way of speaking; they literally mean that we are created by the Earth. And as I reflected on that, as a scientist, I've come to realize how profound that insight is, and how it is completely corroborated by the best science that we have. We are created by these basic elements of the earth. . . . We need a fundamental shift in the way we live on this planet. We need to recognize our complete dependence on nature.[24]

Despite Suzuki's referencing aboriginal ecological insights as essential to the survival of the human species, most Indigenous representatives did not believe that their knowledge of biodiversity and sustainable development was embodied in the conference's advocating the creation of "free-trade zones" for the commercialization of genetic resources.

Fearing that the language of "benefits sharing" and "open access" promoted by the CBD signified not the democratization of ecological knowledge but the expansion of biocolonialism, Harry and fourteen endorsing Indigenous organizations issued a press release from Kuala Lumpur, announcing, "Sadly, all we can do is call upon Indigenous peoples to prepare themselves. The biopiracy regime is coming. They must do whatever is necessary to protect their resources and knowledge at the local level. Their most basic rights of self-determination are not going to be recognized at this level" (Harry 2004).

At the national level, Harry participates in numerous conferences and symposia. Among these was a panel discussion at Summit II, where she discussed the IPCB's efforts to inform Indigenous communities about the dangers of the new trends in genetics technologies and identified commonalities between her organization's goals and those of the environmental justice movement's. Like the women environmental justice activists who question the genetic reductionism inherent in the NIEHS-sponsored research projects that focus on defective genes rather than on air pollution to explain high rates of childhood asthma in Harlem, Harry argues that the "genomania" that has overtaken the world of biomedicine has succeeded in diverting attention away from finding solutions to what she argues are preventable problems:

I think a lot of Indigenous people tend to be skeptics; generally we know what's killing us and it's not our genetic makeup. It's living in contaminated environments. It's living in societies that continue to oppress us, that take our land, that take everything that we need to survive. We're living under conditions of economic oppression. We have elders who still freeze in their homes in the wintertime because they can't afford heat. We have children who die from preventable diseases because they have no access to commonly available healthcare that exists in other parts of society. So, we're not looking at genetics as the solution; we don't expect to find the cures in a bottle.[25]

Although participants at Summit II shared her criticisms, Harry felt that many environmental justice activists believed that with proper ELSI protocols in place and if more people of color entered the field of genetics and conducted the research themselves, positive outcomes for environmental justice communities would result. Hopeful that the mutual concerns of environmental justice activists and Indigenous organizations can lead to productive partnerships, Harry concludes that at present the issues of genetics research, biotechnology, and the patenting of genetic materials stand out as issues that resonate more intensely as threats for Indigenous peoples worldwide. This difference between the two movements, she believes, in part turns on their different relationships to the state. Many Native Americans, for example, see themselves as inhabiting complex identities and living within a "multidimensional cultural world that is postcolonial as well as characterized by internal colonialism, nuclear colonialism," and now genetic colonialism (Kuletz 2004, p. 300). As Kuletz has argued, "whether acknowledged or unacknowledged by the U.S. government, Indian communities . . . construct and conduct themselves as nations *independent* of the United States" (p. 300). For many Native Americans, therefore, conducting genetic research on racially or tribally coded populations as though they are biologically distinctive becomes not just a questionable act of genetic reductionism, but also an assault on Indigenous peoples' rights of self-determination. Citing evolutionary biologists' contention that human evolution reflects a long history of population admixture, Harry stresses that "a tribe is a social and cultural construct, not a biological one."[26] The sovereign status of tribes in the United States has been recognized in numerous treaties, legislation, and court decisions defining the complex nation-to-nation relationship of Native nations to the U.S. government. But, attempts to erode the sovereignty of Native nations are a regular occurrence. Today many Native American communities continue their battle for tribal recognition in the face of the U.S. government's ongoing policies of state-imposed blood quantum calculations and termination (Churchill 2002; Lyden and Legters 1992). The struggles for tribal sovereignty, self-determination, and land rights, therefore, raise particular concerns for Native Americans, as compared with other marginalized groups in the United States, explaining, in part, their hesitation to enthusiastically endorse government-funded genetics research aimed at "improving" their lives.

Moreover, many Indigenous activists argue that the geneticist's hubris of claiming to have unveiled "the language in which God created life"[27] confronts the right of self-determination—the construction of the "self"—at the most fundamental level. Rather than describing genetic material as usable "samples" or the human genome as a set of 20,000 discrete and isolatable entities, many Native epistemologies understand genetics as genealogy: the story of where we come from, our connections and interrelationships with our communities and with our environments, and the historical narrative of our relationships to our past, present and future. These are contrasting stories of what counts as "self-determination"—opposing views that produce profound cultural discord for many Indigenous communities and, at the same time, produce unique and valuable perspectives on the role of science in determining who we are and how we should organize our societies.[28]

"Knowledge and Wisdom are not the Same":[29] Defining the "Science" of Environmental Justice

The role and status of modern science and technology and the conduct of the scientific research process are issues that Indigenous scholars and activists address in depth, especially the extent to which Indigenous and Western technosciences can be integrated (Smith 1999; Arquette et. al. 2002). Although Harry and the IPCB identify particular technoscientific inventions—for example, genetic engineering, the Human Genome Diversity Project, and the Environmental Genome Project—as potentially harmful to humans and the earth and as contrary to Native peoples' philosophy of interdependence and the inalienability of all natural elements, they deem other modern technologies beneficial and "appropriate" for cultural development and especially for political empowerment (Kuletz 2004). Many Indigenous organizations are making use of new media and communication and information technologies to build international networks and document their "presence," their activism, and their agency in contemporary politics.

With the goal of enabling Indigenous peoples "to voice their critiques and their hopes and dreams for their own communities in relation to the new threat of genetic research and its negative impacts on our world,"[30] Harry collaborated with the London-based Independent Film company, Yeast Directions, and filmmakers Max Pugh and Marc Silver to produce *The Leech and the Earthworm*. Released in 2003, the film deploys the modern technological inventions of digital video and computer graphics to provide counter-arguments to what Indigenous peoples from different nations consider to be the dangers of genetic engineering and corporate-driven biotechnology to the future of humanity and the earth itself. The film is a fast-paced hybrid of sophisticated computer graphics, animation, techno soundtracks, archival anthropological documentary footage, and interviews with Indigenous activists from the United States, Canada, Aoteorea/New Zealand, Vanuatu, the Philippines, South Africa, and Columbia. Enacting the "multidimensional" positionality of Indigenous identity and experience, *The Leech and the Earthworm* embraces the instruments and aesthetics of modern visual technologies while calling for a moratorium on the destructive elements of modernity and a revival of lost or eroding Native epistemologies and lifeways.

The film opens with a shot of Chief Viraleo Boborenvanua, the leader of the Turaga Nation from Pentecost Island, Vanuatu, being interviewed on his island nation recounting the Turaga version of the history of colonialism, a cautionary tale portrayed as the ill-fated relationship between a deceitful leech and an unsuspecting earthworm. This opening scene then fades into a vibrant, animated depiction of the chief's story providing the primary narrative and the central metaphor of the film: you can't put old wine (colonialism) into new bottles (corporate-driven biotechnology) and expect people to fall for it again. In Chief Viraleo's words,

This story has existed for centuries. We learnt it from our ancestors. A leech and an earthworm were talking beneath the ground. The leech knew that the earthworm couldn't go to the surface when the sun was very hot. So, the leech told the earthworm, "It's raining on the surface, don't worry, it's raining. You don't need to worry, I'll take care of everything." So, when the earthworm got to the surface, there he found a big, hot sun. And he died. This is how the white man treated us at the beginning. They came and told us, "Life will be better if you come with us. Follow us, life will be better. And we'll take care of everything."

An unconventional documentary, *The Leech and the Earthworm* allows the voices of the Indigenous activists interviewed on film to construct the analysis that like the earlier forms of colonialism, the new corporate-driven biocolonialism continues its historic patterns of deception promising salvation, modern improvements for a better quality of life, and the assurance that "you don't have to worry, we'll take care of everything." But, as the film shows, while the promises of miracle cures for painful diseases are rampant in the justifications for collecting blood samples of "vanishing" Indigenous tribes, rarely do tribes experience any follow-up after having donated their blood. Most often, after having overstated the truth about the likelihood of genetic research being able to offer relief from debilitating diseases, the "forked-tongued" scientist fades into the sunset. In a particularly vivid segment of the film, members of the Nuu-chah-nulth people from British Columbia explain how in 1985 they were visited by Dr. Richard Ward, now deceased and who then served as the head of the Institute of Biological Anthropology at Oxford University, who took blood samples from over 833 tribal members, all of whom had given written permission to use their DNA for research on treatments for rheumatoid arthritis, a condition suffered by approximately two-thirds of the community.[31] Regrettably, as several tribal members testify, the researcher never returned to the community or presented the people with any results. Even worse, explained Nuu-chah-nulth tribal elder, Larry Baird, the community learned that their DNA samples were now being used for research unrelated to arthritis biomarker screening, a violation of the consent agreement previously approved by tribal members. With obvious sadness in his voice, Baird says, "There's no respect, honor, or dignity... They're eager to take our blood, but they're not eager to come back and tell us what happened... even to give us a blank piece of paper and say 'sorry, no conclusion.' Do they think we're so unsophisticated that we can't understand what's written?"

One of the fundamental arguments presented in *The Leech and the Earthworm* is that there is little evidence that the biotechnological vision of progress and "improvement" of human health or the "protection" of the environment has anything to offer except for greater control over Indigenous peoples' lives, traditional knowledge, and resources and greater profits for pharmaceutical and biotechnology corporations. As Maori elder Mahinekura Reinfelds states in the film, "[A]s far as I can tell, genetic engineering is not done for the good of the people but for the good of capitalism." Biotechnology, therefore, reveals itself to these Indigenous activists as the scientific patron supporting the new wave of biocolonialism. This critical perspective on genetics research presented in the film conveys not a naïve reaction to modern science, but an informed position based on many years of experience battling colonial invasions and attempts at cultural annihilation. Not only do many of the new genetics research studies clearly promote biocolonialism, they also run counter to the epistemological tenets of many Indigenous cultures that understand the discipline of genetics as the study of "genealogical inter-connections" or what the Maori call *whakapapa*. Translated as the "ability to see layer upon layer," *whakapapa* is the word most commonly used by Maoris to conceptualize genes and DNA (Mead 1996, p. 51). In the film, legal scholar Angeline Ngahina Greensill explains

Our whole world view is based on *whakapapa*; it's based on relationships that are genealogically tied to the beginning of time. We believe in a genealogical con-nection to everything—to the land, to the trees, to the sea, to other people; we need each other to survive. Our past, our present, and our future are connected, it's a cycle. In fact, if we genetically modify organisms, we change the past, pres-ent, and future.

Grounded in the concept of *whakapapa*, the concern for future gener-ations becomes central to Indigenous scientific worldviews and explains their critique of the disingenuous appeals to "progress" that are fre-quently invoked to promote the advance of corporate-controlled genetic engineering. In a scene that invariably makes nonindigenous audiences wince, Chief Viraleo recounts his trip to the United Nations in New York City and makes clear that he was exceedingly unimpressed with the out-comes of "progress" that he witnessed while visiting the wealthiest coun-try in the world.

If the United Nations is talking about life for the people of this planet, and for all the different countries of the world, what they're talking about is not repre-sented in what I saw in New York City. Right outside the United Nations I saw people who didn't have homes, who didn't have food; they were living on the streets. There were big buildings, but they housed offices, cars, lots of papers, and hotels. But what is the purpose of housing books, papers, cars, and tourists, if we cannot even look after our own people? The western education system, which is what the world development model is built on, can talk about "progress," but as I see it, it is only for a few people, and it's not done for the peaceful coexistence of everybody as a community, so that they can all live together and *progress* together.

Rejecting this colonial view of "progress," where some gain and most lose out, and the damage it has wrought on his own community, Chief Viraleo then describes his nation's revitalization of its own agricultural, medicinal, economic, trade, and educational systems. With the reintro-duction of a locally produced diet—crab, fish, taro root, bananas, papayas, wild pig—rather than imported, packaged foods (or cures derived from genetically altered sheep), the community has "drastically reduced its rates of diabetes and other health problems." Examples such as this, says Harry, demonstrate that Indigenous social and environmental management systems may be "the living alternative" to corporate globalization. Moreover, by providing tangible evidence of the continued existence of sustainable community development models in many Indigenous societies, the film "counters the myth of the 'vanishing' native, which has been fueling much of the rush to collect DNA from Indigenous populations."[32]

In a graphic interpretation of Chief Oren Lyon's 1992 speech to the United Nations General Assembly calling upon all nations to abide by the fifteenth-century risk-assessment philosophy developed by the Haudenausaunee confederation that a society's decisions must be made "on behalf of the seventh generation to come," the film shifts the spotlight from a critique of biocolonialism to an invitation for all nations to benefit from the reliable knowledge systems developed through experimentation over millennia by Indigenous peoples. With the translucent blue waters of the Northern Paiute Reservation's Pyramid Lake as a backdrop, Harry wistfully observes, "I'm optimistic about the Indigenous future, but I'm concerned about what's going to happen in broader society." The broader society has "lost its way," laments Chief Viraleo, and has "abandoned the knowledge necessary to care for all its people," yet if it will listen, it could learn from the centuries-old wisdom of the Indigenous communities from around the world.

In the film's eye-catching finale, a split-screen montage brings home the message that, while still forced to expend precious time and resources in resisting the biocolonial onslaught, Indigenous peoples are rebuilding their languages, governments, and knowledge systems for sustaining life, for coexisting with the environment, and for the benefit of future generations. Ending with Chief Viraleo's assertion that "we need to share our knowledge with the west because otherwise the future does not exist," the Indigenous voices in the film are reminiscent of an earlier plea by Marcos Terena, a member of the Pantanal Terena people of Brazil and the sole representative from the Indigenous world invited to speak at the United Nations Conference on Environment and Development (UNCED) in Rio de Janeiro in 1992. Allotted only five minutes to speak to the assembly,

Terena made his case that the only proven path for protecting and enhancing all life on earth, including that of the nonindigenous world, will be the advancement and further development of Indigenous people's wisdom about the interconnectedness of humans and their environments. In his brief appearance at the podium, he proffered,

This temple of centuries-old wisdom, this life code that no scientist has ever managed to unveil rests with the Indians. . . . You don't have to look any further or research any further and spend millions of dollars on new research. We the Indians would like to offer you our science, our wisdom for your civilization. . . . Is the contemporary world prepared to listen to what we want to convey after 500 years of silence?"[33]

Resisting Biocolonialism, Seeking a Postcolonial Science for the People

Having endured more than 500 years of colonization, Indigenous communities worldwide are concerned about the arrival of yet another weapon in the arsenal of colonialism, this time the goal being to possess "the secret of life," thus striving to control the definition of what it means to be human and our understanding of "life itself." The Indigenous activists appearing in *The Leech and Earthworm* question whether new biotechnological innovations such as the Human Genome Project or the EGP do in fact provide us with the "wisdom" to sustain a healthy, peaceful, biodiverse, and socially just planet. Has the abundance of knowledge amassed in the "gene age" equipped us with the epistemic tools to advance the goals of environmental justice? Ending on a hopeful note, the film suggests that Western environmentalism's oft-stated goal of "sustainability" could be achieved by thinking and acting as though humans are interdependent with, not isolated from, their environment, a cornerstone of most Indigenous epistemologies (LaDuke 1999; Goldtooth 1995; Hunter 2004).

The Native American poet John Trudell offers an interpretation of the meaning of DNA that expands on its more common molecular or chemical descriptions and expresses this idea of interdependence. He writes,

DNA: Descendants Now Ancestors. . . . We are the descendants and we are the ancestors. D and A, our DNA, our blood, our flesh and our bone, is made up of the metals and the minerals and the liquids of the earth. We are the earth. We truly, literally and figuratively are the earth.[34]

Deploying a different vocabulary of genetics, Trudell speaks of DNA (Descendants Now Ancestors) in the terms of relationship, genealogy, and materiality. For many Native peoples, the "secret of life" does in fact lie in our DNA, but it is not a truth about nature that was discovered by the U.S. government or Celera Genomics. Understanding DNA in this sense is to see our "selves" simultaneously as descendants and ancestors, living on the earth as though we are a part of it and as though we are already ancestors who have left a legacy that we can be proud of; these are the "secrets" of DNA that when integrated with the chemical and molecular ones, may have a better chance of ensuring life—and the future—itself.

Expounding on their "holistic" approach to environmental problem solving, Akwesasne Mohawk activists Brenda LaFrance and Katsi Cook participated in the Human Genetics and Environmental Justice conference, offering an alternative to the genetics-as-root-cause model for improving the environmental health of communities of color (Arquette et al. 2002). The First Environment Restoration Initiative challenges the NIEHS's "susceptibility gene" theory of illness as well as the EPA's standard models of risk assessment, and instead defines environmental health as the integration of spiritual, cultural, ecological, political, and physiological—including genetic—components. Although critical of the genetic reductionism inherent in the NIH's research initiatives, LaFrance and Cook understand the importance of blending diverse environmental knowledges. Perhaps in such a hybridization of different knowledge systems—environmental health genetics and genealogy or *whakapapa*—lies the hope for a genuine, postcolonial "science of environmental justice." But, to return to this chapter's earlier questions: On whose terms? Whose environmental sciences are enlisted? And, "Is the contemporary world prepared to listen?"

Notes

1. Debra Harry et al. (2000, p. 5).

2. For example, the environmental justice organizations West Harlem Environmental Action (www.weact.org), the Louisiana Bucket Brigade (www.labucketbrigade.org), Communities for a Better Environment (www.cbecal.org), and the Center for Health, Environment, and Justice (www.chej.org), among others, mobilize scientific resources in their organizing strategies while retaining a critical perspective.

3. The Human Genome Diversity Project was first proposed in 1991 by a group of U.S. geneticists and evolutionary biologists as a nongovernmental, international collaborative effort to sample and archive human genetic diversity, especially the "diversity" inherent in the extant Indigenous populations of the world. Led by Stanford University geneticist Luca Cavalli-Sforza, the group hoped to preserve the genetic material of "isolated indigenous populations" (later referred to as "isolates of historic interest") before they "disappear as independent units, because of disease, economic or physical deprivation, genetic admixture, or cultural assimilation . . . so that their role in human history can be preserved" (quoted in Guerrero 2003, p. 178). Despite its lofty goals of "better understanding our species" and "obtaining information of potential or actual medical interest . . . directed to the health and welfare not only of the individuals or groups sampled, but also of the rest of the world" (Serjeantson 1994, p. 85), and despite the provision of hefty start-up funds by the National Science Foundation, the National Human Genome Research Center, and the Department of Energy to support a series of international meetings, by 1993 the initiative had accumulated a considerable amount of criticism, perhaps most poetically voiced by the World Council on Indigenous Peoples, which labeled the project "the Vampire Project." For analyses of the Human Genome Diversity Project, and its descent into relative obscurity, see Reardon (2001), Cunningham (1998), and Guerrero (2003).

4. See the United Nations Convention on Biodiversity (CBD), "Article 8(j): Traditional Knowledge, Innovations and Practices." Available online at www.biodiv.org/programmes/socio-eco/traditional/default.asp.

5. This phrase was coined by Evelyn Fox Keller (2000).

6. Kenneth Olden, "The Role of Gene-Environment Interaction in Health Disparities." Presentation at the Conference on Human Genetics, Environment, and Communities of Color, Columbia University, New York, February 4, 2002.

7. See the NIEHS website for descriptions of its new genetics research initiatives, available online at http://www.niehs.nih.gov/envgenom/home.htm. Also see the National Human Genome Research Institute (NHGRI) website for descriptions of other genetic research advances it promotes, including the International Hap Map Project and Cancer Genome Atlas, available at www.genome.gov/10001688. For a more in-depth discussion and analysis of the EGP, see Di Chiro (2004c).

8. These are cell samples, usually taken from blood, that have been subjected to a series of chemical, bacterial, or genetic manipulations that promote continual replication, thereby providing the researcher a steady supply of the particular cell line.

9. National Institutes of Health News Advisory (October 10, 1997). Also see Olden and Wilson (2000).

10. Also see the National Center for Toxicogenomics website, available online at http://www.niehs.nih.gov/nct/home.htm

11. The volatile organic compounds polycyclic aromatic hydrocarbons, which include the known carcinogens benzene and benzo (a) pyrene, are particularly

hazardous components of diesel exhaust. Comprising a proportion of the harmful air particulates to which children in Harlem and Washington Heights are exposed, these substances contribute to the high rates of respiratory problems in these New York City communities.

12. Author's interview with Debra Harry, February 5, 2002.

13. For excellent accounts and analyses of these episodes in the history of scientific racism, see Roberts (1997), Paul (1995), Kevles (1985), and Jones (1981).

14. National Human Genome Research Institute website, www.nhgri.nih.gov/ELSI/aboutels.html. For more information about ELSI and the EGP, see Sharp and Barrett (2000).

15. Moana Jackson, interviewed in *The Leech and the Earthworm,* film produced by Debra Harry, filmmakers Max Pugh and Marc Silver, Yeast Directions, London, (2003).

16. *Akwé: Kon Guidelines,* Secretariat of the Convention on Biological Diversity, Montreal, Canada, 2004, available online at www.biodiv.org/doc/publications/akwe-brochure-en.pdf.

17. Arthur Miller Lecture on Science and Ethics presented at MIT, Cambridge, Mass., October 24, 2002.

18. Harry et al. (2000, p. 5).

19. See "Sensitivities and Concerns of Research in Native American Communities," Panel Discussion at the National Bioethics Advisory Commission Meetings, Portland, Oregon, July 14–15, 1998. Available online at www.georgetown.edu/research/nrcbl/nbac/transcripts/.

20. For more information on these organizations, see Call of the Earth (www.earthcall.org/en/index.html) and Council for Responsible Genetics (www.genewatch.org/).

21. Author's interview with Debra Harry, July 17, 2003.

22. Convention on Biological Diversity, http://www.biodiv.org/programmes/socio-eco/benefit/?print=1.

23. Michael Williams, CBD press release, February 20, 2004. Available online at www.biodiv.org/meetings/cop-07/press/.

24. David Suzuki, "The Challenge of the Twenty First-Century: Setting the Real Bottom Line," Keynote address, UN CBD COP-7, Kuala Lumpur, Malaysia, February 7, 2004. Available online at www.biodiv.org/doc/speech/2004/sp-2004-02-07-cop-en.pdf.

25. Debra Harry, MIT lecture, 2002.

26. Author's interview with Debra Harry, July 17, 2003.

27. Statement by President Bill Clinton at the press conference announcing the successful sequencing of the human genome through a collaboration between the NIH and Celera Genomics, Washington D.C., June 26, 2000. Available online at www.genome.gov/10001356.

28. Debra Harry recounts the story, for example, of archaeologists at the University of California and the Nevada State Museum, who are interested in studying the DNA of "Spirit Cave Man" (which is the human skeletal remains of a man dated at approximately 11,000 years old found in 1940 in Shoshone and Paiute territory in western Nevada). One archaeologist has already hypothesized that genetic testing will conclude that this ancient inhabitant of the region that is now Nevada is not related to the current day Paiutes or Shoshones who claim him as their ancestor and who demand that he should be repatriated and properly buried. The Fallon Paiute-Shoshone Tribe has taken the lead in the repatriaton of the "Spirit Cave Man" and is supported by all Nevada tribal governments. The tribes are concerned that the use of genetic markers to refute the genealogical continuity of ancient remains with current populations could be used to deny or overturn Native American land rights claims, which are based on long-term inhabitation of a particular territory. For an analysis of the issues from the perspective of the Nevada BLM, see www.nv.blm.gov/cultural/spirit_cave_man/SC_final_July26.pdf. For the Fallon Paiute-Shoshone perspective, see www.cr.nps.gov/nagpra/review/RCNOTICES/RCF5.htm.

29. This phrase is borrowed from Debra Harry's research on a doctoral dissertation from the Maori and Indigenous Research Institute at the University of Auckland.

30. Author's interview with Debra Harry, July 17, 2003.

31. For more on this case and a discussion of conflicts between geneticists and American Indians from a bioethicist's point of view, see Schmidt (2001). In 2000, the tribe demanded the return of their blood samples from Oxford University, which Ward had promised to do. The samples ultimately were returned to the tribe by Ward's spouse after his death in 2003.

32. Debra Harry, MIT lecture, 2002.

33. Quote by Marcos Terena from the video, *Yakoana*, Under Your Nose Productions, Produced and Directed by Anh D. Crutcher, New York: Parabola Video, 1997.

34. Speech delivered by John Trudell on the occasion of the memorial for Judi Bari, Martin Luther King Jr. High School, Berkeley, Calif., April 26, 1997. Available online at sisis.nativeweb.org/sov/trudbari.html.

References

Adamson, J., M. M. Evans, and R. Stein, eds., *The Environmental Justice Reader: Politics, Poetics, and Pedagogy* (Tucson: University of Arizona Press, 2002).

Agyeman, J., *Sustainable Communities and the Challenge of Environmental Justice* (New York: NYU Press, 2005).

Arquette, M., M. Cole, K. Cook, B. LaFrance, M. Peters, J. Ransom, E. Sargent, V. Smoke, and A. Stairs, "Holistic Risk-Based Environmental Decision Making:

A Native Perspective," *Environmental Health Perspectives* 110, supplement 2 (April 2002): 259–264.

Brown, P., *Health and the Environment*. (London: Sage Publications, 2002).

Churchill, W., *Struggle for the Land: Native North American Resistance to Genocide, Ecocide, and Colonization* (San Francisco: City Lights Publishers, 2002).

Corburn, J., *Street Science: Community Knowledge and Environmental Health Justice* (Cambridge, Mass.: MIT Press, 2005).

Cunningham, H., "Colonial Encounters in Postcolonial Contexts: Patenting Indigenous DNA and the Human Genome Diversity Project," *Critique of Anthropology* 18, no. 2 (1998): 205–233.

Di Chiro, G., "Introduction: Environments," in R. Eglash, J. Croissant, G. Di Chiro, and R. Fouché, eds., *Appropriating Technology: Vernacular Science and Social Power* (Minneapolis: University of Minnesota Press, 2004a), 191–205.

Di Chiro, G., "Local Actions, Global Visions: Remaking Environmental Expertise," in R. Eglash, J. Croissant, G. Di Chiro, and R. Fouché, eds., *Appropriating Technology: Vernacular Science and Social Power* (Minneapolis: University of Minnesota Press, 2004b), 225–252.

Di Chiro, G., "Producing `Roundup Ready®' Communities?: Human Genome Research and Environmental Justice Policy," in S. Rachel, ed., *New Perspectives in Environmental Justice: Gender, Sexuality, and Action* (New Brunswick, N.J.: Rutgers University Press, 2004c), 139–160.

First National People of Color Environmental Leadership Summit. "Principles of Environmental Justice" (Washington DC: United Church of Christ Commission for Racial Justice, 1991). Accessed online September 1, 2005, at www.weact. org/ej_principles.html.

Goldtooth, T., "Indigenous Nations: Summary of Sovereignty and its Implication for Environmental Protection," in B. Bryant, ed., *Environmental Justice: Issues, Policies and Solutions* (Washington D.C.: Island Press, 1995), 188–196.

Guerrero, M. A. J., "Global Genocide and Biocolonialism: On the Effect of the Human Genome Diversity Project on Targeted Indigenous Peoples/Ecocultures as "Isolates of Historic Interest," in A. J. Aldama, ed., *Violence and the Body: Race, Gender, and the State* (Bloomington: Indiana University Press, 2003), 176–194.

Harry, D., "Acts of Self-Determination and Self-Defense: Indigenous Peoples' Responses to Biocolonialism," in S. Krimsky and P. Shorett, eds., *Rights and Liberties in the Biotech Age* (Lanham, Md.: Roman and Littlefield, 2005), 87–97.

Harry, D., "CBD's International Regime: Indigenous Activist Organizations Call for No Access Zones to Genetic Resources and Indigenous Knowledge," Press Release (February 19, 2004). Accessed online August 1, 2005, at www.ipcb. org/issues/agriculture/htmls/2004/pr_cop7.html.

Harry, D., S. Howard, and B. Shelton, *Life, Lineage and Sustenance: Indigenous Peoples and Genetic Engineering, Threats to Food, Agriculture, and the Environment* (Nixon: Nev.: Indigenous Peoples Council on Biocolonialism, 2001).

Harry, D., S. Howard, and B. Shelton, *Indigenous Peoples, Genes and Genetics* (Nixon: Nev.: Indigenous Peoples Council on Biocolonialism, 2000).

Harry, D. and Kanehe, L. M., "The BS in Access and Benefit Sharing (ABS): Critical Questions for Indigenous Peoples," in B. Burrows, ed., *The Catch: Perspectives in Benefit Sharing* (Edmond, Wash.: Edmonds Institute, 2005), 102–122.

Heiman, M., "Science by the People: Grassroots Environmental Monitoring and the Debate Over Scientific Expertise," in R. Eglash, J. Croissant, G. Di Chiro, and R. Fouché, eds., *Appropriating Technology: Vernacular Science and Social Power* (Minneapolis: University of Minnesota Press, 2004), 207–223.

Hofrichter, R., ed., *Reclaiming the Environmental Debate: The Politics of Health in a Toxic Culture* (Cambridge, Mass.: MIT Press, 2000).

Hunter, A. A., "Teaching Indigenous Cultural Resource Management," in D. Abbott Mihesuah and A. Cavender Wilson, eds., *Indigenizing the Academy: Transforming Scholarship and Empowering Communities* (Lincoln: University of Nebraska Press, 2004), 140–155.

Jones, J. H., *Bad Blood: The Tuskegee Syphilis Experiment* (New York: Free Press, 1981).

Juma, C., *The Gene Hunters: Biotechnology and the Scramble for Seeds* (Princeton, N.J.: Princeton University Press, 1989).

Keller, E. F., *The Century of the Gene* (Cambridge, Mass.: Harvard University Press, 2000).

Kevles, D., *In the Name of Eugenics: Genetics and the Uses of Human Heredity* (New York: Knopf, 1985).

Krimsky, S. and P. Shorett, eds., *Rights and Liberties in the Biotech Age* (Lanham, Md.: Roman and Littlefield, 2005).

Kuletz, V., "Appropriate/d Technology, Cultural Revival, and Environmental Activism: A Native American Case Study," in R. Eglash, J. Croissant, G. Di Chiro, and R. Fouché, eds., *Appropriating Technology: Vernacular Science and Social Power* (Minneapolis: University of Minnesota Press, 2004), 287–304.

Kuletz, V., *The Tainted Desert: Environmental Ruin in the American West* (New York: Routledge, 1998).

LaDuke, W., *All Our Relations: Native Struggles for Land and Life* (Cambridge, Mass.: South End Press, 1999).

LaDuke, W., "Voices from White Earth: Gaa-waabaabiganikaag," in H. Hannum, ed., *People, Land, and Community* (New Haven, Conn.: Yale University Press, 1997), 22–37.

Lyden, F. J., and L. H. Legters, eds., *Native Americans and Public Policy* (Pittsburgh: University of Pittsburgh Press, 1992).

Mead, A., "Genealogy, Sacredness and the Commodities Market," in J. Friedlaender, ed., *Cultural Survival Quarterly* 20, no. 2 (1996): 46–53.

Muldowney, S., "Debra Harry: Environmental Leader," *Winds of Change* (autumn 2001): 90–91.

Niezen, R., *The Origins of Indigenism: Human Rights and the Politics of Identity* (Berkeley: University of California Press, 2003).

Olden, K., and S. Wilson, "Environmental Health and Genomics: Visions and Implications," *Nature Reviews in Genetics* 1 (November 2000): 149–153.

Paul, D. B., *Controlling Human Heredity: 1865 to the Present* (Atlantic Highlands, N.J.: Humanities Press, 1995).

Peña, D. G., *The Terror of the Machine: Technology, Work, Gender, and Ecology on the U.S.-Mexico Border* (Austin: University of Texas, 1997).

Pérez-Peña, R., "Study Finds Asthma in 25% of Children in Central Harlem," *New York Times* (April 19, 2003): A1.

Posey, D., "Ethnobiology and Ethnoecology in the Context of National Laws and International Agreements Affecting Indigenous and Local Knowledge, Traditional Resources and Intellectual Property Rights," in R. Ellen, P. Parkes, and A. Bicker, eds., *Indigenous Environmental Knowledge and Its Transformations: Critical Anthropological Perspectives* (Amsterdam: Harwood Academic, 2000), 35–54.

Reardon, J., "The Human Genome Diversity Project: A Case Study in Coproduction," *Social Studies of Science* 31, no. 3 (2001): 357–358.

Riley, M., ed., *Indigenous Intellectual Property Rights: Legal Obstacles and Innovative Solutions* (Walnut Creek, Calif.: Altamira Press, 2004).

Roberts, D. E., *Killing the Black Body: Race, Reproduction, and the Meaning of Liberty* (New York: Pantheon Books, 1997).

Schmidt, C., "Toxicogenomics: An Emerging Discipline," *Environmental Health Perspectives* 110 (2002): A750–A755.

Schmidt, C., "Indi-Gene-Ous Conflicts," *Environmental Health Perspectives*, 109 (2001): A216–A219.

Second National People of Color Environmental Leadership Summit. "Environmental Justice Principles of Working Together," Washington D.C., October 23–27, 2002. Available online at http://www.sric.org/voices/2003/v4n1/principles.html.

Serjeantson, S., "The Human Genome Diversity Project: Facts versus Fiction," *Search* 25, no. 3 (1994): 85–87.

Sharp, R., and C. Barrett, "The Environmental Genome Project: Ethical, Legal, and Social Implications," *Environmental Health Perspectives* 108 (2000): 279–281.

Shiva, V., *Biopiracy: The Plunder of Nature and Knowledge* (Cambridge, Ma.: South End Press, 1997).

Shiva, V., *Monocultures of the Mind: Perspectives on Biodiversity and Biotechnology* (London: Zed Books, 1993).

Shostak, S., "Locating Gene-Environment Interaction: At the Intersections of Genetics and Public Health," *Social Science & Medicine* 56, no. 11 (June 2003): 2327–2342.

Smith, L. T., *Decolonizing Methodologies: Research and Indigenous Peoples* (New York: St. Martin's Press, 1999).

Sze, J., and S. Prakash, "Human Genetics, Environment, and Communities of Color: Ethical and Social Implications," *Environmental Health Perspectives* 112, no. 6 (May 2004): 740–745.

Sze, J., S. Prakash, and P. Shepard, "Introduction: Human Genetics, Environment, and Communities of Color," in *Human Genetics, Environment, and Communities of Color: Ethical and Social Implications: Conference Program and Resource Guide* (New York: West Harlem Environmental Action, 2003).

Tickner, J. A., ed., *Precaution, Environmental Science, and Preventive Public Policy* (Washington, D.C.: Island Press, 2003).

Tokar, B., ed., *Redesigning Life?: The Worldwide Challenge to Genetic Engineering* (London: Zed Books, 2001.)

10

Globalizing Environmental Justice

J. Timmons Roberts

By now readers of this volume know that the environmental justice movement began in the U.S. South in the 1980s with landmark struggles of poor, often rural, African American communities against some of the world's largest corporations and unresponsive government agencies (Bullard 1990, 1994; Roberts and Toffolon-Weiss 2001; Cole and Foster 2001). The definition of the movement first began as "environmental racism," a phrase coined by Benjamin Chavis during the now legendary Warren County, North Carolina, protests in 1982. The "bigger tent" term, "environmental justice," expanded the movement to include Hispanic, Native American, and poor white groups facing the unfair distribution of environmental "bads." The idea of unequal exposures by class was not new, since they were documented in the 1970s; however, because the United States is a nation that lives in denial of class-based inequality, the movement did not take off until it was strengthened by the strong sense of the term "justice," built by the civil rights movement's attack on racism. The difference, some social movement theorists in sociology would argue, was that the earlier movement lacked an effective "master frame" to mobilize members and important allies, and to neutralize response from their potential opposition.[1] Of course, this movement and frame have gotten only so far.[2]

More recently, an important new development has been the application of the "environmental justice frame" to understanding and fighting unequal environmental exposures around the world. Two levels of inequality are being cited: transnational and global environmental inequalities. First, oil, mining and other extraction-based corporations are expanding their operations into the farthest reaches of rainforests and mountains in Africa, Asia and Latin America. Enabled by ongoing improvements in electronic communications, we increasingly are hearing about the consequence of this expansion through the intermediary work of international environmental and human rights groups that are connecting environmental justice communities far and near. Perhaps seen by some activists as an extravagance in the past, I will argue below that this kind of transnational "solidarity" work is critical to the environmental justice movement making substantial progress in the future. This is true because it provides new approaches to fight corporate backlash in the United States, the possibility of the formalization of the term environmental injustice, and the (perhaps long-term) prospect of some kind of binding international agreements.

The second type of expansion of the environmental justice movement is to describe and resist global patterns of inequality in environmental exposures, where the world's poorest, often nonwhite regions face a triple threat. The exhaustion of the most economically viable reserves of resources from the "core" richer nations is driving the expansion of extraction in the world's "peripheral" nations. Further, there has been an enormous increase in the most energy- and pollution-intensive stages of processing those minerals into intermediate products, not only by transnational but also by national and state-owned firms. Finally, there is an enormous manufacturing boom going on in China and other low-wage nations, resulting in some severe exposures of workers and downstream and downwind communities. The restructuring of the world economy in the current phase of increasingly global production is leading to an increasingly global pattern of environmental injustice.[3]

Besides being more exposed to the known and unknown hazards of agricultural and industrial chemicals, radiation, and other hazards, "Third World" people are less able to predict, prepare for, respond to, and cope with industrial exposures and cataclysmic disasters, including those caused by climate change (Blaikie et al. 1984; Kasperson and Kasperson 2001; Roberts and Parks, 2007). An extensive literature in geography has examined the differential "vulnerability" of nations, regions, and communities around the world. Much of this literature has attempted to explain why the same level of earthquake or hurricane can cause few deaths and few disruptions in wealthier nations while devastating economies and societies in poorer ones. Only part of the answer is wealth; much of the reason lies in corrupt and weak states, unorganized civil societies, and inequality (Roberts and Parks, 2007). Driven in part by a society that has left them without viable options, the "dispossessed" often have been forced to use the resources they do have access to in an extremely unsustainable way. Examples are peasant farmers forced to clear forests and "mine" their soils, and periurban slum dwellers building on deforested hillsides or floodplains, which collapse or are inundated with heavy rains or rising seas. So whether the "culprits" are emitters near or far away, poor nations and especially their poorest people increasingly are suffering environmental injustices in a globalized economy. The fact that they are least responsible for the pollutants, and benefiting least from the consumption which is driving this increasing inequity, further exacerbates the injustice.

This new global environmental justice also has the potential to bring important new players into the environmental justice struggle. As Faber (2004) has usefully pointed out, understanding global environmental injustice opens the movement and its academic field of study to go beyond oppression based only upon race and ethnicity in our narrow national(ist) perspective. Tying environmental harm to economic injustice built into the very structure of the world economic system and national class inequalities can open new avenues of coalition building (Schnaiberg and Gould 1994; Gould, Lewis, and Roberts 2004). Efforts to bring together environmental and social justice movements under the environmental justice flag suggest that U.S. environmental justice and mainstream environmental groups can learn from the methods and styles of organizing used by those in other nations.

These are the core points of this chapter, which proceeds as follows. I first discuss difficulties in the U.S. environmental justice movement that are based on its lack of consensus on the definition of terms and the legal standing of the issue, which is due in part to movement dynamics, a weak agency effort, and an effective backlash by business lobbies. Second, I identify the tremendous range of issues to which the environmental justice frame is being applied internationally, including struggles against oil and mining firms, free trade, and environmental treaty formation. I then describe in some detail the climate justice issue and the emerging social movement around the issue. The last section begins with a description of a Brazilian environmental justice network begun in 2001, because it is revealing of the successful transplantation of explicitly environmental justice ideology abroad. I then discuss why conservative U.S. environmental groups partner with more radical environmental justice groups in poorer nations but not at home and explore some implications of that divide. Finally, I conclude with some speculation on what the globalization of environmental justice ideology might mean for the movement abroad and at home. My conclusion is that international environmental justice struggles hold promise for a movement that has lost some traction in the United States, and are in fact some of its greatest hopes for its future. They must not be neglected.

A Contested Idea, A Movement Losing Traction

As several authors have described it, environmental justice embraces the concept that every individual—regardless of race, ethnicity, or class—has the right to be free from ecological destruction and deserves equal protection of his or her environment, health, employment, housing, and transportation.[4] In 1991, the landmark People of Color Environmental Leadership Summit (Summit I) drafted seventeen core Principles of Environmental Justice (Appendix A). Holistic and universal, these principles emphasize that the movement was not just about environmental issues. The goals of the movement include broader social justice issues, such as economic and cultural liberation for all people of color.[5] The principles stress the importance of increased participation of people of color as equals at all levels of decision making. Finally, they made clear that, although pollution and environmental degradation does not belong in communities of color, it also does not belong anywhere else. The movement thus dedicated itself to reducing environmental hazards for all people and, to do that, its focus would be on defending those least protected.

The reason why the environmental justice movement does not focus only on the natural environment as it is often narrowly defined by mainstream environmentalists is because activists see that the economic and social disparities that surround an individual's life are rooted in hundreds of years of economic and political inequalities. Since the first coining of the phrase in the United States, the idea behind environmental justice has been that the racism and injustice created by unequal exposures to environmental "bads" can be conscious or unconscious, intended and unintended. Many critics misrepresent this most central point: environmental racism does not solely refer to actions that have a racist intent, but also includes actions that have a racist impact, regardless of their intent. This impact can manifest in two ways. Environmental injustice can be the "the great disparity in the siting of waste facilities, polluting industries, other facilities having a negative environmental effect."[6] It can also be the uneven "enforcement of environmental law between People of Color communities and White communities," as suggested by a 1992 study by the *National Law Journal*.[7] That study of 1,177 Superfund toxic waste sites found that "[W]hite communities see faster action, better results and stiffer penalties than communities where blacks, Hispanics and other minorities live. This unequal protection often occurs whether the community is wealthy or poor," but poor communities clearly tend to suffer more of society's environmental "bads" while getting less of the "goods."

How a movement develops a definition of their core term is one thing; how policy-making agencies define what the term is going to mean in practice is quite another. President Clinton's landmark 1994 Executive Order 12898 decreed that "all communities and individuals, regardless of economic status or race are entitled to a safe and healthy environment."[8] The order required every department of the federal government to "make achieving environmental justice part of its mission." Still, exactly what environmental justice means for this executive order remains contested today, over a decade later.

Clinton's Environmental Protection Agency (EPA) head, Carol Browner, and her staff were charged with leading the effort to enact the order, and the struggles of many communities persistently forced her and the EPA to decide whether they constituted cases of environmental injustice (Roberts and Toffolon-Weiss 2001). Because Executive Order 12898 was extremely broad and vague, it took the EPA more than six years to issue regulations and instructions to state environmental agencies outlining how to handle environmental justice claims, and both their "Interim Guidelines" and "Draft Guidance" have made it exceedingly difficult for communities to legally claim environmental injustice. This is in large part because of the efforts of industry groups claiming that the order could hinder efforts to bring economic development to the very communities that the government was trying to help with programs such as "enterprise" and "empowerment zones." U.S. Chamber of Commerce president Thomas J. Donahue, for example, claimed the guidelines would have "significant adverse impact on economic growth and job opportunities in low-income and minority communities" (U.S. Chamber of Commerce 1998a). Other business leaders echoed the claims, deriding the movement and its leaders (Roberts and Toffolon-Weiss 2001).

The movement continues to struggle in the face of a solidifying Republican opposition, which is now in power in the White House and both houses of the U.S. Congress. Moreover, the environmental justice movement faces several other important problems (Foreman 1998). One is that the major environmental laws in the United States were constructed in the early 1970s without any provisions about racism and justice. Executive Order 12898 and the accumulation of case law and agency decisions are the basis for the movement's claims to justice. The "seats at the table" were all taken by mainstream environmental groups by the time the environmental justice movement came along in the late 1980s. There is also the difficulty the movement has in prioritizing all the pressing concerns and claims of injustice from different communities. This will likely be a problem for both branches of the globalizing environmental justice movement as well.

Exporting the Environmental Justice Frame

A wide range of struggles by non-U.S. communities against corporate or government polluters are being recast as environmental justice struggles, for various reasons and with varying results. Four cases exemplify the variety of struggles around the globe. Some activists have cast rubber-tapper and labor leader Chico Mendes' struggle in Brazil's Amazon forest against deforestation by ranchers a case of environmental justice. In Nigeria, the Ogoni people, formerly led by Ken Saro Wiwa, have struggled against Shell Oil; Greenpeace has joined activists there with environmental justice community activists from the United States, including NORCO, Louisiana. In Colombia, the U'Wa peoples have fought for years against Occidental Petroleum in consortium with Shell drilling in U'Wa ancestral lands (Roberts and Thanos 2003; Gedicks 2002; Faber 2004). Years of protest on both sides of the Pacific sought justice in the form of restitution and improved environmental protection from mining giant Freeport McMoRan's Grasburg mine in Irian Jaya, Indonesia (Gedicks 2002; Clark 2002). So, in broad terms, these struggles frequently feature indigenous populations displaced by huge dams and other megaprojects that are built by governments and corporations.

While there have been "ups" (especially around the Rio Earth Summit of 1992) and "downs" in global environmentalism, the efforts are diverse, arising "from social conflicts on environmental entitlements, on the burdens of pollution, on the sharing of uncertain environmental risks, [and] on the loss of access to natural resources and environmental services."[9] Jean Martinez-Alier refers to these historical and contemporary incidents as "ecological distributional conflicts."[10] Martinez-Alier and Ramachandra Guha insist that conflicts like these have been particularly widespread and acute throughout the developing world, in turn fostering a new breed of Third World environmental justice perspectives. The emerging terminology in academia is perhaps illustrative: "livelihood ecology,"[11] "liberation ecology,"[12] "subaltern environmentalism"[13] and the so-called environmentalism of the poor[14] are among a much longer list of attempts to invent new environmental justice frames. This diverse terminology suggests the attempt to shift environmental attention to human issues and inequality, away from what was often perceived to be an excessive attention to "green" issues of habitat preservation by an essentially elitist environmental movement headquartered in the global North.[15]

For the environmental justice movement, there also can be an expansion beyond culture and race to economic position in the global economic system. What's more, these struggles often occur at levels both above and below that of the national state. They are localized struggles, which frequently pit a globalizing corporation against a local community attempting to gain the support of an international social movement. We need better theories to explain them, where they appear and especially where they do not. Following the growing literature on international social movements, I would describe these as transnational environmental movements.[16]

From the U.S. side, some environmental justice activists have reached out internationally. Robert D. Bullard of Clark Atlanta University, a prominent environmental justice activist and author, reports that he increasingly works with minorities in other nations. He cites the conference on racism in Durban, South Africa, in 2000 as a critical point for environmental victims around the world to realize that environmental justice was a global problem and to begin to create international networks (Bullard 2001; personal communication). Individuals such as Bullard are important bridge builders in this movement, a crucial group for the success of these kinds of cross-border (and usually cross-class and cross-race) coalitions (Bandy 2004; Rose 2000). United Nations and World Social Forum conferences have been important fora for such bridge building to take place. As part of the corporate and product-focused campaigns mentioned above (such as against Shell or PVC, polyvinyl chloride plastics), Greenpeace International also has been connecting victims of corporate polluters worldwide, bringing to the U.N. Commission on Human Rights victims of Shell from the United States and Nigerians from the Ogoniland.[17]

A growing but still uncertain part of the international environmental justice effort has been legal strategies. The victims of the terrible accident at Union Carbide's Bhopal, India, agrochemicals plant in 1984 are still trying to gain a decent settlement, now from the firm that bought the company, Dow Chemical. Victims of poisoning from agrochemicals exported to Central America in the 1980s continue to press for justice in U.S. courts. A critical question remains of what legal standing these plaintiffs hold in U.S. courts (Roberts and Thanos 2003), because the International Criminal Court is almost routinely ignored, especially by large powerful nations. In the United States, a divide has emerged in environmental justice cases between those communities that secure public interest lawyers and those that turn to private injury lawyers and file class-action lawsuits (Toffolon-Weiss and Roberts 2004). It remains to be seen whether such a stark divide will emerge in cases with foreign plaintiffs attempting to sue in U.S. and international courts.

Discussed above was the important vulnerability of poorer nations to the effects of climate change, including drought, hurricanes, and especially rising sea levels. Beginning in 1992, the government of the tiny Pacific atoll nation of Tuvalu, facing rising oceans that are making their native lands uninhabitable, began speaking out in international fora about the controversial topic of global warming. Tuvalu's capital atoll of Funafuti, home to half the country's 10,000 citizens, is a sliver of land just 400 meters across at its widest, the crest of a long dormant volcano edging above the waves. In 2002, they teamed up with Greenpeace to sue the U.S. and Australian governments and several huge oil producers in the International Court of Justice for endangering their homes. It is unclear how far this strategy will take them, but they have located important support in the legal community and have appealed to the U.N. High Commission on Human Rights, the International Criminal Court, and U.S. courts at different levels (Malone and Pasternak 2004; Roberts and Parks, 2007).

Lawsuits also can be part of a broader "corporate campaign" strategy of singling out one company to target and attack in as many ways as possible. With the restructuring of the global economy, where nearly all manufacturing and extraction are being rapidly "offshored" from wealthy to poorer nations where there is extraordinarily cheap labor (and sometimes very lax environmental protection), it is possible that environmental injustice claims also will become increasingly "offshored." For the "corporate campaign" strategy to work, therefore, environmental and environmental justice activists are having to "go international." Greenpeace and Friends of the Earth have been the most visible of groups with strong U.S. chapters in building transnational campaigns against corporate polluters.

Assembling Global Action to Confront Global Injustice: The Case of Climate Change

Beyond transnational are global environmental justice issues and movements. The cry for "climate justice"—that is, environmental justice on the issue of climate change—is growing louder as impacts are being increasingly felt in poor nations threatened by the changes.[18] These nations are at the same time tragically unable to cope with and respond to climate disasters (Roberts and Parks, n.d.), such as spreading drought and agricultural instability (most notably affecting sub-Saharan Africa), sea level rise (Pacific island atolls and Bangladesh being the most vulnerable), and hurricane risk (IPCC 2001; Kasperson and Kasperson 2002; Parks and Roberts, 2007).

The San Francisco–based group Corporate Watch launched an initiative to redefine the global warming issue as a question of local and global justice. They released a report, *Greenhouse Gangsters vs. Climate Justice*, which was "designed to create a framework from which indigenous peoples, the environmental justice movement, fenceline communities affected by oil refineries, students, and antiglobalization activists can begin to assert leadership on the global warming issue." The report focused on the oil industry and institutions such as the World Bank with respect to how they help create climate disasters and fail to help people prepare for them. In November 2000, Corporate Watch coorganized the First Climate Justice Summit in the Hague, bringing together representatives from the United States and Southern countries from communities already adversely impacted by the fossil-fuel industry to join the climate change debate.

Corporate Watch also applied the tactic discussed above of connecting people in distant places to the case of climate change, attempting to "bring to life the connections between the local effects of oil and the global dynamic of climate change." Their report merits examination:

In the Spring of 2001, CorpWatch brought two environmentalists from opposite ends of the Earth on a Climate Justice Tour. Oronto Douglas from Environmental Rights Action in Nigeria's Niger Delta and Sarah James from the Gwich'in Steering Committee in Arctic Village, Alaska traveled with CorpWatch to seven cities, passionately bringing to life the connections between the local effects of oil and the global dynamic of climate change. They met with oil-impacted communities in the San Francisco Bay Area, Louisiana and Texas; they challenged Chevron at its annual shareholders meeting; and they told it like it is on CNN and in other media. ... The tour was sponsored by the Southwest Network for Environmental and Economic Justice, Indigenous Environmental Network, the Environmental Justice Resource Center, Southern Organizing Committee for Economic and Social Justice and the Asian Pacific Environmental Network.

In this case, Corporate Watch appears to have borrowed a page from Greenpeace, but applied it creatively to attempt to build transnational coalitions.

In the United States, a coalition of twenty-eight small and medium-sized groups, varying from local to national in scale, called the Environmental Justice and Climate Change (EJCC) Initiative is being organized under the leadership of the San Francisco group Redefining Progress. This EJCC Initiative is made up of a range of traditional U.S. environmental justice groups, but no mainstream environmental groups: the group has reached out in an entirely different direction.[19] In 2002, Redefining Progress held an EJCC Forum on November 17 at the Kyoto treaty follow-up meeting in the Hague, and in March 2004 the first academic conference on EJCC was organized at the University of Michigan's School of Natural Resources and the Environment. Graduate students working under Bunyan Bryant, sociologist and a founder of the U.S. environmental justice movement, organized the conference in cooperation with Redefining Progress. At the conference a number of academics and activists from environmental justice and indigenous groups began a process of understanding and strategizing on the issue. The Climate Justice Declaration was drafted there, building on two earlier documents, the Bali Principles of Climate Justice and the Climate Change Initiative's "10 Principles for Just Climate Policies in the U.S." These in turn were built on the original Principles of Environmental Justice, which have been influential around the world, declaring that environmental protection and justice must be addressed together.

A far more international network is the London-based Rising Tide Coalition for Climate Justice. It consists of environmental and social justice groups from around the world (especially Europe).[20] The make-up of the Climate Justice Network is somewhat similar; it contains many environmental groups, environmental justice organizations, and social justice organizations.[21] Indeed, to understand the movement for climate justice, one must look outside the United States, and eventually outside the wealthy nations, because the greatest brunt of climate change's effects will be felt (and are being felt) by the world's poorest people. The global South's entire notion of and antagonistic approach to the climate change debate is rooted in their colonial and postcolonial "development" experiences. With the dawning of the "development decades" following World War II, the North laid out a "blueprint for national economic development" (McMichael 1996, p. 147) with ostensibly universal application.

Unfortunately, the gap between winners and losers in the postwar global economy, which developed nations had promised would narrow, has not closed (Kapstein 1998/1999; Firebaugh 1999; Wade 2004), casting a great deal of Southern doubt upon the North's seemingly empty promise and model. Today, we live in a world where the three richest individuals in the world hold assets greater than the combined wealth of the poorest forty-eight countries.[22] Jamaican President Michael Manley suggests that it is precisely for this unifying reason that we see Southern solidarity during international negotiations. He argues, "[T]here is an underlying and binding cement to be found in their common experience of imperialism and colonialism together with the common disadvantage they suffer under the present world economic order" (Manley 1991, p. 9).

The high-water mark of the infant climate justice movement so far may have been when on October 28, 2002, thousands of activists marched for "climate justice" in the streets of Delhi, India, during the prepcom on the Kyoto treaty. In their Delhi Declaration, they affirmed that "climate change is a human rights issue—it affects our livelihoods, our health, our children and our natural resources." They declared that they would "build alliances across states and borders to oppose climate change inducing patterns and advocate for and practice sustainable development." They tied climate change to economic injustice: "We reject the market-based principles that guide the current negotiations to solve the climate crisis: Our World is Not for Sale!" (Khastagir 2002).

The coalition in Delhi was described in the network's own literature this way:

Participants traveled from around India to engage in the Summit: Fisherpeople from the National Fishworkers' Forum came from Kerala and West Bengal. Farmers came from the Andhra Pradesh Vyavasay Vruthidarula Union (Agricultural Workers and Marginal Farmers Union). A delegation of adivasis (indigenous peoples) from Narmada Bachao Andolan (Save Narmada Movement [victims of dams]) came from the Narmada Valley. Indigenous peoples of the North-East Territories of India and from mining-impacted areas of Orissa brought their music and dance and folk art with them. NGO delegates from over 20 countries came to participate. This is the human face of the rising movement for Climate Justice. (Khastagir 2002)

Photos from the event showed representatives of Delhi's Cycle Rickshaw Union, the Center for Science and Environment, Urban Poor and Sustainable Transportation workshop, and the Transportation and Urban Poor workshop at the Climate Justice Summit.

Climate justice has yet to be seriously seized upon by either mainstream U.S. environmentalists or environmental justice groups. Although a substantial number of environmental justice groups and smaller environmental groups are listed in these networks, it is unclear how many resources they are putting into advancing the agenda. Environmentalists working in the area appear to be focusing on building coalitions with religious, indigenous, and international social justice groups. Even that coalition appears to be extremely difficult to mobilize, because it includes those affected by climate disasters in poor nations, "fenceline" minority communities in industrial countries, and mainstream environmentalists. Some larger environmental groups are dabbling in the issue of climate justice, but few have made it the sole focus of their organizing work. So far the efforts to address the injustice of climate change appear to lack a strong grassroots groundswell.

Overall, the movement is made up of a series of coalitions, which sometimes appear to exist mostly on paper (or on a website). This movement has some important elements—a "master frame" in which to claim injustice, substantial but still emergent cross-border links, some key resources in these networking groups, grassroots energy, and academic skills. It lacks, however, a core NGO (nongovernmental organization) whose mission is centered solely on this issue of climate justice as well as the serious resources required for successful campaigning (Faber 2004). The issue is still new, so this could change.

Moreover, international organizing of the victims and potential victims of climate disruption is very difficult to do, because most "natural" disasters are seen as inevitable and "God-given." The worst of them are also predicted to hit the world's poorest nations, whose populations are typically very difficult to organize because they have little time, energy, or resources to fight for justice. So the coalition seems quite tenuous indeed: some Northern environmentalists, the poorest of the world's poor who are likely to suffer worst and first, and future generations.

Perhaps as a result, some groups are taking a decidedly top-down approach, such as suing nations or firms believed to be driving poor victims to the edge of climate disaster. As Klaus Töpfer, executive director of the United Nations Environment Programme said, laws already in place can be used to move forward the issue of environmental justice and climate change. "For example, it is illegal under international law for one State to cause harm to another State. It is illegal under domestic law in many countries for polluters to cause nuisances to the public and to market defective products, and damages must be paid. International and domestic laws prohibit human rights violations. Domestic laws impose duties on directors of bodies, such as insurance companies or pension funds, to act in the best interests of shareholders who may suffer financial harm as a result of climate impacts."[23] The Climate Law Programme puts it bluntly: "The biggest culprits are the rich and the developed countries."[24]

Still, the coalition for climate justice seems weak and dispersed. This is especially the case when this quite new movement is compared to the organization and resources of the industrial and government lobbying groups they face in trying get these justice issues incorporated in the next round of climate change treaty negotiations.

Conclusion: Globalizing Environmental Justice and Environmentalism

In October 2001, a network of Brazilian academics and social movement organizers called the first congress on environmental justice in that nation, which was held in Niteroi, just outside Rio de Janeiro. The group explicitly chose the terms "environmental justice" and "environmental racism" to attempt to bridge the gap between "green" issue environmentalists and social justice activists. Experts from the U.S. environmental justice movement were brought in, and principles were drafted based on those first released at the landmark Summit I. The network now has dozens of groups, mostly in Brazil but also stretching across the continent.

The network's strength is based on active collaboration between a strong existing umbrella organization called FASE (Foundation for Advancement in Science and Education), local communities, smaller activist groups, and academic faculty. The work is largely in denunciation of negative behavior by firms and government agencies, with a series of groups posting calls for action, such as on behalf of those affected by dams, industrial contamination, deforestation, and industrial reforestation. The group publishes hard-hitting books and magazines and organizes collaborative denunciations of the worst cases it comes across. The hundreds of issues that have been posted on their network, however, suggests that the Brazilian environmental justice movement is suffering some of the same problems as the U.S. movement: there are too many issues, too many demands for the efforts of core activists, little financial resources to sustain rigorous campaigns, and little legal precedent or support for satisfactory outcomes of these struggles. A few campaigns are considered successes; most are not.

So we have seen how the environmental justice frame is increasingly being adopted internationally: to describe ongoing environmental struggles with an equity element; within nations such as Brazil to bring social justice/green agenda activists into an integrated movement; in transnational environmental and social justice networks; and globally on issues such as climate change. The environmental justice approach may be important and potentially potent for reviving the weakened Kyoto treaty on global warming. The application of international law and injury lawsuits across borders holds substantial but uncertain potential.

The prospects for the international and global use of the concept of environmental justice could be very good. It opens possibilities for new networks, as shown in the cases of the Brazilian environmental justice network and the climate justice coalitions. Environmental justice has been shown to be a concept with substantial "traction" in the politicized, manipulated landscape of community and customer relations for corporations. It also may have some legs in the international relations world of treaty negotiations. And, of course, we must address the environmental issues for the world's most disempowered if we wish to stop firms from simply moving around the globe to locate in places with the weakest regulations (Gould 2001).

Finally, focusing on the internationalization of environmental justice opens interesting avenues on the question of whether environmentalism and environmental justice are compatible. Some "mainstream" U.S. environmental groups, such as the World Wildlife Fund and the Nature Conservancy perform some very serious coalition work in their efforts to preserve natural areas and species in poor nations. Some of the groups with whom they partner are in fact social justice–based organizations, rural unions, and so on. An often-used example is Chico Mendes' Rubbertappers Union in Acre, Brazil. The efforts and demands of his organization went far beyond simply the preservation of the forest; however, United States–based environmentalists realized that they needed to reach beyond their typical zone of comfort in making these cross-border links, and this kind of lesson has been applied to protected area management around the world.

There are three different forces driving mainstream U.S. environmental organizations to make these kinds of links. First is the pressure from members of organizations such as the Nature Conservancy and World Wildlife Fund to "do something about" issues like tropical rainforest destruction, which requires these organizations to get more aggressive in attempting to show some progress.[25] Second, they need local groups to partner with, if they are to gain credibility and more traction in local struggles. Third, these more radical coalition partners are far away, and these organizations' boards of directors and membership do not know anything about them. If and when these organizations pair with local U.S. civil rights groups (like the NAACP, Urban League, and so forth), they risk alienating more conservative or racist members of their groups, especially influential board members who might be otherwise "moderate" or conservative. The same may be true if these mainstream environmental groups were to form strong coalitions with labor unions in the United States, coalitions in which they would have to truly stand up for labor in contract disputes, protracted strikes, or legislative battles (Gould, Lewis, and Roberts 2004).

To move to the broader point of globalizing environmental justice, we need to think through the potential of this movement. There is clear and growing evidence of savage inequalities in the distribution of benefits and environmental risks in society—locally, nationally, and globally.[26] Social movements are beginning to develop to address this environmental inequality: environmental justice in the United States, the internationalization of the environmental justice movement, the "climate justice" network, and many other specific issue-networks, such as Oilwatch, indigenous issues networks, and so on. They still are rather small and somewhat weak movements and face often rapid and effective backlashes or "greenwashes" (especially from industry) at the local, national, and global levels; however, international institutions may provide even solely domestic environmental justice movements some leverage: international courts and the use of national courts, international treaties, and U.N. agencies such as the Human Rights Commission have rapidly expanding potential (Malone and Pasternak 2004). It may be that the U.S. movement for environmental justice requires these new external levers and the new emerging international norms of environmental injustice to accomplish some sort of an end run around the business interests that have successfully stalled the efforts of the environmental justice movement to gain retribution from legislators, regulatory agencies, and industry at home. They may also gain from the structural perspective of international movements, which tie unjust environmental burdens to unjust economies and the politics of superpower domination.

Notes

1. Snow and Benford (1992, pp. 137–139) describe how "collective action frames" simplify and condense the world by "selectively punctuating and encoding" events, accentuating certain injustices, attributing blame and laying out a direction for those responsible to correct it. Master frames are broader and common to a number of groups.

2. Faber (2005) argues that the identity-based focus on race and ethnicity has limited the effectiveness of the environmental justice movement in the United States.

3. For more on transnational and truly global environmental issues, see Taylor and Buttel (1992) and Yearley (1996).

4. Bullard (1999); Washington (1997).

5. Bryant (1993).

6. Robinson (n.d.).

7. Lavelle and Coyle (1992, p. 51).

8. Available online at www.epa.gov.

9. Martinez-Alier (2003).

10. Martinez-Alier (2003).

11. Gari (2000), cited in Martinez-Alier (2000).

12. Peet and Watts (1996).

13. Pulido (1996).

14. Guha and Martinez-Alier (1997).

15. This issue has been and continues to be much debated. For an early discussion see Bullard (1990).

16. See, for example, Keck and Sikkink (1998).

17. Greenpeace also brought Japanese neighbors of Shin-Etsu Corporation to Louisiana to meet with poor African Americans facing the construction by the same firm of a huge chemical plant there.

18. The term "climate justice" apparently was first used in the academic literature by Henry Shue (1992). Another early work was Weiss (1989); see, also, Weiss's chapter in Choucri (1993).

19. These organizations have joined the Environmental Justice and Climate Change Initiative (as of summer 2004): Black Leadership Forum; Church Federation of Greater Indianapolis; Church of the Brethren; Communities for a Better Environment; CorpWatch; Corporation for Enterprise Development; Council of Athabascan Tribal Government; Deep South Center for Environmental Justice at Xavier University; EcoEquity; Environmental Justice Resource Center at Clark Atlanta University; Georgia Coalition for the Peoples' Agenda; Indigenous Environmental Network; Intertribal Council On Utility Policy; Just Transition Alliance; National Black Environmental Justice Network; Kids against Pollution; Native Village of Unalakleet; New York Public Interest Research Group; North Baton Rouge Environmental Association; Redefining Progress; Southern Organizing Committee for Economic and Social Justice; Southwest Network for Environmental and Economic Justice; Southwest Workers Union; United Church of Christ Justice and Witness Ministries; United Methodist Church; West County Toxics Coalition; and the West Harlem Environmental Action (WE ACT).

20. As of Summer 2004, these groups include: Asociación para la Acción Climática—AAC, Uruguay; A SEED, Europe; A SEED, Japan; the Bet; Carbusters; the Corner House, UK; Corporate Europe Observatory; Climate Collective, the Netherlands; Ecologistas en Accion, Spain; Engage!, the Netherlands; Environment and Social Development Organization-ESDO, Bangladesh; Eurodusnie, the Netherlands; eyfa; Friends of the Earth, Melbourne, Austialia; GAIA, Portugal; Groenfront! Activists, the Netherlands; Korean Ecological Youth; Mediterranean SOS Network; Mouvement Ecologique Life, Luxembourg; oo_y_o Zero°, the Netherlands; People & Planet Cymru; Rising Tide, the United Kingdom; Rising Tide, Bonn, Germany; Sudanese refugee groups; Transnational Institute; World Information Service on Energy (WISE).

21. The (2004) steering committee of the Climate Justice Network includes the following individuals and organizations: Robert Bullard, National Black Environmental Justice Network, U.S.; Ricardo Carrere, World Rainforest Movement, Uruguay; Chee Yoke Ling, Third World Network, Malaysia; Patrina Dumaru, Pacific Concerns Resource Center, Fiji; Tom Goldtooth, Indigenous Environmental Network, North America; Olivier Hoedeman, Corporate Europe Observatory, the Netherlands; Kate Hampton, Friends of the Earth International, UK; Joshua Karliner and Amit Srivastava, CorpWatch, U.S.;

Ricardo Navarro, Friends of the Earth International, El Salvador; Isaac Osuoka, OilWatch Africa, Nigeria; S. Bobby Peek, groundWork, South Africa; Steve Sawyer, Greenpeace International, the Netherlands; Ruben Solis, Southwest Network for Environmental and Economic Justice, the United States; Ivonne Yanez, OilWatch International, Ecuador.

22. Pew Center on Global Climate Change (1999).

23. Available online at www.climatelaw.org.

24. The Environmental Law Alliance Worldwide (elaw.org) has taken up climate justice, attempting to support the legal challenges against climate change leaders. A look at these coalitions and choices of targets is informative. In June 2004, Germanwatch and BUND (Friends of the Earth Germany) "have begun a legal action to force the German government to disclose the contribution to climate change made by projects supported by the German taxpayer through its export credit agency Euler Hermes AG" (http://www.climatelaw.org/media/german.suit). "The International Centre for Technology, along with Greenpeace and the Sierra Club, have begun an action against the Environmental Protection Agency seeking mandatory reductions of greenhouse gases through the Clean Air Act" (http://www.icta.org). In 2002, "Friends of the Earth, Greenpeace and affected individuals have been joined by the cities of Boulder, Oakland and Arcata in suing the US export credit agencies for funding fossil fuel projects under the National Environment Policy Act" (http://www.climatelawsuit.org).

To understand the depth of these movements and their funding, a look at their donors is informative. E-LAW U.S. is run by Friends of the Earth International, Greenpeace International, and WWF International. The funders for E-law's Climate Justice Initiative include: the Gerling Foundation; Fondation de Sauve; the Heinrich Böll Foundation; the Ecological Foundation; JMG Foundation; Ben Goldsmith; Polden-Puckham Charitable Foundation; the Network for Social Change; and the Esmee Fairbairn Foundation.

E-law describes itself as a service for "hundreds of grassroots lawyers and scientists around the world" who are "protecting the environment through law across borders." The E-LAW network provides "legal and scientific tools, resources and advice." The E-Law network is funded by the AVINA Foundation, which was founded by Stephen Schmidtheny, a Swiss investor who inherited Eternit, an asbestos-centered construction materials manufacturer. He moved his investments to Swatch, made another fortune, and now "prefers to spend his time trying to incorporate ethical, environmental and social goals into private enterprise. Has donated more than $400 million to the cause" (Forbes.com). In 2003, his net worth was estimated at $2.5 billion dollars, making him one of the world's wealthiest people (Forbes.com 2003).

25. In 1990 I was hired as a consultant to write a piece for the World Wildlife Fund about the complex issue of Amazon deforestation and what the organization was doing about it.

26. Some NGOs, especially in poor nations and among ecoradicals in Europe, are proposing the idea of the ecological debt. This is the debt accumulated by

Northern, industrial countries toward Third World countries on account of resource plundering, environmental damages, and the free occupation of environmental space to deposit wastes from the industrial countries (such as greenhouse gases). One leading proponent of this idea is Joan Martinez-Alier of Accion Ecologica, of Ecuador (Martinez-Alier 2001). This concept has much conceptually to support it (Roberts and Parks, 2007), but moving the agenda of the payment or consideration of the ecodebt as compensation for rich nation technology and aid transfers in future environmental treaties or trade agreements will require that the poor nations who are owed the debt work coherently together for some remuneration. This is going to be very difficult indeed.

References

Bandy, J., "Paradoxes of a Transnational Civil Society in a Neoliberal World: The Coalition for Justice in the Maquiladoras," *Social Problems* 51, no. 3 (2004): 463–485.

Blaikie, P., T. Cannon, I. Davies, and B. Wisner, *At Risk: Natural Hazards, People's Vulnerability, and Disasters* (London: Routledge, 1994).

Bryant, P., "Tenants and Toxics: New Orleans, LA," *Southern Exposure* (winter 1993).

Bullard, R. D. Personal communication with author. 2001.

Bullard, R. D., "EJ 101: An Outline Presentation," *EJ Resource Center* (1999), accessed online May 15, 2005, at www.ejrc.cau.edu/ej101.html.

Bullard, R. D., *Unequal Protection: Environmental Justice and Communities of Color* (San Francisco, Sierra Club Books, 1994).

Bullard, R., *Dumping in Dixie: Race, Class, and Environmental Quality* (Boulder, Colo.: Westview Press, 1990).

Clark, J. P., "On Ecocide and Cultural Genocide as Responsible Corporate Policy: The Case of Freeport McMoRan in West Papua," in *International Conference: Reflections on the Social Impact of American Multinational Corporations*, Grenoble, France, January 11, 2002.

Cole, L. W., and S. R. Foster, *From the Ground Up: Environmental Racism and the Rise of the Environmental Justice Movement* (New York: NYU Press, 2001).

Faber, D., "Building a Transnational Environmental Justice Movement: Obstacles and Opportunities in the Age of Globalization," in J. Smith and J. Bandy, eds., *Coalitions across Borders: Transnational Protest and the Neoliberal Order* (Lanham, Md.: Roman and Littlefield, 2005), 43–68.

Firebaugh, G., "Empirics of World Income Inequality," *American Journal of Sociology* 104 (May 1999): 1597–1630.

Foreman, C. H., *The Promise and Peril of Environmental Justice* (Washington, D.C., Brookings Institution Press, 1998).

Forbes.com "Stephan Schmidtheny, 55, inherited and growing." (2003), accessed online May 15, 2005, at www.forbes.com/finance/lists/10/2003/LIR.

Gari, J. A., The Political Economy of Biodiversity: Biodiversity conservation and Rural Development at the Indigenous and Peasant Grassroots (D.Phil. Thesis, School of Geography, University of Oxford, 2000).

Gedicks, A., *Resource Rebels: Native Challenges to Mining and Oil Corporations.* (Cambridge, Mass.: South End Press, 2002).

Gould, K., "Environmental Justice: Empowering Those at the Bottom," *Rio de Janeiro: Colóquio Internacional sobre Justiça Ambiental, Trabalho e Cidadania* (2001).

Gould, K., T. Lewis, and J. T. Roberts, "Blue-Green Coalitions: Constraints and Possibilities in the Post 9-11 Political Environment," *Journal of World-System Research* 10, no. 1: (2004) 90–116.

Guha, R., and Martinez-Alier, J., *Varieties of Environmentalism: Essays North and South* (London: Earthscan, 1997).

IPCC. *Climate Change 2001: Third Assessment Report of the Intergovernmental Panel on Climate Change, including Reports of All Three Working Groups* (London: Cambridge University Press, 2001).

Juneau, D., "Government by Oxymoron," *Louisiana Association of Business and Industry* (June 22, 1998), accessed online May 15, 2005, at www.labi.org/default.html.

Kapstein, E., "A Global Third Way Social Justice and the World Economy," *World Policy Journal* 14, no. 4 (winter 1998/1999), accessed online May 15, 2005, at www.worldpolicy.org/journal/kapstein.html.

Kasperson, R. E., and J.X. Kasperson, "Climate Change, Vulnerability, and Social Justice," in *Stockholm: Risk and Vulnerability Programme* (Stockholm Environment Institute, 2001).

Keck, M. and K. Sikkink, *Activists across Borders: Advocacy Networks in International Politics* (Ithaca, N.Y.: Cornell University Press, 1998).

Khastagir, N., "A Human Face to a Human Problem: Climate Justice Summit," *India Resource Center/CorpWatch* (November 1, 2002), online at http://www.indiaresource.org/issues/energycc/2003/humanfacehumanproblem.html.

Lavelle, M., and M. Coyle, "A Special Investigation: Unequal Protection, the Racial Divide in Environmental Law," *National Law Journal* (September 21, 1992): S1.

Malone, L. A., and S. Pasternak, *Defending the Environment: Civil Society Strategies to Enforce International Environmental Law* (Ardsley, N.Y.: Transnational Publishers, 2004).

Manley, M., *The Poverty of Nations* (London: Pluto Press, 1991).

Martinez-Alier, J., "Environmental Conflicts, Environmental Justice, and Valuation," in J. Ageyman, ed., *Just Sustainabilities: Development in an Unequal World* (London: Earthscan, 2003), pp. 201–208.

Martinez-Alier, J., *Accion Ecologica, Ecuador* (2001), online at http://www.cos-movisiones.com/DeudaEcologica/a_whatis.html.

Martinez-Alier, J., "Environmental Justice, Sustainability and Valuation," *Harvard Seminar on Environmental Values* (March 21, 2000), accessed online May 15, 2005, at http://ecoethics.net/hsev/200003txt.htm.

McMichael, P., *Development and Social Change: A Global Perspective* (Thousand Oaks, Calif.: Pine Forge 1996).

Parks, B. C. and J. T. Roberts, "Globalization, Vulnerability to Climate Change, and Injustice," *Society and Natural Resources* (2007).

Peet, R. and M. Watts, *Liberation Ecologies: Environment, Development, Social Movements* (New York: Routledge, 1996).

Pew Center on Global Climate Change, "Turning Down the Heat: Finding Solutions for Global Warming," (April 22, 1999), accessed online May 15, 2005, at http://www.pewclimate.org/press_room/speech_transcripts/transcript_heat.cfm.

Pulido, L., *Environmentalism and Economic Justice: Two Chicano Struggles in the Southwest* (Tucson: University of Arizona Press, 1996).

Roberts, J. T., and B. C. Parks, *A Climate of Injustice: Global Inequality, North–South Politics, and Climate Policy* (Cambridge, Mass.: MIT Press, 2007).

Roberts, J. T., and M. Toffolon-Weiss, *Chronicles from the Environmental Justice Frontline* (Cambridge: Cambridge University Press, 2001).

Roberts, J. T., and N. Thanos, *Trouble in Paradise: Globalization and Environmental Crises in Latin America* (London: Routledge, 2003).

Roberts, R. E., M. Conrecode, and C. Leftwich, "Environmental Justice and EPA's Title VI Guidance: What Must Be Done" (1998), online at http://www.sso.org/ecos/publications/oldECOStates.htm.

Robinson, F. T., and North Baton Rouge Environmental Association, "Concepts of Environmental Justice," n.d.

Rose, F., *Coalitions across the Class Divide: Lessons from the Labor, Peace, and Environmental Movements* (Ithaca, N.Y.: Cornell University Press, 2000).

Schnaiberg, A., and K. Gould, *Environmental and Society: The Enduring Conflict* (New York: St. Martin's Press, 1994).

Schweizer, E., "Interview with Robert Bullard," *Earth First Journal, email version* (July 6, 1999).

Shue, H., "The Unavoidability of Justice," in A. Hurrell and B. Kingsbury, eds., *The International Politics of the Environment* (Oxford: Oxford University Press, 1992), 373–397.

Sissell, K., "Equity Programs Strain State Resources," *Chemical Week* (July 28, 1999): 36.

Snow D. A. and R. D. Benford, "Master Frames and Cycles of Protest," in A. Morris, and C. Mueller, eds., *Frontiers of Social Movement Theory* (Yale University Press, 1992), 133–155.

Taylor, P. J., and F. H. Buttel, "How Do We Know We Have Global Environmental Problems? Science and the Globalization of Environmental Discourse," *Geoforum* 23 (1992): 405–416.

Toffolon-Weiss, M., and J. Roberts, "Toxic Torts, Public Interest Law and Environmental Justice: Evidence from Louisiana," *Law and Policy* 26, no. 2 (2004): 259–287.

U.S. Chamber of Commerce, "U.S. Chamber Urges President to Withdraw EPA Environmental Justice Policy," press release (May 5, 1998a).

Wade, R. H., "Is Globalization Reducing Poverty and Inequality?" *World Development* 32, no. 4 (2004): 567–589.

Washington, R. O., "When Environmental Justice Confronts Risk Communication" (unpublished manuscript, 1997).

Weiss, E. B., "Intergenerational Equity toward an International Legal Framework," in N. Choucri, ed., *Global Accord: Environmental Challenges and International Responses* (Cambridge, Mass.: MIT Press, 1993), pp. 333–354.

Weiss, E. B., *In Fairness to Future Generations: International Law, Common Patrimony, and Intergenerational Equity* (Ardsley, N.Y.: Transnational Publishers, 1989).

Yearley, S., *Sociology, Environmentalism, Globalization: Re-inventing the Globe* (London: Sage, 1996).

Conclusion
Working Together and Working Apart

Phaedra C. Pezzullo and Ronald Sandler

The goal of this collection is to revisit the environmental justice challenge to the environmental movement and catalyze discussions about the future of the relationship between the two movements. In this conclusion, we provide our interpretation of the story the chapters in this collection tell. Although not all of the authors, us included, agree with each other on every point, certain commonalities do emerge from the collection as a whole. Overall, we believe the chapters provide evidence of (1) undeniable and irreconcilable differences between the environmental justice and environmental movements, challenging the prospects or even the desirability of the environmental movement radically reorienting its core mission in response to the environmental justice critiques as well as integrating or merging the two movements into one single, unified movement; and (2) the ways that campaign or issue-specific collaborations or alliances between the two movements can enhance, in a wide range of situations and on a wide variety of issues, the effectiveness of both movements' efforts. In other words, for these two movements to work well together, they must also come to terms with the ways they must work apart.

To clarify and elaborate on this conclusion, we begin by revisiting the question of collaboration raised at Summit I. We then defend this conclusion on the basis of what the contributors have told us about the movements' relationship in both U.S. and global contexts. Finally, we gesture toward possibilities for future research.

Collaboration: Working Together or Betraying One's Roots?

col·lab·o·ra·tion

1. the act of working together with one or more people in order to achieve something

2. the betrayal of others by working with an enemy, especially an occupying force[1]

The idea of "collaboration" is tricky, embodying both the promise of working together to achieve desirable goals and the risk of acting unfaithfully or duplicitously to one's own beliefs and commitments. Tellingly, and evidenced by the language both in the letters to the Group of Ten and at Summit I, "collaboration" tends not to be the term of choice by representatives of either movement to characterize how the environmental movement ought to respond to the environmental justice challenge or the type of relationship either movement wants. The letters called for "frank and open dialogue," as well as "mutual strategizing"; Pat Bryant called for "coalition and cooperation"; John Adams stated the need for "a common effort"; Michael Fischer charged both movements "to work and look into the future" instead of being divided and conquered; and Dana Alston argued for a "just partnership." So, although there is a mutual desire to work together, there is also a shared feeling that such efforts should not be to somehow combine the movements by redefining their core values and practices.

There have been attempts within both movements to more precisely articulate the type of relationship that is desired. For example, the Sierra Club Environmental Justice Program Site Selection Committee wrote a document called "Guidelines of Environmental Justice Grassroots Organizing" in 1999, to define the goals of their Environmental Justice Program and outline the relationships of the Sierra Club volunteers, staff, and community representatives affiliated with it (Appendix B). In addition, at Summit II in 2003, delegates and participants developed a new set of principles called "Principles of Working Together," with the intent of identifying the ideal conditions for building alliances (Appendix C).[2] Although these documents provide some indication of the general approaches warranted to foster better relations and positive collaboration between the movements, they have not yet been discussed or circulated as broadly as the Principles of Environmental Justice from Summit I.

Both the Guidelines and the Principles of Working Together articulate many of the same themes that emerge from this collection: mutual respect for the goals, methods, and capabilities of the other movement and what they can provide in a joint effort; acknowledgment of the distinctiveness of the two movements; recognition of the effectiveness of working together, under particular circumstances; and insistence that working together should not involve cooption or subsumption of either movement's voice, leadership, or goals. What the contributions to this collection add to this general picture is a more concrete account of the distinctiveness of the two movements, the space available for creating alliances under the rubric of "environmentalism," and the factors (the how, when, and why) that seem to contribute to effective cooperative efforts. This collection not only supports the vision in these documents, but also fills them out with more details on the limitations, hopes, and approaches to enacting them.

Working Apart

First, expanding on the formative events and challenges discussed in the introduction, Allen, Daro, and Holland reiterate from their interviews in North Carolina that many grassroots environmental justice activists came into their activist identities through an understanding of environmental concerns as social justice issues and in a time when the environmental movement generally did not appreciate their voices or contributions. This social justice orientation and feeling of exclusion was manifested in direct statements and in the small, everyday practices (for example, the Styrofoam cup and S.H.I.T. versus H.E.L.P) of grassroots activists that illustrated their different "figured worlds." This divisive history cannot be erased or merged easily into one movement, nor should it be. These accounts offer lessons insofar as they illustrate how racial, cultural, and economic differences can shape political activism from the ground up. If the environmental justice and environmental movements are going to work together productively in the future, as many authors in this collection and elsewhere note, this history and the differences it manifests and engenders must continue to be acknowledged.

Further, the institutionalization of racism, classism, and sexism is bigger than either movement. Here is Robert Bullard on this point:

We've made a lot of progress since 1990 when a letter was written to them charging them with environmental racism, elitism, looking at their staff, looking at their boards and saying that we need to talk. And there's been some talking and sharing and working together along the way. We've made progress but there's still a lot of progress that needs to be made because to a large extent the environmental movement, the more conservation/preservation movement, really reflects the larger society. And society is racist. And so we can't expect a lot of our organizations not to somehow be affected by that.[3]

Bullard's statement is crucial to bear in mind as engagements between the two movements progress. Because sexism, classism, and racism permeate society as a whole, it is not just the environmental movement's racism, classism, or sexism that is at stake. This is not to let the environmental movement off the hook. It merely is to contextualize things in a way that reminds us that these problems do not start or end with the environmental movement.

Second, DeLuca's essay emphasizes that the environmental justice movement's focus on social justice can be used to marginalize nonanthropocentric concerns about wildlife and wilderness, which are central to the history and, he argues, future of the environmental movement. One might take issue with his characterization of the whole environmental justice movement (for example, indigenous cultures, as Di Chiro points out and DeLuca recognizes in his footnotes, tend to be less anthropocentric and a belief in the sacredness of Mother Earth is part of the Environmental Justice Principles) or of the fate of the environmental movement (for example, environmental organizations sometimes can and do balance their preservation work with environmental justice). DeLuca's manifesto does, however, provide an important reminder that some prominent voices of the environmental justice movement have been known to deride "saving" a whale or a tree as less worthwhile than, for example, issues of lead paint, affordable housing, and employment. This line of criticism does signal that there really are ethical, spiritual, and political divides between them. Further, DeLuca points out that it is not just the environmental justice movement that poses challenges to the environmental movement, rather environmentalism also poses challenges to the environmental justice movement. Finding productive ways for these two movements to work together, therefore, would seem to require recognition that there are at least some significant differences in the value orientations and priorities of the two movements.

Recognizing these practical and philosophical points of divergence favors the conclusion that the two movements should not be merged. As important as finding ways to work together—and indeed imperative to being able to do so—is appreciating that both movements also, at times, have to work apart. For example, as Roberts indicates, we need an adequate response to both the environmental aspects of global warming and the social inequities exacerbated by climate injustice. But it does not follow from this that these are best pursued as one package. Perhaps both goals are better served by independent, but mutually informed, efforts. As these chapters illustrate, in some situations, the compromises that would have to be made to present a unified effort would undermine what makes each movement effective in its own way. In some cases, the two movements might be more effective working separately, even while endorsing and assisting each other when appropriate.

One thing that is certain to undermine successful attempts to work together in the future is arguing over which movement's priorities are more urgent or values are superior. If the aim, instead, is advancing two sets of worthwhile goals for two different—though related—movements, the issue becomes not which set of goals is more important to pursue or who needs to transform in the direction of whom, but how these two movements can advance both of their agendas while working together. In some cases, these opportunities are obvious. For example, it is relatively easy for environmentalists to support a Native American community when the issue is preserving a sacred site such as a mountain or wilderness area or an African American community when the topic is the toxic pollution of water and air.[4] In other cases, however, working together is more challenging. For example, dilemmas arise when indigenous sovereignty rights are invoked to justify the commercial development of public lands or when communities of color support efforts that compromise ecological standards.[5] In these instances, matters are often further complicated by the fact that neither movement is homogeneous nor monolithic. There often exist disagreements even within each movement regarding what is the right thing to do.

For all of these reasons, neither a radical revision of the environmental movement's core mission nor unification of the environmental justice and environmental movements into one movement are likely prospects or desirable goals. This is not an indictment of either movement. It is simply an outcome of their existence as distinct social movements, with different histories, values, practices, and visions.

Working Together

Nevertheless, as Wenz and Jamieson demonstrate, there is no inherent or necessary reason that the environmental justice and environmental movements cannot work together or be mutually supportive on a wide variety of issues. Jamieson argues that a commitment to justice is in fact central to environmentalism and that a focus on justice may even help alleviate some of the tensions within environmentalism. Wenz emphasizes that, on a host of issues ranging from mass transportation to job creation to building new energy-efficient technologies, environmental policies need not harm the poor and can often help them. Schwarze provides a specific instance of this with regard to asbestos activism, where he sees possibilities for environmental and environmental justice groups working together to create new legislation and increase corporate accountability. Jamieson and Wenz also emphasize that there are frequent opportunities for the two movements to come together in opposition to a common foe. Cox illustrates in detail such an opportunity in the context of international trade agreements, where both movements have a stake in resisting neoliberal economic policy and already have served as allies with each other and other movements, such as labor and human rights. Faber sees such opportunities as well in the interests of both movements to challenge entrenched state and corporate power structures and the root causes of environmental degradation and political marginalization.

Moreover, recent studies have debunked the myth that people of color are uninterested with nonlocal environmental issues. In fact, there is strong support for environmental protection among minority communities.[6] In some cases, such as those described by Peterson et al., a community may not even distinguish between environmental and environmental justice issues or describe themselves as an environmental or environmental justice community, even as outside observers would be inclined to make those distinctions and characterizations. In such cases, there already is de facto integration of "environmental justice" and "environmental" concerns at the grassroots level.

Identifying mutual investments and efforts is not the same as one movement sustaining or adopting the other's goals. They are cases where both movements would be challenging or supporting the same entities and policies individually. In these contexts, working together mobilizes a larger political base and set of resources for them both. That the two movements often can be brought effectively together in these ways is further evidenced by the fact that they already have shared some campaigns and victories. For example, Kenyan environmental activist Wangari Maathai—who was mentioned by Fischer at Summit I—was celebrated in 2004 by both environmentalists and environmental justice activists as the first environmentalist and first black African woman to receive the Nobel Peace Prize, for her thirty years of activism as a leader of the Green Belt Movement. Likewise, when the "Cancer Alley," Louisiana grassroots community NORCO received a settlement in 2002 from Shell Oil Company for compensation and relocation, both national environmental and environmental justice organizations were thanked by local activists for their support in helping to achieve that victory.

So, the significant differences between the two movements not withstanding, there is a substantial range of issues and situations in which activists from the two movements should, in theory and practice, be able to find common ground to work together in support of converging goals. The question then becomes, how can these movements accomplish this?

Faber and Roberts, in particular, provide examples of when the environmental justice and environmental movements have worked together successfully. From these essays, three general conditions emerge as conducive to productive alliances. First, activists from both movements need to respect what the other can bring to a collective effort in a specific context. For example, Faber describes how, in the commonwealth of Massachusetts, local environmental activists were able to use their experience and resources to lobby for environmental justice, antitoxics and regional equity legislation, while environmental justice activists were able to use their experience and resources to educate the affected public and mobilize grassroots support for the legislation. In this case, the expertise, resources, and capabilities of the participating organizations were complementary and synergistic, and the importance of each group's contribution was mutually recognized.

Second, activists from each movement must respect what the other is trying to accomplish more generally, as well as each other's standing to formulate their own approach to doing so. The effects of the absence of respect are apparent in the Environmental Genome Project and genetic research on Indigenous peoples, as described by Di Chiro. As long as one group supposes it is positioned to determine for others how their goals—for example, community health—are best achieved, the efforts easily could become misguided (for example, focused on genetics rather than obvious and more easily addressed environmental factors) and exploitive (for instance, the misuse of genetic information). In contrast, a positive example is, again, provided by the Massachusetts alliance. Crucial to the success of the Massachusetts collaboration, as Faber describes it, is that it involves a true partnership, from defining the aims of the alliance, to drafting the legislation, to strategizing how to promote the legislation. Likewise, drawing on observations from international arenas, Roberts emphasizes the importance of not only concrete roles that require specific skills to reach a particular goal, but also a willingness to reach across one's comfort zones to broaden a base of support.

Third, in each of the instances when the two movements have been able to work together successfully, they were involved in well-defined campaigns. Whether it is antitoxics legislation, free-trade opposition, or climate justice, productive partnerships in the examples presented in this collection are galvanized around specific issues in specific contexts. Moreover, it is just such a focused goal-oriented campaign that

Schwarze envisions for environmental and environmental justice groups working together on asbestos, as is the case of groups working together in response to the environmental problems associated with September 11.

So, instead of supporting the idea that the environmental movement should try to champion environmental justice goals by incorporating them into their central mission, the contributions in this collection favor the conclusion that the environmental movement is most effective when it does not fall into the trap of betraying one's roots or collaboration in the negative sense. When groups from both movements come to work together with respect for the other within the context of a well-defined, campaign-specific effort, domestically or internationally, a just partnership is not only possible, but desirable.

Opportunities for such mutually enhancing, context-specific alliances vary not only across geographical regions and environmental issues, but also with the structures and missions of the groups themselves. Some major environmental organizations—such as the Wilderness Society, National Audubon Society, and National Wildlife Federation—have a strong wilderness and wildlife focus. As a result, there are fewer opportunities for them to build effective alliances with environmental justice groups (though there are some, of course, such as working with the Gwich'in on what can be preserved of the Arctic National Wildlife Refuge) than there are for other major environmental organizations, such as the Sierra Club, Friends of the Earth, Natural Resource Defense Council, and the Environmental Defense Fund, which have broader missions. The Sierra Club, as many contributors to this volume note, tends to cross paths with the environmental justice movement more frequently than most other environmental organizations. This is not just due to its broadly defined mission, but also because it is organized with local groups, state chapters, regional structures, national leadership, and international involvement. Local environmental groups that have autonomy over their agenda and are not pulled along by institutional inertia may also find more opportunities for effective alliances than major wilderness-oriented environmental organizations. For its part, the environmental justice movement has sought to expand beyond its grassroots and establish a national organization to represent all communities and regional networks involved, which increases the possibilities of alliances on issues at the national level; and, as Roberts discusses, the environmental justice frame has begun to be widely exported, increasingly the possibilities for alliances at the transnational and global levels.

Moving Forward

The intent of this collection is not to provide resolution and shut down debate. Even taken together, the contributors in this volume constitute only an initial study of appropriate responsiveness by the environmental movement to the continuing environmental justice challenge and the possibilities and conditions under which the two movements might work effectively together. There are many more contexts and campaigns to be studied, and a wider range of perspectives need to be considered. Di Chiro's description of the marginalization of indigenous communities' perspectives from discussions on genetics research is cautionary on this point. Moreover, as Schwarze and Peterson et al. attest, the discourses, goals, and practices of the environmental justice and environmental movements still do not exhaust all the current possibilities of what social and political struggles in relation to the environment may involve. Further, although the environmental topics and campaigns discussed in this volume are expansive, they are not exhaustive. The environmental justice challenges to environmentalism in the context of issues such as war, food production, deforestation, conservation refugees, ecological refugees, and immigration need to be explored more fully than they have been here. Finally, we need to continue to revisit the differences and similarities between the environmental justice and environmental movements in order to assess how they—both separately and together—can help improve our relationships with each other and the environment.

Notes

1. Encarta World English Dictionary, 1999 Microsoft Corporation. Developed for Microsoft by Bloomsbury Publishing Plc.

2. One of us, Pezzullo, worked with a small group of committed activists on these Principles at Summit II. Although at the time it was not apparent to her that

the delegates were able to come to complete consensus to adopt these Principles formally, accounts from Summit II organizers since the gathering confirm that they were. (See, for example, the websites of the Environmental Justice Resource Center and the Southwest Research and Information Center "Voices from the Earth.")

3. Schweizer (1999).

4. Robert Gottlieb (2005) has made a case for food, transportation, and globalization as key issues where social justice and environmental concerns converge and thereby provide opportunities for reenvisioning what environmentalism could be.

5. For example, there is an ongoing controversy concerning Makah whaling off the state of Washington coast, where some animal rights groups (for example, the Sea Shepherd Conservation Society) support a complete ban on the hunting of whales, one environmental organization supports only subsistence whaling (Greenpeace), one environmental organization refuses to oppose the practice (the Sierra Club), while the majority of an indigenous community—though not everyone in it—claims that any limitations to their whaling practices is a violation of their treaty rights (the Makah). Also, since 2003, there have been at least two instances where Native American tribes have wanted to develop on designated public lands. For example, the Eastern Band of Cherokee Indians has applied multiple times for the transference of the Ravensford tract of land in the Great Smoky Mountains National Park for use of development (National Park Service 2002). A nonnative example of the level of discord that can be reached when environmental standards and social justice struggles diverge is the Belmont Learning Center controversy in Los Angeles, California, where some local Latino/a leaders and organizations such as MALDEF (Mexican American Legal Defense and Education Fund) supported the building of a much-needed new high school for the community's children, while many environmentalists worked to delay its development because of public health concerns about the site as a former oilfield and polluted industrial site (Anderson 2000).

6. Mohai (1990, 2003); Parker and McDonough (1999); Jones and Carter (1994).

References

Anderson, S., "The School that Wasn't: Politics and Pollution in LA," *Nation* (June 5, 2000), accessed online April 19, 2006, at www.thenation.com/doc/20000605/anderson.

Gottlieb, R., *Forcing the Spring: The Transformation of the American Environmental Movement; rev. ed.* (Washington D.C.: Island Press, 2005).

Jones, R., and Carter, L., "Concern for the Environment Among Black Americans: An Assessment of Common Assumptions," *Social Science Quarterly* 75 (1994): 560–579.

Mohai, P., "Dispelling Old Myths: African American Concern for the Environment," *Environment* 45, no. 5 (2003): 11–26.

Mohai, P., "Black Environmentalism," *Social Science Quarterly* 71 (1990): 744–765.

National Park Service, "Great Smoky Mountains National Park: Briefing Paper," (February 22, 2002), accessed online April 19, 2006, at data2.itc.nps.gov/parks/grsm/ppdocuments/CherokeeLandSwap02-02.doc.

Parker, J., and McDonough, M., "Environmentalism of African Americans," *Environment and Behavior* 31 (1999): 155–177.

Schweizer, E., "Environmental Justice: An Interview with Robert Bullard," *Earth First! Journal* (July 1999), accessed online April 19, 2006, at www.ejnet.org/ej/bullard.html.

Appendix A
Principles of Environmental Justice

Adopted at the First National People of Color Environmental Leadership Summit Washington, DC, October 24–27, 1991

We, the people of color, gathered together at this multinational People of Color Environmental Leadership Summit, to begin to build a national and international movement of all peoples of color to fight the destruction and taking of our lands and communities, do hereby reestablish our spiritual interdependence to the sacredness of our Mother Earth; to respect and celebrate each of our cultures, languages and beliefs about the natural world and our roles in healing ourselves; to insure environmental justice; to promote economic alternatives which would contribute to the development of environmentally safe livelihoods; and to secure our political, economic and cultural liberation that has been denied for over 500 years of colonization and oppression, resulting in the poisoning of our communities and land and the genocide of our peoples, do affirm and adopt these Principles of Environmental Justice:

1. Environmental justice affirms the sacredness of Mother Earth, ecological unity and the interdependence of all species, and the right to be free from ecological destruction.

2. Environmental justice demands that public policy be based on mutual respect and justice for all peoples, free from any form of discrimination or bias.

3. Environmental justice mandates the right to ethical, balanced and responsible uses of land and renewable resources in the interest of a sustainable planet for humans and other living things.

4. Environmental justice calls for universal protection from nuclear testing, extraction, production and disposal of toxic/hazardous wastes and poisons and nuclear testing that threaten the fundamental right to clean air, land, water, and food.

5. Environmental justice affirms the fundamental right to political, economic, cultural and environmental self-determination of all peoples.

6. Environmental justice demands the cessation of the production of all toxins, hazardous wastes, and radioactive materials, and that all past and current producers be held strictly accountable to the people for detoxification and the containment at the point of production.

7. Environmental justice demands the right to participate as equal partners at every level of decision-making, including needs assessment, planning, implementation, enforcement, and evaluation.

8. Environmental justice affirms the right of all workers to a safe and healthy work environment, without being forced to choose between an unsafe livelihood and unemployment. It also affirms the right of those who work at home to be free from environmental hazards.

9. Environmental justice protects the right of victims of environmental injustice to receive full compensation and reparation for damages as well as quality health care.

10. Environmental justice considers governmental acts of environmental injustice a violation of international law, the Universal Declaration on Human Rights, and the United Nations Convention on Genocide.

11. Environmental justice must recognize a special legal and natural relationship of Native Peoples in the U.S. government through treaties, agreements, compacts, and covenants which impose upon the U.S. government a paramount obligation and responsibility to affirm the sovereignty and self-determination of the indigenous peoples whose lands it occupies and holds in trust.

12. Environmental justice affirms the need for an urban and rural ecological policy to clean up and rebuild our cities and rural areas in balance with nature, honoring the cultural integrity of all our communities, and providing fair access for all to the full range of resources.

13. Environmental justice calls for the strict enforcement of principles of informed consent, and a halt to the testing of experimental reproductive and medical procedures and vaccinations on people of color.

14. Environmental justice opposes the destructive operations of multi-national corporations.

15. Environmental justice opposes military occupation, repression and exploitation of lands, peoples and cultures, and other life forms.

16. Environmental justice calls for the education of present and future generations which emphasizes social and environmental issues, based on our experience and an appreciation of our diverse cultural perspectives.

17. Environmental justice requires that we, as individuals, make personal and consumer choices to consume as little of Mother Earth's resources and to produce as little waste as possible; and to make the conscious decision to challenge and re-prioritize our lifestyle to insure the health of the natural world for present and future generations.

Appendix B
Sierra Club Guidelines of Environmental Justice Grassroots Organizing

A working document adopted by the Sierra Club Environmental Justice Program Site Selection Committee in 1999 to define the goals of the Program and outline the relationships of the Sierra Club volunteers, staff, and community representatives affiliated with it

The Sierra Club's relationship with the communities it assists will be governed by the following principles:

1. We will hire grassroots organizers to serve as a bridge linking the Club to communities fighting for environmental justice; and we will encourage qualified applicants from these communities to apply for these positions.

2. We will enter a community to provide grassroots organizing assistance only when invited to do so by the community.

3. We will respect the right of the community to define its agenda to address its environmental problems. We will not be present to persuade the community to work on "our" issues, but rather provide support to the community as it seeks to define its own issues and lead its own campaign.

4. Our grassroots organizers will work to link activists from Sierra Club groups, chapters, and Regional Conservation Committees with the citizens of the community.

5. We will work as a supporting collaborator with the community facing environmental injustice. This may mean providing training and support to meet the needs defined by the community.

6. We will encourage the empowerment of the members of the community and will seek to nurture that empowerment.

7. We will respect the comfort level of the community in responding to requests for tactical assistance. For example, in providing media assistance, we will strive to avoid even the appearance of making public relations capital out of the community's misfortune.

8. We will seek to foster community self-reliance and will be prepared to leave the community at any time as requested.

Appendix C
Principles of Working Together

Adopted at the Second People of Color Environmental Leadership Summit Washington, DC, October 26, 2002

Principle 1: Purpose

1A. The Principles of Working Together uphold the Principles of Environmental Justice, including the commitment to eradicate environmental racism in our communities.

1B. The Principles of Working Together require local and regional empowered partnerships, inclusive of all.

1C. The Principles of Working Together call for continued influence on public policy to protect and sustain Mother Earth and our communities and also honor past promises and make amends for past injustices.

Principle 2: Core Values

2A. The Principles of Working Together commit us to working from the ground up, beginning with all grassroots workers, organizers and activists. We do not want to forget the struggle of the grassroots workers. This begins with all grassroots workers, organizers and activists.

2B. The Principles of Working Together recognize traditional knowledge and uphold the intellectual property rights of all peoples of color and Indigenous peoples.

2C. The Principles of Working Together reaffirm that as people of color we speak for ourselves. We have not chosen our struggle, we work together to overcome our common barriers, and resist our common foes.

2D. The Principles of Working Together bridge the gap among various levels of the movement through effective communication and strategic networking.

2E. The Principles of Working Together affirm the youth as full members in the environmental justice movement. As such, we commit resources to train and educate young people to sustain the groups and the movement into the future.

Principle 3: Building Relationships

3A. The Principles of Working Together recognize that we need each other and we are stronger with each other. This Principle requires participation at every level without barriers and that the power of the movement is shared at every level.

3B. The Principles of Working Together require members to cooperate with harmony, respect and trust—it must be genuine and sustained relationship-building. This demands cultural and language sensitivity.

3C. The Principles of Working Together demand grassroots workers, organizers and activists set their own priorities when working with other professionals and institutions.

3D. The Principles of Working Together recognize that community organizations have expertise and knowledge. Community organizations should seek out opportunities to work in partnerships with academic institutions, other grassroots organizations and environmental justice lawyers to build capacity through the resources of these entities.

Principle 4: Addressing Differences

4A. The Principles of Working Together require affirmation of the value in diversity and the rejection of any form of racism, discrimination and oppression. To support each other completely, we must learn about our different cultural and political histories so that we can completely support each other in our movement inclusive of ages, classes, immigrants, indigenous peoples, undocumented workers, farm workers, genders, sexual orientations, and education differences.

4B. The Principles of Working Together require respect, cultural sensitivity, patience, time, and a willingness to understand each other and a mutual sharing of knowledge.

4C. The Principles of Working Together affirm the value in our diversity. If English is not the primary language, there must be effective translation for all participants.

Principle 5: Leadership

5A. The Principles of Working Together demand shared power, community service, cooperation, as well as open and honest communication.

5B. The Principles of Working Together demand that people from the outside should not come in and think that there is no leadership in the grassroots community. The people in the community should lead their own community and create a legacy by teaching young people to be leaders.

5C. The Principles of Working Together demand that people from grassroots organizations should lead the environmental justice movement.

5D. The Principles of Working Together demand accountability to the people, responsibility to complete required work, and maintenance of healthy partnerships with all groups.

Principle 6: Participation

6A. The Principles of Working Together demand cultural sensitivity. This requires patience and time for each group to express their concerns, and their concerns should be heard.

6B. The Principles of Working Together require a culturally appropriate process.

6C. The Principles of Working Together have a commitment to changing the process when the process is not meeting the needs of the people.

The changes should be informed by the people's timely feedback and evaluation.

Principle 7: Resolving Conflicts

7A. The Principles of Working Together encourage respectful discussion of our differences, willingness to understand, and the exploration of best possible solutions.

7B. The Principles of Working Together require that we learn and strengthen our cross-cultural communication skills so that we can develop effective and creative problem-solving skills. This Principle promotes respectful listening and dialogue.

7C. The Principles of Working Together affirm the value in learning and strengthening mediation skills in diverse socio-economic and multicultural settings.

Principle 8: Fundraising

8A. The Principles of Working Together recognize the need for expanding sustainable community based avenues for raising funds, such as building a donor base, membership dues, etc.

8B. The Principles of Working Together oppose funding from any organization impacting people of color and indigenous communities. In addition, the Principles oppose funding from any organization that is the current target of active boycotts or other campaign activity generated by our allies.

8C. The Principles of Working Together encourage larger environmental justice organizations to help smaller, emerging environmental justice organizations gain access to funding resources. We encourage the sharing of funding resources and information with other organizations in need.

Principle 9: Accountability

9A. The Principles of Working Together encourage all partners to abide by shared agreements, including, but not limited to, oral and written agreements. Any changes or developments to agreements/actions need to be communicated to all who are affected and agreed upon.

9B. The Principles of Working Together encourage periodic evaluation and review of process to ensure accountability among all partners. Any violation of these agreements or any unprincipled actions that violate the EJ principles either must attempt to be resolved among the partners or will end the partnership if not resolved and, then, will be raised to the larger EJ community.

Index

Urban and Industrial Environments

Series editor: Robert Gottlieb, Henry R. Luce Professor of Urban and Environmental Policy, Occidental College

Eran Ben-Joseph, *The Code of the City: Standards and the Hidden Language of Place Making*

Nancy J. Myers and Carolyn Raffensperger, eds., *Precautionary Tools for Reshaping Environmental Policy*

Kelly Sims Gallagher, *China Shifts Gears: Automakers, Oil, Pollution, and Development*

Kerry H. Whiteside, *Precautionary Politics: Principle and Practice in Confronting Environmental Risk*

Ronald Sandler and Phaedra C. Pezzullo, eds., *Environmental Justice and Environmentalism: The Social Justice Challenge to the Environmental Movement*